Crested China

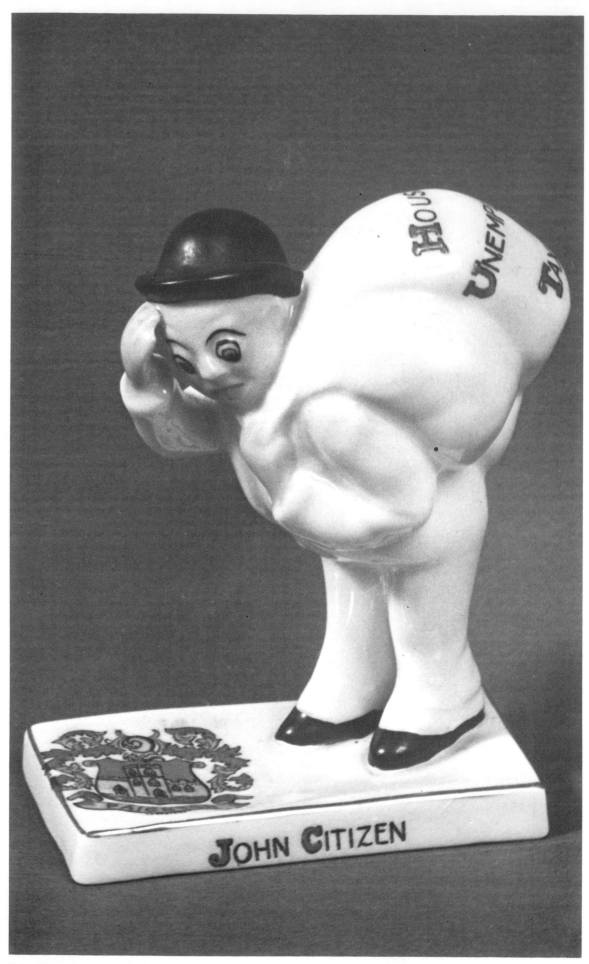

'John Citizen', carrying the burdens of 'Housing, unemployment and taxes'. Carlton 95 mm

Crested China

*The History of
Heraldic Souvenir Ware*

Sandy Andrews

Springwood Books
in conjunction with
Milestone Publications

Prepared by Nicholas Pine

Published by Springwood Books Ltd
11 Garrick Street, London WC2E 9AR

in conjunction with
Milestone Publications
Goss & Crested China Limited
95 Seafront,
Hayling Island, Hants. PO11 0AW.

ISBN No. 0 9059 47 38 X

Design Brian Iles
Factory Marks Janet Ward
Photography Michael Edwards

Text set in 11/13 pt VIP Palatino, printed and bound
in Great Britain at The Pitman Press, Bath

Colour section printed by
Kestrel Graphics, Fleet, Hants.

Other Milestone Publications
Goss China, Arms, Decorations & Their Values
Nicholas Pine
The Price Guide to Goss China
Nicholas Pine
The Goss Record War Edition
Goss for Collectors—The Literature
The Goss Record Eighth Edition
A Pictorial Handbook of Goss Cottages

In preparation
The Price Guide to Crested China
(For use in conjunction with this volume)

Take me back to dear old Blighty
The First World War through the eyes of
the Heraldic China Manufacturers.
R. D. Southall BSc.

Contents

List of illustrations on dust jacket

Front cover

DJ1 Alexandra Bulldog with a Union Jack draped over his back.

DJ2 Carlton. 'Ye Oldest Chemists Shoppe in England, Market Square Knaresborough' inscribed on reverse. This model has a beautiful matching crest and is a good example of the part coloured buildings made by Wiltshaw and Robinson.

DJ3 Willow. A stick of Great Yarmouth Rock, a most unusual model not found in any other range.

DJ4 Savoy. 'Model of 14th Century Salt Pot found at Penrith now in Carlisle Museum'. This named model has been beautifully decorated with border patterns and a carnation design instead of the usual crest.

DJ5 Arcadian. Black boy with 'Cigarettes' container (see Comic/Novelty).

DJ6 Carlton. Felix on mother of pearl lustre sofa with B.E.E. crest (see Cartoon/Comedy Characters)

DJ7 Arcadian. Girl standing by hip bath wearing towel, note the face on what appears to be a sponge (see Comic/Novelty).

DJ8 Carlton. Woody Woodpecker, not named (see Cartoon/Comedy Characters).

DJ9 Carlton. Lustre gramophone in cabinet with lucky white heather device (see 'Modern' Equipment).

DJ10 Leadbeater. Art Coloured Parian footballer on base (see Sports).

Back cover

A colour advertisement for Arcadian Black cats which appeared in a company catalogue produced around 1920.

I would like to dedicate this book to my much loved father J. A. Doughty, who died before it was finished. He was always happy to find one of my 'quaint little pots' at a bargain price. It was he who gave me my first interesting model, a Billiken rather poignantly inscribed: 'The God of Things as they ought to be'.

Preface

After collecting crested china in a very modest way for sometime I became fascinated by the trademarks used. It seemed a simple exercise to look them up in an encyclopaedia of British Pottery Marks and find out who had manufactured them and when. Most of the marks just were not there, so I turned to fellow collectors and dealers and asked them for information. They, I found, knew as little as I did and since there were no reference books on the subject I set out to investigate the marks, to try to list the models, and to find out as much as I could about crested china. So many kind collectors listed their collections for me and so many people gave me information, advice and help that I was encouraged to write this book to share the information I had managed to discover.

I am well aware that I am only at the beginning of my researches, and that models not listed here will be found in many a collection. So I offer the book as an introduction to crested china and hope that others will now do research on the manufacturers and retailers, taking the trouble to record any models not found in these lists, and pass on the information to my publisher so that revisions can be made.

I do hope that collectors, general antique dealers, those interested in china commemoratives and souvenirs, or just feeling rather nostalgic will find this book informative and even perhaps entertaining.

Acknowledgements

This book would never have been written without the encouragement, experience and enthusiasm of Lynda and Nicholas Pine, who having recently researched, written and published the most exciting and learned books on Goss saw no reason why someone should not fathom the depths of crested china from lesser potteries. Lynda and Nicholas, who are the leading dealers in Goss and crested china, persuaded, cajoled and I suspect even bribed all the busy collectors listed below to catalogue their collections and later answer my endless queries. Without this assistance it would have been impossible for me to have contacted so many people and to try to record all known models. I owe them an enormous debt of gratitude and hope that this book in some way justifies their faith in me.

I must thank Robert Southall for his kindness in allowing me access to his researches into Great War Souvenir China; R. E. Alexander for his very valuable contribution to the listings, John Galpin and Douglas Goodlad for checking the text and saving me from some dreadful howlers.

I would also like to thank the following collectors, in Great Britain and the United States for listing their collections or allowing Nicholas Pine, R. E. Alexander or myself into their homes to do so: Mrs C. Adams, Mrs J. Allison, Mrs I. Applin, D. Ashton, G. Atkinson, D. Barker, Mrs C. Barnes, F. Bartlett, Mrs K. S. Blacklock, Mrs H. L. R. Brenchley, A. Broadley, Mrs R. L. Brook, I. Brown, Mrs J. Buckle, Mrs P. C. Bullock, Dr G. Burrow, D. Caroline, Mrs J. Caswell, A. W. T. Chapman, E. Chambers, M. J. Coombes, J. B. Cornish, Mrs A. Courtenay, V. B. Curson, Mr and Mrs P. Dobson, Mrs I. H. Donnelly, Mrs M. S. Elliot, B. Fawkes, Mrs J. Fellows, D. R. Foster, R. Fresco-Corbu, H. B. Gallier, Mr and Mrs V. Garside, Mr and Mrs B. Gilham, N. Gillingwater, R. Glendinning, T. Goddard, Miss J. Godfrey, D. Goodlad, Mrs A. A. Green, Mr and Mrs R. Green, B. J. F. Greet, Mrs B. Hacking, R. Haddock, S. R. Harden, Mrs K. J. Harris, Canon B. H. Hawkins, Mr and Mrs K. Hill, P. Holloway, T. Hood, Mrs E. Hooper, Mrs A. L. Jarman, I. Johnson, M. Johnson, R. Jones, Mr and Mrs W. M. Jones, K. Kirk, Mrs R. M. Lain, Mrs M. Latham, W. Llewellyn, E. Locke, Mr and Mrs J. Lory, A. Lowe, M. and J. Lowther, Mrs J. G. Marr, J. Matthews, J. McGregor, Mrs V. Miles, D. W. Mitchell, K. D. Mitchell, Mrs S. Morgan, C. Morris, J. G. Morris, Mrs P. Osborne, V. Partington, S. D. Phelps, Mr and Mrs R. A. Piller, Mr and Mrs R. Pope, M. G. Powell, J. Proud, R. Ralph, H. Ray, M. Regnard, G. Reid, Mr and Mrs W. R. Richards, Mrs R. Riley, Master Simon Riley, Mrs D. Robinson, F. Rowley, Mrs P. Russell, Mrs J. P. Samson, Mrs J. Saunders, Mrs E. L. Sherwin, A. C. Smith, C. L. Smith, Mr and Mrs J. Smith, J. R. C. Smith, K. Southall, Mrs V. Sprigg, Mrs J. Stetson, Mrs J. R. Stevens, Mrs

P. A. Taylor, C. Tetlow, R. J. Toms, B. Triptree, Ms B. Varley, J. Varley, R. Watts, Mrs M. Webber, R. Wellsted, Mr and Mrs J. Wheeler and Mrs M. Winfield.

A group of good friends and dedicated collectors kindly allowed us to photograph items from their collections to illustrate this book. I would therefore particularly like to thank Peter Holloway, Tom Hood, Gwyn Jones, John Proud, The Riley Family, Rita and John Smith for their help, hospitality and enormous patience.

All other pieces illustrated are from the collection or stock of Lynda and Nicholas Pine or my own collection.

An old postcard showing the
Goss agency in Chelmsford

The crested china stall at
Brighton west pier in Edwardian
times

Right Carlton. Lustre flat iron
with lucky white heather device
and a lustre kettle with a colour
transfer print of Windsor Castle

Left Carlton. Pearl lustre trumpet
vase with orange lustre inside
and lucky white heather device

Heraldic Porcelain to Crested China

China miniatures with applied coat of arms were popular souvenirs in Britain from around 1890 to 1930, the collection of these becoming almost a craze before the First World War.

China mementoes of tours and holidays had been popular all through the latter half of the reign of Queen Victoria, with the coming of the railways and slightly enlightened employers giving workers more holidays there certainly was a market for cheap souvenirs. The china was mostly ornate and was often made by the Germans, who were, in fact, the main producers of the pink pictorial china which was sold all over Great Britain. For some reason, which the British manufacturers never quite understood, the Germans could produce reasonable ware very cheaply. Probably their use of hard paste porcelain rather than bone china, more modern kilns and cheaper labour had a great deal to do with their commercial success. The Germans seemed much more concerned with producing wares that would appeal to the general public than the English firms who were more concerned that their products were 'artistic and in good taste'.

In the 1880's Adolphus Goss a traveller for the firm of W. H. Goss hit on the idea of producing china with the coat of arms of the tourist area or resort where it would be sold. His father William Henry Goss had developed a fine ivory porcelain which he had already used to make small pots with applied arms for the towns where public schools and University Colleges were located. The black outline of the arms was transfer printed onto the china and coloured by hand. Adolphus very cleverly decided to make china miniatures of ancient artefacts found in local museums and sold the idea to a good china shop in each town, producing the heraldic porcelain models for that shop alone in the area. Other models were added to the range, including local buildings, monuments and regional symbols such as 'The Bear and the Ragged Staff' of Warwickshire. Coloured buildings were introduced in 1893.

There can be no doubt that these models would be very much in the Victorian taste, appealing perhaps more to the white collar workers than the masses. Other well known fine china manufacturers were not slow to follow the Goss example and by the turn of the century heraldic china was being sold in all the best china shops who advertised it as 'Heraldic china in quaint and antique shapes'.

At this time the German china manufacturers had begun producing comic animals, often referred to as grotesques, miniature soldiers and other military models to commemorate the South African War. The 'Bazaar Trade', as it was called at the time, was clamouring for inexpensive china and many English earthenware manufacturers turned their hand to producing crested wares. Most producers of tableware

Such was the importance of crested china that Arcadian took the whole front page of the Daily Mail on Saturday April 3rd 1920 to advertise their wares

One of the pages of an original catalogue issued by Arcadian china in the 1920's showing some of the hundreds of pieces that retailers could select from to stock their bazaars, tea rooms, newsagencies etc.

made badged goods for hotels and other institutions which were often quite elaborate. The techniques for applying badges were very similar to those for adding crests, a little more hand painting was necessary. It was not difficult to get engravings made of any arms and travellers for the various firms would offer a range of plain white or ivory ware and suggest having the local arms engraved free of charge for an order of an agreed value. At the turn of the century the manufacturers of earthenware applied arms to small domestic items but later many of them copied the Goss shapes and gradually added animals and other small miniatures to their range.

Goss and other respected companies took great pains to apply correct coats of arms. If a town had no arms then a seal was used, if all else failed Goss had invented a type of seal (Reg. No. 77966) that could be used for any town. Less scrupulous firms would design a coat of arms to suit and some rather odd creations can be found masquerading as correct heraldic devices.

The German manufacturers were very quick to provide a range of suitable china miniatures and to offer to apply crests. They also copied the Goss idea of making miniatures of buildings for sale in souvenir shops or in the buildings themselves. It is amazing that in 1905 a German firm could take an order for a building in Britain, send back a post-card or photograph of the building and an example of the crest required and have the order in the shop within a fortnight. It certainly amazed their British competitors, whose main defence for slow delivery was that British china was much better anyway. One of the most over-used advertising slogans of the British potters at that time was 'Best English China at foreign prices'.

By 1910 *Crest Ware* as it was now called was extremely popular. Good china shops were selling *Goss* if they had their agency or china from another manufacturer of fine china. Souvenir shops, fancy goods shops, bazaars and the like were selling the cheaper and more vulgar pottery miniatures and the German hard china wares.

The Pottery Gazette was already predicting that the 'craze for crest ware' would soon be over and indeed the popularity of the more tasteful antique shapes was certainly not as great. Most manufacturers were turning to much more exciting miniatures, comic figures, sporting items, grotesques and regional souvenirs. Seaside souvenirs were of course very popular, lighthouses, ships, shells, lifeboatmen and Punch and Judy booths all being produced.

Designers were very quick to pick up any new public interest. Billiken for instance had been designed in America in 1908 by Florence Pretz. The happy little 'God of Luck' had caught on across the Atlantic and was introduced to Britain, he was soon found 'crested' in all the cheaper ranges.

The Great War one might think would have finally ended the passion for crested china but on the contrary it gave it a new impetus. The English manufacturers freed at last from German competition could sell as much cheap china as their works could make, which was not as much as they would have liked as the work force was sadly depleted by more and more men being called up. Naturally during the war many firms who had specialised in producing tableware turned to making china miniatures.

Clever businessmen like Harold Taylor Robinson, who was fast becoming a pottery tycoon, were quick to produce models of the new weapons of war. Tanks, monoplanes, bombs and hand grenades were all reproduced in china. China soldiers, sailors and nurses, very reminiscent of those produced by the Germans at the turn of the century, now reappeared with crests applied. These models would probably have sold without crests but the happy coincidence of a novelty which was also a souvenir was not lost on the retailers.

After the war many firms concentrated on reproducing the war memorials which were erected in many towns, but weapons went on selling into the mid twenties which is rather incredible when one considers what a blood bath it had been. Interest in crested china was fading and many firms started concentrating on producing Nursery Ware (children seem to have been invented in the twenties) and dressing table ware for the newly liberated women who were using make up openly for the first time.

From the mid twenties the crests on models really became quite immaterial, a simple 'souvenir from . . . .' inscription would have done just as well. The public, when they could afford to buy them, were looking for more colourful and amusing souvenirs. The most successful manufacturers were making models of flappers, 'cute' children, comic figures and joke items, adding more and more colour and often adding a lustre finish for good measure. Cartoon characters were also made. Bonzo Dog, Felix the Cat, Winkie the Gladeye Bird and Lucky Black Cats can all be found in crested china.

At this time firms were offering to apply the transfer devices 'Lucky White Heather' and 'Lucky Black Cats' to models instead of crests. 'View ware' was also offered as an alternative, colour transfer views having survived from before 1900. German competition was again very much in evidence. They were now producing heavily lustred wares with 'Lucky White Heather' devices.

Firms were still advertising crested goods right up to 1930 but the last things people could afford then were china novelties. One by one after 1930 the firms who had particularly specialised in crested china and other fancy wares became bankrupt. The craze was finally over.

Introduction to Marks, Manufacturers and Recorded Models

These have been arranged by marks, placed in alphabetical order, with information on the manufacturer and known models after each mark.

The models have not been listed alphabetically but have been grouped into types of souvenirs and have been arranged for the most part in the order they would have been made. The headings are as follows:

Unglazed/Parian
Parian busts are also found under this heading.

Ancient Artefacts
Models of historic interest as produced by W. H. Goss.

Buildings—Coloured

Buildings—White

Monuments (including crosses)

Historical/Folklore

Traditional/National Souvenirs
These have been listed in the following order: British, England, Ireland, Scotland, Wales, Other Countries.

Seaside Souvenirs
These have been listed in the following order: Bathing Machines, Crafts, Fishermen/Lifeboatmen, Lighthouses, Shells, Luggage, People and Punches.

Countryside

Animals
These listings include animals which are really regional symbols such as the Sussex Pig. Most collectors would include these in an animal collection.

Birds (including Eggs)
These listings also include regional or national emblems such as the Kiwi.

17

Great War

These models have been grouped as follows: Personnel, Aeroplanes/ Airships/Zeppelins, Ships/Submarines, Armoured Cars/Red Cross Vans/Tanks, Guns/Mortars, Small arms, Shells, Bombs, Grenades, Mines, Torpedoes, Personal Equipment.

Memorabilia

Memorials

Florence Nightingale statues are always included in Great War collections although she died before 1914. Certainly the statue was offered for sale at the same time, so it is listed under this heading.

Home/Nostalgic

Comic/Novelty

Cartoon/Comedy Characters

Alcohol

Sport

Musical Instruments

Transport

'Modern' Equipment

'Modern', that is, at the time it was made.

Miscellaneous

Miniature Domestic

Under these headings models are listed alphabetically, if that is possible. All short inscriptions are written in italics, verses or long inscriptions are in inverted commas.

If a model is best described by its inscription this will be placed at the beginning of an entry in italics.

Sizes are height unless otherwise indicated.

Crested China Manufacturers

Abbey China

Trademark used by Hewitt & Leadbeater, Willow Potteries, Longton for a fancy goods wholesaler or retailer in Tewkesbury.

For details of this china and manufacturer see Willow Art and Willow China. C C of Tewkesbury must have been a wholesaler as crests from several places have been recorded; these include Cheddar, Devizes, Upton on Severn and Wincombe as well as Tewkesbury. Possibly the firm owned a chain of souvenir shops. No view ware or late transfers have been found on models with this mark. (Stock Numbers where found are the same as those found on *Willow* models.)

Abbey Models

Seaside Souvenirs
Lighthouse Pepper Pot. 110 mm. (There is almost certainly a matching Salt Pot.)

Animals
Cat, sitting, one ear down. 102 mm.

Home/Nostalgic
Grandfather Clock, inscribed: *Make use of time let not advantage slip. Shakespeare.* No. 149. 140 mm. (This is rather larger than the usual *Willow* model.)

Cartoon/Comedy Characters
Baby with arms outstretched, inscribed: *Cheerio.* Some colouring on face. 125 mm. (Great War Cartoon Character, could be 'Pooksie'.)

Miscellaneous
Schoolboy's Cap. 62 mm long. (Some collectors think these caps are actually cricket caps.)

Adderleys

Trademark used by Adderleys Ltd., Daisy Bank Pottery, Longton.

Used 1912–1926

Used 1912–1926

Adderleys Ltd established in 1906 manufactured china and earthenware throughout the 'crested china' period. They did not as far as is known manufacture crested ware but they did produce a range of 'smalls' to commemorate the Great War, these are inscribed: 1914 EDITION, and are often found in Great War china collections.

Right Albion. Yacht 125 mm

Left Albion. Lancashire clog
80 mm long

Right Anglo Heraldic. Ladies
18th Century Slipper

Left Aldwych. Unnamed
Tommy's Steel Helmet, with the
Arcadian version of the
'Aldwych' mark and the usual
City of London crest

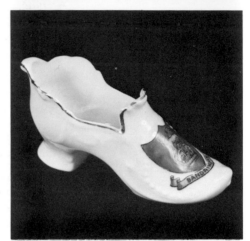

Right Anglo Heraldic. Bear
sitting. 80 mm

Left Anglo Heraldic. A fierce
model of a British Bulldog

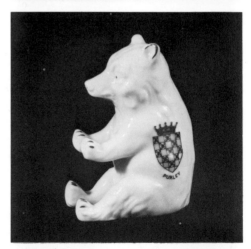

Right Avon. Reverse of double
headed bust usually inscribed
'Votes for Women'

Left Avon. Votes for Women,
double bust, not inscribed

Albion China

Trademark used by Robinson
and Beresford, Baltimore Works, Longton.
Subsequently a branch of J. A. Robinson Ltd.

1907–1910

In 1901 Mr W. H. Robinson set up as a china manufacturer in Longton, specialising in *Queens White Ware*. In 1903 Mr Robinson had need to take into partnership a Mr Beresford and the firm was then known as Robinson and Beresford. The firm seems to have been under financed from the start and by 1907 Harold Taylor Robinson (see Arcadian China) had gained control and merged Robinson and Beresford with Charles Ford (see Swan China). In 1910 these firms were made branches of J. A. Robinson Ltd.

All known models with the *Albion China* mark are exactly the same as *Arcadian* and *Swan* pieces. It is unlikely that Robinson and Beresford made crest china before the merger, and as only early models and 'smalls' have been recorded it seems that the *Albion* mark was not used after 1910.

Numbering System The stock numbers found on the base of *Albion* models are exactly the same numbers as found on Arcadian models. They are listed below. The dashes and other pointed symbols found near the trademark are paintresses' marks.

Albion (Robinson and Beresford) Models

Ancient Artefacts
Glastonbury Bowl, inscribed: *Model of bowl from the ancient British lake village near Glastonbury*. No. 55. 50 mm.
Loving cup originated by Henry of Navarre King of France. 2 or 3 handled. No. 579. 40 mm.
Newbury Leather Bottle. Inscribed: *Model of leather bottle found on battlefield of*

Newbury 1644 now in museum. No. 83. 65 mm.
Silchester Vase, inscribed: *Model of vase from Silchester in Reading museum*. No. 54. 60 mm.

Historical/Folklore
Ancient coaching hat, model of. No. 687. 65 mm long.

Albion China

Trademark used on china
made for a Scottish
wholesaler by Taylor and
Kent (Ltd), Florence Works, Longton.

Usual mark 1913–25

Mark only rarely found and thought to be a variation used by the firm.

ALBION
CHINA
ENGLAND

For details of this china and manufacturer see FLORENTINE CHINA.

'Smalls' and models found with this mark have Scottish crests or coloured transfer printed views. Some useful crested domestic ware has been recorded including plates, beakers, bagware vases and a money box with a handle 70 mm long. (Stock numbers were not used by Taylor and Kent.)

Albion (TC and P) Models

Traditional/National Souvenirs
Lancashire Clog. 88 mm long.

Seaside souvenirs
Portmanteau. 60 mm long.

Animals
Cat, sitting, very furry coat. 90 mm.
Dolphin Jug. 100 mm.
Frog Jug. No details of size.
Hare. 95 mm long.

Birds
Pelican Jug. 83 mm long.

Great War
Shell. 75 mm.

Home/Nostalgic
Firebucket. 65 mm.
Old Armchair, The with verse 'I love it, I love it and who shall dare to chide me for loving the Old Armchair'. 85 mm.
Pillar Box, not found with inscription. 76 mm.

Miscellaneous
Carboy. 76 mm.

Miniature Domestic
Coffee Pot. 76 mm.
Tea Pot. 60 mm.

Alexandra. 'Tower Bridge'
140 mm long

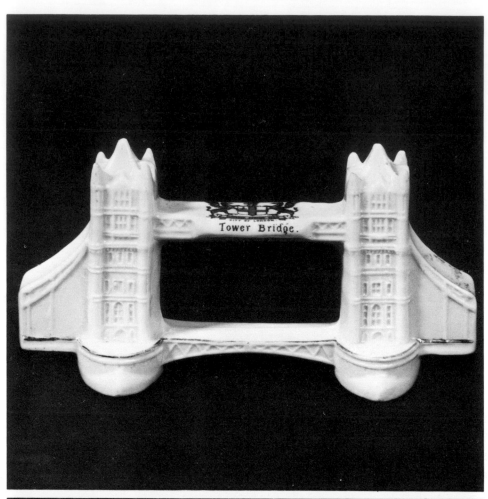

Alexandra. 'St. Paul's Cathedral'.
'The Monument' and
'Westminster Abbey, West Front'

Aldwych China

Mark used on wares manufactured by Arkinstall & Son Ltd

Mark used on wares manufactured by Birks, Rawlins & Co

Mark used on wares manufactured by Wiltshaw & Robinson Ltd

Trade name used by the retailer, Samuels, The Strand, London, on crested china. Manufactured by Arkinstalls and Son Ltd (see Arcadian China) Birks, Rawlins and Co. (see Savoy China) and Wiltshaw and Robinson Ltd (see Carlton China).

Samuels either changed their supplier often or all three companies produced crested wares for them at the same time. For details of the china and manufacturer see the appropriate entry in these lists. Many 'smalls' have also been recorded. (Stock numbers where known coincide with those on other models made by these firms.)

Aldwych (A and S) Models
Manufactured by Arkinstall (Arcadian China)

Animals
Tortoise. Rd. No. 456065. 72 mm long.

Birds
Cock standing, legs modelled separately, inscribed: *Cock o' the South*. Some colouring to head. 100 mm. (This is usually found inscribed *Cock o' the North* on Arcadian models.)

Great War
Cannon Shell, inscribed: *Jack Johnson* (Reigning heavyweight boxing champion of the World during the Great War). 90 mm.
Steel Helmet with EP on side. 70 mm long and only 24 mm high. (Not the usual Arcadian model.)

Home/Nostalgic
Grandfather clock, inscribed: *Make use of time let not advantage slip. Shakespeare.* 108 mm.

Miscellaneous
Horseshoe. 55 mm long.

Aldwych (BR and Co) Models
Most pieces found with this mark are small vases etc. Only one model has been recorded. Manufactured by Birks, Rawlins and Co. (Savoy China).

Countryside
Acorn, model of. No. 110. 56 mm.

Aldwych (W and R) Models
Only one model recorded. Manufactured by Wiltshaw and Robinson Ltd (Carlton China).

Monuments
Nelson's Column with four lions at base. 165 mm.

Alexandra China

Marks used on china made by Hewitt Bros

Trademark used by a wholesaler, china manufactured by several leading producers of crested china.

CEB must have been a wholesaler for souvenir china with showrooms in London. Many such companies advertised in the Pottery Gazette, but so far I have been unable to place these initials. Alexandra China has presented an enormous problem for researchers, the china is of good quality and many of the buildings are not found in other ranges. All the buildings with the exception of the Bottle Oven are to be found in London, and many *Alexandra* models carry London crests. Once one had realised that the china was not made by one manufacturer and that the buildings were probably (with the exception of the Bottle Oven) made by Hewitt Bros (see Willow China) this mark is not so problematic.

It would seem that before the war *CEB* probably sold cheaper German china wares as there are very few early 'crested' models in the range.

Right Alexandra. 'Ad Astra' RAF Memorial. Golden eagle on brown globe on a white glazed base

Left Alexandra. Cat with ruff of fur round neck 100 mm

Left Alexandra. Bottle oven 82 mm

Alexandra. Torpedo 150 mm long

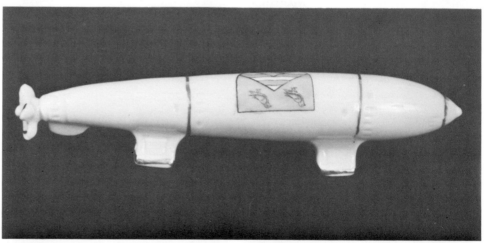

Right Atlas Heraldic CR & Co. Sabot with turned up toe

Left Alexandra. Red Cross Van 98 mm long with 3 red crosses

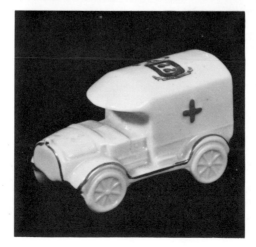

Mark found on some domestic ware

ALEXANDRA CHINA
MADE
IN
ENGLAND

Mark thought to be used by Sampson, Hancock & Sons

Most of the models in the Great War, animals and home or nostalgic categories appear to have been made for the firm by Sampson Hancock and Sons (see Corona China) during the war years. Many of the Alexandra models listed below will also be found in the *Corona* range including that puzzling Bottle Oven. Hewitt Bros seem to have become the supplier after the Great War, working to a higher standard than usual. The buildings are not recognisably *Willow* but one finds that hardly any London buildings are found marked Willow, the exception being Nelson's Column. I have been unable to compare a *Willow* Nelson's Column with an Alexandra model but they are the same size. A Cenotaph has been found bearing a Willow mark as well as an *Alexandra* mark which goes some way to proving this theory correct. Later 'smalls' and models with 'Lucky Black Cat' transfers were very obviously made by Hewitt Bros, the paintresses' marks and the stock numbers being identical. Many of the models listed below will also be found in the Willow range.

It is quite probable that other manufacturers made china for this wholesale firm and hopefully other clues will indicate which these were.

No view ware, foreign or military crests have been found with these marks. Later wares not only include the 'Lucky Black Cat' transfers but other decorations on domestic ware and models including all kinds of floral patterns. No 'Lucky White Heather' devices have been found.

Numbering System Unfortunately stock numbers have not been recorded with any regularity. This is a pity as they would help in identifying manufacturers. Numbers are given where known.

Alexandra Models

Ancient Artefacts
Aberdeen Bronze Pot, not named. No details of size.

Buildings—White
Marble Arch, can be found unglazed except for top. 75 mm.
Bottle Oven. No. 233. 82 mm.
St. Pauls Cathedral. 135 mm.
Tower Bridge. 140 mm long.
Westminster Abbey, West Front. 90 mm.

Monuments
Cleopatra's Needle, not recorded named. 130 mm.
Monument, The. 159 mm.
Nelson Monument Trafalgar Sauare. 165 mm.

Historical/Folklore
Man in the Moon. 55 mm.

Traditional/National Souvenirs
Welsh Harp. No. 292. 95 mm.

Animals
Cat, sitting and smiling. 106 mm. (Could be an un-named Cheshire cat.)
Cat, sitting, with ruff of fur round neck. 100 mm.
Cat, sitting, with very long neck. 68 mm. (This cat, found in most manufacturers' ranges, was a model of the cat mascot of a Destroyer during the Great War.)
Dog, Bulldog, standing. 63 mm.
Fish, 120 mm long.
Fish Vase. 63 mm.
Pig, standing. 80 mm long.

Rabbit, crouching, ears back. 67 mm long.
Shetland Pony. 110 mm long.

Birds
Swan. 51 mm.

Great War
Monoplane, with movable prop. 145 mm long.
British Airship on stand. 130 mm. long.
Lusitania. 163 mm long.
Submarine, inscribed: *E4.* 110 mm long.
Red Cross Van. 98 mm long.
Tank with inset trailing wheels. 100 mm long.
Field Gun. 120 mm long.
Torpedo. 150 mm.
Bell Tent. 85 mm.
Gurka Knife. 140 mm long.
Ad Astra. RAF Memorial with inscription: *Unveiled by HRH Prince of Wales July 16th 1923.* This model is only found in this range. The Memorial takes the form of an eagle with outstretched wings, standing on brown circular globe on a white glazed base. 170 mm.
Cenotaph, inscribed: *The Glorious Dead MCMXLV. MCMXLX* with green wreaths. 2 sizes: 145 mm & 184 mm.
Edith Cavell Memorial London. 2 sizes: 115 mm & 155 mm.
Florence Nightingale Statue. 146 mm. (These last two must be named but have not been recorded as such.)

Home/Nostalgic
Baby, in Bootee. 76 mm.

Grandfather Clock. 138 mm.
Sundial with verse:
"I mark not the hours unless they be
bright.
I mark not the hours of darkness and
night.
My promise is solely to follow the sun
And point out the course his chariot
doth run."
112 mm. (Same inscription found on
'Willow' models.)
Watering Can. 70 mm.

Alcohol
Barrel on Stand. 65 mm.

Transport
Petrol can. No. 249. 66 mm.

Modern Equipment
Gas Cooker. 70 mm.

Miscellaneous
Ladies' Button Boot. 65 mm.
Ladies' 18th Century Shoe. 70 mm long.
Sabot. 102 mm long.

Miniature Domestic
Cheese Dish, 1 piece. 50 mm.
Cheese Dish and Cover. 2 sizes: 50 mm &
60 mm.
Coffee Pot, with lid. 75 mm.

Anglo Heraldic Co
Trademark used by Sampson
Hancock (& Sons), Bridge
Works, Stoke

For details of this china and the manufacturer see THE CORONA
CHINA.

Sampson Hancock appear to have used this mark before the Great
War, as most pieces found with this mark are 'smalls'. Ancient artefacts
(unfortunately un-named and therefore not often recorded as such) and
the usual animals, shoes, etc. made before 1914.

Some pictorials and views are found on china with this mark but as yet
only monochrome (black) transfers have been recorded. (Stock Numbers
are the same as *Corona* models, and are listed where known.)

Anglo Heraldic Models

Ancient Artefacts
Canterbury Leather Bottle, not named. No.
156.

Animals
Bear, sitting. 80 mm.
Cheshire Cat always smiling, The. 95 mm.
Dog. Bulldog, standing. 112 mm long.
Pig, standing. 84 mm long.

Home/Nostalgic
Coal Scuttle. 64 mm.
Milk Churn. No. 168. 70 mm.
Watering Can. 70 mm.

Miscellaneous
Ladies' Button Boot. 65 mm.
Ladies' 18th century Shoe. No. 146. 90 mm
long.

Miniature Domestic
Cheese Dish and Lid. 50 mm.

Arcadian China
Trademark used by Arkinstall
& Son Ltd, Arcadian Works,
Stoke on Trent, subsequently
a branch of J. A. Robinson &
Sons, later Cauldon Ltd, and
finally Coalport China Co.
(John Rose & Co.) Ltd.

From 1903

Arkinstall & Sons were the biggest British producers of crested china
over the longest period, therefore, it follows that the history of the firm
and its wares is of great importance to collectors and anyone interested in
the development of popular china souvenirs from the early part of this
century to just before the Second World War. The story of Arcadian China
has to be the story of its owner Mr Harold Taylor Robinson, possibly the
most interesting and important person in the Potteries during the period
crested china was made. He was the central figure in the production and
promotion of cheap china souvenirs for the lower end of the market. One

Probably introduced 1910

Probably introduced 1912

Arcadian China

Mark used on models with small bases 1903–20's

ARCADIAN CHINA

Mark used on models with small bases 1920's

ARCADIAN

Mark found on late domestic wares

cannot imagine that he did so with the integrity and enthusiasm for quality of some Potters, the Goss family for example; he was first and foremost the entrepreneur, a brilliant and daring business man (his critics would add almost reckless) interested in china only as a marketable commodity. During his amazing career he managed to draw many of the most important crested china manufacturers, including Goss, into his enormous empire; a study of his business dealings and eventual bankruptcy does much to explain why so many identical pieces of crested china can be found with different marks.

Harold Taylor Robinson began his career as a traveller for Wiltshaw & Robinson (the makers of *Carlton China*) in 1899 when he was twenty-two years old. He was paid £156 per annum plus commission, and one can only assume that he managed to earn a huge amount of commission because he was able, four years later, in 1903 to start out on his own as a china manufacturer. With capital of approximately £1,500, which he claimed represented his savings, he formed the company Arkinstall & Son. Using the tradename 'Arcadian', Arkinstall produced china novelties and souvenirs, and was probably the only company formed specifically to manufacture crested china. Mr Robinson continued some kind of association with Wiltshaw and Robinson Ltd and became a partner in that firm by 1906. (The early *Arcadian* and *Carlton* crested wares were very similar.) Mr Wiltshaw seems to have been unwilling to be taken over and he managed to keep the ownership and control of the company in his own hands. From 1903 to 1920 however Harold Taylor Robinson was interested alone or jointly in the acquisition of a number of china and earthenware manufacturing concerns, either for resale or to form new companies to take them over and run them.

He was particularly active in 1910; having gained control of Robinson & Leadbeater (*R & L*) he merged this firm with Arkinstall. This explains the number of *R & L* parian busts found with *Arcadian* marks. Later in August of that year having gained control of more firms he formed a new company, J. A. Robinson and Sons, Ltd (J. A. Robinson was his father, the directors included Harold Taylor, his father and his brother, Hubert Alcock Robinson), to carry on the businesses of Robinson & Leadbeater, Charles Ford (*Swan China*) and Wardle's Art Pottery Ltd. Arkinstall became a branch of J. A. Robinson in 1912 and Ford & Pointon (*Coronet*), having been taken over by Mr Robinson, became yet another branch in 1919. From the dates of their amalgamation models marked Arcadian, Coronet and Swan are from the same moulds and were obviously produced in the same works.

At the 1920 British Industries Fair, J. A. Robinson presented a huge exhibit showing all types of ornamental and domestic china and earthenware, but this was just proof of the first stage of Harold Taylor Robinson's empire building. In April of that year he bought Cauldon (Brown, Westhead, Moore & Co) Ltd for £100,000 and promoted Cauldon Potteries Ltd to amalgamate most of the concerns he by then either owned or in which he had controlling interest. These included J. A. Robinson & Sons, Ltd and branches, F. R. Pratt & Co. Ltd (Greekware and sundries for chemists), Henry Alcock Pottery Co. (Fancy Goods), Grindley Hotel Ware (Hotel Vitrified Ware), Geo. L. Ashworth & Bros (Manufacturers of *Masons* ironstone), and Brown Westhead, Moore & Co. (*Cauldon China*, earthenware and fire proof ware).

Between 1920 and 1930, through a series of share deals, which although not dishonest were rather questionable morally, as he was often the Managing Director of the firms buying and selling the shares,

Right Arcadian. Small cream jug with a very rare transfer of two hens. Inscribed on reverse 'Elp yerself to tha crame'

Left Arcadian. 125 mm model of a bronze pot with the most perfect butterfly print

Arcadian. Top row: Mauve lustre cottage, blue lustre crocodile (very rare model even more rare in lustre)
Bottom row: Two handle vase, deep orange lustre with lucky black cat transfer, yellow lustre pot with black cat and sunset, pale orange vase with sitting black cat transfer

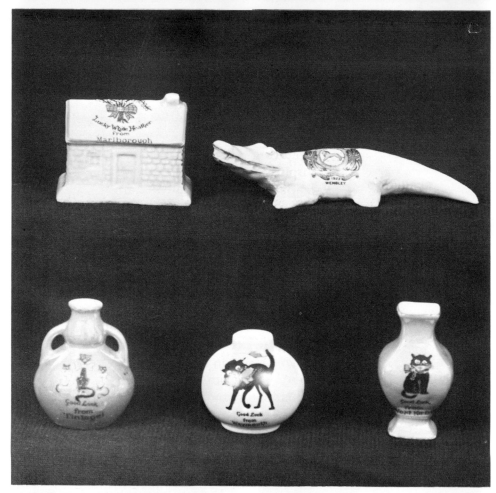

Right Arcadian. Delicate mug with a really beautiful colour transfer scene. Inscribed 'Gift from Withernsea'. 80 mm

Left Arcadian. Examples of bird and vine decoration and the pretty floral patterns

he managed to gain control of some of the bigger names in the china industry. Ridgways (Bedford Works) Ltd, Wedgwood & Co. Ltd, Tunstall (not to be confused with Josiah Wedgwood & Sons), Bishops & Stonier Ltd, The Coalport China Co., Royal Crown Derby Porcelain Co. Ltd, and Royal Worcester Porcelain were all in some way controlled by him. He moved into the sanitary ware side of the business too, gaining control of F. Winkle & Co. Ltd and Baker & Co. Ltd.

On the way he picked up the almost bankrupt firms of W. H. Goss and Hewitt Bros (*Willow*), forming in 1925 Willow Potteries Ltd as part of the Cauldon group and in 1930 W. H. Goss Ltd. He continued to use the moulds and marks of both companies, but from this date the quality of Goss China was never what it had once been. Most of these late Goss pieces are marked *Goss England* but this is not always the case. Models from the *Arcadian* and *Willow* ranges are often found with the *Goss* mark. (For some inexplicable reason Goss collectors who would not dream of buying Arcadian or Willow China, will pay enormous sums of money for models made from these firms' moulds but bearing the Goss mark!) The production of late coloured crested *Arcadian* and *Willow* China was obviously combined at the Arcadian Works, the only difference between late Arcadian or Willow Black Boys being the mark printed on the base. The *Willow* mark was not used after 1930, there being no demand for it as crested china was already out of fashion.

During this period, 1920–30, Harold Taylor Robinson had become the largest employer in North Staffordshire, his interest in the fine china trade being such that he dominated it. His turnover during these years was between £850,000 and £900,000 per annum and he was the director of thirty-two companies. His ultimate scheme was to form an amalgamation of all the companies of which he obtained control into one huge company (perhaps he was a little before his time; such companies exist in the china industry today). It is not surprising, given his speculative genius, that at this stage he started buying into the companies of his suppliers, Parkhouse Collieries Ltd and Goldenhill & Clive's Marl Co. Ltd in order to provide cheap fuel and clay for his works.

Mr Robinson told the court during his bankruptcy hearing that he had been assured by a very important and respectable accountant that if outside events had not overtaken him he would by 1932 have been a millionaire; who could doubt it? Unfortunately, like so many other large concerns at the time, this enormous monument to enterprise he had so cleverly built came crashing down in that year, unable to withstand the crippling effects of world depression. He had had to face a series of disasters, beginning with the coal strike in 1921; the loss of foreign markets, notably America, Australia, West Canada and Brazil, as trade internationally was unsettled; the loss of the 'West End' trade in London (for the Depression hit the rich as well as the poor), and Britain going off the gold standard in 1924. He is quoted in the Pottery Gazette at his Bankruptcy Proceedings in 1932:

'When I saw the depression was developing to the extent it was, I left my country house and came to live practically next door to the works and I have been working fifty weeks out of fifty-two to try and circumvent the terrible effects of that depression.'

'When you get down to basic facts you will realise that as the largest potter in North Staffordshire I have been the largest victim.'

In his frantic efforts to save his empire, his financial dealings became more and more wild. He borrowed money from the banks that he had no hope of repaying, he distributed money and stocks from one of his firms to another in an enormous and over optimistic attempt to keep afloat. His efforts came to nothing and when he was declared bankrupt most of his firms were already in the hands of the Receiver.

Throughout his bankruptcy and discharge proceedings (for which he petitioned in 1934) no one had call to question his honesty, but his dealings could only be described as unorthodox and disturbed and often puzzled the judge, but not as much as his behaviour while still a bankrupt. The Secretary of the Cauldon Potteries had been buying up the debts on the debtors' behalf for very small sums. Fifty-three creditors had sold their debts amounting to £3,733 for £593. Rates varied alarmingly, ranging from 1s. 5d to 20s. in the £. Some of these people were creditors who would have received nothing out of the bankruptcy, whereas preferential creditors got nothing at all.

'Do you suggest that he is only acting for the debtor in this matter?' asked the judge.

'I say that he is the bankrupt's catspaw', answered a very heated Official Receiver.

Harold Taylor absolutely denied any knowledge of the transactions. The judge refused to discharge Mr Robinson for a further two years.

Proving once more that it had been impossible to keep a 'good' man down, Mr Robinson had already been appointed Sales Organiser of the newly formed company, George Jones and Sons Ltd in 1933 when the old established firm of George Jones had been merged with Bishops & Stonier. The new company continued to use the Crescent Potteries that had always been the home of the George Jones firm. Mr Robinson must have been a fairly good Sales Organiser, for George Jones and Sons Ltd soon bought up the old and well-known firm of Allertons. Later in 1933 Cauldon merged with Coalport China Co. (John Rose & Co.) Ltd; the *Arcadian* trade mark was still being used, as was *Goss*. One could almost guess what would happen next! In 1937 the Coalport China Co. was amalgamated with George Jones and Sons, *Cauldon*, *Coalport*, *Allertons*, *Crescent* and *Goss* china were all produced at the Crescent Pottery. It has lately been discovered that the range of ladies marked 'Goss England' are made from Coalport moulds. *Arcadian* had disappeared without trace and the Goss trademark was not listed by the firm after the Second World War. It probably was not used after 1939. What happened to Harold Taylor Robinson after 1933 is not clear: an employee at the Crescent Potteries in the late thirties has no recollection of him, and he is certainly not listed as an officer of that firm. He was by then in his sixties and it may well be that he had retired. The two surviving companies from this last merger have both been sold, Cauldon Potteries Ltd was acquired by Pountney & Co. Ltd of Bristol in 1962 and Coalport became a division of the Wedgwood Group in 1977.

Having considered his career it is not at all surprising to learn that Mr Robinson made a huge commercial success out of his first company, Arkinstall and Sons. W. H. Goss had agents in every reasonably sized town in Britain; Arkinstall's *Arcadian* was sold in just about every conceivable retail outlet; bazaars, lending libraries, cafés, pubs, seaside kiosks, stationers, fancy emporiums, pharmacies, sub-post offices as well as china shops. The wares of the company were not advertised in trade journals, probably because *Arcadian* retailers were unlikely to read them, and Harold Taylor Robinson relied on a large team of travellers to bring back the orders. They obviously left no stone unturned!

Arcadian China is not particularly fine, it cannot be compared with Shelley or Grafton wares, but it is adequate and really quite well produced when one considers the selling price. ('Smalls' were usually sold for less than a shilling.) Early wares for the most part were copies of the historic shapes being sold by Goss on the one hand and the small animals and grotesques of the German souvenir industry on the other. It is very difficult to assess which of these early models were original *Arcadian* moulds and which were brought to the firm as a result of all the mergers. It was during the war years that Mr Robinson showed his flair for innovation, when Arkinstall's provided the war-minded public with an enormous range of crested military souvenirs. Often these models were designed from newspaper descriptions and are therefore very unlike the real thing, but as the public hadn't seen them either no one seemed to mind. As each new weapon was brought into the war Mr Robinson showed great speed in making a china model of it. The day after the 'Daily Mail' ran a photograph of the first tank, Mr Robinson registered his model (Rd. No. 658588). The tank had seen some action and had lost one of its steering wheels. Unfortunately this was not explained, and the first china tanks also had only one wheel, and looked very odd! Mr Robinson had the copyright on models of British tanks, so I doubt if he lost much sleep over it as he collected the dues from all the other manufacturers. (Nearly all the early tanks carry the same registration number.)

It was during the War years and immediately afterwards that *Arcadian* became the brand leader in the china souvenir field. (They were particularly busy after the war making the Memorials which were sold for many years.) In 1921 Arkinstall's were described to the trade as 'Manufacturers of Arms China Miniatures and Coats of Arms Tea Ware.' and apart from Goss they were the only firm who made little else. By the mid 1920s they were offering models with a great deal of colouring and introduced their popular Black Cat series. A catalogue from this period has been discovered; although undated it must have been produced around 1925. It is particularly short on words but visually it provides us with an enormous amount of information. The Black Cats were obviously a new and important line as they were the only items illustrated in colour. The cheapest Black Cats sold for 12/- per dozen to the retailer, the most expensive for 18/-. 'Smalls' were only 4/6 per dozen and small animals 6/-, whereas models of St. Paul's were as much as 36/- per dozen. Certain items were sold to retailers as singles, these being large domestic pieces such as fern pots and tobacco jars; one of these, a delightful Art Deco 'Ballet Girl Puff Box' priced at 5/- has not as yet been found by collectors, presumably few were made as they were so expensive. At this time the catalogue offers any of the models in 'Arms China, Black Cat, 'Good Luck From', Lucky White Heather or Coloured Views'.

After 1925, for the most part, only coloured models were added to the range. These include Black Boys, cute children and novelty, joke items, all unique to this firm and particularly appealing. The crests found on these models are purely incidental and one suspects they would have sold just as well with a simple 'Souvenir from' message. The craze for crests was nearly over so it is surprising to find a large advertisement in the 'Daily Mail' 22nd May 1928 for 'Arcadian Arms China'. It reads:

'Arcadian Arms China can be obtained from over 10,000 Retail Fancy Goods Stores in practically every town and village in Great Britain, decorated in correct colours with local Coat-of-Arms.

Arcadian. Two smalls and a cream jug showing tropical bird transfer prints

Arcadian. Three examples of coloured transfer prints on smalls and in the middle a Canterbury Roman Vase, from left to right 'St. Olaves Bridge', 'Crowthorne Church' and 'Stonehenge'

Arcadian. Cockerel transfers, middle jug shows motto on reverse

Arcadian. A small vase, thistle and small Cheshire cat all decorated with poppies

If not already collecting Arcadian Arms China, START AT ONCE! It is a fascinating hobby.
The collection of Arcadian Arms China creates an added interest and preserves pleasant recollections of a holiday. Friends will appreciate nothing better than a gift of Arcadian Arms China on your return. No other souvenir is so conveniently carried home'.

Arcadian China can be found decorated with a great number of other devices and designs. View ware, both monochrome (black only) and polychrome, was produced throughout the life of the company. A huge number of views and pictorials of reasonable quality can be found, usually on small vases and named artefacts but occasionally on animals, Great War and other unlikely models. Transfer prints of a regional nature are very desirable; these include: 'Devonshire Dumplings', 'Hampshire Hog', 'Somerset Cuckoo', 'Trusty Servant', 'Yorkshireman's Advice', Royal Stewart Tartan and 'Welsh Teaparty'.

Later, other transfer prints were introduced, the most popular being the Lucky Black Cats which can be found in great quantity on small pieces and domestic ware. Less easily found transfers are the range of tropical looking birds on branches; these can be coloured yellow, yellow and brown, pink and brown and pink and blue; they are usually found inscribed: 'A Gift from . . .' or more unusually 'A Souvenir from . . .'.

Other transfer prints have some hand colouring added, the same technique as used on crests. These include 'Lucky White Heather', 'Raphael Tuck Cartoons' and an early range of beautifully and brightly coloured cocks and hens. The Lucky White Heather device is found on many small models and domestic ware, either of which can have a lustre finish or be made in cream ware. The Raphael Tuck cartoons, usually of a small Dutch boy and girl, or Derby & Joan figures in Dutch costumes are found on small and domestic china including nursery ware. 'By Special Permission of Raphael Tuck & Sons Ltd', is usually found printed on domestic ware. Various mottoes accompany these cartoons, including such gems as:

'He that is satisfied is rich.'
'None but the brave deserve the fair.'
'No life can be dreary when work is a delight.'
'Deeds are fruits, words are but leaves.'
'A good life and health are a man's best wealth.'
'Tis deeds alone must win the prize.'
'He loves me! He loves me not! He loves me!'

Cockerel or Hen transfers have only been found on small vases and jugs of various sizes and they are quite rare. These too are found with rather trite mottoes and sayings, but oddly not the same as the ones above. They are:

'Joy, temperance and repose slam the door on the Doctor's nose.'
'If you can't be aisy, be as aisy as you can.'
'All the world's a stage and man in his time plays many parts.'
'Little and often fills the purse.'
'To err is human to forgive divine.'
'A handsome shoe often pinches the foot.'

How many relatives were irrevocably offended by receiving one of these offerings is not recorded.
Floral transfer decorations are also rarely found, red poppies being the most common, but forget-me-nots and much later floral designs of

sprays of mixed flowers were also used, although they are difficult to find, as are the transfer prints of butterflies, but they do exist.

In 1921 Arkinstalls advertised 'Nursery Rhyme Ware', but very little of this has survived. The only piece I have seen is a child's plate with a charming hand coloured transfer print of 'Ride a Cock Horse'.

Pieces with transfer prints other than Views can be found edged in colour rather than gilt, orange (Black Cats and Lucky White Heather); green (Black Cats, Flowers, Nursery Ware, Cockerels and Cartoons) and black (tropical birds).

Arcadian was exported and many foreign crests have been recorded; models for non-English speaking countries were marked *Porcelaine Arcadienne*. Crests of the Allies are often found on models made during the Great War, as are Military Crests. These are much collected by Great War enthusiasts; the following have so far been recorded:

The Royal Military College, Camberley.
The Inns of Court O.T.C.
Army Service Corps.
East Kent Mounted Rifles.
Imperial Yeomanry.
Machine Gun Corps.
Queens Royal West Surrey Regiment.
Staffs. Regimental Insignia.
R.A.F. Ewshott.
H.M.S. Queen Mary.
H.M.S. Thunderer.

Apart from Great War flags of the allies transfer 'United we stand', very few commemoratives seem to have been produced, the only ones known being: South Africa 1900–1901 and British Empire Exhibition 1924 and 1925.

As more and more collectors are being priced out of the Goss market they are turning to *Arcadian* which offers a similar range of wares (history repeats itself!). So it is not surprising that the very late products of the firm are eagerly sought and have risen in price over the last few years. Unlike other firms Arkinstall did not make a range of uncrested coloured models in the early 1930s, except for female figures. These are of particular interest as they are very like the Goss England ladies and were made at the same time. The *Arcadian* ladies are more detailed and of a rather higher quality than the Goss England versions. Models recorded so far are:

Ballet Girl, seated on three-legged stool, wearing a crimson dress. 164 mm.
Balloon Lady, old lady in pink dress, mauve apron and green shawl, holding balloons. 145 mm.
Bridesmaid, wearing pink dress and holding flowers. 135 mm.
Cherry Ripe, wearing yellow dress and holding a basket of flowers. 175 mm.
Doris, wearing bonnet and holding skirts. No details of size.
Market Woman, old lady in blue dress and red shawl, holding a basket of fruit. 155 mm.
Miss Ascott, wearing large Ascot hat. No details of size.
Miss Prudence, wearing a green dress and pink hat, holding a spray of flowers. 175 mm.
Tinker, wearing yellow trousers. 150 mm.
Tulip Girl, Dutch girl in national costume, with basket of tulips at her feet. 130 mm.

Late lustre ware marked *Arcadian* is suspiciously like that marked *Goss*, and one wonders if they were produced by the same hands. Vases, bowls and domestic ware can be found, but not all that often, with mother-of-pearl, orange, green, mauve, purple and yellow lustre finishes.

Numbering System Printed stock numbers are found on early models and these have been given where known in the following lists. It must be emphasised that registration numbers printed on later *Arcadian* models are notoriously unreliable and are often found not to be the number that the piece was actually registered under. Mr Robinson registered up to twenty models at a time and given that more moulds became available with each new merger presumably no one could be bothered to check that the correct number was being used on each model. (Printing any number or 'Registration applied for' was an indication that the model was registered and therefore copyright.) The Registration Number most often found on a model, whether it is the correct one or not, has been given in the lists—hopefully this will help with identifying an un-named item. The tiny numbers, initials and marks often found painted on the base of *Arcadian* china are paintresses' marks.

Arcadian Models

Parian/unglazed

Busts

Bust of King Edward VII, later models found with inscription: 'King Edward VII born Nov. 9th 1841. Died May 6th 1910. Reigned from Jan. 22nd 1901 to May 6th 1910.' On circular glazed base. 140 mm.

Bust of King Edward VII, in Military Uniform on circular glazed base. 130 mm.

Bust of Queen Alexandra, on circular glazed base. 2 sizes: 120 mm and 140 mm. Smaller size can be found named in blue lettering.

Bust of King George V, can be found with a glazed circular or keyhole base. With inscription: 'King George V. Born June 3rd 1865, ascended the throne May 6th 1910.' 135 mm.

Bust of Queen Mary, can be found with a glazed circular or keyhole base, with inscription: 'Queen Mary, born May 26th 1867'. 135 mm.

Bust of Prince of Wales (later Edward VIII) in midshipman's uniform, inscription in red and blue: 'HRH Prince of Wales. Born June 23rd 1894.' On glazed circular base. Rd. No. 583045/8. 135 mm.

(Any of the above can be found with crests on their glazed bases.)

Bust of Burns, found with poem by Wordsworth. On circular glazed base. 120 mm.

Bust of King of the Belgians on square glazed base, sculpted by W. C. Lawton. 175 mm.

Bust of Sir John Jellicoe on square glazed base, sculpted by W. C. Lawton. 175 mm.

Bust of General Joffre on square glazed base, sculpted by W. C. Lawton. 175 mm.

Bust of Lord Kitchener on square glazed base, sculpted by W. C. Lawton. 2 sizes: 155 mm and 175 mm. Smaller size has been found with crest on base.

Bust of Lord Roberts on square glazed base, sculpted by W. C. Lawton. 155 mm.

(Any of the above busts can be found undermarked 'R & L' or 'Cauldon Parian'. It seems likely that R & L moulds were used.)

Buildings

First and last refreshment house in England. H. T. James. 98 mm long.

Queen's dolls house, Model of. 140 mm long. (Undermarked 'Cauldon Parian'.)

Wells Cathedral, stone coloured, with some colouring on doors and windows. 110 mm long.

Monuments

The Globe, Swanage, on glazed base. 88 mm.

Saxon lady and child, both with swords, on glazed circular base, not named. 153 mm (a very rare unglazed model).

Ancient Artefacts

These models are often found not named and numbered. Models, named and otherwise can be found with transfer print views and other decorations instead of crests. Most inscriptions begin: *Model of*, so this will not be repeated throughout the list.

Aberdeen Bronze Pot, no details available.

Ancient Tyg. No. 58. 70 mm (1 or 2 handles)

Ancient Urn. No. 85. 35 mm.

Ashbourne Bushel, inscribed: *His Majesty King Charles 2nd's Royal standard bushel fastened to the Ashbourne Market Cross in the year 1677* No. 99 67 mm dia. (not often found).

Bath Roman Ewer, no details available.

Right Arcadian. Big Ben, not named 130 mm and 'The Clock Tower. St. Albans' 125 mm

Left Arcadian. Top: 'Ye Olde London Bridge'
Middle: 'Model of Marble Arch, Hyde Park, London'
Bottom: 'The Old Curiosity Shop' with inscriptions

Right Arcadian. Top: Norwich Cathedral not named
Bottom: Wimborne Minster not named

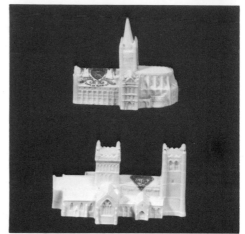

Arcadian. 'King Alfred's Tower', 'Temple Bar', and 'The Smallest House in Great Britain'

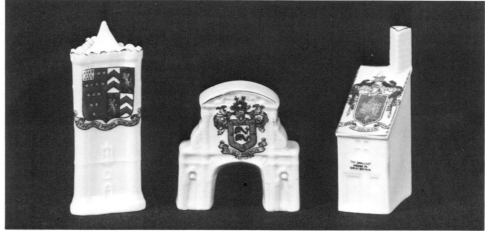

Right Arcadian. Top row: York Roman Ewer No. 57, Chinese Vase No. 292 Scarborough Jug No. 82
Bottom row: Ancient tyg, one handle No. 58, Canterbury Roman Vase No. 282. Ancient tyg, two handles No. 58

Left Arcadian. 'Martello Tower, erected for Coast Defence 1804'

British bronze pot (not found numbered). 71 mm.

Butter pot, old, of 17th century. (Not found numbered.) 45 mm

Cadogan teapot, working model of. With further inscription: 'This Teapot pours but not until you find how the way to fill.' Rd. No. 472329. 70 mm.

(This is lidless and is filled from the base. Lady Cadogan surprised guests with such a pot, originally brown and gilded Rockingham ware. Not often found.)

Cambridge Roman Jug, inscribed: *Model of Roman Jug found at Cambridge.* No. 67. 2 sizes: (smaller size 60 mm).

Canterbury Roman Ewer, inscribed: *Roman ewer found near Canterbury original in Canterbury museum.* No. 23. 60 mm.

Canterbury Roman Vase, inscribed: *Roman vase found near Canterbury original in Canterbury museum.* 3 different shapes: No. 32, 63 mm; No. 24, 66 mm; No. 29, 60 mm.

Chester Roman Vase, inscribed: *Roman vase now in Chester museum.* No. 136. 60 mm.

Chinese vase, original in Hanley museum. No. 127. Rd. No. 449545. 38 mm.

Colchester vase, no details available.

Derby Roman Vase, inscribed: *Roman vase found at Little Chester Derby.* No. 26. 63 mm.

Devon Oak Pitcher, inscribed: *Oak pitcher peculiar to Devon.* No. 165 60 mm.

Dogger Bank Bottle, inscribed: *Ancient bottle dredged up near the Dogger Bank.* No. 206. Rd. No. 449300. 70 mm.

Dorchester Jug inscribed: *Old jug found in North Square Dorchester.* No. 66. 55 mm.

Eddystone Spanish Jug, inscribed: *Spanish jug dredged up near Eddystone now in Athenaeum Plymouth.* No. 585. 60 mm.

Egyptian urn. No. 130. No details of size available.

Egyptian vase, ancient, about 230 BC. (number not known). 45 mm.

Egyptian water bottle. (Number not known.) 60 mm.

Exeter Vase, no details available.

Fountains Abbey Cup, inscribed: *The abbots cup from the original at Fountains Abbey.* (Number not known.) 50 mm.

Glastonbury Bowl, inscribed: *Bowl from the ancient British Lake Village near Glastonbury.* No. 55. 40 mm.

Glastonbury Bronze Bowl, inscribed: *Bronze bowl from the ancient British Lake Village near Glastonbury.* No. 74. 40 mm.

Glastonbury Vase, inscribed: *Vase from the ancient British Lake Village near Glastonbury* (copyright). No. 642. 55 mm.

Grecian bronze pot found at Pompeii. No. 138. 50 mm.

Greek cauldron. Ancient. No other details available.

Hastings Kettle, inscribed: *Ancient kettle dredged up off Hastings 1873 in Hastings museum.* No. 237. 62 mm.

Hereford Terracotta Kettle. No details available.

Highland whiskey jar. No. 679. 72 mm.

Highland quaich or whiskey bowl No. 529. 134 mm wide.

Irish bronze pot, ancient. No. 62. 45 mm.

Irish kettle (number not known). Rd. No. 473068. 70 mm.

Jersey milk can, ancient. No. 523. 72 mm.

Kendal Jug, inscribed: *Jug in Kendal museum dated 1602.* No. 9. 75 mm.

Lichfield Jug, inscribed: *Ancient jug dug out of the foundation of Lichfield museum.* No. 60. No details of size available.

Lincoln jack from original in museum. No. 50. 62 mm.

Loving cup originated by Henry of Navarre King of France. 2 or 3 handled. No. 379. 40 mm.

Newbury Leather Bottle, inscribed: *Leather bottle found on battlefield of Newbury 1644 now in museum.* No. 83. 65 mm.

Phoenician vase original in Stoke-on-Trent museum. No. 25. 60 mm.

Plymouth Jug. No details available.

Pompeian Vessel, inscribed: *1st century AD Pompeian vessel original in Wedgwood museum Burslem.* No. 208. 43 mm.

Pompeii lamp. No. 603. 90 mm long.

Portland vase now in British Museum (usually found unnamed). No. 52. 60 mm.

Puzzle jug original in South Kensington museum. No. 147. 70 mm.

Salisbury jack, no details available.

Salisbury kettle. No. 90. 107 mm.

Salt Maller, no details available.

Scarborough Jug, inscribed: *Jug about 600 years old found in the ancient moat of Scarborough.* No. 82. 50 mm.

Shakespeare's Jug, No. 120. 54 mm.

Shrewsbury Salopian Ewer, inscribed: *Roman Salopian ewer found at Uriconium now in Shrewsbury museum.* No. 618. 75 mm.

Silchester Vase, inscribed: *vase from Silchester in Reading museum.* No. 54. 60 mm.

Southwold Jar, inscribed: *Ancient jar washed out of cliff near Southwold.* No. 627. 95 mm.

Toby Jug, inscribed: *This jug is an exact copy in miniature of the old Toby jug.* No. 253. 61 mm.

Upstones Jug, inscribed: *Ancient jug found near Upstones, Staffs.* No. 73. 60 mm.

Wedgwood Roman Vase, inscribed: *Ancient Roman vase now in Wedgwood museum Burslem 1st century AD.* (copyright). No. 202. Rd. No. 489060. 60 mm.

West Malling Elizabethan jug or stoup. Hallmarked London 1581. Sold for 1450 guineas by permission of Messrs Crichton Bros., London. No. 152. 75 mm.

Winchelsea Roman Cup, inscribed: *Roman cup found near Winchelsea.* No other details available.

Winchelsea Vase, inscribed: *Vase found near Winchelsea.* 2 sizes: No. 68, 55 mm & No. 87, 75 mm.

Winchester Vase, inscribed: *Vase found near Winchester.* No other details available.

Windsor Roman Urn, inscribed: *Roman urn dug up at Old Windsor from original in Windsor museum.* No. 128. No details of size.

York Roman Ewer, inscribed: *Roman ewer from original in Hospitium found at York.* No. 57. 55 mm.

Arcadian. Top: 'Windsor Castle' and 'Rochester Castle'
Bottom: 'Hasting Castle Ruins' and 'Rowton Tower'

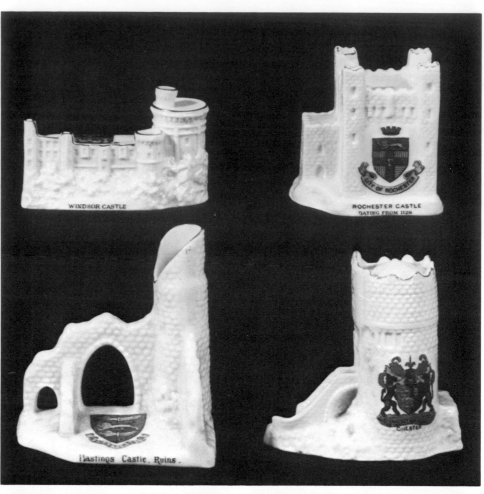

Right Arcadian. 'The Market Cross Richmond Yorks' and Banbury Cross with verse 'Ride a cock horse'

Left Arcadian. One of the range of unrecognisable figures thought to be famous statesmen. Inscribed on the reverse 'Industry is the parent of success'

Right Arcadian. Lady standing by chest, the heroine of folk stories, lustre with transfer of shamrock

Buildings—Coloured

These buildings are not normally found crested.

Dean Goodman's Birthplace, with inscription: 'Birthplace of Dean Goodman founder of Ruthin Grammar School in the year 1574' (rare).

First and Last House with annexe. 100 mm long.

Guildhall, Thaxted. 83 mm (rare).

Old Star Inn, Alfriston. 80 mm (rare).

Shakespeare's House. 2 sizes: 63 mm & 127 mm long.

Buildings—White

It is probable that all of these buildings can be found named, but I have only recorded this where an example has been reported. (Many of the buildings listed here as named can be found unnamed.) It is quite likely that some *Willow* moulds were used after 1925.

Aberystwyth University. 110 mm long (not often found).

Ann Hathaway's Cottage. 83 mm long.

Alton, Round House. 80 mm.

Big Ben, also found inscribed: *City of London.* 3 sizes: 92 mm, 130 mm & 150 mm.

Blackpool Tower. Rd. No. 585476/7. 144 mm.

Blackpool Tower with Buildings. 107 mm.

Blackpool Tower with Buildings on heavy base. 2 sizes: 135 mm & 165 mm.

Boston Stump. 114 mm.

Bunyan's Cottage. 95 mm.

Canterbury Cathedral. West front. 126 mm.

Canterbury, *Westgate.* 93 mm.

Chester Cathedral. 120 mm long.

Chesterfield parish church AD 1037, Model of. Plus long description. 125 mm.

Clifton suspension bridge. 175 mm long.

Cottage, usually found with no inscription, but can be found inscribed: *Model of Highland cottage* or *Welsh cottage.* Size varies between 50 mm–63 mm. The Highland version has been found numbered 27 and Rd. No. 570859.

Ely Cathedral. 140 mm long.

First and last refreshment house in England. E. James, is often found without 'refreshment' in inscription. 73 mm long. Also found with annexe, with 'copyright E. James'. 2 sizes: 100 mm long & 138 mm long with same colouring.

Forth bridge, with very long inscriptions about its cost and construction. 158 mm long.

Gloucester Cathedral. 128 mm long.

Grimsby hydraulic tower, with long inscription. 170 mm.

Hastings Castle ruins. 96 mm.

Hastings, clock tower. 2 sizes: 152 mm. Small version not named. 135 mm.

Hop Kiln. 86 mm.

Houses of Parliament. Rd. No. 712455. 73 mm long.

Irish round tower. 106 mm.

King Alfred's tower. 92 mm.

Lantern Hill Church, inscribed: *Model of ancient church, Lantern Hill, Ilfracombe.* 98 mm long.

Lincoln Stonebow. 88 mm long.

London bridge, Ye olde. Rd. No. 712455 (same number as Parliament!) 2 sizes: 88 mm & 170 mm long.

Marble arch. 65 mm.

Martello tower with inscription: 'Erected for Coast Defence 1804' often found unnamed. 73 mm dia.

Mundesley-on-Sea Castle Ruins, with verse: 'On the grass of the cliff at the edge of the steep'. 105 mm.

Norwich Cathedral. 105 mm long.

Old curiosity shop. Immortalized by Charles Dickens. No. 14, Portsmouth Street. 95 mm long.

Old Pete's cottage (near Ramsey). 75 mm long.

Pegwell Bay, clock tower. 135 mm.

Plymouth, clock tower. 150 mm.

Portsmouth, Guildhall. Model of. 60 mm long.

Queen Mary's dolls house, model of. Often found with BEE crest. 3 sizes: 75 mm, 95 mm & 118 mm. Two smaller sizes are often found as boxes with loose roof lids. (These models can be found with the 'Cauldon' mark as well as 'Arcadian'.)

Rochester castle, dating from 1126. 70 mm.

Rowton Tower, with inscription: 'King Charles 1st stood on this tower, Sept. 24th 1645 and saw his army defeated on Rowton Moor'. 88 mm.

St. Albans. The clock tower. 125 mm.

St. Nicholas Chapel, Ilfracombe. 100 mm long.

St. Pauls Cathedral. No. 114. 3 sizes. 72 mm, 95 mm & 130 mm.

St. Tudno's Church, Llandudno. 73 mm.

Salisbury Cathedral. 120 mm long.

Shakespeare's House. 2 sizes: 50 mm & 83 mm long.

Skegness, clock tower. 125 mm.

Smallest house in Great Britain. 2 sizes: 88 mm & 115 mm.

Southampton, the Bargate. 66 mm.

Temple Bar. 2 sizes: 60 mm & 95 mm.

Tom Tower, Christchurch, Oxford, with inscription: 'contains Great Tom Bell from Osney Abbey 1633 AD.' 88 mm.

Tower Bridge. Reg. applied for. 2 sizes: 115 mm & 135 mm long.

Tower of Refuge, Douglas I.O.M. 68 mm.

Tudor House, L shaped. (Part of the Rows in Chester.) 80 mm.

Wembley Stadium, with inscription: 'Wembley Sports Stadium cost £400,000 capacity 125,000 persons, one and a half times the size of the Roman Coliseum and the largest sports stadium in the world.' Reg. applied for. 136 mm long. (Much sought after by collectors.)

Westminster Abbey. 2 sizes: 70 mm & 115 mm.

Westminster abbey, West Front. 118 mm.

Wimborne Minster. 127 mm long.

Windmill with movable sails. Very rarely found inscribed: *Windmill. Woodhouse.* 85 mm.

Windsor castle. 80 mm.

Windsor, round tower. 2 sizes: 58 mm & 90 mm.

Worcester Cathedral. 2 sizes: 127 mm & 140 mm long.

York Minster. 105 mm.

Right Arcadian. 'Lifeboatman' bust

Left Arcadian. 'Peeping Tom' bust, a souvenir of Coventry

Right Arcadian. Bust of judge and judge in box both with inscription 'Defend the children of the poor' etc

Left Arcadian. Man in stocks 'AD 1600'

Arcadian. Three very evocative seaside souvenirs, a bathing machine, a shell inkwell with a colour transfer print and a whelk shell inscribed 'Listen to the sea'

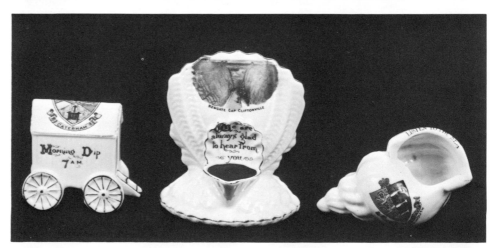

Right Arcadian. Model of a Japanese girl with fan and parasol

Left Arcadian. 'Lady Godiva, Coventry' on circular base 95 mm

Monuments (including Crosses)
These too could be *Willow* moulds after 1925.

Banbury Cross, with nursery rhyme: 'Ride a cock horse.' 160 mm.

Bloody Corner, Ilfracombe with very lengthy inscription of slaying of King Hubba on all 3 sides. Same mould as Rufus Stone. 100 mm (rare).

Bunyan statue. 140 mm.

Caister on Sea Lifeboat Memorial. 150 mm.

Castleton village cross. 140 mm.

Celtic Cross. Rd. No. 629157. 125 mm.

Conway *Seven are we* Grave, with inscription: 'The Grave immortalised by Wordsworth's Poem' and poem 'Two of us in the churchyard lie'. This is a triangular tube shaped tomb with seven small towers. 110 mm long (rare).

Drake statue. 160 mm.

Fishermen's Memorial, not named but probably Hull. 160 mm.

(The) Globe, Swanage. Model of. 80 mm.

Iona Cross. 142 mm.

Irish Monument, not named but appears with Irish Crests. Circular base with man standing on top. 138 mm. (I have not seen this so cannot guess who it may be.)

King Alfred the Great, Statue, Winchester. Rd. No. 521701. 170 mm.

Maiwand memorial, Forbury Gardens, Reading. (Lion on Base) 100 mm. (Often found in animal collections.)

Moffat Ram Memorial, ram mounted on rock. 108 mm. (rare).

Margate Surf Boat Memorial, with inscription to the memory of men who died in the capsizing of the surf boat in 1897. 125 mm.

Nelson's column. 102 mm.

Newton Monument. 165 mm.

Richmond, Yorks, Market Cross. 125 mm.

(The Great) Rock of Ages, Burrington Coombe, near Cheddar. Som. Model of, with three verses of hymn. 83 mm.

Rufus Stone, with lengthy inscription on all 3 sides. 100 mm.

Sailor's Stone, Hindhead, with inscription: 'Erected in detestation of a barbarous murder' etc. 100 mm.

Series of at least three figures standing on a square plinth. (These are not easily identifiable and could be statesmen, industrialists or literary figures) inscribed: *Industry is the parent of success.* Edged in green. 135 mm.

Stowmarket memorial gates. 110 mm long. (rare).

Historical/Folklore
Archbishop of Canterbury's Chair, Model of. 146 mm.

Coaching Hat, can be found inscribed: *Model of ancient coaching hat.* No. 687. 65 mm long.

Ducking stool, 2 pieces, hinged together. With long details of its last employment in Leominster in 1809 and 1817. Rd. No. 652243. 120 mm long (very rare).

English Folksong Bride beside chest. Not named. 93 mm. (This very rare model is thought to be of the bride in folksongs who played hide and seek, and hid in a chest. The skeleton was not found until many years later. When I was a child in Worcestershire, my aunt sang this song at Christmas, it was called 'All under the Mistletoe Bough'.)

Execution block with axe. 50 mm (very rare).

Henry V cradle. Rd. No. 392347. 78 mm.

Jenny Geddes stool 1637, 3 legged. More often found unnamed. 40 mm.

Judge bust, with inscription: 'Defend the children of the poor and punish the wrong doer.' Copy of inscription of New Bailey Court, London. Rd. No. 486001. 2 sizes: 55 mm & 70 mm.

Lady Godiva, Coventry, on horseback on circular base. (This is a popularised version of the statue in Coventry.) 2 sizes: 75 mm & 95 mm.

Lady Godiva on heartshaped base. 80 mm.

Miner's Lamp, inscribed: 1836. 85 mm.

Mother Shipton, can be found with verse: 'Near to Knaresboro dropping well I first drew breath as records tell'. 2 sizes: 76 mm & 115 mm.

Peeping Tom, bust. 110 mm.

Man in Pillory, can be found inscribed: *Time for reflection, AD 1600.* Rd. No. 572151. 190 mm.

Man in Stocks, can be found inscribed as above and very rarely *Berkswell stocks*. 88 mm.

Trusty servant on ornate rectangular base, with verse. Fully coloured and without crest. 137 mm (very rare and much sought by collectors).

Trusty servant on small square base, can be found with verse. Fully coloured with crest and unglazed. 130 mm (rare and equally sought after).

Yorick's Skull, inscribed: *Alas poor Yorick.* 57 mm.

Traditional/National Souvenirs
John Bull, bust. Rd. No. 537470. Some colouring on face. 3 sizes: 65 mm, 85 mm & 100 mm. Largest size found with black hat.

Blackpool Big Wheel. 110 mm.

Cheddar cheese, prime. 60 mm.

Cheddar cheese, prime, with slice out. 60 mm.

Cornish pasty, with inscription: 'This is a pasty. Don't 'ee see. Will 'ee ave a piece of me. There's more in the kitchen.' 98 mm long.

Devonshire dumpling, Model of and verse. 45 mm.

Isle of Wight, relief map standing upright on pintray. Coloured. 106 mm long.

Lancashire Clog, usual type. Rd. No. 570859. 94 mm long.

Lancashire Clog, high narrow type. Rd. No. 607828. 140 mm long (very detailed).

Lancashireman's Jug with verse, no details of size.

Lincoln imp. 110 mm.

Lincoln imp, on square stand. 125 mm.

Luton boater, usually found unnamed. 2 sizes: 78 mm & 102 mm dia.

Right Arcadian. Manx Cat, this particular model has not got a coloured face as is more usual

Left Arcadian. Cat with blue bow sitting on oval base

Right Arcadian. 'The Cheshire Cat' with orange bow and inscription on tail 'The smile that won't come off' 95 mm and grotesque cat very like the Cheshire cat with bow left uncoloured and no inscriptions 75 mm

Left Arcadian. Two angry cats, front and back view showing inscription

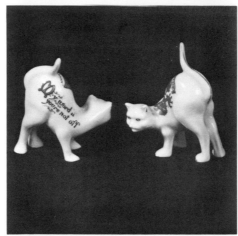

Right Arcadian. Scottie dog wearing blue tam o'shanter, King Charles Spaniel on cushion large size, and Staffordshire bullterrier

Left Arcadian. Fox on square plinth

Arcadian. Dog with curly tail and blue collar, collie dog lying down and 'Model of Bill Sykes Dog' small size

Manx Legs on stand. 101 mm.

Manx Legs on rock. 51 mm.

(Manx) *Tynwald Hill, Model of,* and inscription: 'This is one of the most venerable objects of antiquity in existence. It is 256 feet in circumference and is composed of earth bought from the seventeen parishes into which the island is divided. In accordance with the ancient Scandinavian custom, every law that is passed by the Manx Government the Tynwald court must be promulgated from the top of this hill, before it can come into force. This ceremony takes place each year on the 5th July. The laws being read in Manx and English.' 115 mm dia. (This possibly could be considered an historical souvenir. It is an extremely rare model.)

Mill Lass, bust, shawl draped round head and shoulders. 60 mm (rare).

Irish Harp with green shamrocks. 108 mm.

Irish jaunting car, Model of with horse and driver. 120 mm long. (Very rare, possibly because it is so easily damaged.)

Irish Lady, bust, inscribed: *My simple graceful Nora Criena.* 85 mm.

Bagpipes. 110 mm long.

Gretna Green, Anvil from and verse. Often found without inscription. 66 mm.

Souter Johnny, sitting figure on chair with verse: 'Here's to all of us! For there is so much good in all of us, and so much bad in the best of us, that it hardly behoves any of us to talk about the rest of us.' Some colouring. 130 mm (could be *Willow* mould).

Tam O'Shanter (bonnet) inscribed: *Tha can sit on the thistle noo.* Coloured heather and pom-pom. 95 mm dia.

Thistle Candlestick. 50 mm.

Thistle, on Stalk base (candlestick or vase) inscribed: *Tha can sit on the thistle noo.* 85 mm.

Thistle Vase, wide necked. 85 mm.

Welsh harp. 80 mm.

Welsh hat, Model of, often unnamed. Can be found with largest Welsh place name round brim. 52 mm. (Very fine china.)

Welsh Lady, bust. Found with inscription: 'Wales! Wales! My Mother's sweet home 'ere. 3 sizes: 65 mm, 80 mm & 100 mm. Larger sizes found coloured.

Welsh Leek, can be found with inscription: 'King Henry V. The Welshmen did goot servace (at Crecy) in a garden where Leeks did grow. Shakespeare'. 2 sizes: 76 mm & 98 mm.

Seaside Souvenirs

Bathing Machine, can be found inscribed: *Morning dip 7 am* and with '32' above the door. Rd. No. 570859. 3 sizes: 50 mm, 65 mm & 85 mm.

Lifebelt. 80 mm dia.

Lifeboat, with blue band and yellow rigging, can be found inscribed with any of the following names: *Bob Newson; Charles Susanna Stephens; The Charlie and Adrian; James Stevens No. 5 or Nancy Lucy.* Rd. No. 572151. 118 mm long.

Rowing Boat. 83 mm long.

Yacht. 125 mm long.

Lifeboatman, bust. 85 mm.

Fishing Basket, found inscribed: *A good catch.* 50 mm.

Fisherman's Creel, with separate lid. 60 mm.

Beachy Head Lighthouse, with black band. 2 sizes: 102 mm & 140 mm.

Bell Rock, Lighthouse. No. 14. 108 mm.

Cove Sea Lighthouse. 136 mm.

Eddystone Lighthouse often found unnamed. 3 sizes: 70 mm, 105 mm & 140 mm.

Pharos Lighthouse, Fleetwood, Model of. No. 255. 2 sizes: 100 mm & 140 mm. Smaller sized (fully inscribed) has been found as a pepper pot.

Crab ashtray. 90 mm long.

Lobster pintray. 90 mm long.

Oyster Shell dish. 72 mm dia.

Nautilus shell on three legs. 80 mm long.

Scallop Shell. 2 sizes: 70 mm & 92 mm dia.

Scallop Shell dish, very ornate. 83 mm dia.

Shell Ink Well, one open shell inverted on another, usually inscribed: *We are always glad to hear from you.* Can also be found inscribed: *We're aye prood to hear fae ye, or pins.* 105 mm.

Whelk Shell, can be found inscribed: *Listen to the sea* or *We alre always glad to hear from you.* Size varies from 80 mm–100 mm long.

Gladstone bag. 82 mm long.

Punch and Judy show. Rd. No. 37083? 90 mm (moderately rare).

Punch, bust. Some colouring. 2 sizes: 65 mm & 80 mm.

Countryside

Acorn. 55 mm.

Beehive on table. Rd. No. 629167. 78 mm.

Farmer with plough on rectangular base, some colouring. 110 mm long (rare).

Hay Stack, circular. 58 mm.

Hay Stack, rectangular 50 mm.

Pinecone, curved. 88 mm long.

Animals

Small models of 'pets' were obviously made in great numbers for many years so the moulds do vary. Large, more exotic animals were much more expensive at the time and so are consequently much more rare.

Bear with Ragged staff. 80 mm.

Bull, Highland. 130 mm long (rare).

Camel (2 humps–Backtrian) 70 mm.

Cat, angry, standing with arched back and green eyes, inscribed: *My word if you're not off.* 63 mm long.

Cat, climbing into boot, which has a mouse peeping out of its toe. Rd. No. 629155. 100 mm long.

Cat, Cheshire. No bow round neck, inscribed: *Keep smiling.* 90 mm.

Cat, The Cheshire. With orange or red bow round neck, inscribed: *The smile that wont come off.* 95 mm.

Cat, long necked and sitting. Inscribed: *My word if youre not off.* 108 mm.

Cat, Manx with coloured face. 70 mm long.

Cat, playing flute. 75 mm.

Right Arcadian. The model collectors describe this as The Cougar, I have a sneaking suspicion it is in fact, a lioness

Left Arcadian. 'King of the Forest' inscription on reverse

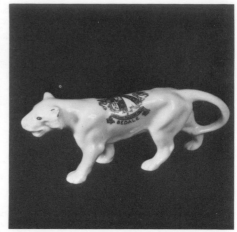

Arcadian. Crocodile (or is it an alligator?) whichever it is the model is quite rare

Right Arcadian. Polar Bear 100 mm long, a very lifelike creature

Left Arcadian. A very rare model, the kangaroo. An illustration of this model along with a range of other zoo or wild animals, appears in the Arcadian Catalogue which has been found

Right Arcadian. Bactrian camel. 70 mm

Left Arcadian. Elephant with trunk modelled free from body. Inscribed on reverse 'Baby Jumbo'

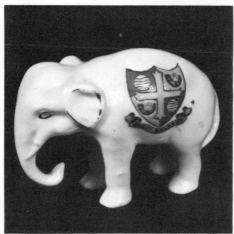

Right Arcadian. A fawn, a delicate model which seems to have sold reasonably well

Left Arcadian. 'Model of Welsh Goat' showing Welsh inscription

Right Arcadian. Tortoise wearing a blue helmet. This was probably a model of a cartoon character of the time

Left Arcadian. Large donkey, 120 mm long, has no saddle. A lovely seaside souvenir

Right Arcadian. Small teddy bear 68 mm with no inscription and 90 mm size inscribed TEDDY BEAR

Left Arcadian. Models of a rabbit and a hare

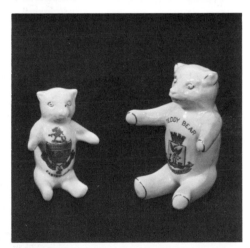

Right Arcadian. Two models one on base and one on its side proving that this Arcadian Rabbit is also a duck

Left Arcadian. Sitting chimpanzee, three wise monkeys and monkey with hands to mouth. Most manufacturers produced models of monkeys and they would make an interesting collection

Arcadian. Otter with fish in its mouth. A most impressive model

Right Arcadian. Tiny golfer on a golf ball 74 mm

Left Arcadian. Monk holding glass with verse 'A jovial monk am I' black skull cap

Arcadian. Top row: 'Model of Sussex pig' with inscription 78 mm long, frog closed mouth and kneeling piglet
Bottom row: 'Model of Sussex Pig' sitting, frog with open mouth and squirrel holding nut

Cat with bow, sitting on plinth. Bow
sometimes coloured blue. 123 mm (very
detailed model).

Cat sitting with tail curled round feet, red
bow and green eyes. No. 77. 67 mm.

Cat sitting and smiling (grotesque, rather
similar to Cheshire Cat), bow round
neck, sometimes coloured orange. Rd.
No. 712455. 75 mm.

Cat sitting with bow round neck. 56 mm.

Black Cats: 2 types of black cats are found
with the Arcadian Mark. The most usual
being from the 'Arcadian Registered
series', they are rather thin implike
creatures performing for the most part
impossible feats. The second small
group are very large, very feline animals
sitting on various popular items. This
second type are undoubtedly from
Willow moulds.

Arcadian Black Cat Registered Series

No. 1. Black Cat on Jug. 60 mm.

No. 2. Black Cat on vertical horseshoe.
76 mm.

No. 3. Black Cat on pillar box posting
letter. 56 mm.

No. 4. Black Cat on telephone. 65 mm
(rare).

No. 5. Black Cat in Canoe. 80 mm long.

No. 6. Black Cat on Wall. 70 mm.

No. 7. Black Cat in boot. 61 mm.

No. 8. Black Cat with bottle, bottle can
have solid or cork top, can be inscribed:
Cheerio from . . . . (can be found in
lustre). 70 mm.

No. 9. Black Cat on milk churn. *New milk*
moulded on churn. 70 mm.

No. 10. 3 Black Cats in bed (quite rare).

No. 11. Black Cat on swing. 63 mm (quite
rare).

No. 12. Black Cat in well. (Can be found in
lustre.) 63 mm.

No. 13. Black Cat operating radio. 63 mm.

No. 14. Black Cat in Pram. 70 mm (very
rare).

No. 15. 3 Black Cats in basket, and 1 on
top. 70 mm (rare).

No. 16. Black Cat on scooter. (Can be
found in lustre.) 70 mm (rare).

No. 17. Black Cat with umbrella. 65 mm
(very rare).

No. 18. Black Cat on bicycle. 80 mm long
(rare).

No. 19. Black Cat in yacht. 96 mm long
(rare).

No. 20. Black Cat on double bass. 70 mm
(very rare).

No. 21. 2 Black Cats on seesaw. 85 mm
long (very rare).

No. 22. 5 Black Cats on a house, their tails
spell: *Good luck.* 65 mm (rare).

No. 23. 3 Black Cats on sledge. (very rare).

No. 24. Black Cat on Piano. 52 mm (very
rare).

(All of the above Cats are completely
coloured on white churns, pianos,
swings and so on. The Cats have red (or
rarely yellow) bows and odd coloured
eyes, one green and one yellow, with
red pupils. They were registered in 1924
obviously in a block of 24 as no two

similar models have the same
registration number printed on their
base, but most Rd. No's begin 70864/5 or
70961/4. It is interesting to note that the
higher numbers were originally more
expensive and are now very difficult to
find. Why the black cat on the telephone
was so unpopular originally is very
difficult to understand. Unpopularity
can be the only reason for their rarity as
they are not easily broken.)

There is also a very similar black cat that is
not part of the Registered series:

Black Cat, wearing kilt and glengarry,
playing golf standing on golf ball.
70 mm. (This is also rare.)

(This is very similar to a range of black cats
marked *Willow* and was probably made
when the two firms had merged.)

Sitting Black Cats can be found on the following:

Armchair. 55 mm.

Ashtray, horseshoe shaped. 93 mm long.

Pouffe, inscribed: *Good luck.* 85 mm.

Trinket box, horseshoe shaped. 70 mm.

(All of these cats have blue/green eyes and
red bows.)

Chimpanzee, sitting. 70 mm (rare).

Cougar (or panther). 102 mm long (rare).

Cow, Jersey. 125 mm long (quite rare).

Crocodile (or alligator). 125 mm long (very
rare).

Bill Sykes dog, Model of, sitting. Sometimes
inscribed: *My word if youre not off.* No.
300. 2 sizes: 63 mm & 103 mm.

Bill Sykes dog, Model of, standing.
Sometimes inscribed: *My word if youre
not off.* No. 300. 3 sizes: 88 mm, 102 mm
& 118 mm long.

Bulldog, black, emerging from kennel
inscribed: *The Black Watch.* 56 mm.

Bulldog, sitting, very thin face. 57 mm.

Bulldog, standing, sometimes inscribed:
"Who said Germans". No. 301. 2 sizes:
115 mm & 130 mm long. (Often included
in G. War Collections.)

Dog, Collie, lying down. 78 mm long.

Dog, Collie, standing, Sometimes
inscribed: *Shetland collie.* Rd. No. 611243.
2 sizes: 60 mm & 95 mm long.

Dog, King Charles Spaniel begging on
cushion. Rd. No. 417592. 2 sizes: 68 mm
& 95 mm.

Dog (Pup), sitting with one ear raised.
68 mm.

Dog, Scottie, standing. 60 mm.

Dog, Scottie wearing Tam o'Shanter. Hat
can be found coloured blue. 85 mm.

Dog, Scottish Terrier, can be found
inscribed: *Scotch terrier* or *As old Mrs
Terrier said to her pup, in all life's
adventures keep your tail up.* 66 mm long.

Dog, standing, facing sideways, curly tail
and blue collar. 80 mm long.

Dog, Staffordshire bullterrier, sitting,
sometimes inscribed: *Daddy wouldn't buy
me a bow wow.* 72 mm.

Donkey. 2 sizes: 80 mm & 120 mm long,
smaller size has saddle.

Right Arcadian. 'Norwich Warbler' with whistle and bubble blower base 126 mm

Left Arcadian. Peacock yellow beak and coloured plume 115 mm

Left Arcadian. Bird perched on circular base 68 mm

Arcadian. Top row: Largest size swan, 'Pretty Polly' parrot and wise owl with verse.
Middle row: Pelican with no inscription, stork with B.E.E. crest and duck
Bottom row: Roosting hen, smallest size swan and chicken hatching from egg

Elephant, trunk attached to body. 55 mm.
Elephant, trunk modelled free from body, sometimes inscribed: *Baby Jumbo*. 50 mm.
Fawn. 50 mm.
Fish, fat. 98 mm long.
Fish, open mouthed. 2 sizes: 80 mm & 108 mm long.
Fish ashtray in shape of plaice, usually inscribed: *A pla(i)ce for the ashes*, but can be inscribed: *Caught at . . .* 125 mm long.
Fish dish in shape of plaice, inscribed: *A pla(i)ce for everything*. 125 mm long.
Fox. 102 mm long.
Fox on square plinth. 114 mm.
Frog, closed mouth. 45 mm.
Frog, open mouth and green eyes, inscribed: *Always croaking*. 2 sizes: 80 mm & 100 mm long.
Goat. 82 mm long.
Hare. 73 mm long.
Kangaroo. 75 mm (rare).
Hippopotamus. 88 mm long (very rare).
Lion, roaring. 85 mm long.
Lion, walking. 2 sizes: 110 mm & 140 mm long. Smallest size can be found inscribed: *King of the forest*.
Monkey, sitting, hand to mouth. 65 mm.
Monkey, wearing coat. 75 mm.
Otter holding fish in mouth. 120 mm long.

Pig, smiling and sitting. 63 mm long.
Pig, short and standing, inscribed: *I won't be druv*. 70 mm. 63 mm long.
Pig, tall and standing, inscribed: *You can push or you can shuv but I'm hanged if I'll be druv*. 78 mm. 63 mm long.
Hampshire hog, Model of, sitting. No. 148C. 70 mm long.
Sussex pig, Model of, sitting, inscribed: *Won't be druv*. No. 148. Rd. No. 454897. 88 mm long.
Sussex pig, Model of, standing fat pig can be found inscribed: *Mochyn bad* with Welsh Crest. No. 148. Rd. No. 454827. 80 mm long.
Sussex pig, Model of, standing thin pig, inscribed: *You can push or you can shuv but I'm hanged if I'll be druv* or *Wunt be druv*. No. 148. 78 mm long.
Wiltshire pig, Model of, sitting up on haunches, alert ears. No. 148. 60 mm.
Piglet, kneeling. 70 mm long.

Polar bear. 100 mm long.
Pony, New Forest, can be found unnamed. 100 mm long.
Pony, Shetland, often found unnamed. 2 sizes: 105 mm & 120 mm long.
Rabbit, lying ears along back. Found numbered 22 and 23. Sizes vary between 65 mm–80 mm long.
Rabbit, sitting, ears apart. No. 13. Sizes vary between 50 mm–68 mm.
Rhinoceros. 90 mm long (very rare).
Russian bear, inscribed: *War edition* and carries Russian Imperial Crest. 70 mm. (Often found in G. War Collections.)
Seal. 102 mm long.
Squirrel holding nut, on base. 65 mm.
Squirrel Jug. 80 mm.
Teddy bear, sitting. 90 mm. Smaller size 68 mm not found inscribed.
Tortoise, Rd. No. 456065. 72 mm long.

Tortoise, standing upright, wearing blue helmet. 75 mm.
Welsh goat, Model of, inscribed *Yr Afr Cymreig*. Rd. No. 497684. 100 mm long.
Wembley Lion, inscribed: *A souvenir from Wembley*. 100 mm long (stylised symbol of the B.E.E.).
3 Wise Monkeys on wall inscribed: *I see no evil, I speak no evil, I hear no evil*. Rd. No. 700306. 76 mm.
Isn't this rabbit a duck. On its base a rabbit, turned on its side a duck. (Can be found in lustre.) Rd. No. 508647. 75 mm. (Really a novelty comic item but usually found in animal collections.)

Birds (including Eggs)

Chick, breaking out of egg. Can be found inscribed: *Just out*. 2 sizes: 63 mm & 86 mm long. Larger size can be found inscribed: *Easter egg*.
Chick and Egg Pepper pot. 58 mm.
Chick, very tiny and completely yellow, sitting on a white egg, inscribed: *Every little helps mother will be pleased*. Rd. No. 723911. 50 mm long. (This is really a novelty coloured item.)
Egg salt and pepper pots. 58 mm.
Egg shell, broken open. 39 mm.
Egg with flat base, can be found inscribed: *Sparrows egg*. 44 mm.
Cock standing, legs modelled separately, inscribed: *Cock o'th North* or *Cock o'th South*. Some colouring to head. 100 mm.
Cock standing, legs modelled together. Some colouring to head. 85 mm.
Hen standing, some colouring, 62 mm. (Matches above.)
Hen roosting. 54 mm.
Bird perched on circular base. (Reputedly a black bird.) 68 mm.
Bird, perched on tree, wings extended. 125 mm. (Very impressive.)
Bird salt pot. 70 mm.
Duck. 86 mm.
Norwich warbler. Canary. 100 mm.
Norwich warbler. Canary on rock, with a whistle and bubble blower base. Often found unnamed. 126 mm.
Owl, baby. 40 mm.
Owl, Barn. 63 mm.
Owl, Horned (long eared). 74 mm.
Owl (Wise), one eye closed, with verse: 'An aged Owl sat in an oak. The more he saw the less he spoke. The less he spoke the more he heard. Would there were more like that old bird.' 98 mm.
Parakeet. 60 mm.
Parrot, sometimes inscribed: *Pretty Polly*. No. 751. 75 mm.
Peacock, yellow beak and coloured plumes. Rd. No. 678582. 115 mm (rare).
Peacock on ashtray. (Can be found in lustre.) 80 mm long.
Pelican, with details of its stomach capacity. 70 mm (rare).
Penguin. No details of size (rare).
Seagull. 76 mm (rare).
Stork. 80 mm.
Swan, 3 sizes: 50 mm, 70 mm & 85 mm.
Swan Posy Bowl. 88 mm.
Turkey, on round base. 60 mm.
Turkey on square base. 76 mm.

Right Arcadian. Model of a clip of bullets. 57 mm

Left Arcadian (Swan/Clifton etc.). Tommy on sentry duty in sentry box

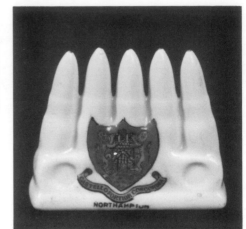

Right Arcadian.'Soldiers Friend' a red cross nurse

Left Arcadian (Swan/Clifton etc.). 'Model of sailor winding capstan'

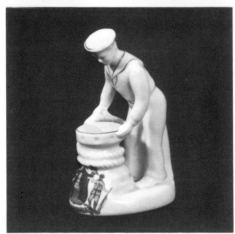

Right Arcadian. Parian bust of 'Sir John Jellicoe'

Left Arcadian. Tommy and his machine gun, one of a series of British soldiers in action

Left Arcadian. Glazed and crested model of Tommy throwing his grenade, with an unglazed model with no crest or inscription. It is possible that this unfinished model was a travellers sample.

Great War

Many of these models are found with the inscription 'War Edition AD 1914' and a crest of 'one of the allied countries.' Some of the soldiers, although sold separately, were based on the same design idea and form a set. They are therefore grouped together in the listings.

British soldier, Model of, more often than not unnamed. 135 mm.
Colonial soldier, Model of. Rd. No. 658685. 135 mm.
French soldier, Model of. Rd. No. 657733. 135 mm.
Scotch soldier, Model of. Rd. No. No. 657744. 135 mm.
Bugler boy, Model of. 135 mm (often sold as pair with drummer, but this is more rare).
Drummer boy, Model of. Rd. No. 65737. 135 mm.
(All of these figures are standing to attention on an oval domed base.)

British cavalry soldier, Model of, on horseback. Rd. No. 658680. 122 mm.
Russian Cossack, Model of, on horseback. Rd. No. 658684. 122 mm.

Belgian Soldier, bust, usually found with Belgian Crest. 80 mm (rare).
Despatch rider, Model of, on motorbike. (Can be found in lustre.) Rd. No. 657737. 120 mm long.
Nurse and wounded Tommy, Model of. Rd. No. 658674. 108 mm long.
Nurse, inscribed: *Soldier's friend.* Red cross on chest. 132 mm.
Old Bill, inscribed: *Yours to a Cinder,* standing figure of Bruce Bairnsfather's cartoon character. Can be found with coloured face and balaclava. 132 mm.
Sailor, bust, found with hatband impressed: *HMS Dreadnought, HMS Lion* or *HMS Queen Elizabeth.* Inscribed: *The Handyman.* Can be found coloured. Impressed version, Rd. No. 653343. Unimpressed, Rd. No. 652244. 92 mm. (This model was obviously made for some time and moulds were changed. The hat can be found tilted to the right or left.)
Sailor standing with hands on hips. 2 sizes: 95 mm & 132 mm.
Sailor winding capstan, Model of. Rd. No. 658675. 105 mm.
Soldier, bust inscribed: *Tommy Atkins* or *Territorial,* either found with verse 'Its the Soldiers of the King my lads.' Some colouring. 90 mm.
Soldier with respirator, bust, inscribed: *Model of new gas mask.* Rd. No. 657652. 95 mm. (This is an almost horrific model which is probably why very few were ordered by retailers. It is very rare.)
Tommy driving a steam roller over the Kaiser, inscribed: *To Berlin.* 120 mm. (This is highly prized by collectors and although not extremely rare changes hands for large sums of money.)
Tommy in bayonet attack, Model of. Rd. No. 658676. 130 mm.
Tommy and his machine gun, Model of. 72 mm.

Tommy on sentry duty, Model of, in sentry box. Rd. No. 657213. 110 mm.
Tommy throwing his grenade, Model of. Rd. No. 638681. 130 mm.

New aeroplane, Model of. Biplane with fixed prop, and roundels in relief. Rd. No. 658683. 120 mm long.
New aeroplane, Model of. Monoplane with revolving propeller. Rd. No. 629137. 153 mm long.
Monoplane, v winged, with revolving prop. Propeller can be found with 2 or 3 blades. Rd. No. 607828. 2 sizes: 118 mm & 140 mm long. (This model has a circular portion added for no other reason than to carry crest.)
Aeroplane Propeller. 150 mm long.
British airship, Model of with suspended engine. Rd. No. 658679. 120 mm long.
British Airship on stand. Rd. No. 652241. 128 mm long.
Observer or Sausage balloon, Model of. Rd. No. 668582. 84 mm (rare).
Super Zeppelin, Model of. Rd. No. 657735. 127 mm long.

Battleship, inscribed: *HMS Queen Elizabeth.* 2 sizes: 115 mm & 160 mm long.
Battleship. 3 funnels and tiny gun fore and aft. 3 sizes: 100 mm, 120 mm & 165 mm long.
Minesweeper, not found named. 126 mm long (not often found).
Torpedo boat destroyer, Model of. Rd. No. 658677. 108 mm long.
Submarine, inscribed: E4. Rd. No. 607828. 95 mm long.
New submarine, Model of, inscribed: E5. Rd. No. 658687. 126 mm long.
Airfield tractor, Model of. 80 mm long (rare).
Armoured car, Model of. Rd. No. 657736. 2 sizes: 95 mm & 120 mm long.
Red Cross Van, red cross on each side and rear. 'EH 139' printed on radiator. 2 sizes: 85 mm & 160 mm long. (The large size is extremely rare.)
Staff Car, 'EH 139' printed on front and rear. 115 mm long.
Tank, Model of. Rd. No. 658588. 5 sizes: 100 mm, 115 mm, 160 mm, 180 mm & 325 mm. Second size found inscribed: *Original made in Lincoln.* 160 mm size can be found in lustre. (The smallest size is quite rare and the largest size is very rare, being so enormous that it must have been made for shop display.)
Tank, Model of, with inset wheels. This model has an exhaust pipe which looks like a gun on the top turret. Rd. No. 658588. 115 mm long.
Tank, Model of, with trailing steering wheels. Also has an exhaust pipe in turret. Rd. No. 658588. 144 mm long.
Tank, Model of, exactly as above but with one trailing wheel. Rd. No 658588. 144 mm long. (Rare as this was only made by mistake!)
Whippet Tank, large hexagonal gun turret at rear. 172 mm long (rare).
Field Gun. Rd. No. 630859. 2 sizes: 120 mm & 140 mm long.
New field gun with screen, Model of. Rd. No. 658686. 105 mm long.

Arcadian. Bugler Boy and Drummer Boy. Only the Drummer Boy is found with a registration number. It seems possible that the Bugler boy was only sold with the Drummer boy as a pair

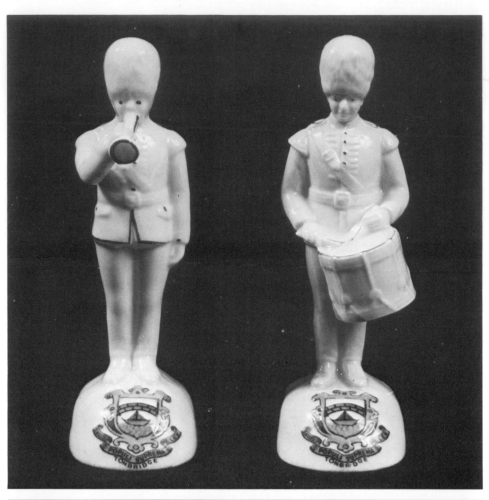

Arcadian. Model of Nurse and Wounded Tommy with B.E.E. crest

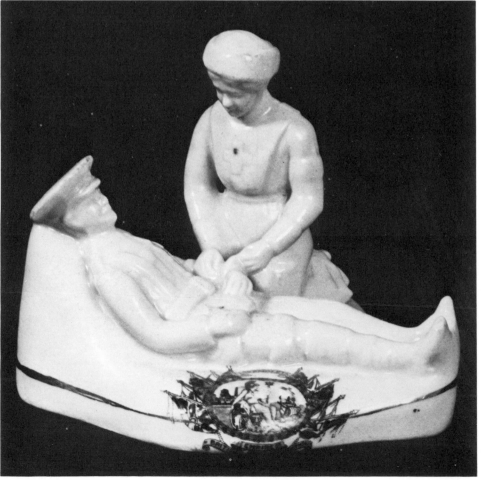

Arcadian. Models of 'French Soldier', 'British Soldier', sailor with hands on hips, 'Tommy in bayonet attack' and 'Scotch Soldier' (sic)

Arcadian. 'Tommy Atkins'. 'Model of New Gas Mask', and 'Territorial'. 'Tommy Atkins' and the 'Territorial' have the verse 'Its the soldiers of the King' on the reverse

Arcadian. 'Model of Russian Cossack' and 'Model of British Cavalry Soldier'. Two very similar models registered at the same time

Arcadian. 'Tommy driving a steam roller over the Kaiser'. This desirable model is full of amusing detail and is also inscribed 'To Berlin'

Right Arcadian. An unnamed plum pudding bomb. This model is more often found unnamed than named

Left Arcadian. Top row: Trench Lamp, water bottle.
Bottom row: Field glasses, sandbag

Right Arcadian. Sheringham bomb 15 mm

Left Arcadian. 135 mm and 90 mm versions of a cannon shell, with the 'Jack Johnson' inscription

Arcadian. Top: British Aerial Bomb, Bury St. Edmunds Bomb, Anti Aircraft shell, Canister Bomb
Bottom: Hand Grenade, German Hand Grenade, Trench Mortar Bomb. Hair Brush Grenade

German howitzer, Model of. 2 sizes: 115 mm & 140 mm long.

Trench mortar, Model of. Rd. No. 657212. 70 mm long.

Machine Gun, not found named. 100 mm long (rare).

Revolver, Model of. Rd. No. 657653, 83 mm long.

Anti aircraft shell, Model of. 98 mm.

Cannon Shell. 3 sizes: 70 mm, 90 mm & 135 mm. The 90 mm size is often inscribed: *Jack Johnson* (Reigning heavyweight boxing champion of the world) and sometimes: *Hartlepool's Bombardment Sep 16th 1914.* (The 135 mm size is rare.)

Cannon Shell Salt and Pepper pots. 70 mm.

Clip of bullets, Model of. Rd. No. 657648. 57 mm.

Trench flying pig, Model of. (Flying pig is thought to be a nickname for the flying rocket.) Rd. No. 657701. 95 mm long. (Extremely rare, only one model is known.)

Bomb dropped from Zeppelin, Model of, inscription sometimes reads 'German Zeppelin'. 75 mm. A parian model with a glazed base is occasionally found. 170 mm.

Bomb dropped from Zeppelin upon Sheringham during first raid on England 8.30 pm Jany, 18th 1915, Model of. Rd. No. 664837. 115 mm.

British aerial bomb, Model of. Rd. No. 657694. 75 mm.

Canister bomb, Model of. Rd. No. 657700. 60 mm.

Plum pudding bomb, Model of. Often found unnamed. Rd. No. 657699. 72 mm (rare).

German hand grenade, Model of. Rd. No. 657697, 92 mm (very rare).

Hair brush grenade, Model of. Rd. No. 657702. 104 mm long (rare).

Mills hand grenade, Model of. Rd. No. 657211. 62 mm.

British aerial torpedo, Model of. Rd. No. 657210. 102 mm long.

German aerial torpedo, Model of. Rd. No. 657651. 88 mm long.

Bandsmans Drum. No. 226. 53 mm. (Probably made originally for the S. African War.)

Bell Tent, inscribed: *Camping out.* 64 mm dia.

Capstan. 56 mm.

Ghurka knife, Model of. 110 mm long.

Pair of field glasses, Model of. Often found not named. 78 mm long.

Sandbag, Model of. Rd. No. 658678. 73 mm long.

Tommy's hut, Model of. Rd. No. 657215. 105 mm long.

Trench dagger, Model of. Rd. No. 657649. 102 mm long.

Trench lamp, Model of. Rd. No. 657696. 70 mm.

Water bottle, Model of. Rd. No. 657695. 65 mm.

Colonial hat, Model of, found inscribed: *Anzacs.* Rd. No. 657738. 38 mm wide.

Glengarry. 90 mm long.

New Zealand Hat. 71 mm dia.

Officer's peaked cap with coloured badge and hatband. 65 mm dia.

Solar Topee. 60 mm.

Steel Helmet. Rd. No. 657630. 65 mm dia.

Anti-Zeppelin Candle Holder. 65 mm.

Fireplace, inscribed: *We've kept the home fires burning.* Rd. No. 658878. 2 sizes: 90 mm & 115 mm.

Angel with raised arms, found with R.A.F. Crest (not named but must be a R.A.F. Memorial.) No details of size (very rare).

Bishop's Stortford *War Memorial.* 132 mm (rare).

Burford War Memorial, with inscription 'In grateful memory of the men of Burford who fell in the War 1914–18'. 128 mm (rare).

Burnham on Crouch *War Memorial.* 146 mm (rare).

Cavell Memorial, inscribed: *Nurse Cavell.* 160 mm.

Cavell *Memorial statue, Norwich,* inscribed: *Edith Cavell—Nurse, Patriot and Martyr.* 175 mm.

Cenotaph, Model of, with green wreaths. 4 sizes: 80 mm, 100 mm, 140 mm & 180 mm. Three larger sizes with inscription: 'erected in Whitehall, London in memory of the fallen in the Great War 1914–1919'. Smallest size with inscription: 'Whitehall London. MCMXIV–MCMXIX.'

Chesham *War Memorial.* 159 mm.

Dover Patrol Memorial. 130 mm.

Dover *War Memorial.* 140 mm.

East Dereham War Memorial, with inscription: 'In honour of the men of East Dereham who fell in the Great War 1914–18.' (Rare.)

Florence Nightingale Statue, inscribed: *The Lady of the Lamp.* 170 mm. 147 mm smaller version from different mould.

Folkestone War Memorial inscribed '*May their deeds be held in reverence*'. No details of size.

Fryatt Memorial, with inscription: 'In memory of Captain Algernon Fryatt Master of the Great Eastern Railway Steam Ship "Brussels" illegally executed by the Germans at Bruges on the 27th July 1916. Erected by the Company as an expression of their admiration of his gallantry.' 125 mm (rare).

Great Yarmouth *War Memorial,* with inscription: 'For God and King and Right. These nobly played their part. They heard their country's call. They gave their all.' 146 mm.

Invergordon *War Memorial.* 148 mm (rare).

Loughborough War Memorial. 155 mm.

Margate *War Memorial* 160 mm.

Newhaven Mercantile Memorial, with inscription: 'This Memorial is erected to the memory of the captains, officers and seamen of H.M. Transports who lost their lives whilst sailing from this port during the Great War 1914–1918 and also in commemoration of the valuable services rendered by the Mercantile Marines of the United Kingdom in the war.'

Arcadian. 'Model of new
aeroplane', monoplane with
revolving propellor and an
unnamed monoplane with V wings
and revolving propellor, with in this
case two blades

Right Arcadian. H.M.S. Queen
Elizabeth. The 'Arcadian' range did
not include a great number of
battleships

Left Arcadian. 'Model of new
aeroplane' a biplane with a fixed
propellor

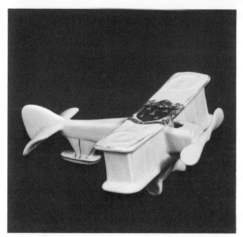

Arcadian. An unnamed battleship
and a 'Model of Torpedo Boat
Destroyer'

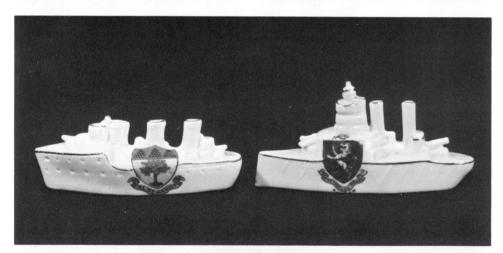

Arcadian. 'E4' and 'E5' submarines.
'E5' is inscribed 'Model of a new
submarine'

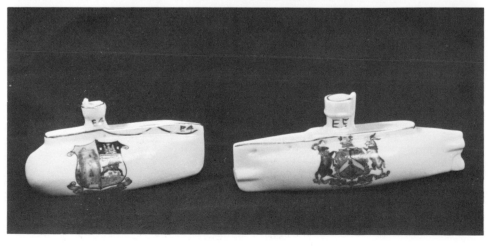

Right Arcadian. Red cross van with 'EH 139' on radiator

Left Arcadian. 'Model of Revolver' 83 mm long

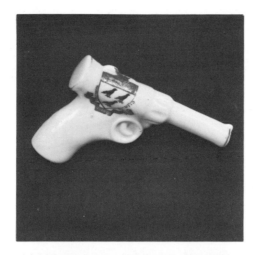

Right Arcadian. 'Model of a trench mortar' with the inscription 'War Edition'

Left Arcadian. 'Model of armoured car'

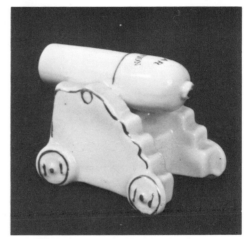

Arcadian. 'Model of Tank' in two sizes, 160 mm and 115 mm long. There are five sizes in all

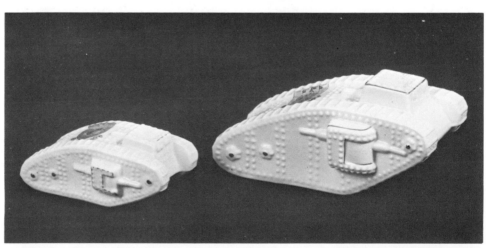

Arcadian. Tank with one trailing wheel, rare, as the makers soon realised that there should be two. This tank was the first made and given the Rd. No. 658588

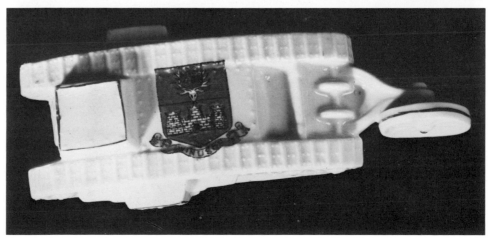

Right Arcadian. 'Model of observer or sausage balloon'

Left Arcadian. Top: British airship on stand
Bottom: 'Model of Super Zeppelin'

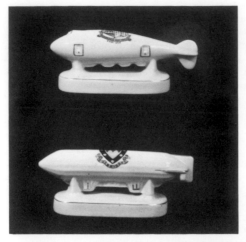

Arcadian. British aerial torpedo and German aerial torpedo

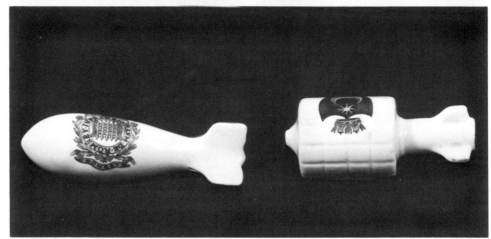

Right Arcadian. 'Model of Cenotaph' and Cavell 'Memorial Statue, Norwich'

Left Arcadian. Invergordon and Loughborough War Memorials

Right Arcadian. Folkstone War Memorial, a most imposing piece

Left Arcadian. Newhaven Mercantile Memorial, Dover War Memorial and Royal Naval Memorial Southsea. 140 mm

Norwich *War Memorial*. 134 mm (rare).
Plymouth *War Memorial*, with inscription:
'He blew with his winds and they were
scattered.' 2 sizes: 125 mm & 178 mm.
Sheringham War Memorial, with
inscription: 'To keep in remembrance of
those men from the parishes of
Sheringham & Beeston Regis who gave
their lives in the course of right and
justice in the Great War, 1914–1918.
Their name liveth for ever. Greater love
hath no man than this.' and inscribed: *H.
H. Palmer, Sculptor Sheringham*. 165 mm
(rare).
Southsea Naval War Memorial. 2 sizes
140 mm & 162 mm.
Woodhouse Eaves. War Memorial with
inscription: 'Their name liveth for
evermore.' 130 mm (rare).

Most of the above Memorials are relatively
rare, possibly because they were ordered
in small numbers by local shops, or were
only made for a short time.

Home/Nostalgic
Anvil on tree trunk base, horseshoe, tongs
etc. against base. 70 mm.
Armchair. 65 mm.
Armchair, inscribed: *The old armchair* and
with verse: 'I love it, I love it and who
shall dare to chide me for loving the old
arm chair.' 90 mm.
Basket. 50 mm.
Basket with twisted handle. 73 mm long.
Bellows. 95 mm long.
Chair, highbacked. 90 mm.
Child in long nightdress, for use as
candlesnuffer. Some colouring. 100 mm.
Coal Scuttle. 50 mm.
Coal Scuttle, sometimes found inscribed:
Coal scuttle. 80 mm.
Cradle. 48 mm.
Dressing Table, Swing Mirror, with
drawer. 50 mm.
Dust Pan. Rd. No. 629144. 95 mm long.
Firebucket. 55 mm.
Fireplace, with teapot, cat, etc. in bold
relief. Inscribed: *There's no place like home*.
Some colouring. 2 sizes. 90 mm and
112 mm.
Fireplace, with cauldron, teapot, etc.
moulded in slight relief. Inscribed:
There's no place like home. Some
colouring. 65 mm.
Fruit basket. Rd. No. 629155. 63 mm.
Grandfather clock, Model of a. Usually
inscribed: *Make use of time let not
advantage slip. Shakespeare*. Can be found
inscribed: 'Top o' the morn. No. 209.
108 mm.
Kennel, can be found inscribed: *Beware of
the dog*. 50 mm.
Lantern. 70 mm.
Lantern, horn, not found named. 85 mm.
Lantern with open side. Rd. No. 659858.
125 mm.
Milk churn. 63 mm.
Pillar Box, with inscription: *If you haven't
time to post a line here's the pillar box*.
Found marked G.R.V. 63 mm.
Shaving Mug. 60 mm.
Spinning Wheel, not found named. 84 mm.

Suffragette handbell, some colouring. See
Swan for details
Sundial, inscribed: *Life's but a walking
shadow*. 2 sizes: 86 mm & 115 mm.
Umbrella, open. 50 mm dia.
Victorian lady and gentleman figure group
on base, inscribed: *He that is satisfied is
rich*. Found with colour transfer of
children. 115 mm (rare).
Village Pump with trough. Rd. No. 629148.
90 mm.
Old warming pan, Model of, inscribed: *Polly
warm the bed*. No. 254. 125 mm.
Watchman's Lamp, inscribed: *Watchman
what of the night!* 85 mm.
Water Pump. Rd. No. 629167. 90 mm.
Wheelbarrow. 100 mm long.

Comic/Novelty
Many of the highly coloured models in this
section were produced in a series, being
of similar style and decorated in the
same way, and these have been grouped
together at the end of the listing. They
are generally models made in the late
1920s.
Alarm Clock, inscribed: *Many are called but
few get up*. No details of size (rare).
Basket of Milk, six bottles, tops can be gold
or brown. 65 mm.
Billiken, often found not named. 63 mm.
Boy Scout, inscribed: *Be prepared*, 105 mm
(quite rare).
Clown, bust, inscribed: *Put me amongst the
girls*. Some colouring. Rd. No. 522477.
80 mm.
Couple in Bed, man sitting up inscribed:
*John is everything shut up for the night—all
but you darling*. 70 mm long (very like a
fairing.)
Couple in bed, woman with all the
blankets, inscribed: *They don't need many
clothes in the daytime but they want'em all at
night*. 70 mm long. (Very like a fairing.)
Fat Lady on weighing scales; scale registers
20 stone. Inscribed: *Adding weight*. Blue
bonnet. Rd. No. 740919. 90 mm.
Japanese Girl, with fan and parasol. No.
250. 64 mm.
Jester, double faced bust, happy and sad
and eyes open and closed. Can be found
inscribed: *Ye Jester awake. Ye Jester asleep*.
Some colouring. Rd. No. 473172. 2 sizes:
65 mm & 90 mm.
Judge in his box reading a book. 82 mm.
Lavatory Pan with brown seat, inscribed:
Ashes. Not found crested. 60 mm (rare).
Negro Minstrel, bust, verse by Eugene
Stratton: 'May be crazy, but I love you!'
Some colouring. Rd. No. 534809.
100 mm (rare).
Policeman, fat and jovial, with raised
hand. Inscribed (on hand): *Stop*. 94 mm.
Policeman hailing, inscribed: *From . . .*
142 mm.
Policeman on duty, with verse: 'A
Policeman's lot is not a happy one.' Can
occasionally be found inscribed:
Controlling the traffic. 148 mm.
Policeman, jovial holding large truncheon.
Uniform and helmet blue. 106 mm
(rare).

Arcadian. Top: Sailor with blue
cap and coloured face, policeman
inscribed 'Stop'
Bottom: 'Ye jester awake, ye
jester asleep', double faced bust,
small monk holding glass (see
Alcohol)

Right Arcadian. Bust of Harry
Lauder, coloured bobble and
thistle

Left Arcadian. Suffragette
handbell, showing 'This one
shall have a vote'. This model
shows the prevailing attitude to
womens suffrage

Right Arcadian. Bust of Ally
Sloper the first English comic
strip character

Left Arcadian. Suffragette
handbell, showing 'Votes for
Women' side

Petrol Pump Attendant, body is pump. Inscribed: *Petrol Sir*. Some colouring. 95 mm.

Pierrot, standing. 100 mm.

Sailor, standing, cap can be found impressed: *Lion*. Blue cap and coloured face. 2 sizes: 95 mm & 195 mm. (This is a nice little naive model of a sailor and is not a G. War souvenir.)

Suffragette double sided bust, front sour old lady, inscribed: *Votes for women*, back pretty young girl, inscribed: *This one shall have the vote*. Much colouring. 98 mm. A smaller version exists with no colouring or inscriptions. 72 mm.

Suffragette candle snuffer, double faced as above. 72 mm.

Suffragette hand bell, double faced as above, with same inscription and colouring. No details of size.

(All the suffragette items must be considered scarce.)

A truck of coal from . . . Wagon of black coal. 80 mm long (coal was rationed during and after the Great War. As it was the fuel mostly used for cooking and heating at that time, it became very precious!)

Comic Ashtrays: Coloured figures on white trays. (All are quite rare.)

Flapper, sitting on bench on heart shaped tray, yellow hat and dress. Rd. No. 678581. 105 mm.

Jester, sitting on heart shaped tray, other card symbols are on tray. 65 mm.

Scotsman, really grotesque, sitting on bench on round tray. Rd. No. 678580. 95 mm.

(Ballet Dancer, Bill Sykes, Puppy, Paddy and Irish Colleen are all illustrated in this series in the catalogue, but have not been reported as found! The Footballer, Golfer and Racehorse which would be under sport have not been found either.)

Comic Cruet sets: Only odd items have been found but these items must have been sold in sets. They are all fully coloured. They are usually marked Rd. No. applied for.

Policeman Salt Pot. 80 mm.

Regimental Sergeant Pepper Pot. 80 mm.

Naval Petty Officer pepper pot. 80 mm.

Sailor, comic figure with green parrot on shoulder with white mustard barrel with lid. 63 mm.

Little birds: these are fully coloured heads popping out of white eggs. They do not seem to match any other series of models, the black boy's face is much more carefully detailed than the black boy's listed below.

Flapper's head hatching from egg, inscribed: *A little bird from* . . . Rd. No. 728917. 50 mm long.

Black boy's head hatching from egg, inscribed: *A blackbird from* . . . Rd. No. 732369. 50 mm long.

(There is a tiny coloured chicken in this series, see under Birds.)

Black Boys—often found marked Rd. No. applied for. All the boys are fully coloured but sit on white boxes, baths and so on. Later models are very brightly and carefully coloured and lightly

glazed. These are marked as late in the listing below. All of these models, except the banjo player and 'A little study in black and fright', are rare.

Black Boy standing with hands in pocket, also found as salt pot. 94 mm (late).

Black Boy playing banjo, boy can be wearing red or blue striped pyjamas. Rd. No. 728916. 85 mm.

Black Boy in bath of ink, towel hanging at side, inscribed: *How ink is made*. 110 mm. (Probably *Willow art mould*.)

Black Boy in hip bath holding yellow soap. Rd. No. 752300. 90 mm (late).

Black Boy in bed with spider, inscribed: *A little study in black and fright*. Boy can have red or blue striped pyjamas. Rd. No. 728917. 70 mm long.

Black Boy being chased up a tree by a crocodile. 80 mm.

Black Boy eating slice of Melon, sitting on soap box. 80 mm (late).

Black Boy sitting at table eating a boiled egg which has chicken popping out. Rd. No. 723910. 70 mm.

Two Black Boys' heads popping out of box, inscribed: *Box of chocolates*. 60 mm. (Probably *Willow art mould*.)

Two Black children, boy and girl sitting on a tree trunk. 80 mm (late).

Black Boy holding container for cigarettes. 100 mm (late).

Black Boy holding container for matches. Rd. No. 740918. 100 mm (late).

Children: very late models, beautifully coloured and detailed children on white armchairs, baths etc. Usually found marked Rd. applied for. They are particularly appealing and unfortunately rare.

Girl and boy sitting in armchair. Girl is wearing a frilly dress and has a large bow on her head; the boy is dressed in top hat and tails. 60 mm.

Girl and boy as above sitting on tree trunk. 87 mm long.

Girl standing by hip bath, wearing towel. 75 mm.

Baby in bath with a coloured transfer of an insect (variously described as a wasp or a fly). Rd. No. 740917. 80 mm long.

Cartoon/Comedy Characters

Ally Sloper, bust, with inscription: 'Good Health Old Man, Vote for Sloper and more of everything. More beer, more bacca more work', some colouring. Rd. No. 522476. 85 mm. (Ally Sloper was the first English comic strip character—pre 1900.)

Harry Lauder, bust. Inscribed: *Stop ye're tickling Jock*. Often found not named. Some colouring. Rd. No. 537473. 83 mm.

Mrs Gummidge, standing figure with inscription: 'A lone lorn creetur & everything goes contrary with her.' 112 mm (rare).

Mr Pickwick, type character, bald headed with spectacles, sitting on neck of bottle. Man fully coloured. Rd. No. 752303. 2 sizes: 80 mm & 95 mm (late and rare).

Right Arcadian. Eighteen seater charabanc with number plate '7734 or 'HELL' read upside down

Left Arcadian. Omnibus, double decker bus with stairs outside

Right Arcadian. Three models of a Lancashire clog

Left Arcadian. Folding camera 60 mm

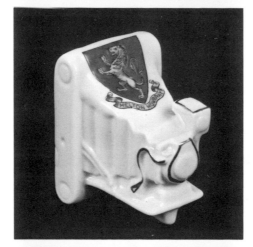

Right Arcadian. Top: Large size fireplace 112 mm
Middle: Small size fireplace 90 mm
Bottom: Fireplace with cauldron 65 mm

Left Arcadian. 'King Alfred the Great' Statue Winchester 170 mm

Mr Pickwick as above climbing into a large basket. 75 mm (late & rare).

(Although the above look like Mr Pickwick they could in fact be a comic or cartoon character of the time who cannot now be identified, or possibly just an invention of an Arcadian modeller.)

Alcohol

Beaker, fluted, with inscription: 'They speak o' my drinkin, but they dinna consider my drouth.' or 'Ye never ken the worth o' water till the well nor is dry.' 78 mm.

Beer Barrel on stand, inscribed: XXX on each end of barrel. Rd. No. 629150. 55 mm.

Beer Bottle and Tankard on horseshoe ashtray, with inscription: 'The more we are together the merrier we'll be.' Silver tankard. 85 mm long.

Bottle with cork. 76 mm.

Man holding tankard on horseshoe ashtray, with inscription: 'The more we are together the merrier we'll be.' Figure fully coloured. Rd. No. 708645. 99 mm long (rare).

Man drinking beer from tankard. Can be on white, or have silver tankard and occasionally found with head coloured as well as silver tankard. 92 mm.

Monk, jovial, and holding glass with verse: 'A jovial Monk am I contented with my lot. The world without this gate, I flout nor care for it one jot.' Rd. No. 537472. 2 sizes: 70 mm & 112 mm.

Soda Syphon. 100 mm.

Tankard, foaming, with verse: 'The more we are together.' 50 mm.

Thistle vase, with verse: 'Just a wee deoch-an doris.' 70 mm.

Toby Jug, sometimes found with verse: 'No tongue can tell, No heart can think, Oh how I love a drop of drink.' 2 sizes: 65 mm & 85 mm (smaller size is exactly the same as Old Toby Jug).

Whisky Bottle, can have a solid or cork top, inscribed: One special Scotch. 100 mm.

Whisky Bottle and Soda Syphon on tray, inscribed: Scotch and soda. 88 mm dia.

Whisky Quaich (or bowl) inscribed: Scuab As'I. 134 mm long.

Sport

Cricket Bag. 80 mm long.
Cricket Bat. Rd. No. 629150. 115 mm long.
Football. Rd. No. 570859. 50 mm dia.
The F.A. Cup. 100 mm.
Golf Ball, often inscribed: The game of golf was first played in the year 1448. 42 mm.
Golf Club. 76 mm.
Golf Club Head. 94 mm long.
Golf Bag and Clubs. 105 mm.
Golfer, with Clubs standing on golf ball. 76 mm.
Golfer's Caddie holding golf bag. Figure coloured. 110 mm (late model.).
Golfer's Caddie, very tiny, holding huge bag of clubs. 88 mm.
Tennis Racquet. 90 mm long.

Musical Instruments

Banjo. 2 sizes: 125 mm & 150 mm long.
Double Bass. 153 mm long.
Guitar. 153 mm long.
Piano, Upright. 70 mm long.
Tambourine. 26 mm dia.
Violin with bow. 125 mm long.

Transport

Car, open tourer (2 seater) inscribed: EH 139; can be found also inscribed: Hell. 110 mm long.
Car, saloon, inscribed: EH 139. 76 mm long.
Charabanc, 18 seater, inscribed: 773H which upside down reads Hell. 138 mm long.
Can of Petrol, impressed: Motor Spirit. 55 mm.
Omnibus, Double decker bus with stairs outside, 130 mm long (rare).

'Modern' Equipment

Camera, folding. 60 mm.
Gramophone in cabinet. 80 mm long.
Horn Gramophone. 112 mm.

Miscellaneous

Hats

Boy Scout's Hat. 73 mm dia.
Mitre. No. 19. 84 mm.
Top Hat. 40 mm.

Shoes

Highboot. 88 mm (could be military, but not named).
High backed narrow shoe. 2 sizes: 90 mm & 130 mm long.
Hobnail Boot. 2 sizes: 65 mm & 80 mm long.
Dutch Clog. 102 mm long.
Sabot, pointed toe. 60 mm long.
Ball of String match holder and striker. 55 mm.
Chess Set. (Complete sets can be found but these are very rare. It is extremely difficult to collect a set with matching crests. Individual pieces are often found however, the rook being the most common; the pawn, strangely, is quite rare.)
King. 88 mm.
Queen. 84 mm.
Knight. 63 mm.
Bishop. 60 mm.
Rook. 55 mm.
Pawn. 52 mm.
Handbell, no clapper. 53 mm.
Horse's Hoof on base. No. 151. 30 mm.
Horseshoe. 55 mm long.
Thimble. 40 mm.

Miniature Domestic

These models can be found with crests, views, black cats and other transfer decorations.
Beaker. 40 mm.
Chamber pot. 38 mm.
Cheese dish, one piece. 50 mm.
Cheese dish and cover. 50 mm.
Teacup and saucer. 40 mm.
Teapot and lid. 60 mm.

Domestic Ware

This is listed as it was made specifically to carry crests. Pieces can also be found with 'Lucky Black Cat,' 'Lucky White Heather' and other transfer decorations, but not usually views. Late pieces are found with the black cat *Arcadian* mark. Lettering is usually in blue.

Ashtrays, can be found inscribed: *Ashtray*.
  Various shapes:
  Clover shapes.
  Club, diamond, heart and spade shaped with crinkle edges.
  Club shaped tray with match box stand.
  Heartshaped bowl.
  Horse shoe.
  Octagonal.
  Round tray with match holder.
  Bulb Bowl, hexagonal.
Candle Snuffer, cone.
Candlesticks, various shapes:
  Column with ornate moulding.
  Octagonal, fluted.
  Short on oblong base with handle.
  Short on fluted oblong base with handle.
  Short on fluted leaf shaped base with handle.
Fern Pots, fluted. 3 sizes.
  Hexagonal. 3 sizes.
Flower Bowl, octagonal.
Hair Pin Box, can be found inscribed: *Hair pins*. Fluted oblong or round.
Hair Tidy, can be found inscribed: *Hair tidy*. Various shapes:
  Hexagonal.
  Octagonal with ornate moulding and blue bow.
  Square, fluted.
Hat Pin Holder, can be found inscribed: *Hat pins*. Various shapes:
  Octagonal.
  Square, fluted.
  Square with ornate moulding.
Inkstand
Inkstand, with penholder base.
Match Holder, can be found inscribed: *Matches*. Various shapes:
  Hexagonal.
  Round.
  Round on base.
Pin Tray, can be found inscribed: *Pins*. Fluted round or oblong.
Pot Pourri, 2 shapes:
  Round vase shaped, lid with knob.
  Round with domed lid (rather like a ginger jar).

Powder bowl, round.
Preserve Jar and lid, round or tub shaped.
Puff Box, can be found inscribed: *Puff box*, hexagonal or round. 2 sizes.
Ring Stand.
Rose Bowl, fluted with brass fittings.
Tableware: Cups and saucers, coffee cans and saucers, and plates are all found in classic and simple shapes. Also the following:
  Beakers, plain and fluted.
  Butter Tub.
Cream Jugs and Sugar bowls (matching) in various shapes:
  Hexagonal.
  Octagonal.
  Round, plain.
  Round, fluted.
These can occasionally be found inscribed: *Help yourself to tha crame/sugar* or *Be aisy wid tha crame/sugar*.
Egg Cup.
Jugs, in a variety of sizes, also bagware.
Mugs. 2 sizes.
Mustard Pots. Various shapes:
  Round with pointed lid.
  Round, fluted and ornate.
  Round, with silver lid.
  Round, tall, with silver lid.
Pepper & Salt Pots, various shapes:
  Cone shaped, small.
  Cone shaped, tall with silver lids.
  Hexagonal.
  Round, fluted and ornate.
  Round, with silver lids.
Plate, with thistles and leeks moulded in relief. Rd. No. 722373.
Sugar Basin on Stand.
Sugar Caster.
Sweet Dishes, various shapes:
  Octagonal, 2 sizes.
  Round, crinkle edged. 2 sizes.
  Round, fluted, 2 sizes.
  Teapots. 1, 2 & 3 cup sizes.
Tobacco Jar, inscribed: *Tobacco*.
Trinket Boxes, can be found inscribed: *Trinkets*. Various shapes:
  Heart shaped. 4 sizes.
  Hexagonal.
  Horseshoe shaped.
  Oblong.
  Oval.
  Round. 2 sizes.
  Square.
  Square with bevelled corners.
  Square, fluted.

Argonauta Porcelain

Trademark used by James
Macintyre and Co. Ltd,
Washington China Works, Burslem.

Very little is known about this firm and the only reference I have been able to find to their products is an advert for the firm in the Pottery Gazette in 1913. They advertise their firm as specialising in Arms Ware, 'School, College or Town Arms on Tobacco Jars, match pots and ashtrays'. This mark has so far only been found on 'smalls'. J. Macintyre and Co. were earthenware manufacturers and the pieces found tend to be rather heavy.

Argosy China

Trademark used by an
unknown manufacturer
possibly using a retailer's mark.

The only manufacturer working between 1900 and 1940 using the initials KB were King and Barratt (Ltd), Bournes Bank Pottery, Burslem. King and Barratt were earthenware manufacturers and it is just possible that they used this mark. The models are unlike the products of other known manufacturers, and they are rather heavy, so it is possible that they were produced as a sideline during the war years by a firm which did not specialise in crested wares.

Most pieces found have been 'smalls' and many of them have carried Southend Crests, so it is possible that the initials SEOS stand for Southend-on-Sea, and that KB was a retailer. Until more models are recorded with details of paintresses' marks and stock numbers the manufacturer will remain a mystery. No device other than crests has been found on china with this mark. (A stock number has been recorded on one model and it is possible that many models carry such numbers.)

Argosy Models

Animals
Elephant, comic standing with sandwich
  boards. 115 mm.

Great War
Colonial Hat. 25 mm.

Miscellaneous
Boot with laces. No. 234. 80 mm long.
  (*Grafton* made a similar boot with the
  stock number 237.)

Miniature Domestic
Teapot. 90 mm long

Asbury

ASBURY
LONGTON

Trademark used by Edward
Asbury and Co., Prince of
Wales' Works, Longton.

Edward Asbury and Co. manufactured china and earthenwares from 1875 to 1925. In the early nineteen hundreds the firm was making transfer printed wares for the fancy goods trade including 'Charles Dickens' Ware—drawings by 'Phiz' on mugs, plates, jugs and beakers. The company obviously made a small range of crested items during the Great War. A Great War Commemorative is often found on 'smalls' and models, consisting of a transfer print of '5 Flags of the Allies' and inscribed: 1914. (No numbering system seems to have been used.)

Asbury Models

Animals
Swan. 65 mm long.

Great War
Tank. 85 mm long.

Novelty
Billiken, flat grotesque type. 68 mm.

Miscellaneous
Sabot. 80 mm long.

Atlas Heraldic China

Trademark thought to have
been used by Taylor and
Kent, Florence Works,
Longton, for a wholesaler in Scotland.

CR and Co. are not known to be china manufacturers (there was an Atlas china works in Stoke on Trent from 1889 to 1906 owned by Chapman and Sons, but they did not use this mark. From 1906 to 1919 the company was known as The Star China Co., and used a different mark together with the initials 'SCC').

Right Arcadian. Vase in pearl lustre, has orange lustre interior with lucky white heather device

Left Arcadian. Parian busts of 'King Edward VII' and 'Alexandra of Denmark'. The King's bust also has an inscription on the reverse giving details of his life and death

Right Arcadian. Parian 'Model of the Globe, Swanage'

Left Arcadian. Raphael Tuck cartoons, 'Spooning', 'Are you Afraid', 'A pleasant sunset' and 'Two Minds But With A Single Thought'

Aynsley. Two military caps and a helmet

Right Aynsley. Tent with open flaps with the badge of the Life Guards

Left Aynsley. Grenade with flames leaping from the top, a most unusual model

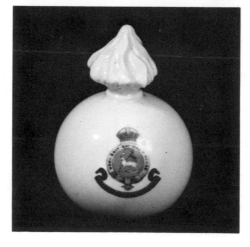

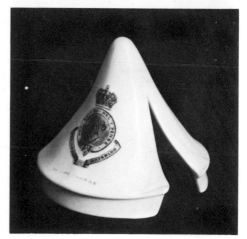

All known models, except the thimble, are identical to *Florentine* models made by Taylor and Kent. (See Florentine China for details.) Taylor and Kent are known to have sold a great deal of china in Scotland so it is quite reasonable to suppose that they used this mark for a Scottish wholesaler.

All known models carry Scottish crests or Scottish colour transfer views. (Taylor and Kent did not use stock numbers.)

Atlas Models

Ancient Artefact
Salisbury Kettle, not named. 100 mm.

Seaside Souvenir
Whelk Shell. 100 mm.

Bird
Pelican Cream Jug. 83 mm long.

Home/Nostalgic
Sofa. 82 mm long.

Miscellaneous
Carboy. 76 mm.
Shoe, Ladies', 18th century. 95 mm long.
Thimble. 40 mm.

Miniature Domestic
Cheese dish and cover. 55 mm.
Coffee pot and lid. 63 mm.
Teapot. 70 mm.

Avon China

Trademark used by Arkinstall and Son Ltd, Arcadian Works, Stoke-on-Trent.

Mark used 1903–1906

Arkinstall more usually used the trademark ARCADIAN CHINA. (See under that heading for details of china and manufacturer.) This mark is very like the earliest known *Arcadian* mark used by the firm and indeed all of the models recorded are 'smalls', except for one vase which was recorded as Model of a Roman Vase No. 285, with no other details. It is probable that Arkinstall tried out this trademark for a time when the firm was first established. (It is unlikely to be a retailer's mark as crests are found from places as far apart as Scotland and Wales.)

Aynsley

Trademark used on china with Military crests by John Aynsley and Sons, Portland Works, Longton.

AYNSLEY

AYNSLEY & SONS

John Aynsley and Sons are the well known firm that produce fine china today. The firm was established in 1864 to manufacture porcelain. In 1903 they advertised a 'number of fancy pieces, plain and white and enamelled in colours'. In 1904 they registered a number of designs of miniature military models as souvenirs of the South African war. These military items and 'smalls' are found with a series of military crests which pre-date the Great War. In 1908 with the introduction of the Haldane Act many of these Regiments disappeared. Obviously these models are of great interest to Military model collectors and they are often found in Great War collections where unfortunately they have no business to be. Military Crests found on Aynsley models are:

Connaught Rangers 88th and 94th Foot
First Middlesex—Victoria and St George Rifles
Fourth Middlesex
Grenadier Guards

Kings Dragoon Guards
Kings Own Scottish Borderers 25th Foot
Queens Westminsters, 18th Middlesex R.V.
Royal Army Medical Corps
Royal Irish Fusiliers
Royal Irish Rifles. 83rd and 86th Foot
Royal Marine Artillery
Royal Scots 1st Foot
Royal Scots Fusiliers
Royal Welsh Fusiliers, 23rd Foot
Second Dragoons
Second V.B. Royal West Surrey Regiment
South Wales Borderers 24th Foot
Staffordshire Imperial Yeomanry
Third Dragoon Guards
Twenty-First Lancers

Aynsley did not produce crests of towns or countries and do not appear to have made crested ware during the Great War. Some black monochrome transfer views can be found on domestic ware but as this firm made such a vast range of china this cannot be considered 'crested china' in the terms of this book.

Aynsley Models

South African War
Hand Grenade, with flames coming from the top. Rd. No. 444522. 88 mm.
Cannon Shell. Rd. No. 444369. 104 mm.
Empty Shell Case. Rd. No. 444366. No details of size.
Bandsman's Drum. Rd. No. 444367. 55 mm.
High boot. Rd. No. 444523. 118 mm.
Tent, with open flaps. Rd. No. 444368. 75 mm.
Waterbottle. Rd. No. 444365. 80 mm.
Colonial Soldier's Hat. Rd. No. 445700. 106 mm long.
Forage Cap. Rd. No. 445680. 85 mm long.
Glengarry. Rd. No. 445079. 90 mm long.

Pickelhaube. Rd. No. 442812. No details of size.
(Although always described as a Pickelhaube and recognisable as such, it is much more likely to be a spiked helmet as worn by some English soldiers before 1908.)
Pith helmet. No details of size.

Miscellaneous
Boot. Rd. No. 446680. 60 mm.
Horse's hoof. Rd. No. 444521. 55 mm
Horse shoe. Rd. No. 446521. 85 mm long.

B

Trademark used by Blairs and Beaconsfield Pottery, Longton

Blairs advertised 'Arms Ware' in 1902 but seem to have made very little. Only two models have been recorded so one can only assume that they sold other models unmarked or used another trademark. Certainly crested ware was only a side line and the firm produced other decorative china, much of it at this time being very Art Nouveau in style. The firm was established in 1880 and was subsequently known as Blairs Ltd in 1911. This firm produced Great War Commemoratives. (See Blairs China.)

B Models

Animal
Pig, standing. 80 mm long.

Miniature Domestic
Cheese Dish, one piece. 50 mm.

Balmoral China

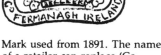

BALMORAL CHINA

R & D
ENGLAND

Mark used 1909–1933

Trademark used by Redfern
and Drakeford (Ltd),
Balmoral Works, Longton.

This mark has only been found on one piece of crested china, and that carries a Wembley British Empire Exhibition crest. It seems likely that this china manufacturer produced a few models purely for the Exhibition.

Balmoral Model

Bird
Goose, standing and very fat. 155 mm.

Belleek

Mark used from 1891. The name of a retailer can replace 'Co Fermanagh Ireland'

Trademark used by Belleek
Pottery (David McBirney and
Co.), Belleek, Co.
Fermanagh, Ireland.

This well known Irish firm employed the noted Goss modeller William W. Gallimore for a short period, during which he imported to Belleek Ivory Porcelain production invented by W. H. Goss. The firm produced a range of crested domestic ware, 'smalls' and probably a few simple models although only two have been recorded. As two of the 'smalls' recorded have a lustre finish it could be that these were made in the twenties but it is much more probable that the range was made at the turn of the century.

Belleek Models

Alcohol
Barrel. 57 mm.

Animal
Terrier standing. 88 mm.

Birks China

THE ORIGINAL
BIRKS 1895   CHINA 1928
STOKE ON TRENT
MADE IN ENGLAND

Trademark used by Birks,
Rawlins and Co. (Ltd), Vine
Pottery, Stoke, previously
L. A. Birks and Co.,
established in 1895.

Birks Rawlins and Co. used the Trademark SAVOY CHINA. (See that entry for details of china and manufacturer.)

This trademark was obviously used in 1928 to trade on the old and respected name of Birks. We know the new company was already in financial trouble by this date. 1928 was rather late to introduce a range of crested ware and this venture did nothing to help the firm's sales. Most pieces recorded are domestic items with only one model being known. One colour transfer view of Hampton Court Palace has been recorded on a teaplate but known crests are from all over England. (*Savoy* china always carry stock numbers but these have not been recorded on *Birks* china.)

Birks Model

Home/Nostalgic
Basket. 48 mm.

Right Arcadian. 'Model of a trench dagger' 102 mm long

Left Arcadian. 'Model of Ghurka Knife' 110 mm long

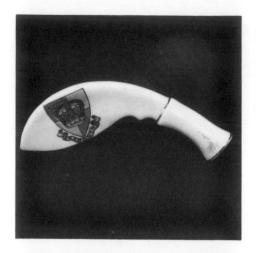 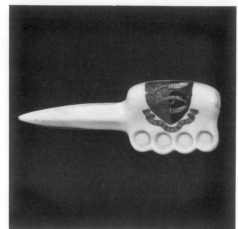

Right Botolph. Model of 'Temple Bar' with City of London crest

Left Balmoral. 155 mm Goose, the only recorded 'Balmoral' model

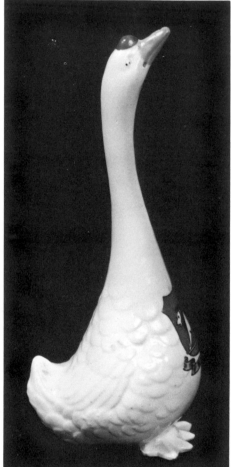 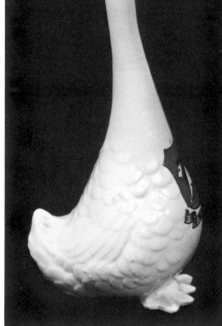

Right Botolph. Model of Cenotaph, Whitehall London. 102 mm

Right Botolph. Model of a tank, which carries the usual registration number '658588'

Left Botolph. Tower Bridge, not named

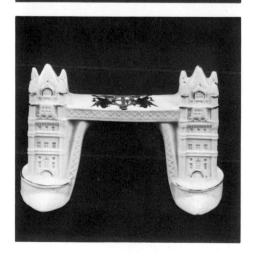 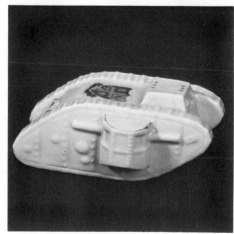

Blairs China

Trademark used by Blairs
Ltd, Beaconsfield Pottery,
Longton.

BLAIRS
CHINA
ENGLAND

1914

Blairs Ltd are not known to have made crested ware, earlier in the firm's history as Blairs and Co. they had done so. (See B.) Blairs Ltd was formed in 1911 and in 1914 they produced a range of 'smalls' with a Great War Commemorative. This transfer print shows four flags of the Allies tied to a rope.

Boots

Trademark used for Boots the
Chemist by an unknown
British manufacturer.

Boots sold a range of crested 'smalls' in their fancy goods departments. Although the trademark would indicate a Great War Commemorative, these pots often carry the crest of a town. A transfer print of Six Flags of the Allies is also found inscribed: *In freedoms cause*. This commemorative often occurs on unmarked wares; it was probably used by one of the known crested china manufacturers who do not appear to have marked their wares. (See Unmarked Crested China.)

Botolph China

Trademark probably used by
J. Wilson and Sons, Park
Works, Fenton.

BOTOLPH
J. W. & Co

Marks used c1914–1926

J. Wilson and Sons were china manufacturers, the firm being in business from 1898 to 1926. This mark was not registered but all the clues point to this firm, the wares being very like those made by other works in Fenton, notably J. Reeves the makers of Victoria China. It seems likely that this manufacturer began production of souvenir items during the Great War when skilled labour was scarce and the lack of German competition made such production very worthwhile. The models with the *Botolph* mark are therefore rather heavy and crude. The similarity to *Victoria* models points to some sort of connection between the two firms and it is possible that J. Reeves sold moulds to *Botolph*. Other models seem to be copies of pieces made by other firms.

Botolph was made mostly for the London retail trade, many crests of the City of London are found and all known buildings are found in London.

No other forms of decoration other than crests are found on *Botolph* models and no military or commemorative crests have been found. (No numbering system was used on models.)

Botolph Models

Buildings—White
Big Ben. 130 mm.
Marble Arch, Model of. 2 sizes: 60 mm &
  80 mm.
Old London Bridge, Ye. 86 mm.
St Paul's Cathedral. 2 sizes: 76 mm &
  127 mm.
Temple Bar. 96 mm.
Tower Bridge. 178 mm long.
Westminster Abbey, Front. 80 mm.

Historical/Folklore
Mother Shipton. 73 mm.

Traditional/National Souvenirs
Yarmouth Bloater. 100 mm long.
Irish Harp. 106 mm.

Seaside Souvenirs
Lifebelt. 85 mm dia.
Lighthouse. 95 mm.
Whelk Shell. 98 mm long.

Right Botolph. Billiard Table, a
rare model not found in other
ranges

Left Botolph. Saloon car showing
gilded display side 85 mm long

Caledonia Heraldic. Armoured
car, again a 'Savoy' model

Right Caledonia Heraldic. Model
of Mons Meg, Edinburgh Castle
135 mm long (This model is
sometimes found in Great War
collections where it has no
business to be)

Left Caledonia Heraldic. Scottish
soldier on circular base, the
model is usually found marked
'Savoy'

Right Caledonia china. Two King
Charles spaniels sitting in top
hat. This model also appears
marked 'Dainty Ware'

Animals
Bulldog. 57 mm.
Dog, puppy, with curly tail, sitting.
   90 mm.
Pig, standing. 55 mm.
Rabbit. 70 mm long.
Tortoise. 70 mm long.

Birds
Chicken. 102 mm long.
Hen, roosting. 52 mm.
Kingfisher. 76 mm.
Owl, baby. 70 mm.
Swan. 63 mm.
Swan Posy Holder. 90 mm long.

Great War
Nurse, inscribed: *A Soldiers Friend*.
   125 mm.
Monoplane, with movable prop. 175 mm
   long.
Observer Sausage Balloon. Rd. No.
   658681. (Same Rd. No. as Arcadian
   model.) 80 mm.
Battleship, 2 sizes: 115 mm & 165 mm
   long. Larger size found with inscription:
   'Great War 1914–1918. The German Fleet
   surrendered 74 warships Nov 21st 1918'.
Torpedo Boat Destroyer. 110 mm long.
Submarine, inscribed: *E4*. 95 mm long.
Submarine, inscribed: *E5*. Rd. No. 658681.
   127 mm long.
Red Cross Van. EH 139 with 3 red crosses.
   88 mm long.
Tank, Model of. Rd. No. 658388. 155 mm
   long.
Tank with small integral steering wheels.
   Rd. No. 658588. 105 mm long.
Field Gun. 120 mm long.
Howitzer. 135 mm long.
Trench Mortar. 70 mm.
Clip of Bullets. 85 mm.
Revolver (Luger). 83 mm long.
Bandsman's Drum. 58 mm dia.

Fireplace, inscribed: *We've kept the home
   fires burning*. 110 mm.
Cenotaph, Whitehall London, Model of, with
   green wreaths, inscribed:
   MCMXIV–MCMXIX. 3 sizes: 80 mm,
   102 mm and 140 mm. Largest size has
   inscription: 'The Blood of Heroes is the
   Seed of Freedom'.
Cavell Memorial Statue, London.
   inscribed: *Nurse Cavell*. 2 sizes: 115 mm
   & 160 mm.

Home/Nostalgic
Girl in bonnet, hatpin holder. 88 mm.
Sofa, no details of size.

Comic/Novelty
Jack in the Box. 95 mm.
Screw, inscribed: *A big fat screw*. 75 mm.
   (Screw meant salary in the 1920's!)
Pierrot, sitting, playing banjo. Some
   colouring on hands and face. 120 mm.

Sport
Cricket Bag. 110 mm long.
Golf Club Head. 2 sizes: 75 mm & 95 mm.
Snooker Table on 6 legs. With 3 balls and a
   cue resting on top. 100 mm long. (Very
   rare.)

Musical Instruments
Grand Piano. 85 mm.

Transport
Car Horn, inscribed: *Pip Pip*. 90 mm long.
Saloon car, always found gilded on one
   side only. 86 mm long.

Miscellaneous
Bishop's Mitre. 55 mm.
Clog with pointed turned up toe. 98 mm
   long.
Shoe, ladies', 18th century. 93 mm long.
Toby Jug. No details of size.

Bow China

Trademark used by Birks,
Rawlins and Co. (Ltd), Vine Pottery, Stoke.

This firm usually used the trademark SAVOY CHINA (see under this heading for details of the firm's history and the china).

A small range of models with this mark has been recorded. They are mostly Great War miniatures but a few domestic items have also been recorded.

Numbering System. Savoy models usually carry printed or pointed stock numbers, Bow China does too. Where models have been found with both marks they carry the same stock number.

Bow Models

Ancient Artefacts
*Lincoln Jack from original in museum, Model
   of.* No. 39. 60 mm. (This has not been
   recorded with the 'Savoy' mark.)

Animals
Elephant and Howdah. 70 mm (rare).

Great War
Battleship found inscribed with one of the

following: *HMS Lion* or *HMS Ramilies*.
   No. 524. 168 mm long.
Submarine, inscribed: *E1*, usually found
   with the inscription: 'Commander Noel
   Lawrence, Large German Transport
   sunk July 30th 1915.' German cruiser
   Moltke torpedoed August 19th 1915.
   150 mm long.

Miscellaneous
Top Hat. No. 339. 44 mm.

C and S C

Trademark used by Taylor
and Kent Ltd.

See Florentine China for details of the firm.

One could normally assume that *C and S C* were retailers, and indeed they may have been, but the crests of the two models recorded suggest this does not seem likely. One model carries a crest of Durban the other Saffron Walden. Taylor and Kent were known to export arms ware and if *C and S C* were retailers they were probably based in South Africa. Presumably this mark could have been used in England if the company needed extra models to complete an order.

C and S C Models

Seaside Souvenirs
Yacht in full sail. 127 mm long.

Great War
Cannon Shell. 75 mm.

Cambrian China

Trademark used for a Welsh
retailer by Wiltshaw and
Robinson Ltd, Carlton
Works, Stoke-on-Trent.

For details of this manufacturer and china see Carlton China.

Only one Welsh souvenir has been recorded with this mark, having obviously been made for a shop in Swansea. (The hat bears this crest.)

Cambrian Model

Traditional/National Souvenirs
Welsh hat, Model of, with largest Welsh
place name round brim. No. 283.
56 mm.

Caledonia China

Trademark used by Taylor
and Kent (Ltd), Florence
Works, Longton for the
Glasgow wholesaler CR and
Co. (See also Atlas Heraldic
China.)

For details of this china and manufacturer see Florentine china.

Taylor and Kent used at least two different marks for this wholesaler, Atlas Heraldic China being the other known one. The *Caledonia* range mainly consists of small domestic ware and small pots and vases. All known crests are Scottish, and some transfer printed Scottish views can also be found on 'smalls'.

Caledonia (CR and Co.) China

Animals
Camel, kneeling. 95 mm long.
Pig, standing. 80 mm long.

Home/Nostalgic
Sofa. 82 mm long.

Miniature Domestic
Cheese dish and cover. 2 pieces. 55 mm.

Can sometimes be found as
Caledonia Heraldic China

Caledonia China

Trademark used by James
Macintyre and Co. Ltd,
Washington China Works,
Burslem, for sale in Scotland.

For details of this china and manufacturer see Argonauta Porcelain.

Models, 'smalls' and domestic ware found with this mark, all carry crests of Scottish towns.

Caledonia (Macintyre) Models

Animals
Polar Bear, inscribed: *Sam*. 88 mm long.
Two King Charles spaniels sitting in top hat.

Birds
Hen, roosting. 51 mm.

Caledonia Heraldic China

Trademark used by a Scottish
wholesaler on crested china
manufactured by leading
arms ware firms including
Birks, Rawlins and Co.,
Hewitt and Leadbeater, and
Wiltshaw and Robinson Ltd.

This mark can sometimes be
found with MADE IN
SCOTLAND printed below.

For details of china and manufacturers see Savoy China, Willow Art China and Carlton China.

Most models carrying this mark are recognisably *Savoy* or *Willow Art* pieces but only one *Carlton* model has been recorded. The domestic ware is unlike that of the two firms and may well have been made in Scotland. All known china has Scottish crests, no views or other transfer devices have been recorded.

Where models are known to be from Birks and Rawlins moulds they have, for the most part, the same stock numbers. However Birks and Rawlins use of stock numbers is at best perplexing (see Savoy China). Willow Art moulds always carry the same stock numbers when they are used.

Caledonia Heraldic Models
NB. Where models are known to be from one of the above manufacturer's moulds this will be indicated by (Savoy), (Willow) or (Carlton) after the description of a model.

Parian/Unglazed
Bust of Burns on square glazed base. 160 mm (actually impressed H and L).
Bust of Scott on square glazed base. 160 mm (impressed as above).
Grace Darlings boat, Model of. Fully coloured boat on brown rocks. 108 mm long (Carlton).

Buildings—White
Burns cottage, Model of. 105 mm long (Willow).
Carnegie's Birthplace, inscribed: *Model of the birthplace of Andrew Carnegie*. 70 mm long.
Cottage, thatched. 60 mm long.
Cottage, inscribed: *Tigh-na-gaat centre of Scotland*. 85 mm.
First and last house in England. 83 mm long (Willow).
Old town house Dunbar, The. 135 mm.

Monuments
The Blackwatch Memorial, Edinburgh. 127 mm (Willow).

Historical/Folklore
James V Chair. Stirling Castle. 100 mm (Willow).
Mons Meg, Edinburgh Castle. No. 162. 130 mm long (Willow).

Seaside
Bathing Machine. 80 mm (Willow).

Animals
Dog, Bulldog, standing with verse: 'Be Briton Still to Britain true, Among ourselves united. For never but by British hands, Maun British wrongs be righted. Burns'. No. 364. 130 mm long (Savoy).
Pig, lying down. No. 559. 80 mm long (Savoy).

Great War
Scottish soldier on circular base. 160 mm (Savoy).
Monoplane with revolving prop. 178 mm long.

Battleship inscribed: *HMS Lion*. 140 mm long (Willow).
Torpedo boat destroyer, Model of. No. 615. 140 mm long (Savoy).
Armoured Car (reputedly a Talbot, but not named). 125 mm long (Savoy).
British motor searchlight, Model of. No. 665. 103 mm long (Savoy).
Tank with trailing steering wheels, inscribed: *HMS Donner Blitzen* and 515 on side. Further inscription on base: 'Model of British Tank first used by British Troops at the Battle of Ancre Sept 1916.' 140 mm long (Savoy).
Tank, no steering wheels. Inscription exactly the same as above. No. 651. 135 mm long (Savoy).
Field gun, Model of. 150 mm long.
Shell, inscribed: *Iron rations for Fritz*. 60 mm (Savoy).
French trench helmet. 82 mm long (Savoy).

Alcohol
Pot with inscription: *A wee deoch an doris*. 44 mm (Willow).

Musical Instruments
Upright Piano. No. 755. 83 mm long (Savoy).

Miscellaneous
Top Hat. 44 mm (Savoy).

Miniature Domestic
Cheese Dish. 2 pieces. 50 mm.
Cheese Dish. 1 piece. 40 mm.

Note: Models offered for sale in dealers' lists as *Caledonia China* could be any of the three marks recorded above. When first recording marks I was only aware of two marks: Caledonia (JM) China and Caledonia Heraldic so three models remain which cannot be properly listed. They are:
Cat pincushion. 70 mm—Either Caledonia CR and Co. or Caledonia Heraldic.
Lighthouse, without crest and inscribed: *Lands End*. 100 mm. Either Caledonia CR and Co. or Caledonia Heraldic.
Dutch Sabot inscribed: *God Speed. Greenock*. 90 mm long. Either Caledonia CR and Co. or Caledonia Heraldic.

Carlton China

Trademark used by Wiltshaw and Robinson Ltd, Carlton Works, Stoke-on-Trent.

c1902–30

MADE IN ENGLAND

From 1928–present day can also be 'China'

Wiltshaw and Robinson started manufacturing in 1890 (a previous trademark used the same bird and initials W and R but did not use the name Carlton). A visitor to the works in 1902 reported that the firm specialised in making a large assortment of fancy goods and that they had been busy filling orders for the coronation. The firm was reported to make 'vases, teapots and waterjugs etc. Also pieces for silver mounting e.g. biscuit boxes'. It was also first in 1902 that Wiltshaw and Robinson 'the Manufacturers of Carlton Ware, Tinted Faience, etc.' advertised their 'latest speciality—Carlton Heraldic China' which could be seen at their London Agents, Messrs Green Bros, 47 Hatton Garden, E.C. This early advert would seem to indicate that Carlton was the first of the big Goss competitors to make heraldic china.

It is surprising that this company managed to remain independent of the *Cauldon* mergers that took place later on in Stoke, especially as Harold Taylor Robinson began his career as a traveller for the firm in 1899 when he was 22. By 1906 he had become a partner in Wiltshaw and Robinson, after having left this firm in 1903 to start his own company. (J. A. Robinson, the manufacturers of *Arcadian*.) But somehow (not publicly disclosed) one of the original owners managed to buy him out, or at least break the partnership, and registered the firms as a private company in 1911. In an advert for Carlton Ware in the same year Mr J. F. Wiltshaw proudly announced he was the sole proprietor of Wiltshaw and Robinson Ltd.

Mr Wiltshaw seems to have been determined to produce unique and novel designs, and his modellers (in fact the owners often designed their own models) were not influenced overmuch by the wares of the other potteries working in Stoke. They continued to produce very individual and (using a term much liked at the time) artistic models. The company seemed very concerned that only correct coats of arms should be used. I have been told that one customer designed a crest for his town and forwarded it to Carlton with an order for china. The order was filled but Carlton finding later that the crest was bogus asked for all the china to be destroyed (not all the models were destroyed however, and one lucky collector must have the only 'Ise Making Ink' with this Bawtry Crest).

By 1920 the Carlton Speciality, lustre ware had been developed, the Pottery Gazette was full of praise for the lustre finishes the firm was using. After this date Wiltshaw and Robinson used lustre finishes on all their wares, including some heraldic china. This was obviously popular and although other firms later added lustre to their range it remained very much a hallmark of Carlton. A great number of heraldic models can be found in lustre, sometimes rather unsuitably on buildings and figures. By 1924 the firm had developed 'twelve very smart colours' in lustre (only five have been found used on crested pieces: mother of pearl, orange, tangerine, turquoise and black).

Throughout the period that Wiltshaw and Robinson produced heraldic china, they also made other decorative pottery. 'There are few factories in North Staffordshire that can claim to produce a bigger or more interesting range of earthenware fancies' (Pottery Gazette). They also produced useful tableware but always in novel shapes or in 'lustrine', and decorated very much in the popular style of the time.

The firm exhibited goods of this kind at the 1924 British Empire Exhibition and appeared to be flourishing, but by 1931 Wiltshaw and Robinson Ltd was put into the hands of the Receiver. Presumably this firm, like many others, had found it difficult to overcome the Depression. Details of the firm's financial state were not made public and quite possibly the liquidation was voluntary, so that a new company could be formed. F. W. Carder ceased to act as Receiver on March 7th 1932 and 'Wiltshaw and Robinson Ltd, Manufacturers of earthenware, etc' merged with 'Birks, Rawlins and Co Ltd', china manufacturers, previously of Vine Pottery, Stoke on Trent (makers of *Savoy* china). The merged company went on using the *Savoy* trademarks as well as *Carlton* for a few years.

Carlton Ware decorative and novelty items have continued to be produced. The ownership of the firm has changed and in 1957 the company became known as Carlton Ware Ltd. Representatives of the company claim that no records of the manufacture of heraldic china have been kept and that they know nothing of the early history of the firm. (In fact two of them did not know what crested or heraldic china was!) One can only hope that the growing interest in collecting Carlton Ware will prompt someone to search through whatever files remain and supply some information, trade catalogues, details of personal and other company trivia, which would be of enormous interest to collectors.

The firm must have survived all these years because of someone's ability to quickly change the style of its products to suit each new public whim and fancy. (The only plan for survival if one is in the fancy goods trade). This is most obvious when surveying their range of crested china. The style of the Carlton models quite noticeably changed to exactly catch the mood of each period over the twenty odd years of production. The early ancient artefacts and historical models are properly labelled and have the right sober Victorian feel about them. The light hearted Edwardian holiday souvenirs are beautifully detailed and touched with colour. The Great War models are heavy with patriotism and yet the post war animals and novelty items are jolly and rather naive. Finally no other company produced quite such vulgar lustre and coloured models to suit the taste of the late 1920's.

Grafton. Three different
Wembley Exhibition crests.
60 mm vase with a simple
Wembley Lion, club shaped pin
box with inscription and 50 mm
vase with a more elaborate device

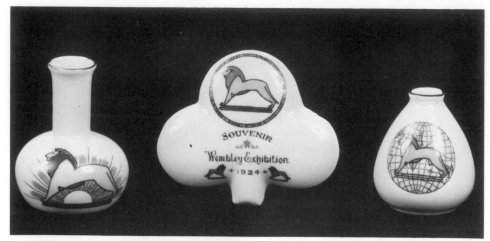

Right Carlton. Globe shaped vase
in brilliant lustre 145 mm,
Carlton were producing these
wares at the same time as crested
china

Left Carlton. A very fine 80 mm
beaker with a colour transfer
print of 'Idol Rock, Brimham
Rocks'

Carlton. Lustre vase with green
shamrock transfer, mug with
coloured transfer print of 'The
Lighthouse, Withernsea and vase
with a commemorative crest of
'Gloucestershire Historical
Pageant, Cheltenham 1908'

Right Carlton. Small bowl in
yellow lustre advertising
Carltonware at B.E.E. Wembley
1924. 65 mm dia

Left Carlton. 'Model of Roman
Jug found at Cambridge' instead
of the normal crest this model
carries Xmas Greetings and is
dated 1912

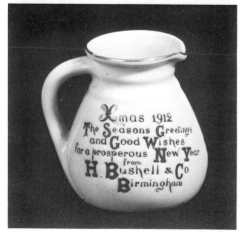

The quality of Carlton cannot be compared with the fine china made by Shelley and Grafton. They produced heavy models and the crests are not always painted carefully, although many examples of fine china and beautiful crests can be found. Carlton were competing for the same end of the market as Arcadian souvenir shops, bazaars and the cheaper china shops. However at its best Carlton can be very beautiful and the detail to be found on models throughout the range is quite extraordinary when one considers how cheaply they were sold.

Early decorations on small models normally found with crests include roses, green shamrocks and forget-me-nots (these can be found forming initials on beakers—a design also used by Goss). Wiltshaw and Robinson produced some View Ware, but as they did not advertise this and there is relatively little around one can only assume that this was an unimportant line for them. (Possibly the production of view ware was only an early activity as these transfers are usually found on small domestic items and very rarely on named models.) This is a pity because the coloured transfer views used by this firm are excellent and compare well with Shelley (possibly the leader in the field). Other coloured transfers used are of a regional nature, such 'Biddenden Maids', 'Welsh Teaparty', 'Grace Darling' and 'The Trusty Servant'. These prints are found on all kinds of models, including buildings, sundials, hats and animals.

Carlton do not seem to have produced a range of Military crests, the exception being the Tank Corps badge which Great War collectors like to see on their tanks. They did however produce a number of Naval crests, including HMS AUSTRALIA, HMS CONQUERER, HMS FURIOUS, HMS LION, RMS LUSITANIA, HMS QUEEN ELIZABETH and HMS TEMERAIRE. (They also made an unusually large range of named battleships—one wonders if the firm had naval connections or whether this interest in the war at sea was due to the number of retail outlets in ports!)

Some foreign crests have been found—Australian Towns, Tasmania, Bermuda and Hawaii—indicating some exporting, but it does not appear that Carlton ware was sold in allied countries during the Great War. There seem to be very few commemorative crests for the collector, only the BEE, Four Flags of the Allies, 'United we Stand' and The Gloucester Historical Pageant 1908 are known. There is however, a commemorative transfer print of the *Titanic* with details of its sinking.

Wiltshaw and Robinson did produce a great number of models with the lucky white heather device rather than a crest. These are nearly always used on lustre pieces, some models, but more often vases, jugs and bowls. To a much lesser extent they also used Lucky Black Cat transfers, but the cats are usually part of a larger design incorporating horseshoes and four-leaf clovers and these again are often found on lustre models.

As Carlton manufactured coloured and non-crested animals, Toby jugs and ladies from 1925 onwards which are difficult to date these have not been listed here, although as they are often of a similar style to crested china they are frequently found in collections. There is also a range of model cars, made after the Second World War, which appeal to collectors but cannot be considered crested china. Anyone becoming addicted to Carlton might well look out for examples of all their products from 1890 to the present day. Early Art Nouveau and the later Deco style wares are already very expensive but items from the 1930's, 40's and 50's are still to be found at bargain prices except for the coloured ladies which are much sought after. Modern items, such as teapots on legs, are to be found in

Right Carlton. Tintern Abbey Ruins with green moss on top of the walls

Left Carlton. British Pavilion at the British Empire Exhibition with matching crest

Right Carlton. 'Model of Hop Kiln' with coloured hop transfer

Left Carlton. Parian bust of Sir Philip Sydney

Carlton. Top row: Dorset Roman Jug, Hastings Kettle, Chinese Vase, Hanley, Roman Pottery
Middle row: Eddystone Spanish Jug, Etruscan Vase, Penmaenmawr Urn, Portland Vase
Bottom row: Roman Pottery 1st Century, Irish Kettle, Chester Roman Vase, Newbury Leather bottle

rather fashionable and expensive gift shops but are worth looking for. Such a collection of items would almost certainly tell the story of 20th century popular taste.

Numbering System. Printed stock numbers appear on early models and can be taken as an indication that a model was made before 1914 at least. (Models that were originally numbered were made after this date but are found with no printed number.) Some early vases, mugs and trays have painted numbers, and these too are probably stock numbers. (Paintresses marks are usually small painted initials and cannot be confused with stock numbers.) Stock numbers are given where known in the following lists.

NB. Domestic ware and later gift items have impressed numbers. (usually four numbers). By the 40's these reach the 1900's, so it is possible to find very late pieces impressed 1910, 1912, etc. Some rather dishonest stall holders will try to explain that this is the date of manufacture—do not be deceived!

Carlton Models

Parian/Unglazed
Unglazed models are mostly busts which are on circular glazed bases, normally carrying crests.

Busts
Bust of King Edward VII, later models found inscribed: *King Edward VII. Born Nov 9th 1841. Died May 6th 1910. Reigned from Jan 22nd, 1901 to May 6th 1910. The Peacemaker.* 135 mm.
Bust of Queen Alexandra. 135 mm.
Bust of King George V. 135 mm.
Bust of Queen Mary. 135 mm.
Bust of Burns, with verse by Wordsworth. 120 mm.
Bust of (Austen) Chamberlain. 115 mm.
Bust of Ruskin. 135 mm.
Bust of Sydney, inscribed: *Sir Philip Sydney. Thy necessity is greater than mine.* 135 mm.
Bust of Wordsworth. 2 sizes: 115 mm & 135 mm. Smaller size impressed: *Wordsworth Poet.*

Monuments
Cavell Memorial Statue. 165 mm.
Captain Cook Statue on glazed square base. 140 mm.
Captain Cooks Monument. An obelisk. Rd. No. 493796. 135 mm (very fine).
Globe, Swanage, with map in relief, on square glazed base. Inscribed: *Model of Globe at Swanage.* 55 mm. dia. 86 mm.
Florence Nightingale on square glazed base, inscribed: *1820–1910 The Lady of the Lamp.* 174 mm.
(John) Ruskin Memorial on square glazed base. Rd. No. 397960. 172 mm.

Ancient Artefacts
These models are often found not named, named models usually have a printed number and this is given where known. Most inscriptions begin: *Model of* so this will not be repeated throughout the list.

Ancient Tyg, 1 handle. No. 184. 66 mm.
Ancient Tyg, 2 handles. No. 245. 66 mm.
Cambridge Jug, inscribed: *Roman jug found at Cambridge.* No. 332. 60 mm.
Chester Roman Jug, inscribed: *Roman jug found in Chester 1892.* Rd. No. 449297. 75 mm.
Chester Roman Vase, inscribed: *Roman vase found at Chester from original in museum.* Found numbered 154 and 286. 60 mm.
Christchurch Harvest Vase, Rd. No. 506865. No. 407. No details of inscription or size available.
Cobham Bottle, no details available.
Colchester Ancient Vases, inscribed: *Ancient vase original in Colchester Museum.* 2 vases: No. 351. Rd. No. 474414. 66 mm. No. 353. Rd. No. 474415. 68 mm. (No model numbered 352 has been found; could this be another Colchester Vase?)
Colchester Famous Vase, inscribed: *The famous Colchester vase in the museum.* No. 80. 36 mm.
Dogger Bank Bottle, inscribed: *Ancient bottle dredged up near the Doggerbank.* No. 251. Rd. No. 449300. 65 mm.
Dorset Roman Jug found in Bath. 70 mm.
Eddystone Jug, inscribed: *Old Spanish jug dredged up near Eddystone—now in Athenaeum Plymouth*, not found numbered. 58 mm.
Elizabethan Jug or Stoup, inscribed: *West Malling Elizabethan jug or stoup, hall marked London 1581 sold for 1,450 guineas.* No. 360. 90 mm.
Fountains Abbey Cup, inscribed: *The Abbots Cup from the original in Fountains Abbey.* No. 238. 50 mm.
Glastonbury Bowl, inscribed: *Bowl from ancient British lake village near Glastonbury.* No. 172. 39 mm.
Grecian Vase. No. 257. 78 mm.
Hampshire Roman Vase, inscribed: *Roman vase found in New Forest Hampshire.* No. 247. 70 mm.
Hanley Chinese Vase, inscribed: *Chinese vase original in Hanley Museum.* No. 263. Rd. No. 499545. 55 mm.

Carlton. A very impressive
model of the Fourth Bridge with
details of construction on base.
166 mm long

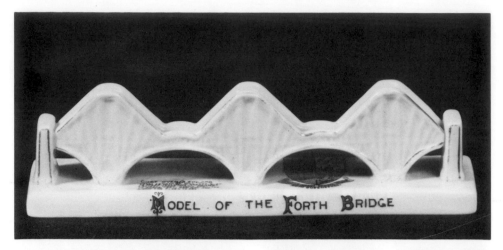

Right Carlton. Fire Engine
House, Leatherhead, not named

Left Carlton. 'West Front, York
Cathedral' and 'Micklegate Bar,
York'

Carlton. 'Tom Tower,
Christchurch Oxford', 'Mallock
Memorial Clock Tower,
Torquay', and 'Douglas Jubilee
Clock' in lustre

Hanley Cyprus Vase, inscribed: *Cyprus vase now in Hanley Museum 900 BC*. No. 374. 45 mm.

Hanley Egyptian Vase, inscribed: *Ancient Egyptian vase now in Hanley Museum. 3,300 BC*. 2 different models: No. 367. Rd. No. 489059. 64 mm (2 large handles from neck to body). No. 368. 63 mm (2 tiny handles on body only).

Hanley Roman Jug, inscribed: *Ancient Roman jug now in Hanley Museum*. No. 370. 55 mm.

Hanley Roman Vase, inscribed: *Ancient Roman vase now in Hanley Museum*. 2 vases: No. 372. 63 mm. No. 373. 55 mm.

Hastings Kettle, inscribed: *Ancient kettle dredged up near Hastings in Hastings Museum*. No. 166. 60 mm.

Hull Suffolk Palace Jug, inscribed: *Antique jug found on site of Suffolk Palace, Hull. Now in museum*. No. 276. No details of size.

(Ancient) Irish bronze pot. No. 183. 45 mm.

Irish kettle. No. 346. Rd. No. 473068. 65 mm.

Jersey milk can, with lid. No. 242. 70 mm.

Lichfield Jug, inscribed: *Ancient jug dug out of foundation of Lichfield Museum*. No. 181. 60 mm.

Lincoln Jack (from original in museum). No. 156. 60 mm.

Loving Cup, 2 handled. Not named. No. 97. 38 mm & 47 mm.

Loving Cup, 3 handled, not named. 38 mm.

Merthyr Tydfil Roman Pottery, inscribed: *Roman pottery excavated at Merthyr Tydfil*. No. 383. 52 mm.

Newbury Leather Bottle, inscribed: *Leather bottle found at Newbury 1644 on battlefield now in museum*. No. 299. 65 mm.

Old bronze porridge pot. No. 221. No details of size.

Penmaenmawr Urn, inscribed: *Ancient urn found on Penmaenmawr*. No. 213. 50 mm.

Phoenician vase (original in Hanley Museum). No. 174. Rd. No. 449298. 70 mm.

Pompeian Vessel, not named. Rd. No. 473329. 60 mm.

Portland vase (now in British Museum), often found not named. No. 89. 58 mm.

Puzzle Jug, not named. 2 sizes: 68 mm & 90 mm. Larger size carries verse: 'Try now to drink and not to spill and prove the utmost of thy skill'. Small size also found in lustre with rust handle.

Roman Pottery, inscribed: *1st Century AD Roman pottery original in Wedgwood Museum, Burslem*. No. 377. 70 mm.

St. David's Vase, inscribed: *Ancient vase found at St. David's*. No. 249. 62 mm.

Salopian Ewer, inscribed: *Roman ewer found at Uriconium now in Shrewsbury Museum*. No. 75. 76 mm.

Shakespeare's Jug: inscribed: *Jug of William Shakespeare*. 70 mm.

Silchester Urn, inscribed: *Roman urn from Silchester in Reading Museum*. No. 193. 54 mm.

Southampton Pipkin, inscribed: *Ancient pipkin dug up at N.P. Bank Southampton*. No. 204. 54 mm.

Spilsby Jug, no details available.

Stoke (14th century) Etruscan vase. No details of size.

(Old) Swedish kettle. No. 344. 70 mm.

Winchelsea Vase, inscribed: *Vase found near Winchelsea*. No. 87. 77 mm.

Winchester Bushel, with Latin inscription around the side. No. 323. 2 sizes: 80 mm & 110 mm dia.

Windsor Urn, inscribed: *Urn found at Old Windsor from original in museum*. No. 284. 50 mm.

Wokingham Tankard inscribed: *Old tankard jug found near Wokingham*. No. 217. 78 mm.

York Roman ewer, inscribed: *Roman ewer from original in Hospitium found at York*. No. 178. 57 mm.

Buildings—Coloured

Carlton do not seem to have produced a range of coloured buildings and only two have been listed below. They did however sometimes introduce coloured detail to what are basically white glazed buildings and these will be found listed in the next section.

Dove Cottage, the early home of Wordsworth, Model of. 50 mm.

(The) Transport and General Workers Union Convalescent Home. Littleport. 112 mm long.

Buildings—White

Arundel Castle, The Keep. 120 mm long.

Bandstand, inscribed: *O listen to the band*. Also found in lustre. 85 mm.

Blackpool Tower, also found in lustre. 125 mm.

Blackpool Tower, inscribed: *Model of Blackpool Tower*. 140 mm.

Blackpool Tower with base, also found in lustre. 164 mm.

Blackpool Tower and Big Wheel on ashtray, inscribed: *Good old Blackpool*. Also found in lustre. 2 sizes: 108 mm & 130 mm (nice and vulgar).

Burns Cottage, Ayr. 70 mm long.

Cairn on Culloden Battlefield, 1746 (model of) and inscription giving details of battle. Rd. No. 493796. 65 mm.

Cottage. 50 mm (very delicate).

Cottage with coloured doors, hedges and windows with a removable roof lid, and inscribed: *Ours is a nice house ours is*, or with verse 'A little wife well willed, A little farm well tilled, A little mouse well filled and I am satisfied'. 70 mm.

Douglas Jubilee clock. 127 mm.

Douglas Tower of Refuge. 73 mm.

Dropping Well, Knaresborough, coloured details and water. 77 mm.

Dutch Cottage, Canvey Island, dated 1621. 75 mm (scarce).

Fire Engine House, Leatherhead. 115 mm (uncommon).

Forth Bridge (model of the) and inscription giving details of bridge. 166 mm long.

Harrogate *Pump House*, inscribed: *A nip and a smell from the old sulphur well*. 75 mm.

Hastings Castle Ruins. 88 mm.

Hastings Clock Tower. 127 mm.

Right Carlton. Parian Ruskin
Memorial Cross on glazed base
172 mm

Light Carlton. Nelson's Column,
not found named 163 mm

Right Carlton. 'Model of Toad
Rock' and 'Model of Cairn on
Culloden Battlefield'

Left Carlton. 'Model of
Flamborough Lighthouse'
115 mm

Right Carlton. Blackpool Big
Wheel, not named 110 mm

Left Carlton. 'Laxey Wheel'
92 mm

Hop kiln (model of) with coloured transfer of hop. Also found in lustre. 96 mm.

Irish round tower (model of). No. 520. 126 mm.

King Charles Tower, Chester. 85 mm.

Laxey Wheel. 92 mm (not often found).

Marble Arch. 127 mm long.

Old Bishops Tower, Paignton. 82 mm (rare).

Oldest chemyste shop in England, Ye. Coloured roof and door. 100 mm long.

Parade, Chester, inscribed: Gods providence is mine inheritance. 108 mm.

Pithead (model of). 110 mm (rare).

Rochester Castle Keep inscribed: Dating from the year 1126. 80 mm.

St. Leonards Tower, Newton Abbot. 123 mm.

St. Nicholas Church, Lantern Hill, Ilfracombe. 98 mm.

St. Pauls Cathedral. 112 mm.

Scarborough Castle (model of). 80 mm.

Skegness Clock Tower. 124 mm.

Smallest house in Wales. 115 mm.

Tintern Abbey, with green moss on walls. 105 mm long.

Tom Tower, Christchurch, Oxford. 127 mm.

Torquay Clock Tower. Inscribed: Model of Mallock Memorial, Torquay. 168 mm.

Upleatham Old Church, the smallest church in England. 80 mm.

Wallace Tower. 140 mm.

Wembley Exhibition Hall. 88 mm long.

Wembley Stadium, inscribed: Model of British Stadium Wembley and details of cost and size. 110 mm long. Also found in lustre.

Windmill with revolving sails. Rd. No. 603779. 103 mm.

York, Bootham Bar. 114 mm.

York Cathedral, West Front. 112 mm.

York, Micklegate Bar. Also found in lustre. 112 mm.

Monuments (including crosses)

Burns Statue, Burns holding a crimson tipped daisy, with verse 'Wee modest crimson tipped flower. Thou's met me in an evil hour. R. Burns'. 160 mm (not often found).

Caister-on-Sea, Lifeboat Memorial. 160 mm.

Colne Market Cross 1822–1902. 125 mm (rare).

Flora Macdonald. Statue. 160 mm (not common).

Garstang Market Cross, inscribed: Model of Market Cross. 135 mm.

Globe, Swanage. (Model of the). 86 mm.

Hull, Fishermans Memorial, with inscription. 170 mm.

Hull South African War Memorial. 170 mm.

Irish Cross (model of). No. 519. 136 mm.

Mallock Memorial, Torquay. Rd. No. 493796. 165 mm.

Nelson's Column, not found named. 163 mm.

Queen Eleanor's Memorial Cross, Northampton. 138 mm (scarce).

Ripon Market Cross, inscribed: Model of Market Cross Ripon.

Rufus Stone with lengthy inscription on all 3 sides. 96 mm.

(John) Ruskin Statue. 120 mm.

Toad Rock (model of). 78 mm.

Sir William Wallace Statue with long inscription. 130 mm.

Wilberforce Statue, Hull. 155 mm.

Historical/Folklore

Biddenden Maids, inscribed: The Biddenden Maids were born joined together at hips and shoulders in year 1100 and a 34Y in 1100. (The twins died within 6 hours of each other aged 34.) 105 mm (rare model, only made by Carlton).

Caveman, standing figure holding club. Brown hair and club. 113 mm. (This is not comic—it is also rare.)

Font, not named. 133 mm.

Fox's chair, inscribed: Model of chair of George Fox the Quaker, original at Swarthmoor Hall Ulverston. 96 mm.

Grace Darling's boat, Model of and description. Boat in blue and white or brown rocks. 108 mm long.

Great Peter, handbell with clapper. No details of size.

Man in Pillory with some colouring. 100 mm.

Sedan Chair, inscribed: Model of 17th century Sedan chair. 70 mm.

Thomas A'Becket Shoe, inscribed: Model of the famous Thomas A'Becket shoe. 105 mm long.

Ulphus Horn (York) on base. 115 mm long (quite rare).

(The) Wallace Sword, inscribed: The sword that seem'd fit for the Archangel to wield was light in his terrible hand. 105 mm long.

Watchman's Lamp, inscribed: Model of 16th century watchman's lamp and Watchman what of the night. 2 sizes: 80 mm & 115 mm.

Witch's Cauldron with Macbeth verse 'Double, double, toyle and trouble fyer burns and cauldron bubble'. 45 mm.

Witch's cauldron on Tripod (rustic). Also found in lustre. 115 mm.

Xit, The historical dwarf with inscription: 'He is said to have been born in the 16th Century. He was under two feet in height, a brother of the giants Og, Pog, Magog. Xit was a noted curiosity at the Tower of London and was knighted Sir Nargissus Le Grande. Model taken from a statue in an old garden at Lewes.' 137 mm (rare).

Xit, The historial dwarf. 137 mm (rare).

Traditional/National Souvenirs

John Bull, bust. Rd. No. 537470. 100 mm.

John Bull with Bulldog, standing figure on oval base. Union Jack waistcoat and black hat, dog has red, white and blue collar. 125 mm.

Blackpool Big Wheel. 110 mm.

Lincoln Imp moulded in relief on Lincoln Jack, inscribed: 'The Imp'

Lincoln Cathedral. No. 156. 60 mm.

Kelly from the Isle of Man. 3 legged man, holding Manx Kipper in hand, fully coloured. 110 mm.

Manx Legs on base. Also found in lustre. 95 mm.

Right Carlton. 'Welsh Spinning
Wheel', one of two Welsh lady
groups

Left Carlton. 'Scotch Fisher Girl
at Work', rather a clumsy Carlton
model

Right Carlton. 'John Bull' bust

Left Carlton. Policeman with
verse on reverse 'A Policeman's
Lot is not a happy one' 'Pirates of
Penzance'

Right Carlton. Model of Pithead,
a rare model

Left Carlton. 'The Fiddler of York
Minster'. A rather clumsy model
to find in the Carlton range, it is
nevertheless sought by collectors
as it is reasonably rare

Right Carlton. 'Ripon Horn'
80 mm

Left Carlton. 'Dropping Well
Knaresboro' a reasonably rare
model

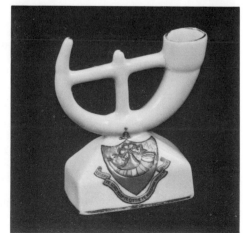

(The) Ripon Horn on square base, inscribed: *The ancient custom of blowing the horn each evening at nine o'clock continues to the present day*. 80 mm.

(The) Ripon horn blower, inscribed as above. Rd. No. 653720. 2 sizes: 80 mm & 120 mm.

(The) Sheffield grinding stone. 80 mm long (rare).

Yorkminster, The Fiddler of. 132 mm (not often found).

Yorkshireman, standing figure holding tankard—often found not named. Found with inscription: *Tak hod and sup lad* and verses 'Here's to me and ma wifes husband, not fo'getting messen' and 'See all, here all, say nowt, Eat all, drink all, pay nowt and if ever tha does out for nowt allus do it for thisen'. Rd. No. 662109. 126 mm.

Irish cabin, trunk more often found without this inscription. 58 mm long.

Irish Colleen, on circular base. 130 mm.

Irish Harp, with green shamrocks. 90 mm.

Irish Jaunting car, with horse and driver, some colouring. 130 mm long. (This is quite rare.)

Irish spinning wheel. Irish lady sitting by spinning wheel. 95 mm.

Bagpipes. 114 mm.

(The) Crown of Scotland with inscription giving details. 68 mm (rare).

Gretna Green, Model of blacksmiths anvil with verse: 'How far, how far to Gretna. Its years and years away and chaise and four shall never more fling dust across the day.' This anvil is often found without inscription or verse. 70 mm. (The Gretna Green verse often appears on models with a matching crest which have otherwise no connection with Scotland.)

Scotch fisher girl at work, coloured fish in barrel. 118 mm.

Scotsman, standing figure, blue tam o'shanter with red bobble and brown walking stick. With verse 'Just a wee deoch an doris'. 130 mm.

Tam O'Shanter (bonnet) with coloured sprig of heather. 80 mm dia.

Thistle Vase. 76 mm.

Jenny Jones, Welsh lady, standing figure with black hat, brown basket and red and green shawl. Rd. No. 651140. 147 mm.

Prince of Wales Feathers. 95 mm.

Welsh hat, Model of, can be found with longest Welsh place name round brim. Rd. No. 450915. No. 283. 56 mm.

Welsh Hat, with orange band. Can be found in lustre with a coloured transfer 'Welsh Teaparty'. 44 mm.

Welsh leek, Model of, leaves coloured green. 93 mm.

Welsh spinning wheel, two Welsh ladies with spinning wheel, coloured hats and shawls. 95 mm.

Welsh tea party, three Welsh ladies taking tea, coloured hats and shawls, etc. 90 mm.

Bermuda sailing ship, can be found with Bermuda crest. 127 mm long.

Gondola. 127 mm long.

Seaside Souvenirs

Bathing Machine, found inscribed: *Morning dip*. Sizes vary from 55 mm to 70 mm.

Lifebelt. 105 mm dia.

Lifeboat. 113 mm long.

Motor Boat on waves. 120 mm long.

Motor Boat with Driver on waves. 102 mm long. Also found in lustre.

Rowing Boat. 108 mm long.

Trawler, inscribed on sail: *SM*. 115 mm long.

Yacht, in full sail, found inscribed: *Saucy Sue*. 115 mm long.

Fisherman on Rock, holding brown net, inscribed: *Son of the sea*. 117 mm (beautifully detailed).

Lifeboatman, bust with colouring on face. Rd. No. 524786. 80 mm.

Lifeboatman in boat on sea, black clothing, lustre. 85 mm.

Lighthouse inscribed: *Sailor beware*. 140 mm.

Beachy Head Lighthouse. 148 mm (no named example found).

Douglas Lighthouse. 128 mm.

Eddystone Lighthouse, Model of, with black band, found inscribed: *Landing of Prince of Orange 1688*. 138 mm.

Flamborough Lighthouse, Model of. 115 mm.

Mumbles Lighthouse and telegraph office. 127 mm.

Pharos Lighthouse Fleetwood, Model of. No. 409. 100 mm. (Identical model, so named and with same stock number can be found as a pepper pot.)

Scarborough Lighthouse. 135 mm.

Scarborough Lighthouse, Model of with rectangular building showing shell holes from Great War. 98 mm.

Withernsea Lighthouse. Can also be found in lustre. 134 mm.

Limpet shell with 2 feet. 23 mm.

Oyster shell, found inscribed: *A Whitstable native* (when it becomes a traditional souvenir). 70 mm.

Whelk Shell, inscribed: *Listen to the sea*. 100 mm long.

Porter's Barrow with luggage. 76 mm long.

Valise (or travelling case) with two straps. 70 mm long.

Bathing Beauty, seated figure with green cap. 110 mm long.

Bathing Beauty lying on edge of lustre shell dish, same colouring on figure. Inscribed: *Washed up by the tide*. 110 mm long.

Boy on Donkey, can be found inscribed: *Gee up Neddy* or more occasionally: *This beats going to school*. Can be found without a base. 98 mm long.

Mr Punch, bust. Rd. No. 524786. 82 mm.

Punch and Judy Booth, with coloured Punch and Judy. Inscribed: *Good morning Mr Punch*. 133 mm. (A much sought after model.)

Countryside

Beehive on square stand, with coloured transfer bee. 64 mm.

Beehive with squat feet. 63 mm.

Pinecone. 79 mm.

Tree Trunk Candleholder. 113 mm.

Tree Trunk Vase. 115 mm.

Right Carlton. An appealing little fieldmouse on base, his features are picked out in gilding.

Left Calton. Bear with ragged staff impressed WARWICK. A beautifully modelled piece.

Right Carlton. 'Russian Bear' inscribed on reverse

Left Carlton. Dog with 'Caesar' on collar and inscribed on the reverse 'I am the King's Dog'

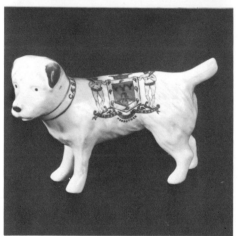 

Right Carlton. Dog with banjo, has red mouth

Left Carlton. Two models of a child on a donkey, the one on a base is inscribed: 'This beats going to school. The one without a base has no inscription. (The base was probably added to make the model more stable)

Right Carlton. Cat wearing black top hat with green shamrock. This model can also be found in lustre

Left Carlton. Pup on hand mirror. 'Me twice'

Animals

Carlton very craftily made new models by placing cats (especially black cats) and dogs on other popular pieces, not only ashtrays as other firms did but chairs, postboxes and sofas. They made two kinds of black cats, the usual type is small and chubby and the other is rather larger and more muscular. Both have red bows and green eyes. These black cats are not so popular with collectors as Arcadian black cats, probably because they are not doing anything but sitting.

Ape (Orang Outang) holding orange, brown face. Can be found in lustre. 58 mm.

Bear, can be inscribed: *Russian bear*. 118 mm long.

Bear and Ragged staff. 85 mm.

Bull, inscribed: *King of the herd*, or much more rarely: *The ox of Oxford*. 103 mm long.

Cat, angry, with back up, inscribed: *My word if you're not off*. 80 mm.

Cat, Cheshire, inscribed: *The Cheshire cat*, and *The smile that wont come off*. 90 mm.

Cat doing hand stand on oblong base, back legs up in the air. Inscribed: *Well what about it*. 115 mm (rare).

Cat, Manx. 75 mm.

Cat playing banjo, inscribed: *Some band*. 83 mm.

Cat sitting, chubby and kittenish. 63 mm.

Cat sitting on square cushion, impressed: *Good luck*. 80 mm.

Cat, sitting with red bow, pepper pot. 70 mm.

Cat sitting, wearing black topper with shamrock, bow tie can be found coloured red or green. Also found in lustre. 88 mm.

Cat sitting with blue bow (bow sometimes left uncoloured). 56 mm.

Cat sitting with Swastika round neck. 59 mm. This cat can be found on a pouffe and inscribed: *Good luck*. 85 mm.

Black Cat, small, found on the following:

Armchair (upholstered) with green swastika and red horseshoe on arms, inscribed: *Jolly good luck*. Can also be found in lustre. 75 mm.

(Old) Armchair with solid arms. 90 mm.

Ashtray, circular with transfer cigarette, inscribed: *Who burnt the cloth*. 110 mm dia.

Ashtray, club shaped, lustre. 90 mm long.

Ashtray, diamond shaped. 95 mm long. (It seems very likely that small black cats will be found on heart and spade shaped ashtrays as well and that all four were made in white and lustre.)

Chair. 90 mm.

Horseshoe Ashtray, inscribed: *Jolly good luck*.

Pillar Box, pillar box can be found painted red. Inscribed: *Good luck*. 110 mm.

Sofa, can also be found painted red. Inscribed: *Jolly good luck*. 80 mm.

Trinket box, inscribed: *Trinkets*. 93 mm long.

Black Cat, large, found on the following:

Oval base with coloured Swastika and horseshoe. Inscribed: *Good luck*. Base can be found in mother-of-pearl or blue lustre. 85 mm.

Pouffe, the cat's bow is found blue instead of usual red. Inscribed: *Good luck*. 90 mm.

Doe on oval stand. 118 mm. (Probably sold as pair with stag.)

Bulldog sitting, inscribed: *Bill Sykes dog*. 95 mm.

Bulldog sitting, thin faced. Inscribed: *Model of Bill Sykes dog* and sometimes found also inscribed: *My word if youre not off*. 51 mm.

Bulldog sitting, sometimes found inscribed: *Slow to start, but what a hold*. 56 mm.

Bulldog standing, inscribed: *My word if youre not off*; can be found inscribed: *Slow to start, but what a hold*. 120 mm long.

Dog (French Bulldog), sitting with pricked-up ears and blue eyes. 57 mm.

Dog looking out of kennel, inscribed: *The Blackwatch*. Dog's head is coloured black. 85 mm.

Dog playing banjo, inscribed: *Some band*. 82 mm.

Dog (Puppy) in slipper. Puppy coloured brown. 100 mm long.

Dog (Puppy) sitting with one ear raised. 83 mm. This puppy can be found on a hand mirror (silvered) inscribed: *Me twice*. 105 mm long.

Dog, Scottie, begging, pink ears and red collar. 74 mm.

Dog, Scottie, begging, wearing a glengarry, some colouring. 105 mm.

Dog, Scottie, sitting, wearing a tartan tam o'shanter with red bobble. 2 sizes: 60 mm & 80 mm. Also found in lustre.

Dog, Scottish Terrier, standing with tail in the air. Found inscribed: *As old Mrs Terrier said to her pup in all lifes adversities keep your tail up*.

Dog, standing, impressed on collar: *Caeser* and inscribed: *I am the Kings dog*. Some colouring. Rd. No. 582915. 106 mm long.

Elephant, walking. 51 mm.

Fawn. 70 mm.

Field Mouse, on base. 54 mm.

Fish (salmon), 112 mm long. (There could possibly be more than one model fish but if so they must all be straight and around this size as all reported models fit this description.)

Fish Ashtray, inscribed: *A plaice for the ashes*. 120 mm long.

Flamboro donkey, with orange and blue rosettes. 88 mm (rare).

Monkey, sitting hands to mouth. 90 mm.

Pig sitting on haunches, inscribed: *Wont be druv* or *You can push, you can shuv but I'm hanged if I'll be druv*. 60 mm.

Pig standing, found inscribed: *Wont be druv*. Also found entirely coloured blue. 65 mm long.

Pig, fat and standing, found inscribed: *Wont be druv*. Rd. No. 454897. 80 mm long.

Rabbit, crouching with pricked ears. 65 mm long.

Shetland pony. 138 mm long.

Right Carlton. Mother of Pearl lustre ape with tan face and orange fruit

Left Carlton. Racehorse on base, obviously often found in animal collections.

Carlton. Stag and Doe on oval stands. Probably originally sold as a pair. It is now much easier to find odd models of the doe, the stags antlers being very easily broken

Carlton. Top row: Hen and turkey
Bottom row: Duck with extended wings, rather comic large duck and realistic small duck
All animals on green bases with some colouring to heads. A model of a cock completes the series

Right Carlton. Wembley Lion on ashtray base with British Empire Exhibition crest

Left Carlton. 'Well What about it' a most energetic cat doing a hand stand. This is a very rare model

Right Carlton. Owl 66 mm, Stork with pink beak 110 mm and Owl with black mortar board with red tassel 75 mm

Left Carlton. Monkey with hands to mouth 80 mm. This model lacks something of the charm of most Carlton models

Right Carlton. 'Winkie the Gladeye Bird'

Left Carlton. Hen 'pepper' pot in cream wear with a lucky white heather device and cock 'salt' pot. Both have features picked out in red. Unfortunately it is quite difficult to find a matching pair

Right Carlton. Three wise monkeys. The monkeys are painted brown with red faces

Left Carlton. Fisherman on rock and lustre lifeboat man in boat. Both models have some colouring

Carlton. Two forms of 'British Machine Gun, showing, the closed and open stands

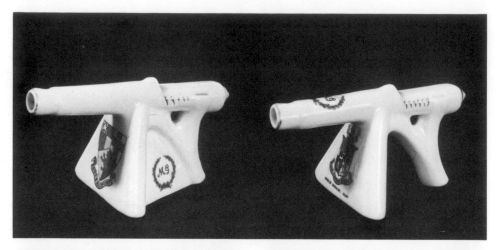

Right Carlton. 'Λre we down hearted? No!' Scottish soldier and soldier standing to attention

Left Carlton. Field gun inscribed 'French 75'

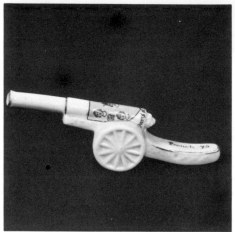

Right Carlton. Munitions Worker. This particular model has no colouring

Left Carlton. 'Old Bill' Bruce Bairns father's cartoon character, coloured face and Khaki balaclava

Left Carlton. Kitchen range with black kettle (no teapot) 70 mm

Stag with large antlers on oval stand.
146 mm. Probably sold as pair with doe,
but less of them around, possibly
because the antlers are easily broken off.
Three Wise Monkeys on wall. Inscribed:
Speak no evil, see no evil, hear no evil. Can
be found coloured brown with red faces
on white wall. 90 mm long.
Welsh Goat on rocky base, inscribed: *Y afr
Cymreig* (The Welsh Goat). No. 391. Rd.
No. 497684. 96 mm. (This is the mascot
of the Welsh Guards.)
Wembley Lion on ashtray base, some
colouring. Rd. No. 338414, 60 mm. (This
was stylised lion symbol of British
Empire Exhibition and is usually found
with BEE crest. It is often included in
animal collections.)

Birds (including eggs)

Carlton made a series of birds on green
bases and these have been grouped
together and listed at the end of this
section.
Hen roosting. 60 mm long.
Hen and Cock, salt and pepper pots, some
colouring. 70 mm.
Chicken hatching from egg. 64 mm long.
Egg cracked open, lying on side. 74 mm
long.
Owl. 66 mm.
Owl, wearing black mortar board with red
tassel. (Models with Irish crests can be
found with red mortar boards.) 75 mm.
Parrot, inscribed: *Pretty Polly.* 74 mm.
Peacock. 63 mm.
Stork with pink beak, standing on one leg.
110 mm.
Swan. Rd. No. 493796. 3 sizes: 55 mm,
63 mm & 76 mm long. Smallest size can
be found coloured red.
Swan Posy Holder. 78 mm.
Cock standing on green base, some
colouring to head. 85 mm long.
Duck standing on green base, yellow beak.
2 sizes: 72 mm & 102 mm.
Duck taking off from green base, yellow
beak. 2 sizes: 80 mm & 102 mm.
Hen standing on green base, some
colouring to head. 85 mm long.
Turkey on green base, coloured beak and
feet. Can also be found in lustre. 70 mm.

Great War

Many Great War models are found with
the following Victory inscriptions: 'The
Victory of Justice, Armistice of the Great
War signed Nov 11th 1918' and 'Victory
of Justice. Peace signed at Versailles June
28th 1919'.
Munitions Worker, inscribed: *Doing her bit*
and *Shells and more shells,* some
colouring. 140 mm. (Only made by this
firm.)
Nurse with red cross, inscribed: *A friend in
need.* 150 mm.
Old Bill, standing figure of Bruce Bairnsfather's cartoon character tommy.
Inscribed: *Yours to a cinder.* Can be found
coloured. 138 mm.
Sailor, bust. Inscribed: *The handy man* and
HMS Dreadnought. 85 mm.

Sailor, crouching and holding submarine,
inscribed: *We've got 'U' well in hand.*
70 mm.
Sailor standing to attention with blue trim.
Inscribed: *Handy man.* 135 mm.
Scottish Soldier, some colouring. Rd. No.
651139. 148 mm.
Soldier leaving trench, inscribed: *Over the
top.* 195 mm.
Soldier standing to attention, inscribed:
Are we downhearted No! and with verse
'Its a long way to Tipperary'. Rd. No.
66210. 153 mm.
Soldier standing to attention with
ammunition belt worn over shoulder.
125 mm (quite rare).
Biplane with movable prop. Rd. No.
657607. 135 mm long.
Biplane, coloured roundels and tailplane
with movable prop. 165 mm long.
Monoplane with movable prop. 136 mm
long.
Monoplane, rounded fuselage and
movable prop. 134 mm long.
Zeppelin or Airship with moulded Iron
Cross on side; can be found with cross
painted black, or left white and RAF in
coloured circles on nose. 118 mm long (2
models for the price of one mould).
*British mine sweeper whose splendid work will
live forever in the annals of British history.*
Can be found inscribed: *HMMS Gowan
Lea* or *HMMS Peggy.* Rd. No. 661565.
115 mm long.
Battleship with 2 funnels, 2 different
moulds, one with 2 guns pointing
diagonally foward fore and aft and the
other with parallel guns. 120 mm long.
Battleship with 3 funnels, 2 guns fore and 4
guns aft, can be found with the
following Victory inscription only:
'Great War 1914–18. The German Fleet
surrendered 74 warships Nov 21st 1918'.
More usually found inscribed with name
of one the following ships: *HMS
Australia, HMS Canada, HMS Inflexible,
HMS Iron Duke, HMS Lion, HMS
Marlborough, HMS Princess Royal, HMS
Queen Elizabeth* or *HMS Tiger.* 165 mm
long. (Can also be found wrongly named
HMS Warspite.)
Battleship with high prow, usually
inscribed: *Dreadnought* but can also be
found inscribed: *HMS Humber, Model of
British Monitor.* Has also been found
with same Victory inscription as above
and not named. 140 mm long.
HM Hospital Ship Anglia, Model of with 2
funnels, often found with further
detailed inscription: 'Model of British
Hospital Ship whose voyage was
disregarded on three occasions by the
German Submarines'. 165 mm long.
(Has been found wrongly inscribed as
HMS Tiger.)

HMS Warspite, 4 guns fore and 2 guns aft.
155 mm long.
RMS Lusitania, 4 funnels. Found with
details of sinking: 'The Lusitania was
sunk by a German Submarine May 7th
1915. Lives lost 1198', or the numerically
incorrect inscription 'Sunk by German

Carlton. Top: 'British submarine' half submerged, inscribed 'E9'
Middle: 'British submarine' blunt nosed can be found inscribed 'E9'.
Bottom: 'E9' with pointed nose and fish tail

Carlton. H.M.H.S. Anglia, the British Hospital ship

Carlton. R.M.S. Lusitania with an inscription giving incorrect numbers of lost and saved

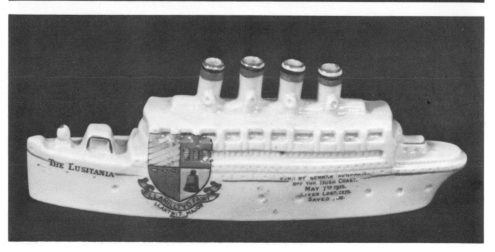

Right Carlton. British Mine Sweeper, as well as the usual inscription it also carries on the reverse the inscription 'Great War 1914–18. The German fleet surrendered 74 warships November 21st 1918'

Left Carlton. H.M.S. Humber, also inscribed 'Model of British Monitor'. Model more usually found inscribed 'Dreadnought'

Carlton. Wrongly named 'H.M.S. War Spite' and correctly labelled 'H.M.S. Iron Duke' on identical models. Carlton do not appear to have taken too much care to label their ships correctly

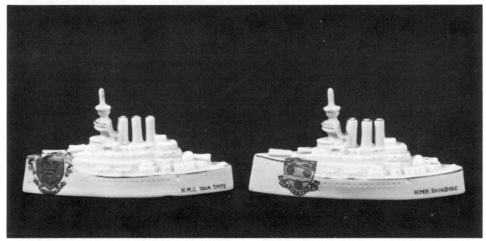

Right Carlton. Monoplane with moveable prop

Left Carlton. Biplane with moveable prop

Right Carlton. Back view of British Naval gun

Left Carlton. Front view of British Naval Gun, which is very rare

 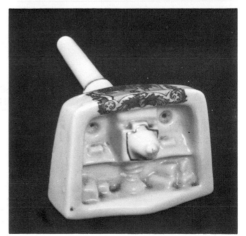

Right Carlton. 'Blighty' Map of England and Wales

Left Carlton. An unusual war memorial in Brighton

Right Top: Glengarry with coloured thistle on reverse and 'Territorials Hat' with coloured hat band
Bottom: 'Colonial Hat' and Australian hat inscribed 'Anzacs for ever'

Left Carlton. 'Shrapnel Villa' modelled from Bruce Bairns father's cartoons

Right Carlton. 'Model of German Incendiary Bomb', 'Model of British 15" Shell' and 'Model of floating mine'

Left Carlton. Zeppelin with black iron cross on side, this model is also found with the cross left unpainted and with RAF roundel

Carlton. Kitbag with Victory inscription on reverse, Circular Bell Tent usually found inscribed 'Tommies Bungalow' and model of British search light, 'The Zeppelin Finder'

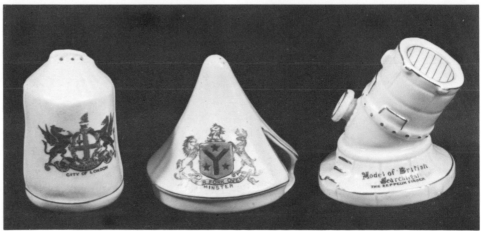

Right Carlton. 'British Trench Mortar' mounted on steps

Left Carlton. Ambulance with the usual red crosses and 'WD' on radiator

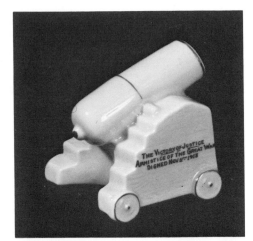

Right Carlton. Top: 'HMLS Creme de Menthe', tank with trailing steering wheels. 130 mm long
Middle: 'H.M. Whippet Tank' 121 mm long
Bottom: 'Tank Bank', tank money box. 156 mm long

Left Carlton. Armoured car with 3 guns on turret. Usually inscribed 'RNAS'.

Left Carlton. 'British Anti-aircraft motor'

Carlton. 'HMLS Creme de Menthe' inscribed, 'The British tank successfully used against the Germans, Combles September 1916'. 134 mm long and 80 mm long small size with no inscriptions

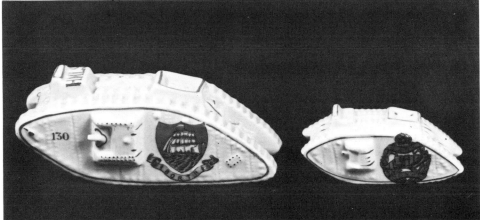

Right Carlton. Stick telephone inscribed 'Hello, hello'

Left Carlton. Fireplace with cloth and dogs on mantlepiece. 85 mm

Carlton. Models with lucky white heather device, bathing machine, basket of fruit and puzzle jug

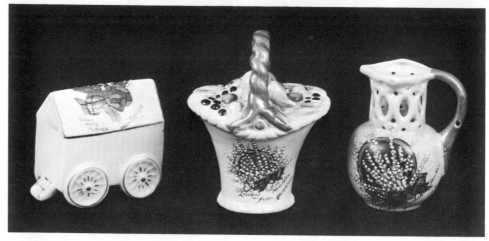

Right Carlton. The lovely Carlton model of a sundial with inscription

Left Carlton. 'Model of Welsh Hat' 56 mm. Welsh Hat with orange outlined band 44 mm and the same hat in lustre with a colour transfer print of a Welsh teaparty

Right Carlton. Two models of chairs inscribed 'The Old Armchair'

Left Carlton. Bisque windmill with revolving sails

Submarine off the Irish Coast, May 7th 1915. Lives lost 1275, Saved 703'. Rd. No. 662104. 168 mm long.

British submarine, Model of, blunt nosed, often found without this inscription but with E9 on side. Submarines found unnamed are found with the following inscription: 'Great War 1914–18. 150 German U Boats surrendered Nov 20th 1918'. 140 mm long.

British submarine, Model of, half submerged, inscribed: *E9.* 124 mm long.

Submarine, pointed nose and fish tail, incribed: *E9.* 146 mm long. (Much rarer than blunt nosed model.)

Ambulance with 3 red crosses and WD on radiator. 100 mm long.

Armoured car with Rolls-Royce type front. 120 mm long.

Armoured car with 3 guns on turret, inscribed: *RNAS.* 116 mm long.

British anti-aircraft motor, Model of, inscribed: *RNAS.* 121 mm long.

Tank with trailing steering wheels, inscribed: *HMLS Creme de Menthe.* 2 sizes: 130 mm & 160 mm long. 130 mm size found with Victory inscription: 'The British Tank successfully used against the Germans, Combles, Sept 1916'.

Tank with no steering wheels, 4 sizes: 80 mm, 100 mm, 134 mm & 156 mm long. (The 80 mm size is quite rare and the 134 mm size is the most common.) The two smallest sizes usually carry no inscription, but the 100 mm size has been found with the *Combles* inscription (see above). The two larger sizes are usually inscribed: *HMLS Creme de Menthe* and can be found also carrying the *Combles* inscription or: *Gave them hell at the Marne, 1918.* The largest size has been found inscribed: *Buy War Bonds.*

Tank Bank, as largest size of tank above but with slot for coins. Inscribed: *Buy War Bonds,* and can be found with *Combles* inscription. 156 mm long.

HM Whippet tank (actually a Renault but named wrongly by Carlton). 121 mm long.

Italian Fiat Tank, not named. 100 mm long (rare).

Vickers Tank, not named. 126 mm long (very rare). The latest model manufactured, approx. 1928–1932.

British machine gun, Model of. MG in green wreaths on barrel. 2 moulds, one with open stand. 100 mm long.

Machine gun, Model of (Vickers), 2 pieces on swivelling tripod. 150 mm long.

British naval gun, Model of. Rd. No. 662103. 88 mm long (very rare).

British trench mortar, Model of, mounted on steps and barrel at an angle. 66 mm.

Trench Mortar, not named, with horizontal barrel. 60 mm.

Field Gun, found inscribed: *French 75.* 2 sizes: 130 mm & 148 mm long.

Field Gun with screen and sighthole, inscribed: *French 75,* 145 mm long.

British 15" shell, Model of. 90 mm.

Cannon shell, Model of. No. 606. 75 mm.

German incendiary bomb, Model of. 75 mm.

British hand grenade. 83 mm.

Floating mine, Model of. Rd. No. 662106. 83 mm.

British searchlight, Model of, sometimes found inscribed: *The Zeppelin finder.* 68 mm.

Dockside capstan, Model of, with brown rope. 70 mm.

Australian Hat, inscribed: *Anzacs for ever.* 75 mm long.

Colonial hat, often found unnamed. Also found inscribed: *Anzacs for ever.* 95 mm dia.

Forage Cap. 80 mm long.

Glengarry with coloured thistle. 78 mm long.

Kitbag with open neck, with verse 'Pack up your troubles in your old kit bag and smile, smile, smile'. 72 mm.

Highboot. 63 mm.

Officer's Peaked Cap, coloured band. 78 mm long.

Royal Flying Corps Cap. 78 mm long.

Bell Tent. 66 mm.

Territorials hat, coloured hat band. 85 mm dia.

Tommies bungalow, Circular Bell Tent. 70 mm.

Blighty, Map of England and Wales, with verse 'Take me back to dear Old Blighty'. Rd. No. 660695. 115 mm.

Kitchen Range, with black kettle but *no* teapot. Inscribed: *Keep the home fires burning till the boys come home.* Rd. No. 659332. 70 mm.

Kitchen Range, with black kettle and brown teapot. Inscribed: *We've kept the home fires burning till the boys came home.* 70 mm.

Shrapnel Villa, Tommies dugout somewhere in France. (From Bruce Bairnsfather's cartoons.) Rd. No. 660613. 83 mm long.

Brighton War Memorial. 105 mm. (Building, not a statue.)

Cenotaph, inscribed: *The Glorious Dead* with 2 green wreaths. 2 sizes: 105 mm & 146 mm.

Clacton-on-sea War Memorial. 148 mm.

Cranbrook War Memorial. 130 mm (scarce).

Douglas War Memorial. 160 mm.

Edith Cavell, statue, inscribed: *Brussels dawn October 12th 1915. Sacrifice. Humanity.* 2 sizes: 140 mm & 163 mm.

Ripon War Memorial, found with Ripon Hornblower inscription. 115 mm.

Tunbridge Wells War Memorial, soldier unglazed on glazed plinth carrying a rifle with fixed bayonet. With inscription: *Our Glorious Dead 1914—1918. Honour, Gratitude, Praise.* 170 mm.

Home/Nostalgic

Anvil on tree stump base. 76 mm.

Basket of fruit, fruit coloured. 88 mm. (Almost Art Deco.)

Bellows. 95 mm long.

Book with lock. 66 mm.

Dog Kennel. 62 mm.

Dust Pan, inscribed: *Who said dust.* 94 mm long.

Fireplace, with a kettle and teapot in the hearth, and dogs and clock on the

Right Carlton. 'Mr. Punch' bust

Left Carlton. Jester or clown bust with some colouring

Right Carlton. 'Thumbs Up'

Left Carlton. Upright unnamed Bonzo Dog with red tongue 110 mm

Right Carlton. 'I'm forever blowing bubbles' blue clothes and bowl and bubble lustre

Left Carlton. Radio Operator inscribed 'Listening In'. No horn or microphone.

Carlton. Scotsman with verse, Yorkshireman, 'Jenny Jones' and John Bull with bulldog

mantelpiece. Found inscribed: *By my ain fireside* but usually with verse: 'East or West, Home is best: The Kettle on the fire is singing. The Old Clock ticks, And the teapot is on the hob, sure its a good old home *Sweet* home.' 85 mm.

Flat Iron, can be found in lustre. 60 mm.

Frying Pan. Rd. No. 337474. 110 mm long.

Grandfather clock, Model of. No. 389. Rd. No. 495195. 2 sizes: 105 mm & 135 mm. Large size found inscribed: *Make use of time. Let not advantage slip. Shakespeare* or more rarely: *Come what, come may, time and the hour runs through the day. Macbeth. Act 1. sc. 3.*

Grandmother clock, inscribed: *Gude morn.* 105 mm.

Kettle, fixed lid, inscribed: *Polly put the kettle on, we'll have some tea.* 80 mm.

Miner's lamp. Rd. No. 624410. 110 mm.

(The) Old armchair, solid arms, with verse: 'I love it, My old Armchair, And who shall dare to chide me for loving "The Old Armchair" '. 88 mm. (Can be found not named.)

(The) Old armchair, open 'barley sugar' arms, with verse as above. 120 mm.

Pillar Box GVR, found inscribed: *If you havent time to post a line heres the pillar box.* 72 mm.

Saucepan with lid. 100 mm long.

Spinning Wheel, found inscribed: *Model of ye olde spinning wheel* or more rarely: *The exact model of 14th Century spinning wheel* (in which case it really belongs in the historical section). 74 mm.

Sundial, round, inscribed: *Model of ye olde English sundial,* and *What's o'clock: lifes but a walking shadow.* No. 525. Rd. No. 593655. 133 mm.

Sundial, square. 86 mm.

Time glass. Rd. No. 449397. 60 mm.

Thimble. 40 mm.

Trug. 75 mm.

Village Water Pump, round. 76 mm.

Village Water Pump, square. 105 mm.

Warming Pan, inscribed: *Sally warm the bed.* 127 mm long.

Comic/Novelty

Baby Girl Handbell, with metal clapper. 100 mm.

Billiken, flat faced grotesque type. 63 mm.

Billiken sitting on high backed chair with thumbs raised, inscribed: *Thumbs up.* Rd. No. 653728. 84 mm.

Choir Boy Handbell. 88 mm.

Clown, Bust, inscribed: *Put me amongst the girls.* Some colouring. Rd. No. 522477. 75 mm.

I'm forever blowing bubbles. Pears advert blue boy blowing bubbles. Clothes blue, bubble and bowl lustre. Rd. No. 681378. 110 mm. (A most beautifully detailed and decorated model.)

Jester, inscribed: *Put me amongst the girls.* Some colouring. Rd. No. 454827. 72 mm.

Jester awake, jester asleep, double faced bust. Rd. No. 473172. 80 mm.

John Citizen, man carrying sack inscribed: *Housing, unemployment, taxes.* Hat and face coloured. 95 mm. (A really original model, which never seems to date!

Unfortunately quite rare.)

Negro minstrel, bust, verse by Eugene Stratton. Much colouring. 85 mm.

Policeman hailing: *From . . .* 138 mm.

Policeman with raised hand, inscribed: *A policemans lot is not a happy one.* 140 mm.

Truck of Coal, *Black diamonds from . . .* Can be found in lustre. 2 sizes: 60 mm & 95 mm long.

Yes we have no bananas, oval dish with yellow bananas. 115 mm.

Cartoon/Comedy Characters

Jackie Coogan, coloured figure of boy film star, attached to white tree trunk; ink well with lid. 73 mm.

Harry Lauder, bust, with red bobble on hat and coloured thistle. Rd. No. 537473. 80 mm.

Ally Sloper, bust, inscribed: *Vote for Sloper etc.* Some colouring. 85 mm.

Bonzo Dog, standing upright, not named. Red tongue. 110 mm.

Felix the Cat, on oval base, inscribed: *Felix kept on walking.* Coloured Felix and swastika and horseshoe on base. 75 mm.

Felix the Cat on lustre Armchair, with Felix inscription. Coloured Felix. 75 mm.

Felix the Cat on lustre pillar box, with Felix inscription. Coloured Felix. 115 mm.

Felix the Cat on lustre sofa, with Felix inscription. Coloured Felix. 80 mm.

Felix the Cat on Trinket box, with Felix inscription. Coloured Felix. 93 mm long.

Felix the Cat on rectangular base, a much larger and well modelled Felix than the above, with Felix inscription. 82 mm (Very rare.)

Winkie the gladeye bird, some colouring. 68 mm.

Woody Woodpecker, fully coloured. 63 mm.

With the exception of 'Winkie' all the items in this section have to be considered rare, they are all much sought after by collectors.

Alcohol

Beer Barrel on stilts. XXX in red on sides. 57 mm.

Bottle with cork. 70 mm.

Drunkard leaning on lamp-post, fully coloured on orange lustre ashtray. Inscribed: *Show me the way to go home. Hic.* 112 mm. (Very, very vulgar.)

Hand holding beaker, inscribed: *Good health.* 88 mm.

Man sitting with beer barrel and glass, some colouring. Inscribed: *Beer Hic Beer Hic Glorious Beer Hic.* 70 mm.

Monk holding beaker with verse: 'A Jolly Monk am I'. Rd. No. 537472. 113 mm.

Mr Pussyfoot, holding umbrella with one foot on bottle of Scotch, inscribed: *No home in Scotland.* 135 mm. (Mr Pussyfoot was an American Prohibitionist—this model is very rare.)

Toby Jug, with verse: 'No tongue can tell. No heart can sing How I love a drop of drink'. Can be found inscribed: *This jug is an exact copy in miniature of the old Toby jug* (when it should really be in artefacts section). No. 413. 70 mm.

Right Carlton china. Lustre sack of meal with a mouse. B.E.E. crest.

Left Carlton. 'Put and Take' one of the British Sports series ashtrays.

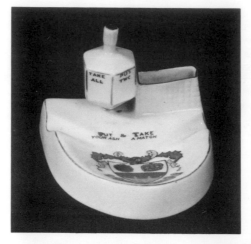

Carlton. Man with beer barrel inscribed 'Beer-hic-beer-hic-glorious beer-hic,' and hand holding tumbler inscribed 'Good Health'

Right Carlton. The F.A. cup, here inscribed as the 'English Cup' on the right and an unrecognisable trophy 130 mm high

Left Carlton. Dog listening to Gramophone inscribed 'His Masters Voice'

Right Carlton. Lustre 'National' cash register

Left Carlton. Dice pin box with B.E.E. crest

Sport
Two pieces have been found labelled British Sports Series. Two can hardly be considered a series so more must have been made. The Ashtrays labelled in this way have been listed separately.

British Sports Series
Games spinner and match holder on shield ashtray, inscribed: *Put and take: yer ash: a match*. Rd. No. 684704. 90 mm long.

Goal with keeper and ball on ashtray, inscribed: *League Football first played 1888*. Some colouring. 100 mm long. (Can be found with a crest or inscription of various teams. Strip appears in club colours.)

Other Sporting Items
Cricket Bag. 105 mm long.

Cricketer carrying bat, flat figure on green base. Some colouring. 115 mm (rare).

Curling stone, inscribed: *Soop-up*. 61 mm dia. (It is not unknown for Great War collectors to insist that this model is a Hand Grenade!)

F. A. Cup. 100 mm.

Golf Ball, can be found inscribed: *The ancient game of golf was first played in 1448*. 50 mm.

Golf Club, can be found inscribed: *Fore*, or as above. 95 mm.

Jockey standing on base, yellow cap and blue shirt. 121 mm (rare).

Jockey on Racehorse, jockeys colours can be blue/green, blue/brown, green/yellow or red/yellow. Very occasionally the horse is found painted black. Can also be found with inscription: for example: *Ala Baculia: St Leger first run 1876*. 160 mm.

Jockey on Racehorse with real hair tail (often missing) on ashtray base, some colouring. Inscribed: *Horsey keep your tail up*. 102 mm.

Racehorse on base. 2 sizes: 118 mm & 140 mm long.

Roller Skate. Rd. No. 565604. 112 mm long.

Tennis Racquet. 140 mm long.

Trophy. 130 mm.

Musical Instruments
It is very odd that only one model has been found, as Arcadian made so many.

Upright Piano, 2 sizes: 64 mm & 90 mm.

Transport
Charabanc, inscribed: *Over the hills and far away*. 'DN999' on radiator. 148 mm long. Found in lustre.

Double Decker Bus, with driver and outside staircase, impressed: *Putney—Charring Cross: Globe Theatre John Bull Thursday: General*. 'DN999' on radiator. 126 mm long. (Very detailed model.)

Motorbike and sidecar. 102 mm long.

Motorbike and sidecar with rider. 112 mm long.

Motorscooter on rectangular base. 110 mm long. (These motorbikes and the motor scooter are often found in Great War collections but they are not military.)

Open Sports Car, 'DN999' on radiator. 106 mm long.

Saloon Car, 'DN999' on radiator. 103 mm long.

Scooter on oval base. 100 mm.

Steam Locomotive. 118 mm long.

Stephenson Locomotive, with detailed inscription 'I Locomotion 1925'. 'This Engine was built by Geo. Stephenson and Son, and was used at the opening of the S. and D. Rly. Sept 27th 1825'. 2 sizes: 88 mm & 110 mm long. (Much sought after model.)

'Modern' Equipment
Gramophone in Cabinet, black record on turntable, inscribed: *Music hath charms*. Found in lustre. 92 mm.

Gramophone, square with Horn, inscribed: *HMV* or *His Masters Voice* with transfer of 'HMV' dog and notes of music. 96 mm.

Gramophone with dog listening to horn, on oval base. Inscribed: *His Masters Voice*. Some colouring. 88 mm long (a much sought after model). Very rarely found in lustre.

National cash register with '£.s.d.' Found unnamed but with '£.s.d.' in lustre. 70 mm (not very common).

Radio Operator, inscribed: *Listening in*. Some colouring. 85 mm.

Radio Operator with microphone, inscribed: *Listening in*. Some colouring. 85 mm.

Radio Operator with horn, inscribed: *Listening in*. Some colouring. 85 mm.

Telephone, stick type. inscribed: *Hellow, Hellow*. 115 mm.

Treadle sewing machine, found inscribed: *Singer*. 80 mm.

It is interesting to note the use of trade names on these models; they are always the brand leaders of the time and one can only wish that there were more examples as they are so indicative of the period.

Miscellaneous
Boot. 2 sizes: 50 mm & 72 mm long.

Sabot. 100 mm long.

Bishop's Mitre. 70 mm.

Boy Scouts hat. 95 mm dia.

Top Hat. 40 mm.

Dice Pin Box. 50 mm square.

Hand holding crinkle topped flower vase (not a tulip as usually found). 85 mm.

Horseshoe. 115 mm.

Miniature Domestic
Cheese Dish (one piece). 45 mm.

Cheese dish with cover. 50 mm.

Coffee Pot with separate lid. No. 271. 78 mm.

Kettle. 60 mm.

Teapot with separate lid. 50 mm.

Right Carlton. Motor Cyclist and sidecar

Left Carlton. Saloon car with DN999 number plate

Right Carlton. Charabanc with DN999 number plate

Left Carlton. Open sports car DN. 999 on radiator. 106 mm long

Carlton. Charabanc inscribed 'Over the hills and far away' and double decker bus impressed 'Putney–Charing Cross' etc

Right Carlton. Locomotive 4-4-0

Left Carlton. 'Model of 17th Century Sedan Chair', a reasonably rare model

Carlton also made a whole range of pin or ashtrays, pill boxes and trinket boxes in club, diamond, hearts and spade shapes. They can be found with crest or transfer views. Very few articles of domestic use, plates, cups etc. have been found but this is probably because they were used and broken. A 108 mm long teapot has been found with elaborate moulding and a miniature swan projecting from lid, and objects like this which are obviously decorative are likely to have survived.

Carmen China

Trademark used for E. A. Green, Rugby by J. A. Robinson and Sons Ltd, Arcadian Works, Stoke-on-Trent.

For details of this china and manufacturer see Arcadian China.

Although most models and 'smalls' found with this mark have a Rugby crest, other English crests are also discovered. E. G. Green, whose name often appears below the *Carmen* mark, was either a wholesaler, or more probably J. A. Robinson used this mark to supply other buyers.

All known models indicate that this mark was not used after the Great War. No devices other than crests have been recorded. Stock numbers where used would be the same as Arcadian models.

Carmen Models

Ancient Artefacts
Model of vase found near Winchelsea. 75 mm.

Monuments
Tom Hughes Monument, Rugby School. 135 mm.

Seaside Souvenirs
Eddystone Lighthouse. 125 mm.

Animals
Dog, Scottish Terrier. 66 mm long.

Birds/Eggs
Egg with flat base. 44 mm.
Hen roosting. 54 mm.

Great War
Battleship, 3 funnels and tiny gun fore and aft. 100 mm long.
Torpedo Boat Destroyer, not named. 108 mm long.
Bomb dropped from Zeppelin. 80 mm.
Bandsman's Drum. 53 mm.
Officers peaked cap with coloured badge and hatband. 65 mm dia.

Comic/Novelty
Clown, no other details. 85 mm. (May possibly be a clown bust or a standing pierrot.)

Cauldon

Trademark used by Cauldon Ltd, Stoke-on-Trent.

'CAULDON IVORINE' or 'CAULDON PARIAN CHINA' may also be impressed or printed

For details of the history of this firm see Arcadian China.

As Harold Taylor Robinson amalgamated most of his concerns and restyled them Cauldon Potteries Ltd in 1920, this mark can be found impressed or printed on china which also carries any other mark he was entitled to use, these include *Arcadian*, *Goss* and *Willow*. The Cauldon mark was mainly used on domestic china none of which has been found with a crest, but plates, cups and saucers and other items were obviously overstamped with other marks and crests applied to fill orders from 1920 onwards.

One 'Cauldon' model with a crest has been recorded in several sizes. This is a model of the Queen's Doll's House, which is most appropriate as Cauldon had been commissioned to produce a miniature breakfast set for the house, each tiny piece having a royal monogram. The same model of the Doll's House can be found marked *Arcadian*.

Late transfer decorations found on china marked *Arcadian* can also be found on Cauldon domestic wares, which include small floral designs and the coloured tropical birds.

Cauldon Models

Buildings—White
Queen's Doll's House, found parian and glazed. 2 sizes: 95 mm & 118 mm.
Queen's Doll's House with removable 'roof' lid. 2 sizes: 75 mm & 95 mm. (Both can be found with the following inscription: 'Replica of the Queen's Doll's House designed by Sir Edward Lutyens, R. A. The original was exhibited publicly for the first time in the Palace of Arts, British Empire Exhibition, Wembley, England from April to October 1924. The decorations, furniture and fittings were executed by the leading artists and craftsmen of the day, who gave their services free. The doll's house and contents were valued at £275,000. Part of the proceeds of the sale of this replica have been given to the charities of her most gracious majesty Queen Mary.' The houses are not normally found with a crest but one B.E.E. 1924 crest and a Windsor crest have been recorded.)

Celtic Porcelain

Trademark used by an unknown manufacturer for ware sold in Scotland and the North of England.

Only three pieces of china have been recorded carrying this mark and one of those is a 68 mm vase. Some form of numbering system appears on the base, but these could well be paintresses marks. (The vase is marked '11'.) Crests so far listed are Cromarty, Keighley and Fort William. Nothing more can be recorded about this obscure mark until more items are found.

Celtic Models

Countryside
Log Vase. 32 mm (with No. 20 on base).

Miscellaneous
Carboy. No details of size.

Ceramic China

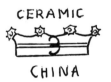

Trademark thought to be used by a German manufacturer.

A two-handled vase with a crest of St Andrews and measuring 45 mm high has been found with this mark. It resembles no other German mark but certainly has a 'continental' look about it. (The only British firm to use the tradename *Ceramic* were the Ceramic Art Co (1905) Ltd and they usually used the initials CA and Co. Ltd). A really rare mark and one which will probably remain a mystery.

Chelson China

1914–1919

Trademark used by New Chelsea Porcelain Co. (Ltd), Bagnall Street, Longton.

This firm is not known to have produced crested china as such, but they did make a range of Great War commemoratives on small domestic pieces and 'smalls'. The commemorative takes the form of a black transfer print of HMS Lion, with four coloured flags of the Allies and inscribed: *For Honour and Liberty*. Some items carry the further inscription: *God Save the King*. Peace commemoratives were also made. These have a transfer print of Britannia, with the flags of the Allies and the inscription: *Peace 1914—1919 Liberty Truth Justice Honour*.

Civic

Trademark used by an
unknown manufacturer.

This mark is mostly found on 'smalls', one animal, a long necked cat also turns up with amazing regularity. The pottery is very heavy and crudely finished and it seems likely that this china was produced by one of the manufacturers who made such crested ware during the Great War, and did not register a mark.

Civic Model

Animal
Cat sitting with long neck. 105 mm. (This is a model of a Destroyer's Ship's mascot which became popular during the Great War.)

Clarence Crest China

Trademark used by Beresford
Bros, Clarence Works, High
Street, Longton.

c1914–c1925

This firm was established in 1900 to produce china and fancy goods. Very little is known about the firm; no mark was registered and the first reference found in the Pottery Gazette is an advertisement in 1920. In 1921 a further advertisement announces Beresford Bros as makers of 'View Ware. "A present from . . .", also Crest Ware'. There is no reference to this firm after 1921 and the Clarence Works belonged to Crown Clarence Porcelain Co. after 1932. One can only assume that Beresford Bros became bankrupt as so many other firms did in the thirties, or that the firm changed its name to Crown Clarence.

This mark is most often found on small vases and domestic ware. The very small range of models bore a close resemblance to those being made by other Longton firms most notably Hewitt and Leadbeater (*H and L* or *Willow Art China*). It is possible that some of these models were purchased from H and L before being decorated and glazed but none has actually been found impressed H and L so it is more likely that designs for models were copied or bought from a freelance modeller.

A commemorative saucer has been found with a transfer print of The Four Flags of the Allies with the inscription: 'For right and freedom' and one suspects that Beresford Bros made a range of such domestic items. Only one transfer print has been recorded, a coloured Kingfisher with the inscription: 'Happy Days at . . .' The two-handled vase with this print is edged in blue rather than gilt. Exactly the same print with inscription and blue edging can be found on *Willow Art*, 'smalls', and another example has been found marked *Clays* (see next entry). This again leads one to look for a connection between Beresford Bros and Hewitt and Leadbeater, but apart from both firms working in Longton no other evidence of such a connection can be found. No view ware has as yet been recorded even though it was advertised. It is possible that little was sold, or that the firm used another trademark or even none at all on view ware.

No numbering systems appear to have been used.

Clarence Models

Animals
Cat, sitting. 78 mm.
Elephant, standing. 78 mm long.

Birds
Swan. 57 mm.

Great War
Nurse, inscribed: *A friend in need*. 130 mm.
Bandsman's Drum. 58 mm.
Kit Bag, with inscription 'Pack up your troubles in your old kit bag'. 70 mm.
Tommy's Steel Helmet. 76 mm long.

Clays

Trademark used on crested
china manufactured by
Hewitt Bros.

CLAYS
ENGLAND

For details of Hewitt Bros china see Willow Art China.

This trademark is very perplexing, a very similar mark having been used by another Longton firm—Green and Clay, Staff Street, Longton. This firm went out of business in 1891. The models found with the *Clays* mark as above are certainly made by Hewitt Bros and some have been found impressed 'H Bros. Willow', and are for the most part Great War souvenirs. One can only guess that there must be some family connection between the two firms indicating that the mark was inherited. Another alternative thought is that Harold Taylor Robinson inherited the mark during his Empire Building days (see Arcadian). Later when Hewitt Bros sold out to him he could have used the *Clays* mark on some unprinted but impressed *Willow* Wares. This obviously needs much more research as it is one of the fascinating mysteries which make crested china marks so interesting.

One transfer print has been recorded, being of a coloured kingfisher with the inscription: *Happy days at . . .* Exactly similar prints can be found marked *Willow Art* and *Clarence* (see Clarence Crest China).

Stock numbers are given where known.

Clays Models

Great War
Battleship, impressed: *HMS Lion*. 140 mm
    long.
British Tank, Model of, with 2 front steering
    wheels. No. 107. 125 mm long.

Cartoon/Comedy Characters
Baby, with arms outstretched, inscribed:
    Cheerio. Some colouring on face.
    125 mm. (Great War cartoon character,
    could be 'Pooksie'.)

Clifton

Trademark used by a branch
of J. A. Robinson Ltd, Stoke-
on-Trent. Subsequently
Cauldon Ltd (see Arcadian
China).

This trademark was not registered, but the china was produced in the Arcadian Works at the same time as *Arcadian* and *Swan* models. (Clifton pieces have been found with badly obliterated 'Arcadian' marks.) The few Clifton models which cannot be recognised as *Arcadian* are invariably found in the *Swan* range. A three-handled loving cup with crests of Edward VII and Queen Alexandra and details of their lives, reign and the 1901 census has been found with the Clifton mark. This is very much in the early *Swan* style and exactly the same loving cup has been found marked *Swan*. One could therefore suspect that this mark was offered by the firm of C. Ford (the makers of *Swan China*) instead of the usual *Swan*.

Clifton is uniformly finer than Arcadian or Swan China and it obviously was a higher class range. The crests are painted with much more care as are the coloured models. Very few Great War souvenirs or late models are found and it is likely that the mark was not used after 1920. (There is one exception listed here, 'A Box of Chocolates' is from a *Willow* mould and this would not have been used in the Arcadian Works until the mid-twenties; why this piece was marked *Clifton* will remain a mystery.)

Some view ware has been found and also two Military crests: Royal Military College, Camberley and Staff College, Camberley. Otherwise all recorded models carry crests.

Numbering System Many of the *Clifton* models are numbered. Printed or painted stock numbers can be found, and these numbers are listed where known. The stock numbers occasionally correspond with the numbers found on similar *Arcadian* or *Swan* models, but this range seems to have been stocked separately. Paintresses' marks are initials painted on the base, where the stock number is also painted, the initial being placed at the end of the numbers. (Beware of the initials O and I.)

Clifton Models
NB. ARC indicates that models are also found marked ARCADIAN.

Ancient Artefacts
Most inscriptions begin: *Model of*, so this will not be repeated throughout the list.
Ashbourne Bushel, inscribed: *His Majesty King Charles 2nd's Royal Standard Bushel fastened to the Ashbourne Market Cross in the year 1677.* (Not found numbered.) 95 mm dia. ARC, but not this size.
Canterbury Roman Vase, inscribed: *Roman vase found near Canterbury original in Canterbury Museum.* 2 shapes: No. 22, 63 mm (with handle); No. 29, 60 mm (no handle). ARC No. 22 and 29.
Carlisle Salt Pot, inscribed: *Old salt pot in Carlisle Museum.* No. 110. 40 mm.
Chester Roman Vase, inscribed: *Roman vase now in Chester Museum.* No. 131. 60 mm. ARC No. 136.
Chinese vase original in Hanley Museum (not found numbered). 58 mm. ARC No. 127.
Fountains Abbey Cup, inscribed: *The Abbots cup from the original at Fountains Abbey.* No. 94. 50 mm ARC.
Glastonbury Bowl, inscribed: *Bowl from the Ancient British Lake Village near Glastonbury.* No. 65, 40 mm. ARC No. 55.
Glastonbury Vase, inscribed: *Vase from the Ancient British Lake Village near Glastonbury.* No. 642. 55 mm. ARC No. 642.
Hastings Kettle, inscribed: *Ancient kettle dredged up off Hastings 1873 in Hastings Museum.* No. 237. 62 mm. ARC No. 237.
Loving cup originated by Henry of Navarre King of France. 3 handled (not found numbered). 40 mm & 50 mm. ARC No. 579. 40 mm.
Nose of Brasenose College, Oxford (not found numbered). 103 mm long.
Pompeian Vessel, not found named. 43 mm. ARC No. 208.
Portland Vase, not found named. 60 mm. ARC No. 52.
Southwold Jar, inscribed: *Ancient jar washed out of cliff near Southwold* (not found numbered). 95 mm. ARC No. 627.
Winchelsea Roman Cup, inscribed: *Roman cup found near Winchelsea* (3 handles). No other details available. ARC.

Buildings—White
Highland cottage, Model of. 60 mm. ARC.

Traditional/National Souvenirs
John Bull, bust, eyes and mouth coloured. Rd. No. 537470. 100 mm. ARC.
Luton Boater, not found named. 78 mm dia. ARC.

Melton Mowbray pie, The. Pie with moulded pastry adornments, with verse 'Though you travel by train or liner. In search of a pie that is finer. North, south, east or west. Melton Mowbray's the best. Here's a genuine one, made in china. 50 mm (late model found marked *Swan* but not as yet *Arcadian*—quite rare).
Welsh Lady, bust, with inscription: 'Wales! Wales! My Mother's sweet home in Wales' etc. With black Welsh hat. 80 mm. ARC.

Seaside Souvenirs
Lifeboat, inscribed: *Margate Lifeboat, friend to all nations.* Rd. No. 572151. 118 mm long. ARC, but not with this inscription.
Clam shell menu holder. 62 mm.
Punch, bust, some colouring—red hearts on cheeks. 80 mm. ARC.

Countryside
Haystack, circular. 58 mm. ARC.

Animals
Cat, long necked and sitting (not found with inscription). ARC. 108 mm.
Elephant walking. Can be found inscribed: *Baby Jumbo.* No. 237. 70 mm.
Frog, open mouth and green eyes, inscribed: *Always croaking.* 80 mm. ARC.
Hare. No. 10. 73 mm. ARC.
Sussex pig, Model of, standing inscribed: *You can push or you can shuv but I'm hanged if I'll be druv.* No. 148. 78 mm long. ARC No. 148.
Teddy Bear, sitting. Rd. No. 548705. 90 mm. ARC.
Pony, Shetland. 2 sizes: 105 mm & 120 mm long. ARC.

Great War
Despatch rider, Model of, on motorbike. 120 mm long. ARC.
Sailor, bust, inscribed: *HMS Dreadnought* and *The handy man.* With verse 'Hearts of Oak'. Rd. No. 539938. 95 mm. (This mould was registered before the Great War, but the inscriptions probably date from the Great War. This model has been found marked *Swan* with the same verse, but not these inscriptions).
Tank, Model of. Rd. No. 658588. 116 mm. ARC.
Howitzer (not found named). 115 mm long. ARC.
Trench Mortar (not found named). 70 mm long. ARC.
Cannister bomb, Model of. 60 mm. ARC.
Colonial hat, Model of. Rd. No. 657738. 88 mm wide. ARC.

Carlton 'Tunbridge Wells War Memorial', Cenotaph and parian 'Florence Nightingale' (see under parian/unglazed models) which is not found glazed

Right Clays. Jug with blue transfer print of a Kingfisher, with inscription 'Happy days at Abbotsbury'. The same transfer and the Happy days inscription can be found with the 'Willow Art' mark and other marks used by Hewitt & Leadbeater

Left Cauldon. Queens dolls house box with lid. British Empire Exhibition crest

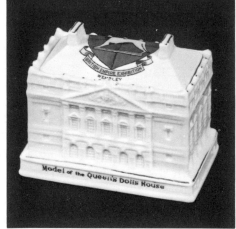

Right Crown. Welsh Hat with beautifully painted crest

Left Clifton WH & S. 'Model of British Tank', with two trailing wheels

Home/Nostalgic
Anvil on circular base. No. 25. 68 mm.
Bucket. No. 92. 75 mm.
Grandfather clock, Model of a, inscribed: *Make use of time let not advantage slip. Shakespeare.* No. 209. 108 mm. ARC No. 209.

Comic/Novelty
2 Black boys heads popping out of box, inscribed: *Box of chocolates.* Much colouring. 60 mm. (ARC/Willow Mould.)
Clown, bust, inscribed: *Put me amongst the girls.* Some colouring. Rd. No. 522477. No. 12. 80 mm. ARC —

Sport
Football. 50 mm dia. ARC.

Recorded Numbered Ornamental Wares
No. 16. Globe Vase. 46 mm.
No. 37. Vase, wide mouth. 50 mm.
No. 45. Trinket Box, spade shaped. 40 mm.
No. 63. Pot on 3 small feet. 41 mm.
No. 72. Jug. 60 mm.
No. 74. Jug. 82 mm.
No. 141. Vase. 47 mm.
No. 145. Vase. 53 mm.
No. 215. Vase. 60 mm.
No. 216. Vase. 60 mm.
No. 217. Vase, flat bottomed. 37 mm.
No. 303. Vase. 52 mm.
No. 532. Jug. 70 mm.
No 587. Taper Vase. 60 mm.
No. 666. Crinkle topped vase. 40 mm.
Found not numbered. Trinket Box, heart shaped. 40 mm.

Clifton China

Trademark used by
Wildblood, Heath and Sons
(Ltd), Peel Works, Longton.

1908–27 (with slight variation)

Wildblood, Heath and Sons (Ltd) made china, mostly hotel and badge ware from 1899 to 1927. Crested china was produced from around 1907 when they first advertised Arms Ware. The production of arms ware seems to have been a small sideline for this firm as few models are found with this mark. Early wares tend to be domestic but in 1920 the firm were advertising china miniatures with crests and most of the named models were made at that date. Many of these models resemble *Willow Art China* made by Hewitt and Leadbeater also in Longton. There is no known connection between the two firms, so one can only speculate whether designs for moulds were bought, sold or borrowed! For the most part the china is heavy and the crests are crudely coloured.

A few pieces of view ware have been recorded, including a nice 'Cat and Fiddle, Buxton' inn sign. These are usually domestic items but transfer prints can be found on other models. Great War inscriptions and commemorative transfers are not found, but one interesting Military crest, 'The Royal Field Artillery' has been recorded.

Numbering System. Hand painted stock numbers are found on models and these are given where known. Paintresses' marks are usually initials painted underneath the stock number.

Clifton China Models

Ancient Artefact
Loving Cup. 39 mm.

Buildings—White
Wainhouse Tower. 135 mm.

Monuments
Burton Statue, Burton on Trent. Inscribed: *Michael Arthur first Baron Burton, born 1837. Died 1909.* 130 mm.

Historical
Burns chair, Model of. No. 49. 90 mm.

Seaside Souvenir
Lighthouse. 110 mm.

Animals
Cat in boot. No. 65. 68 mm.
Elephant, walking. 75 mm.

Bird
Canary on rock, unnamed Norwich Warbler. No. 23. 98 mm.

Great War
British tank, Model of. 140 mm long.
British tank, Model of, with trailing steering wheels. Rd. No. 658588. No. 120. 130 mm long.
Field Gun with screen. No. 214. 115 mm long.
Shell. No. 114. 70 mm.
Kit Bag with verse: 'Pack up your troubles'. 72 mm.
Tommy's Steel Helmet. 75 mm long.

Home/Nostalgic
Anvil. 88 mm long.
Watering Can. No. 126. 75 mm.

Novelty
Billiken, The god of luck. 75 mm.

Right Clifton. Policeman
inscribed 'Controlling the traffic'

Left Clifton. Bust of John Bull

Left Clifton WH & S. Shoe
115 mm long

Clifton. Parian busts of King
George V and Queen Mary on
small round glazed bases

Alcohol
Barrel on legs. No. 85. 60 mm.
Barrel on stand. No. 83. 63 mm long.

Domestic Wares
Hexagonal and octagonal salt pots can be found inscribed: *Salt*. Jugs, beakers and small vases can also be found.

C L Reis and Co.

C L Reis and Co. could be a manufacturer but is probably an Irish retailer.

An obscure mark, only one small pot on three feet measuring 45 mm with a Dublin crest has been recorded. The pot is made of very fine porcelain and is very white, indicating a strong possiblity that it was made in Germany or perhaps even Ireland.

COLLINGWOOD
MADE IN
ENGLAND

1924–30

Collingwood

Trademark used by Collingwood Bros (Ltd), St George's Works, Longton.

Collingwood Bros manufactured china from 1887 to 1957. The firm was not known to produce crested ware, but they did make 'smalls' with the Wembley Lion symbol to celebrate the Wembley British Empire Exhibition 1924. Such souvenirs are very popular not only with crested china collectors but collectors of British Empire Exhibition memorabilia.

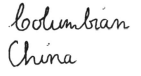

Columbia China

Trademark used by an English manufacturer for export to British Columbia.

Only one small square vase measuring 60 mm has been found with this mark and a crest of British Columbia.

Any of the firms known to have made crested china for the Colonies could have produced this china.

The Corona China

Trademark used by Sampson Hancock (and Sons), Bridge Works, Stoke and later at the Gordon Works, Hanley (renamed Corona Pottery).

Sampson Hancock and Sons was an old established firm of earthenware manufacturers, founded in 1858. On May 9th, 1900 Mr Sampson Hancock a prominent Wesleyan died, and the business was then carried on by his sons. The firm made domestic pottery of all kinds and later introduced high class semi-porcelain and ivory ware to their range, producing an extensive range of decorated dinner ware, toilet ware, flower pots, vases and jugs for the home, Australian and colonial markets. Before the Great War they were represented in London by M. V. V. Adams and had showrooms at 9 Charterhouse Street, Holborn Circus. Hancocks seem to have produced crest china in quantity as an emergency measure to see them through the war years when skilled labour was unavailable. Unlike other established potters they do not appear to have advertised this line, although as early as 1906 they announced that they made 'Art Trinket Wares'. Hancocks exhibited their 'Corona Ware' at the 1920 British Industries Fair but there is no indication that crested china formed a large

Mark used between c1910–1937. The mark is sometimes found without the manufacturers name but with the addition at the base of the initials RBW – These may possibly be retailers initials.

Right Corona. Mouse with hands to mouth

Left Corona. Ghurka Knife 140 mm long

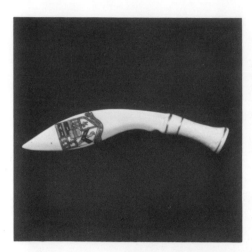

Corona. Left: 77 mm crinkle taper top vase with flags of Allies commemorative
Centre: 60 mm crinkle top globe vase with '12th Lancers' transfer
Right: 65 mm crinkle top vase with '1st Life Guards' transfer
Note the decorative borders designed with flags of the allies

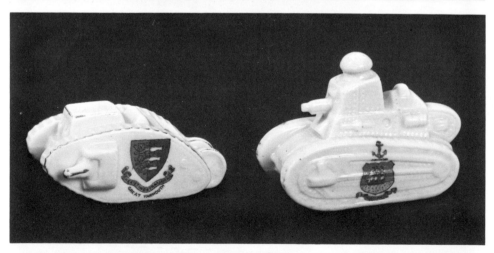

Corona. Tank with inset steering wheels and Renault tank

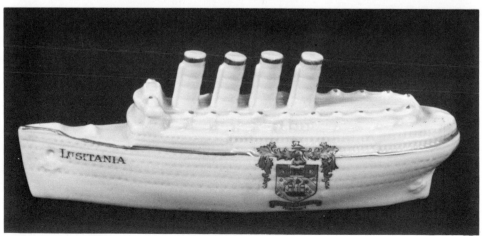

Corona. Lusitania 163 mm long

114

part of the display. In 1924 the firm bought out a large part of the display. In 1924 the firm brought out a parian statuette of 'Our Prince', in civilian clothes complete with walking stick, modelled by P. Bryant Baker. The statuette came in three sizes and was specially designed to be sold to visitors to England for the British Empire Exhibition. (No record can be found of the firm actually exhibiting at Wembley in 1924 or 1925.) As yet no parian or unglazed models marked *Corona* have been recorded including 'Our Prince', although a glazed model of the Prince of Wales at his Investiture exists marked 'Duchess', which was another trademark used by the firm (see THE DUCHESS CHINA).

S. Hancock and Sons (Potters Ltd), Hanley, a title used from 1935, was put into the hands of the Receiver, R. E. Clark on 23rd March, 1937–yet another victim of the Depression.

The *Corona* models are not very original, showing the usual range of animals, Great War and miscellaneous souvenirs in reasonably fine china with pleasant crests. It seems likely that the firm stopped making china miniatures in the early twenties as models have not been found decorated with other devices. There are a few pieces bearing coloured views but these are small pots and jugs and would have been made before the War. Hancocks did make a large number of Great War commemoratives: usually four flags of the Allies and inscribed: 'European War 1914'. These have an unusual border of European flags in scallops around the necks of vases and jugs. A vase bearing a transfer print of General French decorated in the same way has been found and probably other Great War leaders were commemorated similarly.

Numbering System. Early crested models and Great War commemoratives can be found with gold or black painted stock numbers. These are recorded where known in the following lists. Paintresses' marks are a series of coloured dots or squiggles found near the trademark.

Corona Models

Ancient Artefacts
Canterbury Leather Bottle. No. 156 (no other details available).
Hastings Kettle. 57 mm (no other details available).

Buildings and Monuments
Bottle Oven (inside of). 82 mm.
Bunyan's Statue. 165 mm.
Tom Hughes Monument, Rugby. 136 mm.

Historical/Folklore
Noah's Ark. 95 mm long.

Traditional/National Souvenirs
Lancashire Clog. 2 sizes: 70 mm & 102 mm long.
Welsh Harp. 90 mm.
Welsh Hat, can be found with largest place name round brim. 45 mm.

Seaside Souvenirs
Canoe. 102 mm long.
Beachy Head Lighthouse, black band. 150 mm.

Animals
Cheshire Cat. 95 mm.
Bulldog, standing. 112 mm long.
Dog, King Charles Spaniel, begging. 69 mm.
Fish Vase. 60 mm.
Hare with raised ears. No. 166. 63 mm long. (Thought by some collectors to be a rabbit!)
Lion, lying down. 140 mm long.
Mouse, eating nut. 44 mm.
Pig, lying down. 65 mm long.
Pig, standing. 84 mm long.
Teddy Bear, sitting, can be found completely brown with no crest. No. 194. 85 mm.
Tortoise. 32 mm.

Birds
Swan. 85 mm.
Swan, Posy Holder. 87 mm long.

Great War
British Airship on base. 128 mm long.
Zeppelin. 134 mm long.
Battleship, 120 mm long.
Lusitania 163 mm long.
Submarine, inscribed: *E4*. Size varies 102 mm–120 mm long.
New submarine, Model of. Rd. No. 658687. 146 mm long. (This is the submarine usually named E5 by other firms.)
Red Cross Van. 98 mm long.
Renault Tank. 115 mm long (rare).
Tank with inset trailing wheels. 100 mm long.
Field Gun. 2 sizes: 120 mm & 140 mm long.
Field Gun with screen. 120 mm long.

Right Corona. The Peace Clock with the time at 3.25, when the peace was signed. This is a most sought after model

Left Collingwood. 63 mm Urn with a yellow Wembley Lion transfer

Corona. Gas Cooker 70 mm

Right Coronet Ware. A Watering Can 70 mm

Left Coronet Ware. Sabot with turned up toe

Right Cyclone. Cyclone Monkey with hands to mouth, a much cruder version of the 'Carlton' model

Left Cyclone. A model of a boxing glove

Cannon Shell. 100 mm.
Torpedo, Model of. No. 285. 2 sizes: 135 mm
& 150 mm long.
Bandmans Drum. 63 mm dia.
Bell Tent, hexagonal tent with open flaps.
No. 209. 85 mm.
Ghurka Knife. 140 mm long.
Trench Lamp. 88 mm.
Water Bottle. 68 mm.
Grandfather clock, same mould as usual
Grandfather clock but clockface transfer
at 3.25, inscribed: *World War 1914–1919.*
Peace signed 3.25 pm June 28th 1919.
128 mm. (Hard to find because clock
collectors as well as Great War collectors
find this very desirable.)
Cenotaph, Whitehall. 140 mm.

Home/Nostalgic
Armchair. 60 mm.
Baby in Bootee. 80 mm long.
Grandfather Clock. 128 mm.
Hip Bath. 95 mm long.
Watering Can. 70 mm.
Writing Slope/Desk top. No. 268. 53 mm.

Comic/Novelty
Cigarette Case. 72 mm long.
Man's Head Cream Jug. 76 mm.

Musical/Instruments
Upright Piano. 63 mm.

'Modern' Equipment
Gas Cooker. 70 mm.
Gramophone, square with no horn.
57 mm.

Miscellaneous
Horseshoe, on slope. 70 mm long.
Horseshoe, wall plaque. 60 mm long.
King, Chess Piece. 115 mm.
Knight, Chess Piece. 70 mm.
(It is possible that all the chess pieces were
offered in the range.)
Ladies Button Boot. No. 149. 65 mm.
Ladies 18th Century Shoe. No. 146. 90 mm
long.
Top Hat. 45 mm.

Miniature Domestic
Cheese dish. 1 piece. 60 mm.
Cheese dish and lid. 60 mm.
Teapot and lid. 65 mm.

Coronet Ware

A trademark used by Ford
and Pointon Ltd, Norfolk
Works, Hanley, subsequently
a branch of J. A. Robinson
and Sons Ltd, and later
Cauldon Ltd (see
ARCADIAN CHINA).

Mark used c1910–1921 but
without initials before 1917

Mark used 1921–c1924

The old established firm of Pointon and Co. Ltd, at Norfolk Works was sold in 1917 and the new company Ford and Pointon Ltd was formed. In 1919 this firm was made a branch of J. A. Robinson and Sons Ltd, a group of companies that already included Arkinstall (*Arcadian China*) and Charles Ford (*Swan China*).

Pointon and Co. Ltd were basically tableware manufacturers but along with practically every other firm of this kind had begun to make crested china miniatures sometime just before or during the Great War.

At Ford and Pointon Ltd crest china production would have continued along with other decorative items and tableware. In 1920 at the British Industries Fair, J. A. Robinson showed a 'New range of Coaching Scenes in the Ford and Pointon China'. When J. A. Robinson was amalgamated with Cauldon Potteries Ltd in 1920, Ford and Pointon was described as making 'Fords' china—useful and ornamental, and a selection of these wares were exhibited at the B.E.E. in 1924 as part of the Cauldon display. This mark was not used on arms ware for more than a year or two at the Cauldon Place Works. The firm seems to have ceased to exist after the Cauldon/Coalport merger in 1933.

Early models are quite unlike *Arcadian* and are very similar to the products of several firms who did not really specialise in arms ware particularly Taylor and Kent (*Florentine China*). (Moulds were often designed and sold by freelance skilled men.) Some late models are probably from Arcadian moulds.

Two early commemoratives have been recorded, 'Festival of Empire, Crystal Palace 1911' and 'Shakespearian Exhibition, Earls Court 1912'.

Flags of the Allies Great War commemoratives are found inscribed: 'War 1914', and one military crest is known—The Kings Own Yorkshire Light Infantry. There is no evidence of any other forms of decoration being used on models other than coloured views and these are rare. (No numbering system seems to have been used.)

Coronet Models
ARC indicates that a model is also found marked *Arcadian*.

Ancient Artefacts
Puzzle Jug. 70 mm.

Buildings—White
Cottage 50 mm.

Monuments/Crosses
Celtic Cross, on square base. 108 mm.
Wallace's Memorial at Stirling. 120 mm.
  (This is actually a tower.)

Historical/Folklore
Judge, bust. 60 mm.
Man in stocks. 102 mm.

National Souvenir
Welsh Hat. 57 mm.

Seaside Souvenirs
Bermudan rigged sailing boat. 125 mm.
Whelk Shell. 95 mm long.
Punch and Judy Booth, with Punch and dog Toby. 90 mm (rare).
Punch, bust, with red nose. 83 mm (quite rare).

Animals
Camel, with 1 hump, kneeling. 56 mm.
Dog, spaniel type, standing. 76 mm long.
Dolphin Vase. 102 mm.
Fish, open mouthed. 102 mm long.
Frog, open mouthed and green eyes. 60 mm. ARC.
Mouse playing Mandolin, on base. 80 mm.
Pig, standing, inscribed: *The pig that won't go*. 84 mm long.
Pig, standing. 95 mm long.
Seal, with ball on nose. No details of size.
Teddy bear. 96 mm.
Toad (or frog) with closed mouth. 50 mm.
Tortoise. 72 mm long.

Birds
Hen, roosting. 55 mm.
Pelican Jug. 80 mm (quite rare).
Swan Posy Holder. 90 mm long.

Great War
Tommy in bayonet attack. 130 mm. ARC.
British Airship, on base. 130 mm long.
Monoplane with movable prop and cross hatching. 145 mm long.
Monoplane with movable prop and no cross hatching. 170 mm long.
Battleship. 115 mm long.
Torpedo Boat destroyer, Model of. Rd. No. 658677. 105 mm long. ARC.

Submarine, inscribed: *E5*. 130 mm long.
Armoured car with turret. 95 mm.
Red Cross Van. 90 mm long.
Tank. Rd. No. 658678. 110 mm long.
Field Gun. 145 mm long.
Zeppelin Bomb. 78 mm.
Bell Tent. No details of size.
Ghurka Knife. 110 mm long.
Peaked Cap. 63 mm long.
Sandbag. 70 mm.
Tommy's hut, unnamed. 105 mm long. ARC.
Water Bottle. 63 mm.
Cenotaph. 100 mm.

Home/Nostalgic
The old armchair, with verse. 86 mm.
Carboy. 75 mm.
Flat Iron. No details of size.
Grandfather Clock. 127 mm.
Shaving Mug. 58 mm.
Stool, 3 legged. 40 mm.
Watering Can. 70 mm.

Comic/Novelty
Baby in hip bath. 100 mm long.
Boy on a scooter. No details of size.
Clown, bust. 65 mm.
Truck of Coal. 90 mm long.
Jack in the Box. 95 mm.

Alcohol
Bottle of Champagne in Ice bucket. 85 mm.

Sport
Cricket Bag. 112 mm long.
Cricket Bat. 115 mm long.
Football. 50 mm.

Musical Instruments
Grand Piano. 82 mm long.
Tambourine. 68 mm dia.

Transport
Saloon Car. 85 mm long.

'Modern' Equipment
Square Gramophone. 55 mm.

Miscellaneous
Ladies' 18th Century Shoe. 95 mm long.

Miniature Domestic
Cheese dish. 2 pieces. 50 mm.
Coffee Pot and lid. 80 mm.
Cup and Saucer. 40 mm.
Teapot and lid. 70 mm.

Craven China

Trademark used by Wiltshaw
and Robinson Ltd, Carlton
Works, Stoke-on-Trent.

For details of this firm and the china manufactured see CARLTON CHINA.

Wiltshaw and Robinson Ltd seem to have only used this mark during the Great War and a few years afterwards. They do not seem to have used the mark for a specific retailer as crests recorded are from all over Britain. Great War models can be found with 'The Victory of Justice Armistice of the Great War signed Nov 11th 1918' inscription.

Craven Models

Great War
Cannon Shell. 75 mm.
Searchlight. 70 mm.

Glengarry, with coloured thistle. 78 mm.
    long.
Kitbag. 72 mm.

Musical Instruments
Lute. 158 mm long.

Crown China

Trademark used by Wiltshaw
and Robinson Ltd, Carlton
Works, Stoke-on-Trent.

For details of this firm and the china manufactured see CARLTON CHINA.

This mark seems to have been used up to the twenties as an alternative trademark to *Carlton*. No view ware or other transfer devices have been found on pieces marked *Crown*.

Crown Models

Traditional/National Souvenirs
Blackpool Big Wheel. 82 mm.
Jenny Jones, Welsh lady, standing figure with black hat, brown basket and red and green shawl. 147 mm.
Welsh Hat, with orange band. 44 mm.

Seaside
Lifeboat, 113 mm long.
Portmanteau. 55 mm.

Animals
Cat playing banjo, inscribed: *Some band.* 83 mm.
Dog (puppy), sitting with one ear down. 83 mm.

Birds
Hen, roosting. 60 mm long.
Owl, wearing black mortar board with red tassel. 75 mm.

Home/Nostalgic
Grandfather clock, inscribed: *Make use of time. Let not advantage slip.* 135 mm.
Village Pump. Round. 76 mm.

Comic/Novelty
I'm forever blowing bubbles. Pears advert blue boy blowing bubbles. Clothes blue, bubble and bowl lustre. 110 mm.
Truck of Coal, *Black diamonds from . . .* 95 mm long.

Alcohol
Beer Barrel on stilts. XXX in red on sides. 57 mm.

Transport
Motorbike and sidecar. 102 mm long.

'Modern' Equipment
Gramophone in Cabinet, black record on turntable, inscribed: *Music hath charms.* 92 mm.
Telephone, stick type, inscribed: *Hello, hello.* 115 mm.

Note: Three Great War models recorded as Crown China in old sales lists are not *Carlton* models. Whether this is a different *Crown* mark needs investigation. Unfortunately I have not been able to locate the purchasers. Possibly the models were wrongly listed.

CROWN···
···DEVON
MADE IN ENGLAND
"TRADEMARK"

Crown Devon

Trademark used by
S. Fielding and Co. (Ltd),
Railway Pottery, Devon
Pottery, Stoke.

S. Fielding and Co. established in 1879, are earthenware manufacturers. The firm were not known to produce a range of crested china and only one model has been recorded. The mark above was registered in 1930 but was probably used long before that. The model seems to have been made in the twenties.

Crown Devon Model

Buildings—White
Tower of Refuge, Douglas I O M, also found in
lustre and always with a Douglas Crest.
68 mm.

The Crown Duchy English China

Trademark used by an
unknown manufacturer.

This mark is found on a range of domestic ware all of which seem to carry a Morecambe crest. There are absolutely no clues as to its manufacturer, and no similar mark has ever been registered.

Crown Staffordshire

Trademark used by Crown
Staffordshire Porcelain Co.
Ltd, Minerva Works, Fenton.
Subsequently Crown
Staffordshire China Co. Ltd.

This very well known firm did not produce a range of crested china, but, like most famous firms, could not disregard the prevailing fashions. A miniature milk jug and sugar basin with crests have been recorded and this would seem to indicate that a range of miniature domestic ware was made. No 'smalls' have been recorded, which is rather odd as most manufacturers would have added crests to small vases and jugs to satisfy customers' demands.

C W and Co.

Trademark used by Charles
Waine (and Co.), Derby
Works, Longton.

For further details see VENETIA CHINA.
This mark has been found on a 72 mm crinkle top vase bearing the Royal Arms with the inscription: *Festival of Empire, Crystal Palace, 1911.*

Cyclone

Trademark used by a
wholesaler on crested china
manufactured by several
well-known firms including
Taylor and Kent and
Wiltshaw and Robinson.

CYCLONE
H. A. A. & S

For details of the above manufacturers see FLORENTINE CHINA and CARLTON CHINA.

The initials AAA L are most certainly those of a large wholesaler who could have been based in London but was more probably in the Potteries at Longton. Models have been recorded as being identical to several well known ranges but most seem to have been made by Taylor and Kent and Wiltshaw and Robinson. A great number of 'smalls' and some domestic ware have been recorded but no transfer devices other than crests have so far been reported, indicating the mark was not used after the early twenties.

**CYCLONE
A.A.A
L
CHINA**

**CYCLONE
A.A.A.**

Three marks recorded may well have been used by different manufacturers.

Cyclone Models

N.B. *Florentine and Carlton* after a listing indicates the piece is identical to one found with the mark.

Ancient Artefacts
Ancient Tyg, one handle, not named. 70 mm.
Chester Roman Vase, not named. 68 mm.

Buildings—White
Cottage. 70 mm long.

Monuments/Crosses
Market Cross, not named. 108 mm.

Historical/Folklore
Man in Pillory. 105 mm (*Florentine*).

Seaside Souvenirs
Bathing Machine. 76 mm (*Florentine*).
Sailing Yacht, in full sail. 127 mm long (*Florentine*).
Lighthouse. 100 mm.
Suitcase. 77 mm long (*Florentine*).

Animals
Cat, very plump. 88 mm.
Cat smiling, could be an unnamed Cheshire cat. 76 mm.
Dog in kennel. No other details.
Elephant kneeling. 82 mm long (*Florentine*).
Monkey crouching, hands to mouth. 90 mm.
Pig, standing, inscribed: *The pig that wont go*. 80 mm long (*Florentine*).
Rabbit. 70 mm long. (This has been reported by several people as being identical to the *Arcadian* model.)
Toad, very flat. 72 mm long only 32 mm high.

Birds
Pelican milk jug. 83 mm long (*Florentine*).
Swan. No details of size.
Swan Posy Bowl. 75 mm long.

Great War
Submarine, inscribed: *E9*. 146 mm long (*Carlton*).
Tank. 125 mm long (*Florentine*).
Drum. 32 mm.
Cenotaph. Inscribed: *The blood of heroes is the seed of freedom*. 2 sizes: 100 mm & 140 mm (*Florentine*).

Home/Nostalgic
Baby in hip bath. 103 mm long (*Florentine*).
Lantern. 65 mm (*Florentine*).
Pillar Box, inscribed: *I cant get a letter from you so send you the box*. 76 mm. (*Florentine*).
Sofa. 82 mm long. (*Florentine*).

Comic/Novelty
Boy on scooter. 106 mm (*Florentine*).

Sport
Boxing Glove. 70 mm long (very rare).

'Modern' Equipment
Square Gramophone. No horn. 53 mm (*Florentine*).

Miscellaneous
Shoe, ladies' 18th century. 95 mm long (*Florentine*).

Miniature Domestic
Coffee Pot. 65 mm.
Tea Pot. 75 mm.

The Dainty Ware

Tradename used by a London wholesaler on crested china manufactured by a number of companies but mainly Taylor and Kent.

**ENGLISH MANUFACTURE
THE DAINTY WARE
EB & Cº
LONDON**

For details of Taylor and Kent see FLORENTINE.

EB and Co., were almost certainly the initials of a London wholesaler. Although the majority of models marked *The Dainty Ware* were definitely made by Taylor and Kent, others seem to have been made by a number of various manufacturers. A 'Japan' crest has been found on a model of a mouse. The crests of the Allies were reproduced during the Great War by J. A. Robinson Ltd but any other manufacturer could have produced them if requested. Several B.E.E. 1924 and 1925 crests have been recorded with this mark, but they are unlikely to have been made by Taylor and Kent. Quite a number of 'smalls' have been recorded but there are no clues as to their manufacturer. For the most part wares with *The Dainty Ware* mark are rather crude and were obviously sold very cheaply.

Dainty Ware Models
N.B. *Florentine* indicates identical model found with that mark.

Seaside Souvenirs
Bathing Machine with figure on steps. 75 mm.
Yacht in full sail. 127 mm long (*Florentine*).

Right Duchess China. A model of Edward VIII at his investiture as Prince of Wales. A rare model

Left Dainty Ware. Two King Charles Spaniels in a top hat with a lucky black cat transfer

Left Devonia. 'Citadel Gateway. in Plymouth 110 mm

Devonia. Armada Memorial and 'Drake' statue plymouth, both with Plymouth Crests

Animals
Dogs, two King Charles Spaniels in a Top
  Hat. 70 mm (*Florentine*).
Mouse. 63 mm long.
Pig. No details of size.
Seal, with ball. 72 mm (*Florentine*).

Birds
Bird, roosting. 80 mm.
Hen, roosting. 63 mm long.
Parakeet. 75 mm (*Florentine*).
Swan. No details of size.
Swan Posy Holder. 88 mm long.

Great War
Machine Gunner, could well be a model of
  Tommy and his machine gun. No details
  of size.
Picklehaube or Spiked Military Helmet. No
  details of size.

Home/Nostalgic
Baby in Hip Bath. 103 mm long (*Florentine*).
Oil lamp. 60 mm (*Florentine*).
Old armchair, with usual verse. 85 m.
  (*Florentine*).
Pillar Box. 76 mm (*Florentine*).

Comic/Novelty
Boy on Scooter. 106 mm (*Florentine*).

Transport
Charabanc with driver. 118 mm long.

'Modern' Equipment
Square gramophone. 57 mm (*Florentine*).

Miscellaneous
Book. 57 mm.

Miniature Domestic
Coffee Pot. 63 mm.

Devonia Art China

Trademark used by Hewitt
and Leadbeater for a
Devonian wholesaler or
agent.

For details of this firm and the china see WILLOW ART CHINA.

It is likely that WB was based in Plymouth, and that Hewitt and
Leadbeater and subsequently Hewitt Bros made crested ware for them
for some time and in some quantity. There are Great War souvenirs and
memorials, and some later models such as Black Cats. 'Black Cat'
transfers were also made for the firm. A great number of 'smalls' have
been recorded. Crests from all over Devon can be found and occasionally
other places.

Numbering System. Willow models can often carry stock numbers and
where these are known they are the same.

Devonia Art Models

Ancient Artefacts
Loving Cup. 3 handled. 40 mm.

Buildings—White
Citadel gateway, Plymouth. 110 mm.
Derry's clock tower, Plymouth. 2 sizes:
  125 mm & 156 mm.

Monuments
Armada memorial. 191 mm.
Drake Statue, Plymouth. 160 mm.

Traditional/National
Bagpipes. 118 mm long.
Lancashire Clog. 88 mm long.

Seaside Souvenirs
Lighthouse. Not named. 110 mm.

Animals
Black Cat, sitting on diamond shaped
  ashtray. Inscribed: *Good luck* and
  Ashtray. Impressed No. 1016, 120 mm
  long. (This is the usual large realistic
  sitting black cat but with a blue bow
  instead of a red one.)
Dog, Labrador. 90 mm. (This has not been
  found marked *Willow Art*.)

Elephant, walking. 52 mm.
Pig, standing. 85 mm long.
Rabbit, sitting, with alert ears. 60 mm
  long.
Teddy Bear, sitting. 76 mm.

Birds
Chicken. No. 911. 40 mm.

Great War
Monoplane with revolving prop. 150 mm
  long.
Battleship. 2 sizes: 116 mm & 140 mm
  long.
Battleship, impressed: *HMS Lion*. 140 mm
  long.
Troop carrier, Liner converted. No. 213.
  140 mm long.
Tank. 120 mm long.
Fireplace, inscribed: *Keep the home fires
  burning*. Some colouring. 100 mm long.
Cheddar War Memorial, with inscription:
  'Praise God and remember the men of
  Cheddar who died for their country in
  the Great War 1914–1919'. 148 mm.
Plymouth Naval War Memorial. 2 sizes
  which are slightly different models:
  140 mm & 160 mm.

Plymouth War Memorial. 3 sizes: 115 mm size inscribed: *Model of Plymouth War Memorial.* 160 mm size inscribed: *War Memorial.* 190 mm size inscribed: *Plymouth War Memorial, he blew with his winds and they were scattered.*

Home/Nostalgic
Coal scuttle, helmet shaped. No. 101. 53 mm.
Sundial on circular base, with inscription: 'I mark not the hours'. 118 mm.

Comic/Novelty
Sack of Meal with Mouse inscribed: *May the mouse ne'er leave yer meal poke wi' a tear drop in its e'e.* 63 mm.

Alcohol
Barrel. 50 mm.
Whisky Bottle. No. 134. 63 mm.

Miniature Domestic
Shaving mug. 63 mm.

Diamond China

Trademark used by a London wholesaler, the china being manufactured by several leading crested ware specialists.

The tradename Diamond China was registered by the Blyth Porcelain Co., Blyth Works, High Street, Longton. However, this firm used the initials B.P. Co. Ltd, and printed the diamond the other way up. So I think we can discount this manufacturer who never actually advertised crested wares.

H.M and Co. Ltd, was in all probability a London wholesaler. Why the mark sometimes carries the initial W is rather a mystery. (It is just possibly the manufacturer's initial, see W.)

Some models with this mark are recognisably made by Birks, Rawlins and Co. (see SAVOY CHINA). Others are definitely made by Hewitt and Leadbeater (see WILLOW ART). Although the majority of known models and 'smalls' in this range were made by these two firms, there are a few models which were not. One model, a man with his feet and head protruding from a barrel looks very like a model made by A. B. Jones and Sons Ltd (see GRAFTON CHINA). Probably many firms supplied this wholesaler.

Crests found are from all parts of the British Isles, but only early models and Great War souvenirs seemed to have been made, indicating that the mark was not used after the War.

One piece of view ware has been recorded which could have been produced by any of the potters mentioned above. A Great War commemorative is found with this mark, taking the form of a transfer of Four Flags of the Allies and inscribed: *United we stand.* This device was used by *Willow Art.*

Stock numbers are given where known.

Diamond Models
NB. If models are known to be from *Savoy* or *Willow* moulds, *Savoy* or *Willow* will appear after the listing.

Historical/Folklore
Bunyan's chair, Model of. No. 42. 90 mm. (*Willow*)
Mons Meg. Edinburgh Castle, Model of. 130 mm long (*Willow*).

National Souvenirs
Tam O'Shanter. 73 mm dia.

Seaside Souvenirs
Lighthouse, on rocky circular base. 110 mm.
Scallop Shell. 76 mm.

Animals
Elephant, walking. 52 mm (*Willow*).
Pig. 70 mm long.
Rabbit. 88 mm long (*Savoy*).

Great War
Airship (observation Balloon), inscribed: *Beta.* 80 mm long. (*Willow*).
British motor searchlight, Model of. 103 mm long (*Savoy*).
Trench Mortar Gun. 98 mm long (*Savoy*).
Glengarry. 2 sizes: 78 mm & 100 mm long. Small size (*Savoy*).

Alcohol
Man with head in barrel, feet and legs protruding. No. 395. 70 mm.

Miniature Domestic
Cheese dish. 1 piece. 45 mm.
Cheese dish and cover. 45 mm.

Disa Art China

Trademark used by Valentine
and Sons, Cape Town. China
manufactured by Hewitt
Bros.

For details of china see WILLOW ART CHINA.

This mark has only been found on 'smalls' and small domestic ware. Fortunately one such small vase has been found with a *Willow Art* mark so one is fairly confident in naming the manufacturer. Crests found are all in the Cape Town area and include Capetown, Simonstown and Grahamstown. One 'Lucky Black Cat' transfer has been found inscribed: *Good luck from Grahamstown*, which indicates that these pieces were supplied in the mid-twenties.

Do! Do! Crest China

Trademark used by a
wholesaler, manufactured by
an unknown English firm.

This wholesaler—LL and L D—also used another mark (see WY NOT CHINA) on wares manufactured by Hewitt and Leadbeater. The one model found with the Do! Do! mark is not known to be a Hewitt and Leadbeater mould. (See WILLOW ART CHINA.)

The one model recorded was made by Birks, Rawlins and Co. (see SAVOY CHINA), but does not carry their stock number. It is quite possible that they used this mark however, their numbering system was nothing if not unreliable. Only a Great War commemorative crest of flags of the Allies has been found on models with this mark. This indicates that the mark was only used for a short time.

Do! Do! Model

Animal
Elephant, sitting. 70 mm.

The Duchess China

Can be found with H & CL under
mark instead of S. Hancock &
Sons above.

Trademark used by Sampson
Hancock (and Sons), Bridge
Works, Stoke and later at the
Gordon Works, Hanley,
(renamed Corona Pottery).

For details of this firm and their products see THE CORONA CHINA.

S. Hancock and Sons usually used the alternative mark *Corona* on crested ware. This mark having been registered as early as 1898. Most pieces recorded are 'smalls', decorative dishes and bagware and it would seem likely that the crests were added to pieces originally designed and marked to be sold plain. Although some English and Welsh crests are found, these pieces usually carry a Great War commemorative, four flags of the Allies with the inscription: *1914 European War*. Two interesting commemorative transfers have also been recorded: 'Soldier of the 12th Lancers' and 'Royal Engineers'. These models do not appear to carry stock numbers. The Rd. No. found on models refers to the mark and not the model, it is Rd. No. 330440.

Right Elite. 'Our Brave Defender' in this case a sailor

Left Disa Art. Coloured transfer print of 'Mountain Tramway, Camps Bay'

Left Etruscan. 60 mm Vase with a black transfer print of 'H.M.S. Achilles'

Right English Souvenir China. Model of a fish with the usual 'Golden West Exhibition' crest

Left English Souvenir China. English souvenir china camel showing the very detailed crest of the Golden West Exhibition of 1909.

Right FP & S. Sabot with turned up toe

Left Fenton China. Very ornate inkwell

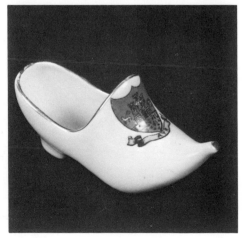

Duchess Models

Ancient Artefacts
Puzzle Jug with verse: 'Try not to spill'.
    70 mm.

Historical
HRH Prince of Wales, future Edward VIII, in
    his investiture costume, standing on
    base. 88 mm long. (Very rare).

Animals
Bear, sitting. 90 mm.

Home/Nostalgic
Watering Can. 75 mm.

Miniature Domestic
Cheese dish and cover. 65 mm.
Kettle and lid. 80 mm.

Elite China Series

Trademark used for a Derby
retailer on china
manufactured by Hewitt and
Leadbeater. (H and L.)

For details of china and manufacturers see WILLOW ART CHINA.

This mark was used by H and L for the Derby retailer D.S.B., mostly
on Great War miniatures. All crests found are Derby or its environs, and
pieces are often found impressed: H AND L WILLOW ENGLAND.

Stock numbers where recorded are the same as those found on *Willow
Art* models.

Elite Models

Great War
Soldier with rifle. inscribed: *Our brave
    defender*. 132 mm.
Red Cross Van, red cross on side. No. 218.
    84 mm long.
Florence Nightingale Statue, Model of.
    inscribed: *Florence Nightingale 1825–1910*.
    No. 225. 185 mm. (This size has not been
    found marked WILLOW ART.)

Home/Nostalgic
Grandfather clock, inscribed: *Make use of
    time let not advantage slip. Shakespeare*.
    112 mm.

Cartoon Character
Baby with arms outstretched, inscribed:
    Cheerio. Some colouring on face.
    125 mm. (Great War cartoon character,
    could be 'Pooksie'.)

Empire China

Trademark used for a
wholesaler or retailer on
china manufactured by an
unknown English firm.

Only two examples of the same model have so far been recorded, both
carrying crests of Edinburgh. Until more pieces are found with this mark,
it is virtually impossible to identify the manufacturer.

Empire Model

Great War
Bell Tent. 67 mm.

English Emporium China

Mark used by F. Phillips,
Bazaar owner, china thought
to have been manufactured
by James Reeves, Victoria Works, Fenton.

ENGLISH
EMPORIUM CHINA
F. PHILLIPS

Mark can also be found without
the rectangular outline.

For details of china and manufacturer see VICTORIA CHINA.

Much crested ware was advertised as being suitable for the Emporium
or Bazaar Trade, so it is rather appropriate that this mark was used. The
china is exactly the same as that marked VICTORIA CHINA which was
thought to have been made by James Reeves. Very few pieces have so far
been recorded and it is very likely that this type of china was usually sold
unmarked.

English Emporium Models

National Souvenirs
Welsh Hat. 62 mm.

Birds
Bird Jug. 70 mm.

English Souvenir China

Trademark used by all
unknown English
manufacturers.

Two models have been recorded with this mark, both have the same commemorative crest—which is an eagle against the sun over a shield decorated with stars and stripes. The pieces carry the inscription: *The Golden West Exhibition 1909—American Industries, Earls Court, London.* Obviously the pieces were made for sale at this exhibition and the mark was probably only used for this purpose. The models recorded offer no clues as to the manufacturer.

English Souvenir Models

Animals
Camel, with 1 hump, sitting. 110 mm.
Fish, with open mouth. 118 mm long.

Miniature Domestic
Mug. 47 mm.

Esbeco

Trademark used by the
retailer S B and Co.,
manufacturer being
unknown.

SB and Co. are not the initials of any china or earthenware manufacturer who are recorded as having made crested ware. The mark is obviously one used by a retailer (or possibly a wholesaler). Unfortunately the one piece recorded could have been made by several of the better-known manufacturers. The details known do not completely correspond to any tank in other ranges. Both Arkinstall (*Arcadian China*) and Birks, Rawlins (*Savoy China*) made similar tanks but not with exactly this inscription. I have not been able to find what crest (or crests) appear on this model. I suspect the town or city begins with G.

Esbeco Model

Great War
British Tank, Model of, with inset wheels.
  Rd. No. 658588. 95 mm long.

Etruscan China

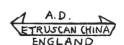

Trademark used by an
unknown manufacturer.
(Possibly Charles Waine,
Longton.)

This mark has not been found on crested ware but a black transfer print of HMS Achilles has been found on a 63 mm vase, with this trademark. No known china manufacturer used the initials A.D. so this vase could have been made by almost any firm for a wholesaler or retailer, with these initials. The vase is more aptly described as earthenware than china and is very similar to the colour transfer ware made by Charles Waine, the mark too being remarkably similar to the 'Venetia' mark this firm used on miniatures and 'smalls' (see VENETIA CHINA), this firm is a possible manufacturer.

Exceller

Trademark used for a retailer
or wholesaler in the south of
England possibly by
Sampson Hancock (and
Sons).

For details of this china see THE CORONA CHINA.

'Smalls' and one model have been found with this mark. It is possible that R.B.W. owned a chain of souvenir shops in southern seaside towns. Crests so far recorded are Littlehampton, Brighton and Lewes. The china looks remarkably like *Corona China* but 'British Manufacture' is so often found on otherwise unmarked pieces that it could have been made by any firm specialising in cheap souvenir ware.

Exceller Model

'Modern' Equipment
Gas Cooker. 70 mm.

Excelsior

Trademark used by an
unknown manufacturer.

This mark looks very like a manufacturer's mark and not one used for a retailer. No known manufacturer however used the initials W.P. and S.L. The mark seems to have been used only during the Great War as all the 'smalls' found have the commemorative: Four flags of the Allies. Until more pieces are recorded it will be impossible to even suggest a manufacturer.

Fairyware

Trademark used by Schmidt
and Co., Carlsbad (Bohemia).

For further details of this china see GEMMA.

Schmidt and Co. used this mark as an alternative to the *Gemma* mark. A great number of small domestic items such as bowls, cups and saucers, vases and ink wells are found with the mark. The china is often very decoratively moulded. Models are often identical to those marked *Gemma* and pieces have been found with both marks. As *Gemma* is stamped over *Fairyware* it seems that the latter was an early mark, the models recorded also indicating that the mark was not used after the War.

Fairyware Models

Ancient Artefacts
Loving Cup, 3 handled. 39 mm.

Historical/Folklore
Coronation Chair. 100 mm.

Seaside Souvenirs
Lighthouse on rocks. 105 mm.

Animals
Cow cream jug. 103 mm long. (Probably a reproduction in miniature of an early Staffordshire 'creamer'.)

Home/Nostalgic
Grandfather clock, with arabic numerals. 105 mm.

Grandmother clock, with arabic numerals. 85 mm.
Watering Can. 65 mm.

Miscellaneous
Griffin Jug. 85 mm.
Winged Sphinx Vase. 85 mm.
(These two are very unusual pieces to find with crests; both are rather 'Victorian' designs and may well have been made before the turn of the century and had crests added later.)

Miniature Domestic
Cheese dish and cover. 55 mm.
Teapot. 60 mm.

Famous Henley China

Trademark used by the
retailer Hawkins,
Henley-on-Thames,
manufactured by an
unknown English firm.

Only one model has been recorded and always with a Henley-on-Thames crest. The two sizes of the pig noted could be the result of shrinkage, but the 14 mm difference is rather larger than usual, so it is more likely that these models were supplied at intervals from slightly different moulds. Similar models were made by all the leading crestware manufacturers and as no stock numbers or other clues have been found it is impossible to suggest a manufacturer.

Famous Henley Model

Animal
Pig, standing. 2 sizes: 80 mm & 94 mm
    long.

Fenton China

Trademark used by
E. Hughes and Co.,
Opal Works, Fenton.

Mark used 1905–1912

1900–1905

E. Hughes and Co. was established in 1889 and were noted for their 'badge ware suitable for hotels, ships, clubs, schools and public institutions generally'. It is not therefore surprising that a firm making such wares would turn to the production of view and arms ware as soon as it became fashionable. The firm started producing 'Arms' ware in white china and in celadon well before 1900. In 1907 they began advertising *Fenton China* Arms Ware and offered to supply the arms of any town, city, county or college. During these years the firm produced a quantity of arms ware, mostly domestic items such as beakers, mugs, vases and shell trays. In 1908, Mr Edward Hughes died and although the firm went on advertising 'correct Heraldic china' for at least the next year they did not specialise in the production of these lines after that date, concentrating rather on tea sets and breakfast ware.

A considerable quantity of crested ware is found with the *Fenton China* mark but for the most part they are small vases, inkwells, dishes and jugs. Such items are very ornately moulded and look rather Victorian. The firm did not make models and although they advertised view ware, none has as yet been recorded. (This is probably because such domestic pieces were used and have therefore not survived.) *Fenton china* was exported and one vase with a Canadian crest has been found.

Fenton Models

Ancient Artefacts
Loving Cup. 39 mm.

Miniature Domestic
Cheese dish and cover. 55 mm.

Florentine China

Trademark used by Taylor
and Kent (Ltd), Florence
Works, Longton.

Can often be found without
'Made in England'

Taylor and Kent, a well known firm which survived the Depression, specialised in producing tableware, toy tea sets, commemoratives and while the craze lasted 'coat of arms ware', at reasonable prices. In 1911 the firm made front page news in the Potteries by persuading the Wallasey Coronation Committee to cancel an order for coronation mugs from a German firm and to fill the order themselves. They gained a great deal of kudos from this order. The firm could hardly have been aware of the longer struggle against Germany in which the whole country was about to embark. A sad sequence of events unfolds in the Pottery Gazette of the next few years. In 1914, Mr John Kent, the traveller for Taylor and Kent in the North of England and Scotland was called up for service. With the rank of Major he commanded the 1st Battery of the 2nd North Midland Division RFA. The Company requested and encouraged customers to send their orders directly to the works. Major John Kent was regrettably killed in action in 1916, his death recorded with many others in the Gazette of that year (yet another victim of that pointless war).

By 1913, Taylor and Kent were making 'Coat of Arms ware and View china' as well as 'Tea sets, Breakfast sets and Domestic China'. A year later large extensions were made to the Florentine Works because of the extra orders the firm were receiving. The new oven could accommodate some 5,000 dozen of porcelain miniatures at each firing. The firm obviously specialised in heraldic, commemorative and view wares throughout the war years and continued into the early twenties. They were recognised as one of the leading Staffordshire firms for souvenir china and one of the biggest suppliers. By 1925, however, Taylor and Kent had recognised the need to emphasise other products and were advertising their 'excellent china tea and breakfast ware suitable alike for home and export trades'.

Florentine china is not particularly fine and was produced as cheaply as possible, often marked with the name or trademark of the wholesaler. The range of models is not particularly original and most of the novelty items are to be found in other manufacturers' lists. (There is a worrying similarity to models made by J. Reeves (*Victoria China*) and even more so with Ford and Pointon Ltd (*Coronet Ware*), which cannot be explained by any known connection between the firms.)

Florentine does present, however, a very representative selection of models but a surprisingly small number of Great War miniatures.

Taylor and Kent made a great amount of crested domestic ware including some early items to which pewter lids and tops were added. View ware made by the firm is pleasant but unmemorable and they also produced a range of transfer prints of a regional nature including 'Welsh costumes' (also found on models marked *Victoria China*). Commemorative transfers of the Great War are often found on 'smalls' and models including the Triple Entente (Flags of Great Britain, France and Russia in shields). There is also an interesting commemorative of the War Museum Exhibition, Crystal Palace.

Many models and 'smalls' are found with 'Lucky Black Cat' transfers but no 'Lucky White Heather' devices have been recorded.

Taylor and Kent produced small china figures and other novelties which were not crested before 1900 and after 1925, although many of

Right Florentine. A fine and large model of a rabbit, it is unusual to find pieces of this quality marked 'Florentine'

Left Fairyware. The Sphinx Jug, a very sophisticated model and quite rare.

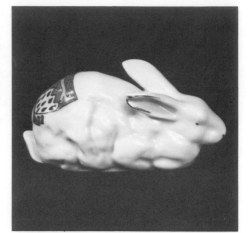

Right Florentine. Dolphin Vase which is also found with many other marks

Left Florentine. 'Mother Shipton' a Knaresborough prophet

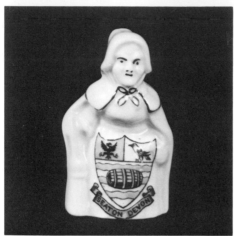

Left Florentine. Boy on scooter 106 mm. A very stylised model

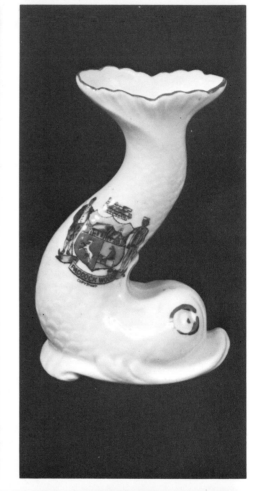

Florentine. Puppy sitting and seal with ball

132

these would be of interest to some collectors, they have not been listed here as they cannot be considered crested china. (No numbering system was used on Florentine china.)

Florentine Models

Ancient Artefacts
Aberdeen Bronze Pot, not named. 58 mm.
Chester Roman Vase, not named. 62 mm.
Loving Cup, not named. 39 mm.
Puzzle Jug. 67 mm.
Roman Lamp. 63 mm.
Salisbury Kettle, not named. 100 mm.

Buildings—White
Blackpool Tower. 117 mm.
London Bridge. No details of size.
Old Pete's cottage, near Ramsey. 75 mm long.
St Pauls Cathedral. 93 mm.
Tower Bridge. No details of size.
Westminster Abbey, West Front. 85 mm.

Monuments (including Crosses)
Caister-on-Sea, Lifeboat Memorial,
    impressed: 1903. 150 mm.
Glastonbury Tor. 90 mm (rare).
Great Rock of Ages, Model of. 135 mm.
Iona Cross. 108 mm.
Nelson's Column. 121 mm.

Historical/Folklore
Brussels Boy, or *Manneken pis,* and so
    inscribed. The famous human 'fountain',
    beloved by tourists. 120 mm.
Man in Pillory. 105 mm.

Traditional/National Souvenirs
Lancashire Clog. 88 mm long.
Mother Shipton. 72 mm.
Thistle Jug. 63 mm.
Welsh Dragon Water Jug, with lid. 120 mm
    (unusual).
Welsh Harp. 100 mm.

Seaside Souvenirs
Basket Beach Chair. 2 sizes: 80 mm &
    100 mm.
Bathing Machine. 76 mm.
Houseboat. 57 mm. (This is most definitely
    a houseboat and not an Ark!)
Yacht, in full sail. 127 mm long.
Fisherman, bust. 84 mm.
Lighthouse, not named. 90 mm.
Whelk Shell. 100 mm long.
Portmanteau. 60 mm long.
Suitcase. 77 mm long.

Animals
Camel, kneeling. 95 mm long.
Cat, Manx. 61 mm.
Cat, sitting. 112 mm.
Cat, with long neck, sitting. 115 mm.
Cheshire cat, The, inscribed: *Always smiling.*
    No details of size.
Dog, bulldog looking out of kennel.
    73 mm. (This has not been found with a
    black dog's head as is more usual.)
Dog, King Charles Spaniel, sitting. 88 mm.
Dog lying in a cradle. 90 mm long (an
    unusual model).
Dog, puppy, sitting. 902 mm.
Dogs, two King Charles Spaniels in a Top
    Hat. 65 mm.

Dolphin Vase. 102 mm.
Elephant, kneeling. 82 mm long.
Fish, inscribed: *Caught at . . .* Can also be
    found inscribed: *The last fish caught in the
    Tyne,* but this is rare. 120 mm long.
Fish Vase. 115 mm.
Pig, lying down, alert ears. 80 mm long.
Pig, sitting. 36 mm.
Pig, standing. 2 sizes: 80 mm & 95 mm
    long. Larger size found inscribed: *The pig
    that wont go.*
Piglet, kneeling. 70 mm long.
Polar Bear. 95 mm long.
Rabbit. 98 mm long.
Seal, with ball. 72 mm.
Shetland Pony. 66 mm.
Tortoise. 74 mm long.

Birds
Bird Cream Jug. 65 mm.
Chicken, hatching from egg. 63 mm long.
Hen roosting. 90 mm long.
Kingfisher with long beak. 80 mm (not a
    common model).
Parakeet. 75 mm.
Pelican Cream Jug. 83 mm long.
Owl. 75 mm.
Sparrow (so described). 63 mm.
Swan. 2 sizes: 65 mm & 80 mm.
Swan Posy Holder. 88 mm long.

Great War
Red Cross Van. 88 mm long.
Tank with trailing wheels. 127 mm long.
Tank. 125 mm long. (Very similar to
    'Victoria' model.)
Shell—75 mm.
Telescope, folded. 70 mm. (This was
    probably not designed as a war souvenir
    but many collectors would classify it as
    such.)
Cenotaph, inscribed: *The blood of heroes is the
    seed of freedom.* 140 mm.
Gravesend War Memorial. 140 mm.
Great Yarmouth War Memorial, with
    inscription on all four sides. 2 sizes:
    145 mm & 175 mm.

Home/Nostalgic
Baby in hip bath. 103 mm long.
Firebucket. 65 mm.
Flat Iron. 76 mm.
Garden Roller. 85 mm.
Lantern. 65 mm
Milk Churn. 72 mm.
Oil Lamp. 60 mm.
Old armchair, The. No details are available
    but it is most likely that this model carried
    the usual inscriptions. 85 mm.
Oriental Lamp (Aladdin's Lamp). 2 sizes:
    100 mm & 198 mm long.
Pillar Box, inscribed: *I cant get a letter from
    you so send you the box.* 76 mm.
Sofa. 82 mm long.
Trowel, with moulded decoration. 145 mm
    long.

Right Florentine. Bunch of keys forming a small dish or ashtray

Left Florentine. Rock of Ages with verse. A very popular model found in most ranges

Right Florentine. Statue of a boy from a fountain in Brussels with 'Bruxelles' crest. Impressed on front 'Manne Kenpis'

Left Florentine. Basket Beach Chair 80 mm

Left Florentine. Screw just meant salary when this model was made

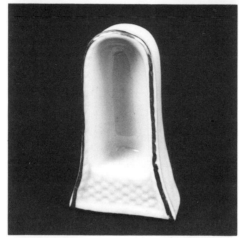

Right Florentine. Telescope folded 70 mm

Left Florentine. Jack in the Box, can also be found marked 'Botolph'

Comic/Novelty
Boy on Scooter. 106 mm.
Jack in the Box. 90 mm.
Pierrot, hands and face flesh coloured, black pompoms on hat and costume. 125 mm.
Screw, inscribed: *You could do with a big fat screw.* 75 mm.

Cartoon/Comedy Characters
Ally Sloper, bust. Not named. 83 mm.

Alcohol
Only one model recorded but a novelty crest 'BEER' has been found.
Bottle of Champagne in Ice Bucket, inscribed: *Something good a bottle of the boy.* 85 mm.

Sport
Cricket Bag. 110 mm long.

Musical
Grand Piano. 85 mm long.

Transport
Motor Horn. inscribed: *Pip Pip.* 88 mm.
Saloon Car. 88 mm long.

'Modern' Equipment
Gramophone, hexagonal, with horn. 90 mm.
Gramophone, square, without horn. 53 mm.
Radio Horn. 102 mm.

Miscellaneous
Bunch of Keys on ring. 46 mm. (An unusual and quite rare model.)
Carboy. 76 mm.
Sabot with pointed turned up toe. 95 mm long.
Shoe, ladies', 18th century. 95 mm long.
Toby Jug. 65 mm.

Miniature Domestic
Cheese dish and cover, 2 pieces. 2 sizes: 45 mm & 552 mm.
Coffee Pot. 63 mm.
Cup and saucer. 40 mm.
Kettle. 85 mm.
Shaving Mug. 52 mm.
Teapot. 3 sizes: 50 mm, 60 mm & 70 mm.

1890–1910

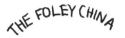

1890–1910

The Foley China

Trademark used by Wileman and Co., Foley Potteries, and Foley China Works, Fenton, Longton, subsequently renamed Shelleys Ltd.

For all details please see SHELLEY CHINA.

c1920–30

Fords China

Trademark used by Ford and Pointon Ltd, Norfolk Works, Hanley. Subsequently a branch of J. A. Robinson and Sons Ltd and later Cauldon Ltd. (see ARCADIAN CHINA).

For details of this firm and the china produced see CORONET WARE.

This mark was mostly used on domestic ware only, and only one model has been recorded. Jugs, trinket dishes, cups and ashtrays are found with crests, transfer views and sometimes coloured transfers of tropical birds found on *Arcadian* pieces. The only known model is most definitely from an *Arcadian* mould.

Fords China Model

Alcohol
Soda Syphon. 100 mm.

Right Gemma. The Coronation Chair

Left Florentine. Red cross van 88 mm long

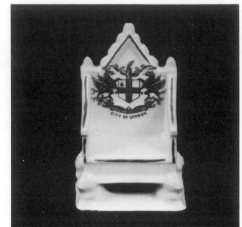

Right Gemma. Despatch riders cap and goggles. Silvered lenses

Left Gemma. Fireman's helmet

Right Gemma. The Frog Prince has green markings on hands and feet and holes in his eyes.

Left Gemma. Cockatoo on branch with rust comb and yellow beak. A very impressive piece of German china

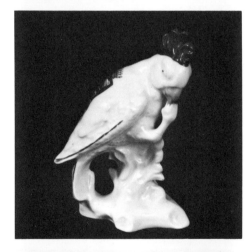

Right Gemma. Ring tree and candlestick. Some fine and delicate domestic pieces are found with the 'Gemma' mark

Left Gemma. Charming model of a dog curled up, holes in the eyes

F.P. and S

Trademark used by Ford and
Pointon Ltd, Norfolk Works,
Hanley, subsequently a
branch of J. A. Robinson and
Sons, Ltd, and later Cauldon
Ltd. (See ARCADIAN CHINA).

F. P. & S.

For details of this firm and the china produced see CORONET WARE.

This mark was probably used by Ford and Pointon Ltd before the Great War. The mark is mostly found on small vases and miniature domestic pieces. No view ware or other transfer prints have been recorded.

F.P. and S Models

Home/Nostalgic
Baby's Cradle. 63 mm long.

Miniature Domestic
Beaker. 39 mm.
Cheese dish and cover. 50 mm.

Miscellaneous
Boot. 35 mm.
Sabot, with pointed toe. 90 mm long.

Furstenberg

FURSTENBERG
GERMANY

Trademark used by a German
manufacturer for German
souvenir china.

This mark has only been found on a small 60 mm vase with the crest Köln Rh. (Cologne). It was obviously made by a German manufacturer for the home market.

Gemma

Often found without
'Czecho–Slovakia' under mark

Trademark used by Schmidt
and Co., Carlsbad (Bohemia).

Established in 1883, Schmidt and Co. were one of the biggest German exporters of crested china. Before the war AUSTRIA sometimes was printed under the mark but after the war it was more acceptable to print the name of the newly formed state of Czechoslovakia. The pottery is now in Eastern Europe and no other information is available.

Schmidt and Co. used the *Gemma* mark mostly on miniatures, especially on domestic ones, but some useful domestic ware can be found with the mark including inkpots, pen stands, pill boxes, ribbon plates and salve pots. (One salve pot has been recorded with a silver rim with a Birmingham mark!). Modern collectors have adopted the scathing attitude to the very white bodied Germany crested china that was prevalent in the period of its manufacture. The attitude is often unfair for, although much *Gemma* china is clumsy and cheap looking, there are some very delicate pieces especially in the miniature domestic range. Some of the coloured animals and lustre models are exceptionally appealing and inventive and should not be overlooked by collectors who like the later crested wares.

Gemma china sold very well in the twenties probably because it was so cheap, and so many of these coloured and lustre finish models are to be found. 'Black Cat' transfers were also used and there are a great number of items with 'Lucky White Heather' usually on lustre but sometimes on a white body. The firm specialised in a yellow shaded lustre, tints varying in depth, but usually shaded from pale lemon, through orange to almost rust. Many bathing beauties are found in this yellow/orange to lustre marked only Germany, but it seems probable that they were made by this

Gemma. Some beautiful examples of Gemma shaded white/yellow/brown lustre models, all with lucky white heather devices except for the really fine watering can. This model has possibly one of the finest Gemma devices a fabulous peacock. Note the two grandmother clocks, the one on the right is a much darker brown than the one on the left, giving some impression of the wide range of shades found

Grays Sports China. Commemorative china recalling football success from 1907 to 1911

Right Heraldic China SH & Sons. Bottle with brown transfer print of Ellen Terry inscribed 'Jubilee 1856–1906 Souvenir' on reverse

Left Griffin. Iona Cross, unmarked

138

firm (see unmarked). Other shades of lustre found on *Gemma* models include pink, blue, dull orange and mother-of-pearl.

Schmidt and Co also produced a range of view ware, and coloured and monochrome (black only) views can be found on *Gemma* models and 'smalls'. Some interesting transfer prints can be found on late miniature models including flowers, crinoline ladies and twenties beauties.

Three interesting commemoratives have been recorded, Festival of Empire, Crystal Palace 1911; Imperial Service Exhibition, Earls Court 1913 and War Museum Crystal Palace. Obviously no Great War commemoratives are to be found, as it was illegal to import German China at the time, but crests of King George V appear. (No numbering system was used on *Gemma* models.)

Gemma Models

Ancient Artefacts
Chester Roman Vase, not named. 65 mm.
Loving Cup. 3 handled. 2 sizes: 39 mm & 68 mm.
Puzzle cup, actually a beaker without a handle, with verse 'Try how to drink and not to spill and prove the utmost of thy skill'. No details of size.
Puzzle Jug, with verse as above. 3 sizes: 50 mm, 70 mm & 80 mm. Large size has 'holes' edged in green.
Puzzle Teapot with verse as above. No details of size.

Buildings—White
Only one building has been recorded, but one suspects that many more were made by this firm but were unmarked.
First and Last Refreshment House, not named. Also found in yellow/orange lustre. 72 mm long.

Historial/Folklore
Coronation Chair. Can also be found in yellow/orange lustre. 98 mm (a very detailed model).

Traditional/National
Welsh Hat. 75 mm dia.

Seaside Souvenirs
Bathing machine Money Box. 83 mm.
Yacht. 102 mm long.
Lobster Ashtray, red lobster. 63 mm long.
Open Bag on four feet. No details of size.

Animals
This manufacturer produced a really interesting range of comic animals, quite unlike the English examples.
Cat wearing Boots (Puss in Boots). Cat has pink face and ears. 84 mm.
Cat in Bowler Hat. Cat coloured as above. 63 mm.
Cat, Manx, as handled on a Jug. Cat coloured. 76 mm.
Cat, in saucepan with black handle. 70 mm long.
Cow cream Jug, some colouring, 127 mm long. (Probably a reproduction in miniature of an early Staffordshire creamer.)
Dog, crossed eyed, with fly on his nose. Can be found with some colouring. 76 mm (really charming model).

Dog, curled up (no particular breed). 98 mm long.
Dog, King Charles Spaniel, sitting. 83 mm.
Dolphin Vase. 100 mm.
Frog Prince (Frog with crown on head). 90 mm.
Pig in Bowler Hat. Pig has pink muzzle and ears. 60 mm.
Pig in saucepan with black handle. Pig coloured pink as above. 57 mm.
Pig sleeping lying on side. 83 mm long.
Pig, standing. Pink muzzle and ears, Can also be found in yellow/orange lustre. 100 mm long.
Shetland Pony. 108 mm long.
Tortoise Trinket Box and lid. 80 mm long.

Birds
Cockatoo on branch. 102 mm.
Swan. 80 mm.
Swan Posy Holder. 90 mm long.

Great War
Dispatch Rider's Cap with Goggles. 65 mm dia. (This is how it is always described by Great War enthusiasts but I suspect that it could be described as a motorbike rider's cap etc.)

Home/Nostalgic
Armchair, straight backed. 50 mm.
Basket. 60 mm.
Basket, star-shaped. 65 mm dia.
Bucket with looped handle. 80 mm (including handle).
Bucket with rope handle. 51 mm.
Clock, bracket. 76 mm.
Coal scuttle, box shaped. 50 mm.
Dressing Stool. 4 legged. 62 mm long.
Fireplace, inscribed: *There's no place like home*. Some colouring. 68 mm.
Flat Iron. No details of size.
Grandmother Clock. Can be found in yellow/orange lustre. 88 mm.
Jardinier, pot and stand. 121 mm.
Kettle. No details of size.
Pillar Box, oval. 90 mm.
Rocking Chair. 60 mm.
Saucepan with silver lid and black handle. 70 mm long.
Sofa, very ornate. 60 mm.
Stool, circular with 3 legs. 55 mm.
Watering Can, also yellow/orange lustre. No details of size.
Wheelbarrow, also in yellow/orange lustre. 2 sizes: 45 mm & 63 mm.

Right Goss Parian bust of
General Gordon 190 mm

Left Parian figure of a nude
bather. Impressed W. H. Goss
Mark

Right Another early Goss group
of three whelk shells

Left An early Goss swan posy
holder. Note the yellow/black
beak

Right One of the earliest Goss
models, The Shrewsbury
Uriconium Ewer with the
Shropshire Coat of Arms 97 mm

Left Goss beaker displaying a
beautiful verse by Adolphus
Goss

 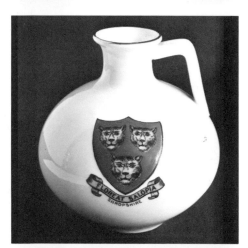

Right A Goss cottage. This one is
the first and last house at Lands
End

Left The Exeter Goblet. 133 mm.
W. H. Goss specialised in
historical shapes such as this
model

Comic/Novelty
Briar Pipe, brown. 76 mm long.
Briar Pipe, brown on leaf tray. 72 mm long.

Alcohol
Beer Mug. 47 mm.

Sport
F.A. Cup, not named. 68 mm.

Musical Instruments
Tambourine Ashtray with gilded discs.
    68 mm long.

Miscellaneous

Shoes
Boot. 2 sizes: 88 mm & 135 mm long.
Dinant Wooden Shoe. 80 mm long.
Dutch Sabot. 88 mm long.
Sabot, high heeled. 80 mm long.
Shoe with buckle. No details of size except
    large.

Hats
Bowler Hat. 82 mm long.
Fireman's Helmet. 74 mm.
Straw Boater. 75 mm dia.
Top Hat, can be a match striker. 45 mm.

Miniature Domestic
Complete tea sets can be found on round or
    square trays. These usually consist of
    teapot, sugar bowl, milk jug and two
    cups and saucers. Usually each piece is
    crested but on really small sets only the
    tray carries a crest.
Cake Dish. Can also be found in
    yellow/orange lustre. 70 mm dia.
Candleholder. 78 mm dia. (Very delicate.)
Cheese dish and cover, round 45 mm dia.
Cheese dish and cover, square. 2 sizes:
    63 mm and 76 mm long.
Coffee Pot. 60 mm.
Dressing Table Set. No details of size but
    very small. (and also very desirable.)
Teapot, also found in yellow/orange lustre.
    3 sizes: 50 mm, 60 mm & 70 mm.
Toast rack. 2 sizes: 39 mm & 70 mm.

W. H. Goss

Trademark used by William
Henry Goss (Ltd), Falcon
Pottery, Stoke.

1862–1930

Printed mark used on small bases
also found as impressed mark

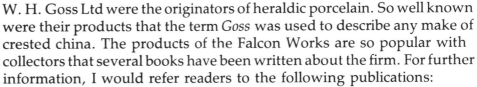

Used from 1930. Can also be
found with the following added;
"Hand Painted," "Royal Buff,"
and "Cottage Pottery"

W. H. Goss Ltd were the originators of heraldic porcelain. So well known were their products that the term *Goss* was used to describe any make of crested china. The products of the Falcon Works are so popular with collectors that several books have been written about the firm. For further information, I would refer readers to the following publications:

1. *The Price Guide to Goss China*, Nicholas Pine, Milestone Publications. 1978.
   Complete listings of *all* Goss wares giving their current values by the leading dealer in Goss china. Many of the wares including dolls, terracotta, parian and domestic items are illustrated. This is the first book to list Goss England models. A must for collectors.

2. *Goss China: Arms, Decorations and their Values.* Nicholas Pine, Milestone Publications. 1979.
   7,000 different arms and decorations are considered, listed and valued. Again an absolute must for Goss Collectors.

3. *Goss China, John Galpin.* Published by the Author. 1972.
   This is a most useful handbook written with great enthusiasm by a well known collector who is the Chairman of the Goss Collectors' Club. A very good introduction to Goss collecting, but be warned—Mr Galpin's enthusiasm is contagious.

4. *Goss Record* 8th Edition (Reprinted) by J. J. Jarvis. Milestone Publications. Originally produced for Goss collectors in 1914.

5. *William Henry Goss and Goss Heraldic China.* Norman Emery FLA. Journal of Ceramic History No. 4.
   A rather learned treatise on William Henry and Goss china. Useful listings of heraldic models and domestic ware, regimental badges and crests of battleships.

6. *The Price Guide to the Models of W. H. Goss.* Roland Ward, Antique Collectors Club 1975.
   A glossy well produced book, short on text but offering a good photograph of nearly all the known named models. This book does not cover the other wares produced by the Goss works.

Right Goss Model of British 6″ Incendiary Shell. 113 mm

Left Goss Model of German Bomb dropped on Bury St. Edmunds in 1915. Note the fragile handle which is often broken

Right Boulogne Wooden Shoe 120 mm long. One of seven named shoes made by Goss

Left Goss Amersham Leaden Measure

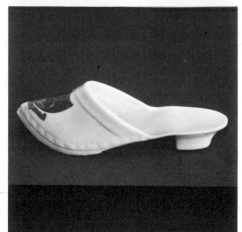

Right The International league of Goss collectors model for 1923. The Egyptian Lotus Vase. One of each model only were sold to league members in the 1920's hence they are now rare and eagerly sought after by collectors

Left Goss Shetland Pony shown with a matching Lerwick Crest

Right A delightful study entitled 'Married Bliss' definitely 'Goss England'

Left A late Goss preserve pot decorated here in orange lustre

The early history of the firm and the lists of models and other wares made by Goss are well covered in these books and so will not be repeated here. But I do feel it necessary to say a few words in praise of Adolphus Goss and to explore the connection between Goss and Harold Taylor Robinson (see ARCADIAN CHINA).

William Henry Goss was an important potter in his day, developing the ivory porcelain body used for heraldic china. He was an industrious and studious man, very much the Victorian. I have the vague suspicion that he was probably a dreadful old bore! The real hero of this book must be his son Adolphus Goss who joined the firm in 1883, it was he who saw the commercial possibilities of heraldic china. The Goss firm had for sometime been decorating small ivory pots with crests of University Colleges and public schools for sale in local china shops and Adolphus rightly saw that these had much wider possibilities. The public interest in archaeology and heraldry could both be satisfied by producing for each town and city miniature historical shapes with applied local coats of arms. Adolphus not only searched the country's museums for suitable ancient artefacts to copy but also found local shops to act as agents. Each agent sold local souvenirs with the correct local crest, but could order other shapes if he so desired. (An exercise in mass-marketing that was years before its time). He also turned his hand to verses to be applied to china but the less said about these the better.

These heraldic porcelains became enormously popular not only in tourist areas, where they made the most perfect souvenir, but in towns and cities all over Britain. The Goss name became famous, but by 1906 many cheap pot versions were being made by other firms who didn't stop at ancient artefacts but applied crests to other, even comic miniatures. W. H. Goss never forgave Adolphus for thus debasing the Goss name: he would have preferred to have been remembered for his Parian wares. Without Adolphus however, the firm would not have prospered and in fact this became evident because in 1906 when William Henry died he left the firm to Adolphus' young brothers Victor Henry and William Huntley, and the story from then on is one of gentle decline.

W. H. Goss left Adolphus £4,000 and commissions, which was dutifully paid, but this left the company very badly financed. With no Adolphus the firm seemed to lack the commercial drive necessary to survive. Goss produced very few miniatures to commemorate the Great War, and although they produced a range of exquisite military badges and crests and even tried making dolls' heads, this period was really the beginning of the end. The other major crested ware manufacturers were making exciting and popular models and the people buying them were not concerned with the beauty of the china. Goss hopelessly failed to catch the style of crested souvenirs popular in the twenties, and so by 1930 the firm was in such financial trouble that the Falcon Works had been foreclosed on by the bank. The trustees of William Huntley sold the business, but obviously not the property to Cauldon Ltd, whose managing director was Harold Taylor Robinson. Mr Robinson arranged the purchase of the business of W. H. Goss from Cauldon Ltd for £2,500. He subsequently bought the Falcon Works from the mortgagee for £4,000. The bank lent him £6,000 to complete the purchase and he then formed W. H. Goss Ltd. The issued capital stood at £6,000 all in ordinary shares all allotted to Harold Taylor Robinson. He acted as director until May 1932 when the firm was put into the hand of the Receiver as the whole Taylor empire crashed. Of the 6,000 ordinary shares he gave 1,000 to his brother, 500 to his father, 500 to his wife, and 1,000 to a business friend. 2,000 shares were transferred to Royal Crown Derby Porcelain Co.Ltd, as part of some rather

List of Colour Illustrations

0

1

2

3

DEPÔT
FOR
THE FOLEY
HERALDIC ENGLISH PORCELAIN

THE WANDSWORTH CREST

4

5

6

7

8

9

10

11

12

13

14

15

16

17

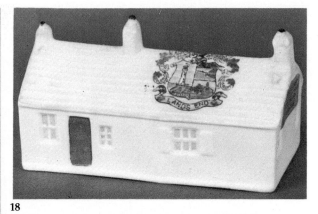

18

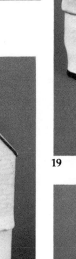

19

20

21

22

23

24

25

26

27

28

29

30

31

32

33

34

35

36

37

38

39

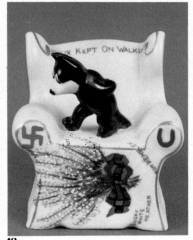

40

41

42

43

44

45

46

47

48

49

50

51

52

53

54

55

56

57

58

59

60

61

62

63

64

65

66

67

68

69

70

71

72

73

74

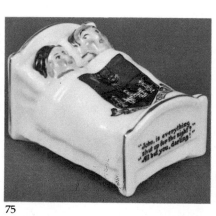

75

76

77

78

79

80

83

81

82

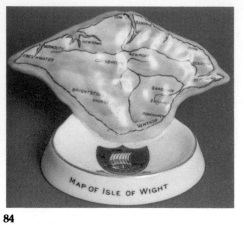

MAP OF ISLE OF WIGHT

84

87

85

86

89

90

88

91

46 Carlton. Black cat on white sofa (see Animals).

47 Rowena. Set of four cartoon characters 'Pa Piggins', 'Oh Jah' or 'Flip Flap', 'Don' and 'Dr. Dromedary'. It is most unusual to find a complete set, Don often turns up on his own (see Cartoon/Comedy Characters).

48 Carlton. The more unusual Carlton Black Cat sitting on an oval blue lustre base. This model also carried a lucky black cat and horseshoe transfer device (see Animals).

49 R & M. Coloured rugby player on ashtray base (see Sport).

50 Carlton. Goal keeper in Goal on ashtray base, one of the British Sports Series (see Sport).

51 Arcadian. Children sitting on tree trunk, the little girl's dress can be found painted in other colours (see Comic/Novelty).

52 Arcadian. Boy and girl sitting in armchair – in this particular model the little girl has no bow in her hair (see Comic/Novelty).

53 Carlton. 'Kelly from the Isle of Man'. Manx three legged man with matching Douglas Crest. Note Manx kipper he is holding in his hand (see Traditional and National Souvenirs).

54 Willow. Scotsman match holder.

55 Arcadian. Grotesque Scotsman on ashtray base, one of a series of comic ashtrays (see Comic/Novelty).

56 German. Girl in basket beach chair. The pink body and face and tan/brown edging to the bathing costume are very typical of crested souvenirs made in Germany during this period. The china is much harder and whiter than English china.

57 Carlton. 'Washed up by the tide' bathing beauty lying on edge of a lustre shell. The tray has a B.E.E. crest (see Seaside Souvenirs).

58 Arcadian. Comic Petrol Pump attendant (see Comic/Novelty).

59 Carlton. Comic horse and jockey on ashtray base, horse has a real hair tail. This model is in lustre with the lucky white heather device (see Sport).

60 Arcadian. Bust of Negro Minstrel with verse 'I may be crazy but I love you' by Eugene Stratton on reverse (see Comic/Novelty).

61 Grafton. Delightful comic dog match holder No. 488 Model more often found without the holder (see Animals).

62 Carlton. Drunk leaning against a lamp post on ash tray base, the inverted top hat acts as a match holder. This is a reasonably restrained model: the lamp is usually in orange lustre (see Alcohol).

63 Grafton. 'The Colonel' a coloured comic figure.

64 Carlton. John Bull and his bulldog, a very patriotic model, presumably made in the days before George Bernard Shaw made his famous remarks about patriotism (see Traditional/National Souvenirs).

65 Arcadian. Jester sitting on heart shaped tray with lucky white heather device (see Comic/Novelty).

66 Arcadian. Baby in a hip bath with coloured transfer of an insect on his leg (see Comic/Novelty).

67 Carlton. The rare and original model of Jackie Coogan, the child film star and ink well in lustre with lucky white heather device (see Cartoon/Comedy Characters).

68 German. Coloured Dutch boy with lustre wheelbarrow with lucky white heather device.

69 Arcadian. Sailor with parrot on shoulder, mustard pot, this model must be part of a full cruet set (see Comic/Novelty).

70 Arcadian. Mr. Pickwick character on bottle with real cork (see Cartoon/Comedy Characters).

71 Arcadian. Comic man drinking beer from tankard on horseshoe ashtray base (see Alcohol).

72 Grafton. Squatting American soldier in this instance shown completely black except for his brown cigar (see Great War).

73 Carlton. 'Xit', 'The Historical Dwarf' this unusual model was taken from a statue formerly in an old garden at Lewes (see Historical/Folklore).

74 Arcadian. Trusty servant with verse on front of base (see Historical/Folklore).

75 Arcadian. Couple in bed, inscribed 'John is everything shut up for the night, all but you darling'.

76 Arcadian. Couple in bed, man sitting up without bed clothes inscribed 'They don't need many clothes in the daytime but they want 'em all at night'.

77 Arcadian. Man drinking beer from tankard, with silvered tankard and fully coloured face. This model is often found all white (see Alcohol).

78 Carlton. Crest faced man 80 mm.

79 Grafton No. 563. Child playing with yacht a rare model (see Seaside Souvenirs).

80 Grafton No. 564. Child playing with bucket and spade, a rare model (see Seaside Souvenirs).

81 Unmarked Parakeet. Fully coloured on plinth 215 mm. An extremely beautiful large model.

82 Willow. Norwich canary, not named with the arms of Norwich (see Birds).

83 Arcadian. Blue lustre crocodile with B.E.E. crest, a rare model and even more rare in lustre (see Animals).

84 Arcadian. Map of Isle of Wight on ashtray base with matching Isle of Wight crest (see Traditional/National Souvenirs).

85 Shelley No. 51. A water pump heavily tinted view ware inscribed 'Surrey scenery' (see Introduction to Shelley wares).

86 Carlton. Fireplace with the unusual inscription 'By my ain fireside' used on models made for Scotland.

87 Carlton. Punch and Judy Booth (see Seaside Souvenirs).

88 Wilton. Grandfather clock completely coloured red with lucky white heather device (see Home/Nostalgic).

89 Carlton. Red coloured hand holding a glass inscribed 'Good Health' (see Alcohol).

90 Carlton. Black cat sitting on red pillar box (see Animals).

91 Carlton. Black cat on red sofa (see Animals).

Goss England. Four small animals usually found marked 'Arcadian'. When marked 'Goss England' they are worth around five times more

Goss England. Small boot, an umbrella and whiskey bottle, all marked Goss England but more usually found marked Arcadian

Grosvenor. Lion model, quite unusual in that he is lying and not standing

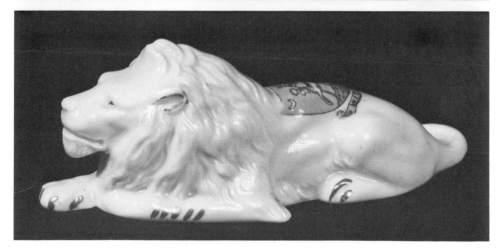

clever deal that Mr Robinson always seemed concerned in. After 1930 the wares marked Goss cannot be considered to be really Goss, the china is not so fine and the moulds used could be from any firm in the Cauldon group.

For history of the firm after 1932 please see ARCADIAN CHINA.

Gladstone China

Trademark used by Taylor
and Kent (Ltd), Florence
Works, Longton.

For details of this manufacturer and china produced see FLORENTINE CHINA.

This mark was only used on domestic and miniature domestic items. No other decoration other than crests have been found on pieces with the mark.

Gladstone Models

Miniature Domestic
Cheese dish and cover. 50 mm.
Mug, one handle. 35 mm.

Grafton China

Trademark used by Alfred B.
Jones and Sons Ltd, Grafton
China Works, Longton, Staffs

1900–1915

1920's on domestic ware

1915–1933

NB Retailers name often appears above these marks for example MEW BROS, SANDOWN I.W.

A. B. Jones and Sons Ltd are one of the few firms, that produced arms ware in any great quantity, to have survived the 1930's and to be still in business today. (They are now trading as Crown Lynn Ceramics Ltd and use the trademark *Royal Grafton*). Although *Grafton China* had a large share of the china souvenir market they always produced other domestic and ornamental lines and presumably they sold enough of these, especially abroad, to keep going through the Depression.

Alfred B. Jones of the Grafton China Works had taken his two sons, Messrs. N. B. and A. B. Jones, Jnr, into partnership on 1st January 1900, the firm was then known as A. B. Jones and Sons Ltd. At that time they announced 'The firm will still make tea and breakfast sets for the Home, Colonial and American Markets, their chief specialities'. They were, however, in 1900 already advertising 'Badge Ware and View Ware' and were obviously producing goods for the lower end of the market (hotel ware and small souvenir items).

By 1906 A. B. Jones and Sons were making a special line of 'Miniature ivory arms china with the arms of any County, City or Borough painted in correct heraldic colours'. The pieces included jugs, loving cups, trays, milk jugs and vases in innumerable shapes. They also supplied 'local views of any locality' and had introduced another interesting speciality the 'zoo' series, animals of all kinds in pure white china, but do not appear to have been applying arms to them at that time.

By 1909, Mr John Walker, their London Representative at the Showroom in Buchanan Buildings, Holborn, was able to display Grafton 'Transparent ivory arms ware' in several hundred different shapes 'antique, pleasing, artistic, useful, quaint and humourous'. So it seems that between 1906 and 1909 Grafton had begun applying arms to more interesting pieces than vases and milk jugs, presumably animals, ancient artefacts and other souvenir items.

Right Grafton. Top: Naked baby
No. 544 Brown hair and blue eyes
(see Home/Nostalgic)
Bottom: Very similar model but
with moulded bathing suit on
blue sea base No. 565

Left Grafton. Baby sitting No. 481

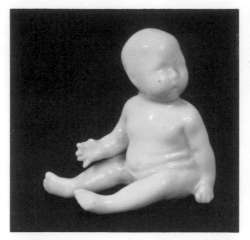

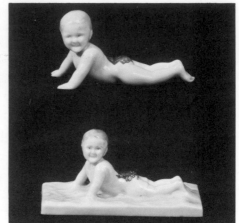

Right Grafton. 'A Cornish Pasty'
No. 340

Left Grafton. Dutchman holding
cheese which carries crest

Right Grafton. 'Ride a cock horse
to Banbury Cross' on base

Left Grafton. No. 331 a water
pump

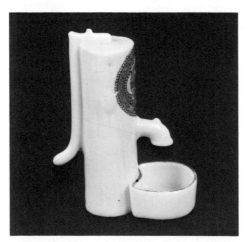

Grafton. Three examples of
colour transfer prints

156

As the craze for heraldic china grew, Grafton appeared to place greater emphasis on its production. In 1919 they introduced crested souvenirs of the Great War and a series of zoo-logical (sic) interest, including, many attractive models of elephants, monkeys, mice and what not else, in all sort of postures!' By 1920 they advertised the firm to the trade as makers of 'heraldic and view wares, miniature mascots, grotesques' and only 'also tea and breakfast ware'.

A. B. Jones were present at the British Industries Fair in 1920 and at the British Empire Exhibition 1924, displaying 'Tea, Breakfast, Dessert, Dinner and Coffee Services and Fancy Goods—coloured, Heraldic and Model Reproductions'. The firm still produces much the same kind of ware today, with the exception of heraldic china which they last advertised in the 1920's. Unfortunately in 1946 there was a fire at the Grafton works and all the records of crested china production were lost, so even this manufacturer, who did not go bankrupt or merge, can offer no detailed information on wares made in the early part of this century. In 1909 A. B. Jones offered in the Pottery Gazette to send 'coloured sheets of illustrations of Grafton China to anyone in the trade writing for them'. Regrettably none of these tantalising sheets have so far been found.

Grafton was one of the major producers of good quality heraldic china, perhaps rivalling Shelley as the main Goss competitor for the better end of the souvenir market. Certainly Grafton models are in the main rather more imaginative and clever than Shelley, and the china tends to be finer. The arms on Grafton models are very well produced and the colours are much more muted and subtle, and therefore rather more attractive than on other china.

Because this firm worked quite independently of any other arms ware manufacturer its wares have a style and character of their own. This is particularly noticeable in the Great War and animal models. The soldiers produced as souvenirs of the Great War are in action: 'Over the Top' and 'The Bomb Thrower' are unlike anything produced by most other firms as are the series of children playing on the beach. The range of white crested animals includes many more grotesque and comical items than are usually found, and Grafton are the only manufacturers to add coloured glass bead eyes to their animals. Many amusing miniature coloured animals were made, but these are invariably without a crest and so have not been listed here. The style is very obviously late 20's, when coloured china souvenirs became more popular. One can only assume that Grafton stopped using crests on such items earlier than the other major manufacturers who went on producing coloured pieces with crests long after the interest in heraldic devices had waned. (This is probably one of the reasons why A. B. Jones survived the Depression. Their souvenir ware must have looked very 'modern' in the 20's.)

Grafton do not appear to have produced Military crests but the following commemoratives are found: Flags of Liberty; Franco–British Exhibition 1905; Latin–British Exhibition, Great White City 1912; British Empire Exhibition 1924/5. Some foreign crests have been found and these are usually marked 'Importe d'Angleterre', and were made for export.

Grafton seem not to have used 'Lucky Black Cat' and 'Lucky White Heather' devices or any other form of decoration on their models, other than coloured transfer views and regional souvenirs such as the 'Somerset Cuckoo'. (View ware too is well produced but the colours are much more vibrant than one would expect from this Manufacturer). Black transfer prints are also found including two unusual portraits of the 'Prince of Wales, President of B.E.E. 1924' and the 'Duke of York, President of B.E.E. 1925' which are really commemoratives.

Right Grafton. Lincoln Cathedral front view

Left Grafton. Lincoln Cathedral back biew showing transfer print 'Old London Bridge' a souvenir of Wembley Exhibition

Grafton. Southampton Bargate 90 mm and Bath Abbey 112 mm

Grafton. Top: No. 139 Brading Roman Vase, No. 309 English Wine Glass, No. 184 Swiss Urn 40 mm
Bottom: No. 160 Roman Vase, No. 186 Ely Drinking Cup, No. 176 Ale Pot

Numbering System. The numbers sometimes appearing on the base of Grafton pieces are stock numbers that occur consistently on certain models. On early china numbers are printed but they are mostly found painted in black and for that reason are not always easy to read. The letter that follows the numbers is obviously the paintresses' mark. The highest number found is 737, but anyone making a numerical list of known models will find that many numbers are missing. The models listed without numbers and domestic ware will account for many of the gaps but nothing has been found numbered 570–632 and one wonders if these were perhaps used on coloured models without crests. Stock numbers are given in the following lists.

Grafton Models

Parian/Unglazed
All known unglazed models are busts which have square glazed bases and do not normally carry crests. Busts are however found with commemorative devices of the Great War on the glazed base, but these are all comparatively scarce.

Bust of John Peel, inscribed: *D'ye ken John Peel with his coat so grey.* 120 mm.

Bust of Albert 1 of Belgium, inscribed: *Albert I.* Usually found with 'Flags of Liberty' commemorative. 125 mm.

Bust of George V inscribed: *George V.* Usually found with 'Flags of Liberty' commemorative. 125 mm.

Bust of David Lloyd George, impressed on back: *Lloyd George.* No. 415. Rd. No. 659418. 135 mm.

Bust of Field Marshall, Sir John French, impressed on back: *French.* 135 mm.

Bust of Admiral Sir John Jellicoe, impressed on back *Jellicoe.* 135 mm.

Bust of General Joffre, impressed on back *Joffre.* 155 mm.

Bust of Lord Kitchener, impressed on back *Kitchener.* 125 mm.

Bust of Lord Roberts, impressed on back *Roberts.* 135 mm.

Ancient Artefacts
These models are often found not named and are quite often found with a coloured transfer view rather than a crest.

Aberdeen Bronze Pot, not as yet found named. No. 267. 65 mm.

Ale Pot, inscribed: *Model of old ale pot.* No. 176. 60 mm.

Brading Roman Vase, inscribed: *Model of Roman vase found at Brading.* 2 vases of different shape: No. 136. 62 mm. No. 139. 55 mm.

British Vase, inscribed: *Model of ancient British vase found in the 4th Century, Uricorium Cemetery.* No. 17. 40 mm.

Butter Pot, inscribed: *Model of old butter pot of 17th Century.* No. 185. 40 mm.

Canterbury Pilgrims' Bottle, inscribed: *Model of Canterbury pilgrims' bottle.* Rd. No. 470749. Can also be found impressed: *Canterbury pilgrims' bottle.* 50 mm.

Chester Roman Vase, inscribed: *Roman vase found at Chester from the original in museum.* No. 165. 60 mm.

Chinese Teapot, inscribed; *Model of Chinese teapot.* No. 77. 54 mm.

Chinese Vase, inscribed. *Model of ancient Chinese vase.* 3 vases of different shapes: No. 276. 86 mm. No. 278. 85 mm. No. 282. 75 mm.

(As no other models have been found with numbers between 276 and 282 it seems probable that there are more Chinese vases to be found.)

Cyprus Vase, inscribed *Vase from Cyprus. 900 BC to 365 AD.* No. 120. 70 mm.

Ely Drinking Cup, inscribed: *Model of drinking cup original in Ely Museum.* 39 mm.

English Wine Glass, inscribed: *Model of Old English wine glass.* 4 glasses of different shape: No. 309. 75 mm (Ale glass). No. 310. 75 mm (Goblet). No. 311? 70 mm (tumbler). No. 312. 70 mm (ovoid bowl).

Egyptian Bottle, inscribed: *Egyptian bottle date about 3,300 BC.* No. 159. 57 mm.

Egyptian Tear Bottle, inscribed: *Model of Egyptian tear bottle.* No. 151. 42 mm.

(These Egyptian models sometimes carry a further inscription:

Egyptian pottery—these specimens were discovered by Doctor Flinders Petra (Sic) in Egypt, manufactured about 4,000 BC. Nos. 152–158 have not been found, except for 156 which was an unmarked vase, so it seems likely that further examples of Dr. Flinders' pottery were made.)

Egyptian Vase, inscribed: *Model of Ancient Egyptian vase.* No. 323. 45 mm.

Hereford Kettle, inscribed: *Model of old terra cotta kettle original in Hereford Museum.* This model has a separate lid. No. 179. 80 mm (can be found wrongly numbered 174).

London Vessel, inscribed: *Model of vessel found during excavations in London.* 3 vessels of different shape: No. 206. 45 mm (pot with 2 handles), No. 209, 70 mm (pot), No. 207? 84 mm (jug).

Loving Cup, not found named. No. 145. 40 mm.

Reading Roman Vase, inscribed: *Model of Roman vase found at Reading.* 50 mm.

Roman Lamp, inscribed: *Model of Roman lamp, Pompeii to 1st Century AD.* No. 119. 60 mm.

Roman Vase, inscribed: *Model of Roman vase. Pompeii to 1st Century AD.* No. 160. 48 mm.

Right Grafton. Ruskin Memorial, a very detailed model

Left Grafton. 'Tonbridge Castle' 88 mm long

Left Grafton. 'Smallest House in Great Britain' with matching Conway Crest

Grafton. Two souvenir models of ripon, St. Wilfred and the Ripon Hornblower

Salisbury Kettle, inscribed: *Model of Salisbury kettle*. No. 174 105 mm (can be found wrongly numbered 179).

Shakespeare's Jug, inscribed: *Model of Shakespere's (Sic) Jug*. No. 124. 76 mm.

Surrey Hill Norman Pot, inscribed: *Model of Norman pot from original in Surrey Hill Museum*. No. 182. 45 mm.

Swiss Urn, inscribed: *Model of urn from Swiss Tacustrine habitation*. No details of size.

Yaverland Vase, no details available.

Buildings—Coloured

These can be found glazed or unglazed and do not carry crests. A few coloured cottages and nightlights have been made since 1945. These are marked *Royal Grafton*, and although they are very collectable, cannot be considered of the same genre as *Grafton* models and have therefore not been listed.

Captain Cook's house Great Ayton re-erected in Melbourne. 95 mm long (rare).

Couch's house, Polperro, on roof, with arms of Polperro.

House on the Props, Polperro. 100 mm long (scarce).

Old Chapel, Lantern Hill, Ilfracombe. 72 mm long.

Old Toll Bar, Gretna Green. 125 mm long.

Buildings—White

Bath Abbey. 112 mm.

Bath Abbey, West front. 105 mm.

Bargate, Southampton. 90 mm.

Carnarvon Castle. 90 mm.

First and Last refreshment house in England, Land's End, found numbered 469 and 627. 75 mm long.

Gynn Inn, Blackpool, inscribed: *Model of Blackpools famous landmark, the old Gynn Inn demolished 1921*. No. 520. 125 mm long.

Houses of Parliament. No. 424. 115 mm.

Largs Tower, (not named) has green shamrocks on base. No. 49. 137 mm.

Lincoln Cathedral, West front. 115 mm.

Old Cornish cottages. 125 mm long (quite rare).

Old Chapel, Lantern Hill, Ilfracombe. 75 mm long.

Old toll-gate house, including path with gate, inscribed: *Ye olde toll-gate house*. No. 498. 130 mm long.

Old Toll-Gate House, as above but not on base with path and gate, and not named. No. 502. 63 mm long.

Oldest chemists shop in England established 1790, also can be found inscribed: *Model of the oldest pharmacy in England, Knaresborough. Yorkshire. Established in the reign of George 1st 1790*. 97 mm long.

Plas Mawr, Conway. 93 mm (rare).

St. Pauls, Cathedral, London. 2 sizes: No. 423. 137 mm. No. 633. 115 mm.

Scarborough Castle Ruins, not named. 104 mm.

Skegness Clock Tower, not named. 127 mm.

Smallest house in Great Britain. No. 560. 92 mm.

Tonbridge Castle. 88 mm long.

Westminster Abbey. No. 422. 121 mm.

Monuments (including Crosses)

Banbury Cross. 141 mm.

Irish Cross, not named, green shamrocks on base. No. 419. 138 mm.

"Lloyd George" statue Carnarvon. Rd. No. 659418. 150 mm.

Ramsgate Lifeboat Memorial (Statue of Lifeboatman), not named but often found with the inscription 'Souvenir from the Imperial Bazaar, Albion Hill, Ramsgate, which was twice wrecked by Zeppelin bombs on May 17th 1915 and June 17th 1917' on base. 140 mm.

Rufus Stone with very lengthy inscription on all three sides. 96 mm.

(John) Ruskin Memorial Stone, inscribed: *John Ruskin MDCCCXIX—MDCCCC* and religious verse. No. 515. 120 mm.

St. Anne's Lifeboat Memorial, inscribed: *Erected in honour of 13 brave men who lost their lives attempting to save the crew of the German barque 'Mexico' December 6th 1886*. No. 495. 161 mm.

Sandbach Crosses, inscribed: *The Saxon crosses, Sandbach ancient legend says these were erected about 650 AD commemorating the conversion to christianity of Peada, son of Penda and his marriage with the daughter of Oswy King of Northumbria*. 130 mm. (This model seems to be quite rare.)

Historical/Folklore

Charles I bottle with removable head lid, not named and thought by some collectors to be Guy Fawkes. No. 209. 96 mm.

Headless Tudor figure (possibly a Beefeater and a ghost!) not named. 60 mm.

President Wilson's Grandfather's chair (Armchair). No. 492. 75 mm.

Ride a cock horse to Banbury Cross (lady on horse). Rd. No. 693636. No. 569. 106 mm long.

Saint Wilfred of Ripon. 136 mm.

Traditional/National Souvenirs

Blackpool Big Wheel, not named. 78 mm.

Cornish Pasty. No. 340. 95 mm long.

Lancashire Clog, sometimes found inscribed: *Model of Lancashire clog*. No. 407. 90 mm long.

Leaking Boot, Cleethorpes (Statue of boy, boot joined to hand by string) Rd. No. 675969, 156 mm.

Lincoln Imp. 108 mm.

Ripon horn blower, often found not named, inscribed: *The horn is blown every night at 9. Formerly it denoted that the watch was set for the night*. 136 mm.

Yarmouth Bloater. 115 mm.

Welsh Harp. No. 418. 80 mm.

Welsh Hat, with blue band and bow, found with longest Welsh place name printed round brim. No. 183. 50 mm.

Welsh Lady Toby Jug, fully coloured. 83 mm.

Seaside Souvenirs

Bathing Machine. No. 256. 55 mm long.

Boat with billowing sail, inscribed: *Polly*. No. 448. 115 mm long.

Boat, flatbottomed with bird's head as figurehead. No. 462. 80 mm long (rare).

Grafton. No. 344 (large size) sitting cat with yellow bow and yellow glass eyes and No. 339 with green bow and only one red glass eye still in place

Grafton. Top row: No. 319 cat with green bow and yellow glass eyes.'The Cheshire cat, always smiling' with one yellow glass eye No. 288, and No. 351 cat with yellow bow and missing bead eyes
Bottom row: Cat singing, red mouth and green bow, standing cat red mouth and blue bow and cat in jar inscribed 'From Chicago Perishable' No. 277

Lifeboat. No. 332. 110 mm long.

Rowing boat, can be found inscribed: *Sant Cybi* (patron saint of Holyhead) on models with a Holyhead crest or: *Robin Hoods Bay* No. 169. 130 mm long.

Fisherman's Creel with lid. No. 292. 72 mm long.

Beachy Head Lighthouse, with black band. 135 mm.

Eddystone Lighthouse. No. 315. 102 mm.

Shell dish. No. 533. 63 mm long.

Oyster Shell, on Coral legs. 51 mm.

Oyster Shell, on stand. 83 mm dia.

Whelk Shell, 4 sizes: No. 65. 45 mm & 85 mm long. No. 528. 70 mm long. No number. 100 mm long.

Bathing Beauty, reclining wearing swimsuit and mob-cap, holding parasol. 135 mm (uncommon).

Boy holding model yacht, coloured hair and yacht. No. 563. 85 mm.

Boy swimming on a rectangular 'sea' base, hair and eyes coloured. No. 565. 120 mm long.

Girl kneeling on 'beach' base, with red bucket and spade, brown hair and red hat brim. No. 564. 75 mm (563–565 are all quite rare).

Toddler on donkey. 85 mm.

Animals

Some 'Grafton' animals were given tiny glass bead eyes, more often than not these are missing, leaving small holes. Even without these beads the models remain very attractive, but obviously a complete model is more desirable. The range of large comical cats with these coloured bead eyes and coloured bows are particularly appealing but are hard to find. I know of only one collector who has managed to amass more than one or two.

Bear, dressed as boy, standing on shell tray. 85 mm.

Bear and Ragged Staff. 2 sizes: 85 mm & 100 mm. The larger version is No. 224 and has bead eyes. (This is much rarer than the small model.)

Calf, not named but mostly found with cartoon transfer of farmer and wife behind gate with bull on the other side. 'Well what shall us do Bill? I spose there bain't nothing else but to cut h's ed off' and inscribed: *Why the natives are called Isle of Wight calves.* No. 287. 100 mm long.

Camel, 2 humps. No. 242. (The same stock number has been found on a stamp box). 120 mm long.

Cat, Cheshire, inscribed: *The Cheshire Cat* and *Always smiling.* 1 yellow glass eye. No. 288. 86 mm.

Cat, Cheshire, with red mouth and nose, one bead eye (green) and one eye closed, inscribed: *The Cheshire Cat.* Found with and without separate shield carrying crest. 100 mm.

Cat, crouching and angry. 55 mm.

Cat, crouching, fat and angry with tail in the air. Found with bead eyes. No. 303. 88 mm long.

Cat in Jar, inscribed: *From Chicago Perishable.* No. 277. 80 mm.

Cat singing, red mouth and green bow. 75 mm.

Cat, sitting and comical, green bow and tail at front with bead eyes (blue or green). No. 319. 2 sizes: 88 mm & 103 mm.

Cat, sitting and comical, yellow bow. Found with verse "As I was going to St. Ives". No. 351. 94 mm.

Cat, sitting and comical, green bow and tail at front with head eyes. No. 339. 154 mm.

Cat, sitting and comical, yellow bow and tail at back with bead eyes No. 344. 2 sizes: 100 mm & 146 mm.

Cat, standing, arched back and tail in the air with green bow. No. 303. 100 mm.

Cat, standing and comical, blue bow and green eyes. 88 mm long.

(Cat) Kitten. No. 211. 50 mm.

Cow standing, not named. 60 mm.

Dog in boater and clothes. 88 mm.

Dog, bottle with separate head lid. No. 232. 100 mm.

Bulldog, British inscribed: *Slow to start but what a hold.* 83 mm.

Bulldog, standing with feet wide apart. No. 391. 51 mm.

Bulldog, sitting with bead eyes (yellow or green). No. 250. 2 sizes: 88 mm & 102 mm.

Dog, Greyhound, standing with front legs on small oval base. No. 709. 102 mm long. (The stock number indicates that this is a late model and probably it was made for a very short period, only one has been found.)

Dog, with 2 heads, one head is smiling and the other is sad. Two models, one with ears down, inscribed: *Two headed dog.* Model with ears up has not been found with inscription. No. 646. 63 mm.

Dog, King Charles Spaniel sitting. No. 390. 53 mm.

Dog, kneeling, wearing a green cap. No. 488. Can be found coloured with match holder. 85 mm.

Dog, Labrador Pup, sitting with bead eyes (yellow or green). No. 355.

Dog, Puppy, sitting one ear raised and scratching with back leg. (Often found coloured with no crest). No. 410. 85 mm.

Dog, Scottie, standing. No. 432. Can be found with bead eyes. 94 mm long.

Elephant sitting and comical. No. 438. 127 mm.

Elephant walking. No. 426. 100 mm.

Elephant walking. No. 470. 2 sizes: 50 mm & 80 mm.

Fish, curved vase. 57 mm.

Fish, curved tail and open mouth. No. 392. 105 mm long.

Fish, curved body and open mouth. No. 393. 80 mm long.

Fish, straight and fat. No. 247. 2 sizes: 88 mm & 110 mm long.

Fish, straight and fat with open mouth. No. 341. 102 mm long.

Fish, straight with open mouth. No. 97. 100 mm long.

Right Grafton. A very rare model of a Greyhound No. 709. The small disc base was probably added to make the model more stable

Left Grafton. Crouching cat with tail in the air No. 303. This particular model has a green painted bow and has lost its bead eyes.

Right Grafton. Two versions of No. 646. two headed dog. Dog on the left has ears down and is inscribed 'Two headed dogs'. The model on the right has pricked ears and no inscription

Left Grafton. A most beautiful model of a fox with yellow bead eyes. No. 462

Grafton. Top row: No. 390 King Charles spaniel, No. 432 terrier standing with yellow glass eyes and No. 391 standing bulldog
Bottom row: No. 410 sitting pup, No. 355 labrador pup with yellow glass eyes and No. 250 sitting bulldog with green glass eyes

Right Grafton. A really comic model elephant No. 438

Left Grafton. Monkey with coat No. 286. This photograph shows the two little holes found in the eyes of Grafton models when the beads are missing

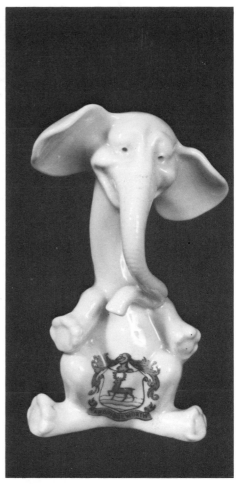

Left Grafton. Standing elephant No. 426

Grafton. Top row: No. 343 Pig standing, No. 417 Pig sitting up Bottom row: No. 338 Pig sitting and laughing. No. 341 fat sitting pig
All of these pigs are inscribed 'Wunt be druv'

Right Grafton. No. 204 Sitting frog with devestating green glass bead eyes

Left Grafton. Camel No. 242 120 mm long

Grafton. Fish No. 392 curved tail and open mouth, fish No. 247 straight and fat and fish No. 393 curved and open mouthed

Grafton. Squirrel No. 327 with blue glass eyes. Seal No. 402 and Mouse No. 210 with green glass eyes

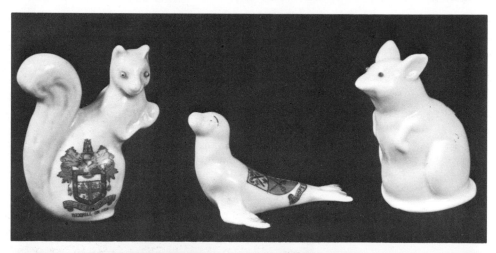

Grafton. Hen on circular base No. 453, Kingfisher No. 670 and cock on circular base No. 454. The hen and cock were probably sold as pairs

Right Grafton. 'Fu Hing God of Happiness' A rare model

Left Grafton. Pierrot playing a banjo with inscription on the reverse 'As I was going to St. Ives'

Right Grafton. Swan, head under wing No. 409 and Duck No. 377

Left Grafton. Bottle with removeable head stopper. Thought to be Charles 1st

Grafton. Top row: Fledgeling with coloured head No. 435, chicken hatching from egg No. 326 with red bead eyes and kingfisher No. 670
Bottom row: Hen on circular base No. 453, Penguin No. 329 and cock on circular base No. 454

Grafton. 'The Bomb Thrower' a
soldier throwing a hand grenade,
beautifully modelled

Grafton. 'Over the Top' a very
exciting and unusual model

Fish, straight and thin. No. 302. 2 sizes:
76 mm & 112 mm long. Large size can be
found with bead eyes.

Fox with bead eyes (yellow). No. 462.
140 mm long.

Frog with closed mouth, can be found with
bead eyes. No. 204. 72 mm.

Lion, standing. 105 mm long.

Monkey with bead eyes (yellow). No. 286.
70 mm.

Monkey, baby with bead eyes (green) No.
210. 67 mm.

Pig, sitting with raised ears. No. 203.
70 mm.

Pig, sitting and laughing, inscribed: *Wunt
be druv*. No. 338. 65 mm.

Pig, sitting, is much fatter than the above.
inscribed: *Wunt be druv*.

Pig, sitting up on hind legs found
inscribed: *Wunt be druv*, or *I Won't be
drove*. No. 417. 70 mm.

(This pig with same inscriptions and Stock
No. can be found made into a salt pot.)

Pig, standing, can be found with no
inscription but normally found
inscribed: *Wunt be druv* or *I won't be drove*.
No. 343. 70 mm long.

Pig, standing, inscribed: *Wunt be druv*.
88 mm long. (This could be a larger
version of 343, but all models have been
reported with no number.)

Polar Bear. No. 102. 105 mm long.

Pony, not named. No. 493. 2 sizes: 70 mm
& 105 mm long.

Rabbit, with bead eyes (yellow). No. 240.
112 mm long.

Seal. No. 402. 70 mm long. (This is a very
delicate model.)

Snail. No. 329, 80 mm long.

Squirrel holding nut, can be found with
bead eyes. No. 327. 75 mm.

Terrapin. No. 253. 92 mm long.

Birds

Bird/fledgling, some colouring. No. 435.
65 mm (very plump and pretty).

Bird posy holder, grotesque chick with
orange legs. No. 737. 68 mm.

Chicken hatching from Egg, can be found
with bead eyes. No. 326. 73 mm long.

Cock on circular base. No. 454. 100 mm
(pair with hen).

Duck, occasionally found inscribed:
Aylesbury duck. No. 377. 96 mm long.

Duck Pin Tray. No. 442. 85 mm long.

Hen on circular base. No. 453. 100 mm
(pair with cock).

Kingfisher on base. No. 670. 62 mm.

Owl on rocky base. No. 687. 132 mm (very
impressive model).

Penguin. No. 329. 88 mm.

Swan, head under wing. No. 409. 85 mm
long.

Great War

American soldier, squatting, fully coloured.
One model found all black except for
cigar and can be found with no colouring
at all. No. 85. 80 mm. (This model is very
rarely found).

Bulldog, British Territorial Bulldog, seated
figure of Tommy with bulldog face, red
and blue bands on hat. No. 262. 88 mm.
(Scarce).

Kitchener Bust (glazed) on circular base,
inscribed: *Lord Kitchener of Khartoum
creator of British Army 1914/1918. Born June
24th 1850. Died serving his country June 5th
1916 by the sinking of HMS Hampshire off the
Orkneys*. No. 395. 2 sizes: 100 mm &
130 mm.

Kitchener Match holder, caricature of
Kitchener with life-belt, some colouring.
No. 214. 95 mm dia. The joke is in rather
poor taste just after Kitchener drowned.
It is included in this section as it is so
popular with great War Collectors.

Sailor seated and holding a model
submarine, hat band impressed: *Victory*
Is often found inscribed: *Weve got 'U' well
in hand*.
Can also be found coloured. No. 452.
80 mm.

Soldier leaving Trench, inscribed: *Over the
top*. No. 403. 118 mm.

Soldier throwing hand grenade, inscribed:
The Bomb Thrower. No. 425. 140 mm.

Biplane, fixed prop. No. 450. 145 mm
long.

Monoplane, fixed prop. No. 414. 135 mm
long.

HMS Dreadnought, ship with high prow.
No. 408. 142 mm long. Same ship with
same stock number found inscribed:
HMS Gosport or *HMS Henry of Blois* or
HMS Victory.

HMS Iron Duke. No. 431. 155 mm long.

Submarine, inscribed: *E9*. No. 406. 145 mm
long.

Motor Ambulance with curtains, inscribed:
*Motor ambulance car given by Staffordshire
china operatives. British Red Cross Society:
St. John Ambulance Association. Load not to
exceed 1 driver, 1 attendant and patients*. No.
397. 98 mm long.

Motor Tractor, inscribed: *Model of motor
tractor used on western front*. No. 456.
80 mm long.

Renault Tank. 100 mm long.

Tank with steering wheels, inscribed: *H.M.
Landship Creme de Menthe*. Rd. No.
658588. No. 413. 118 mm long.

Tank, no steering wheels, inscribed: *H.M.
Landship Creme de Menthe*. Rd. No.
658588. No. 413. 98 mm long.

Whippet Tank, inscribed: *Model of Whippet
Tank*. No. 449. 115 mm long.

Alpine Gun with moving wheels, inscribed:
Model of Alpine gun. No. 394. 105 mm long
(rare).

Desert Gun. No. 430. 155 mm long.

Field Gun on sledge, inscribed: *French 75*.
No. 412. 2 sizes: 140 mm & 160 mm
long.

German Gun captured by British. No. 403.
153 mm long.

Trench Howitzer (found with Ramsgate
Imperial Bazaar inscription. see:
Ramsgate Lifeboat Memorial) No. 404.
75 mm long.

Cannon Shell. No. 400. 76 mm.

Cannon Shell, inscribed *Jack Johnson*. No.
399. (Jack Johnson was a heavy-weight
champion). 90 mm.

German Incendiary Bomb. No. 405.
80 mm.

Right Grafton. 'Model of Motor Tractor used on Western Front'

Left Grafton. 'Model of Whippet Tank' 115 mm long

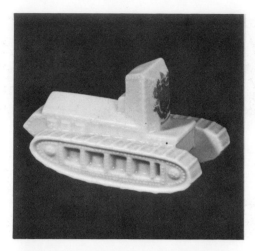 

Right Grafton. Motor Ambulance given by Staffordshire china operatives

Left Grafton. Desert Gun 155 mm long

 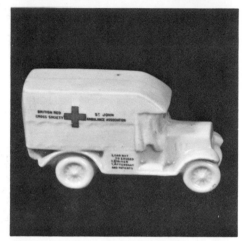

Grafton. 'German Gun captured by British' and 'French 75'

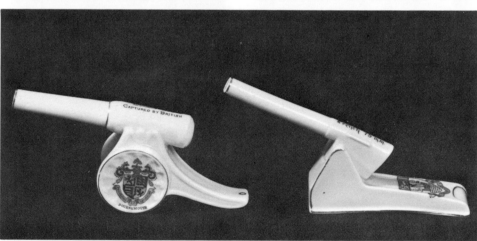

Grafton. H.M. Landship Creme de Menthe with and without trailing wheels

Right Grafton. 'Dreadnought', this model is also found inscribed with the names of famous battleships

Left Grafton. Battleship H.M.S. Iron Duke, this particular model is not always named

Right Grafton. Very realistic model of 'Mills Hand Grenade' with metal pin

Left Grafton. Submarine E9. 145 mm long

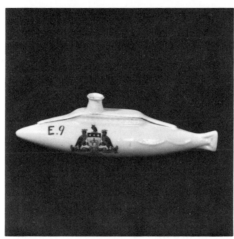

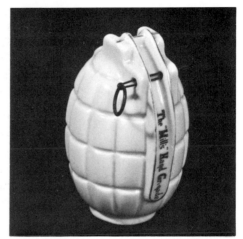

Grafton. Parian busts of 'David Lloyd George', 'Joffre' and 'Kitchener'. The last two both carry flags of liberty devices

Grafton. 'British Territorial Bulldog' with red and blue bands on hat and sailor seated holding a model submarine

Right Grafton. President Wilson's Grandfather's Chair, not found in other manufacturers ranges

Left Grafton. Whisky flask with Franco British Exhibition 1908 commemorative and horses hoof with a commemorative of the Anglo American Exposition 1914

Grafton. Charabanc with the inscription 'Dreadnought' indicating the discomforts of early motor travel

Right Grafton. Footballer with ball on small base, not found numbered

Left Grafton. Rather cruel Kitchener Match Holder, coloured ropes and hat band

Left Grafton. A gruesome model, the Lincoln Imp

Mills hand grenade with removable metal pin, often found without inscription. Rd. No. 657211, No. 411. 83 mm (Very life like piece this. Thank goodness previous owners resisted the temptation to throw it after removing the pin!)
Bandsman's Drum. 45 mm.
Bell Tent with open flaps, with or without base. No. 239. 2 sizes: 65 mm & 140 mm.
Boot with Puttee. No. 389. 75 mm.
Colonial Soldier's Hat. No. 238, 89 mm long.
Water Bottle. No. 234. 80 mm.
Cenotaph, inscribed: *MCMXIV–MCMXIX—The Glorious Dead* and 3 coloured flags on reverse. 2 sizes: 135 mm & 155 mm.

Home/Nostalgic
Anvil on heavy base. No. 352. 70 mm.
Baby crawling naked, Brown hair, blue eyes. No. 544. 110 mm long.
Baby sitting up. No. 481. 63 mm.
Baby's rocking cradle. No. 294. 62 mm long.
Basket with handle. No. 29. 52 mm.
Grandfather Clock. 110 mm.
Horn Lantern, inscribed: *Model of old horn lantern*. No. 306. 76 mm.
Rocking Horse. 125 mm long.
Village Water Pump. No. 331. 80 mm.
Wing Chair. 73 mm.

Comic/Novelty
Billiken. No. 291. 44 mm (Most like the original American concept).
Chinese Man Pepper Pot, some colouring. No. 726. 70 mm. (There must be a matching Salt Pot somewhere.)
Dutchman sitting cross legged, and holding cheese. No. 230. 85 mm.
Fu Hing God of Happiness? Chinese Priest sitting upright, holding baby, some colouring. 115 mm (rare).
Head, Comic Salt Pot, miserable face and droopy bow tie. No. 255. 85 mm. (Matches below).
Head, Comic Pepper Pot, happy face and perky bow tie. No. 258. 85 mm. (Matches above).
Pierrot sitting cross legged on box playing banjo, some colouring. Found with inscription: 'As I was going to St. Ives'. No. 566. 103 mm.
Teapot Man, face on lid, spout and handle form arms, some colouring. 48 mm.

Alcohol
Bottle Stopper. No. 715 . 68 mm.
Champagne Bottle. No. 221. 102 mm.
Champagne Bottle Pepper Pot. No. 225. 102 mm.
Man in Barrel, head and feet protruding, inscribed: *No beer*. 115 mm.

Sport
Canoe. No. 169. 125 mm long.
Footballer with ball on small base. 130 mm.
Golfer holding bag of golf clubs, comic figure, inscribed: *The Colonel*. Can be found fully coloured. No. 352. 90 mm. (This is probably a model of a popular comic or cartoon character.)

Golf Ball Salt Pot. 52 mm.
Golf Ball Pepper Pot. No. 293. 52 mm.
Tennis player, lady holding racquet (reputedly Suzanne Lenglen). 133 mm.

Transport
Car, inscribed: *Dreadnought*. 102 mm long.
Charabanc, with 5 rows of seats, inscribed: *Dreadnought*. No. 568. 100 mm long.

Miscellaneous
Boot. No. 237. 80 mm long. (This is a really detailed model.)
Sabot, pointed. No. 170. 95 mm long.
Shoe, lady's 18th Century. No. 50. 83 mm long.
Handbell. No. 15. 82 mm.
Horse's Hoof. No. 236. 72 mm long.

Miniature Domestic
Beaker. No. 73. 52 mm.
Cheese dish and cover. (2 pieces) No. 78, 65 mm long.
Cup. No. 147. 39 mm.
Cup and Saucer. No. 122. Cup: 36 mm. Saucer: 67 mm dia.
Mug with one handle. No. 36. 48 mm.
Mug with one handle. No. 143. 41 mm.

As quite a large number of people collect Grafton they will probably be interested in a list of other numbered items that have been reported; indeed some of the pill boxes and trays are very attractive and will be of interest to most general collectors. A good number of the ewers, jugs and pots described below are likely to be un-named historical shapes and hopefully named models will be found in the future.

Numbered Domestic and Ornamental Wares
No. 3. Jug, elongated spout. 80 mm.
No. 5. Bagware Vase. 45 mm.
No. 8. Vase. 61 mm.
No. 10. Vase, shaped. 70 mm.
No. 13. Jug. 67 mm.
No. 19. Vase, shaped. 65 mm.
No. 22. Bulbous Vase. 50 mm.
No. 23. Vase, with moulding. 60 mm.
No. 25. Vase, 2 handles. 60 mm.
No. 27. Vase, bulbous. 60 mm.
No. 45. Bagware Jug. 40 mm.
No. 53. Ewer. 76 mm.
No. 67. Tray, diamond shaped. 121 mm long.
No. 68. Tray, heart shaped. 100 mm long.
No. 71. Vase, 2 handles. 40 mm.
No. 74. Pot with 3 blunt feet. 47 mm.
No. 75. Jug. 39 mm.
No. 86. Bowl. 48 mm dia.
No. 88. Vase. 40 mm.
No. 91. Vase. 39 mm.
No. 92. Tray, hexagonal. 69 mm dia.
No. 94. Vase. 44 mm.
No. 95. Globe Vase, crinkle top. 43 mm.
No. 96. Taper Vase. 45 mm.
No. 100. Tray, spade shaped. 78 mm long.
No. 104. Vase. 65 mm.
No. 106. Jar. 60 mm.
No. 121. Vase, 2 handles. 70 mm.
No. 127. Vase, long neck. 62 mm.

No. 140/6 *Hair tidy*. 90 mm.
No. 156. Vase. 63 mm.
No. 177. Vase, bulbous. 40 mm.
No. 184. Vase, 5 sided. 40 mm.
No. 242. Stamp Box. 47 mm long.
No. 263. Salve Pot. 45 mm dia.
No. 297. Pill box, oval. 45 mm long.
No. 299. Pin Box, 5 sided. 28 mm.
No. 300. Stamp Box. 5 sided. 50 mm dia.
No. 301. Vase, bulbous. 50 mm.
No. 302. Vase. 48 mm.
No. 318. Pill box, decorated with angels' heads. 63 mm.
No. 348. Jug. 63 mm.
No. 349. Jug, slim. 66 mm.
No. 367. Pin Box, oval. 90 mm long.
No. 372. Jug, slim neck, 76 mm.
No. 374. Jug, fluted base, 73 mm.
No. 378. Sauce Boat. 120 mm long.
No. 387. Candlestick. 160 mm.
No. 502. Mustard Pot with lid and spoon. 70 mm. (This number also appears on a Toll Gate).

No. 504. Vase, octagonal. 60 mm.
No. 507. Taper Vase, octagonal. 60 mm.
No. 529. Vase, with moulding. 45 mm.
No. 531. Vase, curious wedge shaped, (almost a whistle). 50 mm.
No. 535. Vase, shaped. 52 mm.
No. 649. Vase, hexagonal wide top. 51 mm (same as 654).
No. 652. Vase, hexagonal shaped top. 57 mm.
No. 653. Vase, pentagonal tapered. 57 mm.
No. 654. Vase, hexagonal wide top. 51 mm (same as 649).
No. 657. Vase, bulbous hexagonal base. 44 mm.
No. 658. Vase, octagonal. 50 mm.
No. 713. Vase 70 mm.
No. 714. Vase. 69 mm.
Not numbered. Pill Box, Ivy leaf shaped. 57 mm long.

Grays Sports China

Trademark used by A. E.
Gray & Co., Glebe Works,
Mayer Street, Hanley.

Mark registered in 1911 but used 1908 onwards

A. E. Gray and Co. were earthenware manufacturers; the company was renamed 'Portmeirion Potteries Ltd' in 1961. The firm do not appear to have made crested china but the mark is included here because the 'Sports China' series very much appeals to collectors of pre Great War souvenir china. Vases, jugs and beakers are found with transfer prints of footballers in the colours of League teams. Each transfer design is registered, the earliest registration number being from 1907–8.

The Griffin China

Trademark used by the
London Wholesalers,
Sanderson & Young,
21 Red Lion Square.

Sanderson & Young were quite well known wholesalers who could have sold wares produced by any English Manufacturer, probably several Manufacturers supplying models during the same period. Crests recorded indicate that the models were sold in the South of England, and, judging by models recorded this mark was not used during and after the Great War. No view ware or other transfer devices have been found.

Griffin Models

Buildings coloured
Cottage. 95 mm.

Animals
Cat, Manx. 83 mm long.
Camel, one hump. 88 mm.

Home/Nostalgic
Watering Can, no details of size.

Sport
Cricket Bag. 115 mm long.

Musical Instrument
Tambourine Rd. No. 525025. No. details of size.

Miscellaneous
Lady's 18th Century Shoe, 90 mm long.

Grosvenor Ware

Trademark used by Sampson
Hancock (& Sons), Bridge
Works, Stoke, and later at the
Gordon Works, Hanley,
(renamed Corona Pottery).

For details of this china and the manufacturer see THE CORONA CHINA.

This mark was used as an alternative to the *Corona* trademark; as crests are found from all over Britain it is unlikely to have been a mark specially used for any specific wholesaler or retailer. No commemorative crests, view ware or transfer devices have been found on models. The mark appears to have been only used during the Great War.

Numbering System. Models can be found with gold or black painted stock numbers. These are recorded, where known, in the following lists:

Grosvenor Models

Ancient Artefacts
Jersey Milk Can. 53 mm.

Buildings—White
Blackpool Tower, on heavy detailed base.
  127 mm.

Animals
Cow Creamer. No. 376. 130 mm long.
Fish. 88 mm long.
Lion, lying down. No. 369. 140 mm long.
Pig, standing. No. 158. 84 mm long.

Great War
Submarine, inscribed E4. 110 mm long.
Renault Tank 100 mm long. (This is quite
  rare: the 'Corona' Renault Tank is usually
  115 mm long, this may be from the same
  mould but 15 mm is an abnormally large
  amount of shrinkage.)
Torpedo, Model of. 150 mm long.
Ghurka Knife. 140 mm long.

'Modern' Equipment
Gas cooker. 70 mm.

Miscellaneous
Horseshoe on slope. 70 mm long.

H & L

Impressed mark used by
Hewitt & Leadbeater, Willow
Potteries, Longton.

H & L

Impressed mark used 1905–1919

For details of this firm see WILLOW ART AND WILLOW CHINA.

Early in its history this firm specialised in parian ware, which carried the impressed mark 'H & L'. Many busts also carry the printed trademark *Willow Art China* so they will be found listed under that heading. Several other models have been recorded with only this impressed mark, but as they are normally found with the *Willow Art* mark they too will be found listed under that heading.

The models listed below have not been found with a printed mark and are not normally found with crests.

H & L Models

Parian/Unglazed
Ann Hathaway's Cottage. Coloured. No
  details of size.
Bust of Shakespeare. 112 mm.
*Font in which Shakespeare was baptized, Model
  of.* 95 mm dia. (found with crest of
  Shakespeare's Arms).
Lincoln Imp, not named. 130 mm.

H & S

Trademark used for a
Plymouth retailer by Hewitt
& Leadbeater, Willow
Potteries, Longton.

For details of this china and the manufacturer see WILLOW ART CHINA.

As two of the models recorded are to be found in Plymouth it is almost certain that the 'P' in 'H & S.P' stands for Plymouth. The only other two crests found on models with this mark are Hastings (often found and always on Hastings Castle Ruins with this mark) and the Island of Royal Manor, Portland, (found only once on a Great War souvenir). It is quite possible that H & S had a number of shops in English resorts, or that Hewitt & Leadbeater used pieces with this mark to complete other orders. The mark does not appear to have been used after the Great War and no transfer devices of any kind have been recorded.

H & S Models

Buildings White
Derry's Clock, Plymouth. 150 mm.
Hastings Castle Ruins. 100 mm.

Monuments
Burns, statue on square base. 170 mm.
Drake, Statue, Plymouth. 160 mm.

Great War
Battleship, impressed: *HMS Lion.* 140 mm long.
Church Bell, inscribed: *Curfew must not ring tonight.* 70 mm.

Hamilton China

Trademark used for
H. Hamilton, Milton &
Amber, Saltburn, and made
by an unknown
manufacturer.

The two models recorded are not recognisably made by any leading manufacturer. Several manufacturers made Kingfishers but the waves on the base have only been found with this mark. These models are always found with the Saltburn by the Sea Crest.

Hamilton Models

Seaside Souvenir
Two curling waves on an octagonal base, inscribed: *The glad sea waves.* 50 mm.

Bird
Kingfisher. 77 mm.

Herald China

Trademark used for a
wholesaler or retailer by an
unknown English
manufacturer.

The two models listed below are very like models made by Alfred B. Jones and Son Ltd, makers of *Grafton China*, but these models have not been compared by experienced collectors and so they cannot be attributed with any certainty. Only one of each model has as yet been recorded, the Dutchman having a Westcliffe-on-Sea crest and the Bronze Pot, a Southend on Sea crest.

Herald China Models

Ancient Artefact
Aberdeen Bronze Pot, not named. 60 mm.

Novelty
Dutchman, sitting cross legged. 85 mm.

Heraldic China

Trademark used by Sampson
Hancock (and Sons), Bridge
Works, Stoke.

For details of this firm and china manufactured see THE CORONA CHINA.

As very few models have been found with this mark and all of them would have been made before 1910 it is probable that the mark was used before the more familiar *Corona* trademark. Most of the pieces found with the 'Herald' mark are 'smalls'. One small vase has been found with a monochrome (brown) transfer print of Ellen Terry, this piece is also inscribed: 'Jubilee Souvenir 1856–1906'. Most models and 'smalls' carry seaside crests.

Heraldic Models

Alcohol
Barrel on legs. No details of size.

Miscellaneous
Queen, Chess Piece. 90 mm. (Other Chess Pieces are found with 'Corona' marks, it is possible that the whole chess range was offered for sale).

Herald Series

Trademark used for a Scottish
wholesaler by Alfred B. Jones
and Sons Ltd, Grafton China
Works, Longton, Staffs.

For details of this china and the manufacturer see GRAFTON CHINA.

Several models and some domestic ware are found with this printed mark, all have Scottish crests. One model has been found with a colour transfer view of Portaskaig, Islay.

Numbering System. Where stock numbers occur they are the same numbers as found on 'Grafton' models. Numbers where known are listed below.

Herald Series Models

Ancient Artefacts
Chester Roman Vase, not found named. 60 mm.

Animals
Dog, King Charles Spaniel, sitting. No. 390. 55 mm.
Dog, Puppy, sitting, with one ear up. No. 410. 85 mm.

Shetland Pony, not named. 105 mm long. (This model can be found with a crest of Shetland.)

Great War
Cannon Shell, inscribed: *Jack Johnson*. No. 399. 90 mm.
Bell Tent with open flaps. No. 239. 65 mm.

E Hughes and Co. China

Trademark used by E Hughes
and Co., Opal Works, Fenton.

For details of this china and manufacturer see FENTON CHINA and ROYAL CHINA.

This mark has only been found on domestic ware and the shell dish listed below. The mark was only used for a short time during the Great War of which a commemorative has been recorded, this is a design with six Flags of the Allies and inscribed: 'In Freedoms Cause'.

Hughes China Model

Seaside Souvenir
Oyster Shell dish. 130 mm long.

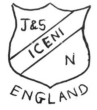

Iceni Crest China

Trademark used for
wholesalers by J. A. Robinson
and Sons, subsequently
Cauldon Ltd.

For details of this china and manufacturer see ARCADIAN CHINA.

This mark appears to have been used from around 1920 to 1925. Crests are found from all over England, it is likely that the initial L stands for London. Coloured transfer views, Poppies and 'Lucky Black Cats' transfers are found on 'smalls' with this mark. Stock numbers where used are the same as *Arcadian* numbers.

Iceni Models

Ancient Artefacts
Goodwins Sand Carafe, not named.
    82 mm.

Seaside Souvenirs
Lighthouse 150 mm.

Monuments
Caister on Sea Lifeboat Memorial. 150 mm.

Animals
Cat, sitting and smiling (grotesque, rather similar to Cheshire Cat). 75 mm.

Sussex pig, Model of, sitting inscribed: *You can push or you can shuv but I'm hanged if I'll be druv.* No. 148. 88 mm long.

Birds/Eggs
Chick, breaking out of egg. 63 mm long.

Great War
Clip of bullets, Model of. 57mm.
Tank. Rd. No. 658588. 110 mm long.
Bomb, not named. 75 mm.

Home/Nostalgic
Chair, highbacked. 90 mm.

Imperial

Trademark used by
Wedgwood and Co (Ltd),
Unicorn and Pinnox Works,
Tunstall, on cheaply
produced souvenir wares

This firm, which is often confused with the famous Josiah Wedgwood and Sons Ltd, manufactured much cheaper earthenwares. The firm specialised in table and domestic ware but obviously turned their hand to crested and view wares when these lines became good sellers. They were already making badged ware, so producing crests would be no problem. The firm began using an 'Imperial' mark in 1909 but used a much more elaborate mark than the one above on tableware. Unlike other manufacturers they did not make models to commemorate the Great War, and it seems likely that the firm was not geared to making these models. There is no evidence that crested ware was produced after the war, and most pieces found with this mark are 'smalls', generally rather heavy and cheaply made. Colour transfer view ware is reasonably well produced, but found on the same heavy pottery 'smalls' and domestic ware.

It is interesting to note that during his most successful period, 1920 to 1930, Harold Taylor Robinson managed to gain some financial control over this firm (see ARCADIAN CHINA).

Imperial Models

Ancient Artefacts
Lincoln Jack, not named. 54 mm.

Seaside Souvenirs
Suitcase, no details of size.

Birds
Pelican Jug. No details of size.

NB. Another *Imperial* Mark has been recorded. This has been found on a very small jug, only 23 mm high. It is quite probable that this trademark was used by another firm, the mark itself was not registered.

Impero

Trademark used by an
unknown German manufacturer.

This mark is mostly found on buildings and monuments and traditional souvenirs usually carrying the crest of the town for which they were designed which is very much what one would expect from a German manufacturer. Models would be made from photographs, postcards or local drawings. The two elephants on the sledge are often found unmarked and is a most attractive comic model.

Impero models are made from the usual white 'hard china' so much scorned by English manufacturers, but the models are very nicely detailed, and for the most part very desirable.

Impero Models

Buildings—White
Boston Stump Church. 125 mm.
Skegness Clock Tower. 122 mm.

Monuments
Captain Cook Monument. No details of
   size.
Hull soldiers' war memorial, with inscription:
   'Erected to the memory of the men of Hull
   who fell in the late South African War.
   122 mm.

Traditional/National Souvenirs
Devil looking over Lincoln. 95 mm.
Lincoln Stonebow. 105 mm long.
The Fiddler, York. 120 mm (rare).

Animals
Two Elephants on Sledge. Comic. 70 mm.

Ionic Heraldic

Trademark used by unknown
manufacturer for a Glasgow wholesaler.

The two other marks with the initials C.R. and Co G. were thought to have been used by Taylor and Kent (FLORENTINE CHINA) for a Glasgow wholesaler. See ATLAS HERALDIC CHINA and CALEDONIA CHINA. The 'smalls' and one model found with the 'Ionic' trademark are not recognisably made by Taylor and Kent, but it is probable that they made them. All items carry Scottish crests.

Ionic Model

Home
Bucket with rope handle. 75 mm.

Ivora Ware

Trademark thought to have
been used by William Ritchie
and Sons Ltd on domestic ware.

For details of this china and manufacturer see PORCELLE.

Many British manufacturers during the early Twentieth Century described their wares as 'Ivory'. Ivory ware, Ivory porcelain and Ivory china are terms found in many advertisements in the pottery gazette at that time. The only manufacturer, other than William Ritchie known to have used the initials W.R. was William Ridgway whose marks were later re-issued by Ridgways, Bedford Works, Shelton. It is unlikely that this firm would have used the term 'British Made', 'Made in England' being the accepted form. William Ritchie however did use 'British Manufacture' as part of their *Porcelle* mark and 'British Make' on *Mermaid*. As the firm were known to use several marks it seems likely that *Ivora Ware* was the mark they used for domestic ware.

Most pieces found with this mark could be described as 'smalls' or domestic ware.

Ivora Model

Miniature Domestic
Cheese dish and cover. 50 mm.

NB. Badly printed marks which appear to
  be *Ivyknot?* are *Wyknot?* (see *Wynot?*).

JBC
Trademark used by an
unknown manufacturer.

This obscure mark is rather a mystery. The pig listed below is not at all like models made by any known manufacturer, so one must conclude that this is not a retailer's mark. The initials J B and C however, were not used by any manufacturer during the 1900 to 1920 period. Until more models are recorded it is unlikely that the mystery will be solved. (The only recorded crest is Burnley which again does not indicate a retailer.)

JBC Models

Animals
Pig, fat and standing. Tail forms a circle and rejoins the body. 80 mm long.

Alcohol
Bottle inscribed: *One special scotch*. 90 mm.

JP
Trademark used by French
Manufacturer for French
Souvenir Market.

One Vase, 70 mm high, has been recorded with this mark with the crest Boulogne Sur Mer.

JW
Trademark used for a retailer
by J. A. Robinson Ltd.

For details of this china and manufacturer see ARCADIAN CHINA.

Only one model with this mark has been recorded, it is very recognisably from an *Arcadian* mould. Unfortunately the crest has not been recorded but one suspects the town begins with the letter R.

JW Model

Great War
Tommy and his machine gun, Model of. Rd. No. 657214. 130 mm. (The 'Arcadian' model had the Rd. No. 658676, but 'Arcadian' Registration numbers were often printed almost at random!)

Keltic
Trademark used by unknown
manufacturer for Irish and
Scottish towns.

Most items found with this mark are 'smalls' or domestic ware. The two models, a camel and the shoe are very like those made by Taylor and Kent. (See FLORENTINE CHINA), and it would seem probable that this firm used the Keltic Mark. All recorded crests are Scottish except for one: Limerick.

Keltic Models

Animals
Camel, kneeling. 95 mm long. (This is often described as lying down.)

Miscellaneous
Shoe, Ladies'. 18th Century. 95 mm long.

Kensington China

Trademark used by Royal
Crown Pottery Co, Burslem.

KENSINGTON
ENGLISH CHINA

No information is available on the history of this firm and the mark was not registered. The Bevington Brothers established a firm called the Kensington Fine Art Pottery Co in 1892 but this was a very short lived partnership, that was dissolved in 1899. The Kensington Pottery Ltd. was established in 1922 in the same Kensington Works in Hanley, and later at Burslem. The name 'Royal Crown Pottery' was not registered until 1952–7 by Trentham Bone China Ltd.

Many of the models with this mark are recognisably from *Arcadian* and *Willow Art* moulds, so it is most likely that this was one of the small firms bought and sold by Mr Harold Taylor Robinson between 1903 and 1920. (See ARCADIAN CHINA). Many of these models carry the same stock numbers as *Willow Art* models and so it seems obvious that either crested ware was produced for the firm at the Willow Pottery or that the mark was used in the same works. (Stock numbers where known will be listed below). Only town and resort crests have been found on *Kensington* models, 'smalls' and domestic ware.

Kensington Models
NB. Models positively identified as being
  from *Arcadian* or *Willow* moulds will be so
  marked.

Seaside Souvenirs
Lighthouse, octagonal. 112 mm.

Animals
Cat, Cheshire, inscribed: *Still smiling.* No.
  159. 95 mm.
Cat, haunched. 70 mm.
Teddy Bear, sitting. 90 mm (*Arcadian*).

Great War
Battleship. 140 mm long.
Field Gun, with screen. 115 mm long.
(These are both probably from WILLOW
  moulds but have not been positively
  identified.)

Home/Nostalgic
Grandfather Clock, inscribed: *Make use of
  time let not advantage slip. Shakespeare.* No.
  149. 128 mm. (*Willow*).

Novelty
Pixie, crouching on a rectangular base.
  78 mm. (Could well be Billiken the God
  of Luck.)

Alcohol
Barrel on Stand. 58 mm (probably *Willow*).

Miscellaneous
Hand holding Tulip. No. 74. 80 mm
  (*Willow*).

King China

Trademark used for a retailer
or wholesaler by Alfred B.
Jones and Son Ltd, Grafton
China Works, Longton,
Staffs.

For details of this china and manufacturer see GRAFTON CHINA.

Only one small fluted vase, 64 mm high has been found with this mark. It is very well produced, the china is delicate and the crest is beautifully printed and painted. The black painted stock number and paintresses mark are indisputably *Grafton*. Like most *Grafton* stock numbers it is difficult to read accurately, the number could be 206, 266 or 286. (206 and 286 have both been found on other *Grafton* models, but any of these could have been as badly painted.)

Right Keltic. Ladies eighteenth century shoe

Left Iceni. Lighthouse with coloured pheasant transfer

Right Kensington English China. 'Teddy Bear' sitting. The usual Arcadian' model marked 'Kensington English China'

Right Kingsway. 'Burns Chair Dumfries' and 'Mary Queen of Scots Chair', Edinburgh Castle

Left Kingsway. Model of King James Vth chair. Usual Willow Art model usually found numbered '200'

Right Kings China. Very delicate fluted vase 65 mm

Left Kingsway. Elephant cream jug

Kingsway Art or Crest China

Trademark used for a retailer
(thought to be W. H. Smith)
by Hewitt and Leadbeater,
Willow Potteries, Longton.

024 and 36 015 are stock numbers
and paintresses marks

For details of this china and manufacturer see WILLOW ART CHINA.

Hewitt and Leadbeater obviously supplied a large range of crested ware for this customer. Crests recorded come from all over Britain and it seems likely that the initials W.H.S. and S. stand for W H. Smith and Sons. The numbers which are found in the mark are either to indicate a particular order or possibly the paintress as it would have been a valuable order and checked more carefully than usual. The same numbers occur on several models and are normally prefixed by 0. Numbers 012, 024 and 030 are most common. (These numbers are not found on *Willow Art* models, where painted stock numbers also occur on models these are the same.)

The range of models indicate that Hewitt and Leadbeater supplied this firm until the end of the Great War. Some Naval crests have been recorded, including HMS CERES, HMS HOOD and HMS VALIANT. No view ware or other transfer devices have been found on models with this mark. Domestic ware and many 'small's have also been recorded.

Numbering System. The numerals from the mark are not recorded as they are found on many different models. Painted stock numbers are listed below.

Kingsway Models

Ancient Artefacts
Salt maller, Model of, no other details of inscription or size.

Buildings—White
St. Botolph's Church, Boston. 112 mm.

Monuments
Princetown, Lifeboatmans Monument. 130 mm.

Historical/Folklore
Burn's Chair, Dumfries. 85 mm.
James V Chair, Stirling Castle, 100 mm.
Mary Queen of Scots Chair, Edinburgh Castle, Model of. 75 mm.

Traditional/National Souvenirs
Bagpipes with turquoise ribbon. 118 mm long.
Burns and Highland Mary, sitting on a rock. 112 mm (rare).
Welsh Lady, bust, with black hat. 110 mm.
Welsh Leek. 55 mm.

Seaside Souvenirs
Yacht in full sail. 122 mm.
Lighthouse on base, not named. 110 mm.
Lighthouse, octagonal. No. 174. 192 mm. (This is a very large lighthouse which has not been recorded with the *Willow Art* mark.)
Eddystone Lighthouse, Model of. 86 mm.
Crab. 83 mm long.

Animals
Cat, Cheshire, inscribed: *Still smiling.* 95 mm.
Cat, sitting. 57 mm.
Cat, standing, with blue bow. No details of size. (Although not described to me as such could be an angry cat, see *Willow Art China.*)
Dog, Scottish Terrier, standing. 90 mm long.
Elephant Jug. No. 78. 70 mm.
Monkey, holding a Coconut. No. 429. 80 mm.
Ram with curly horns. 90 mm long.

Birds
Goose. 95 mm. (Not found in this size in *Willow Art.*)
Owl. 115 mm. (No other details available but too large to be usual *Willow Art. Wise Owl.*)

Great War
It is odd that no models of weapons are found with this mark, but the Edith Cavell Statue indicates that the mark was used during the Great War. Weapons are found in a range marked Norfolk (See NORFOLK CREST CHINA) also made by Hewitt and Leadbeater for W.H.S. and S.
Bugle. 70 mm long.
Edith Cavell, nurse. Patriot and Martyr, Memorial Statue, Norwich. 115 mm. (Found impressed 296.)
Florence Nightingale Statue, Model of. 160 mm.

Home/Nostalgic
Pillar Box, inscribed *GVR* and *If you haven't time to post a line, here's the pillar box.* No. 18. 80 mm. (This model has not been found marked *Willow Art.*)
Sundial, circular on circular base, with inscription 'I Mark not the hours'. 118 mm.
Thimble, no details of size (not found marked *Willow Art* without alcoholic inscription).

Comic/Novelty
Dutch Girl. 80 mm. (It is very probable that the Dutch boy was also made with this mark, but has not yet been recorded.)
Sack of Meal with mouse, inscribed: *May the mouse ne'er leave yer meal poke wi'a tear-drop'n its e e.* 63 mm.

Alcohol
Beer Barrel. 60 mm.
Foaming Tankard, inscribed: *The more we are together the merrier we will be.* 58 mm.

Sport
Cricket Ball. 48 mm.

From 1913

"LAWRENCE SHERIFFE" WARE

Kyle Series

Trademark used by Charles Waine (and Co.), Derby Works, Longton.

For further details see VENETIA CHINA.

This mark has only been recorded on one 50 mm vase with a crest of New Milton.

Lawrence Sheriffe Ware

Trademark used by an unknown English manufacturer.

Lawrence Sheriffe Ware could have been produced by any of the major crest china makers, but none in fact advertised such a line. The only piece recorded with this mark also carried the retailers mark Hands and Son, Rugby, with a crest of Rugby.

Lawrence Sheriffe Models

Ancient Artefacts
Loving Cup, 3 handled. 37 mm.

1920–4

Leadbeater Art China

Trademark used by Edwin Leadbeater, Drewery Place, Commerce Street, Longton.

Mr Edwin Leadbeater was the son of the senior partner of Robinson and Leadbeater ('R and L', makers of parian ware) and worked for that firm until 1905 when he left to go into partnership with Mr Arthur Hewitt, his brother in law. Hewitt and Leadbeater at Willow Potteries was a reasonably successful firm specialising in arms ware (see WILLOW ART AND WILLOW CHINA). Edwin Leadbeater left this partnership and started up on his own at Drewery Place in November of 1919, to manufacture heraldic china and ivory porcelain. It was a small one oven pottery started on £300 capital. This business was in fact very short lived, but there is a surprising amount of information in the Pottery Gazette about Drewery Place during this period, quite out of proportion to its size and importance. While he was a partner at Hewitt and Leadbeater that firm too was often mentioned in the Gazette, one can only speculate as to whether Mr Leadbeater was a friend of the Editor or just very good at selling himself as newsworthy.

In 1920 the Pottery Gazette reported:

'. . . he has some 80 different models in small-wares to offer, which he is decorating with crests, coat-of-arms, and various emblematic devices. These goods he is offering to all branches of the distributing trades, laying himself out specially for those retailers who can buy only in relatively small quantities. Apart from the tiny miniatures, which used to be popular selling lines at 6½d, Mr Leadbeater is bringing out models of monuments, notable buildings etc, for souvenir and commemorative purposes. These are quaintly tinted up by hand, very often quite realistically, although they are always very moderate in price. It is surprising how quickly, with enterprising zeal, some of these new models can be produced. A little time ago, Mr Leadbeater was asked by a big buyer to copy a model for a seasonal trade. Within 10 days the first sample was in the buyer's hands, and the latter was prompted to admit that it reminded him of how the German manufacturers of such wares used to handle their enquiries in the years before the war'.

In adverts for the trade at that time Mr Leadbeater announced that he specialised in arms china, miniatures, reproductions of War Memorials and historical buildings.

Edwin Leadbeater became bankrupt early in 1924, his business having run at a loss since it started. He had borrowed a great deal of money from friends and business acquaintances, and even £50 from a Bailiff to try to keep going, as he was still getting orders. Mr Leadbeater said he found he was 'selling his stuff too cheaply'. He seems to have been a bad businessman and it must be said that he was not much of a potter either.

Leadbeater Art China is often very heavy and on the whole not very well finished, but what it lacks in quality it makes up for in originality. The firm obviously got a large number of orders for War Memorials in the early years after the war and some of these were not modelled by any other manufacturers.

The firm collapsed before the vogue for 'Lucky Black Cats', 'Lucky White Heather' and other transfer devices, so these are not found marked Leadbeater. No commemoratives or view wares have been recorded either. However there is some evidence that some view ware marked 'Wagstaff and Brunt' was made by Edwin Leadbeater. (see PANORAMA).

Numbering System. Painted stock numbers were sometimes used and where these have been recorded they will be found in the following lists. The paintresses' mark is the number painted directly below the stock number.

Leadbeater Art Models

Buildings—Coloured
These are of a much higher quality than other works in the range, and Shakespeare's House and Ann Hathaway's Cottage are illustrated in the Gazette, but neither has yet been recorded. Coloured buildings can be glazed or unglazed.
Gate House, Stokesay Castle. 102 mm long.
Isaac Walton's Cottage, Shallowford. 114 mm long.
Old Market Hall, Church Stretton 1617–1839. 2 sizes: 95 mm & 105 mm long.

Buildings—White
Burns Cottage, with inscription. 70 mm long.

Monuments
Sir Walter Scott. Statue. 178 mm.

Historical
James Vth Chair, Stirling Castle, Model of. 102 mm.

Traditional/National
Welsh Hat. No. 57. 60 mm.
(Traditional figures with impressed: *England* and *Scotland,* and Leaking Boot, are illustrated in The Pottery Gazette, but have not yet been recorded).

Seaside Souvenirs
Lifeboat, no details of size.
Lighthouse, 110 mm.

Animals
Cheshire Cat, inscribed: *Still smiling.* 85 mm.
Lion, walking. 114 mm long.
Pig, fat. 102 mm long.

Great War
Red Cross Van. No. 105. 88 mm long.
Cumberland and Westmoreland war memorial. 148 mm.
Derby war memorial. 150 mm.
Harrogate war memorial, on unglazed obelisk on base with spiral steps. 153 mm.
Nottingham war memorial. 150 mm.
Nurse Cavell, Memorial. 200 mm. (This is an exact replica of the Memorial in St. Martin's, London; other Manufacturers only reproduced the top half of the Monument.)
Plymouth naval war memorial with inscription: 'He blew with his wind and they were scattered.' No. 107. 168 mm.
Ulster War Memorial with inscription: 'They died that we might live.' 140 mm.

Home/Nostalgic
Anvil. No. 78. 58 mm.

Miscellaneous
Sabot. 80 mm long.
School Boy's Cap. 67 mm long.

Lion China

Trademark used by Wittshaw
& Robinson Ltd, Carlton
Works, Stoke-on-Trent.

For details of this china and manufacturer see CARLTON CHINA.

This mark has been recorded on only one model, listed below; this has a Brighton Crest.

Lion Model

Animal
Dog. (Puppy) sitting on a glass hand mirror.
   Inscribed: *Me twice.* 105 mm long.

LIVERPOOL RD
POTTERY LTD
FINE BONE CHINA

Liverpool Rd, Pottery Ltd

Trademark used by Liverpool
Rd. Pottery Ltd.

No information is available on this firm. They were not known to register a mark and do not appear under this name in the directory of British Pottery Manufacturers published in the Twenties and Thirties. C. J. Biss & Co. (see UNMARKED) worked at 82 Liverpool Rd, Stoke during the Twenties; it is just possible that this firm used the name 'Liverpool Rd. Pottery Ltd'. The registration Number on the only model found with this mark is very late, well into the Thirties when the craze for crested china was well and truly over. It is not surprising that only one item of crest china with this mark has been recorded; there must have been little call for it at the time it was sold.

Liverpool Model

Seaside Souvenirs
Scallop Shell standing upright. Rd. No.
   925353. 110 mm long. (This carries a map
   as well as a crest of Norfolk.)

c1895–1900

Locke and Co.

Trademark used by Locke and
Co. (Ltd), Shrub Hill Works,
Worcester, and subsequently
taken over by The Worcester
Royal Porcelain Co. Ltd in
1904.

This firm, established in 1895, would have made a small range of what they described as Arms ware. In 1904 they advertised 'A variety of arms ware in heraldic colours on ivory ground, and there are original shapes amongst them.'

Many 'smalls' and some domestic ware are found with this mark. The porcelain is very fine and the crests well produced. Some vases and jugs have been found with cream, biscuit and buff grounds, these are particularly attractive. The Porcelain was exported and one Australian crest has been recorded. A coloured transfer print of the Flag of the Admiralty has been found and view ware was also produced by the firm.

Numbering System. Stock numbers were used but unfortunately these have not been recorded. Stock numbers where known are given in the list below.

c1900–1904

Locke Models

Ancient Artefacts
Newbury Leather Bottle, not named.
    70 mm (found with biscuit ground).
Roman Lamp. 100 mm long (found with
    biscuit ground).

Alcohol
Tankard, very ornate. 70 mm.

Miscellaneous
Dutch sabot. 60 mm long.

Numbered ornamental and domestic wares
No. 16. Large Pot. 65 mm.
No. 36. Vase. 41 mm.
No. 41. Cream Jug. 63 mm.
No. 43. Vase, no details of size.
No. 95. Vase. 63 mm.

M

Trademark used by an
unknown English
Manufacturer.

This very obscure and unusual mark has only been found on one Great
War Commemorative. No manufacturer was known to use the initial M in
1914, and no firm used a mark anything like the unicorn above.

The colour transfer print of five flags and a field gun is found on a mug
with a large handle, 59 mm high, inscribed: *Allies United 1914.*

Marine Art China

Trademark used for a
Brighton retailer by an
unknown manufacturer.

One small jug 55 mm high has been found with this mark and with a
Brighton crest. The Jug has no identifying marks and could have been
made by any English manufacturer. The 'Art' in the mark could indicate
this was made by Hewitt and Leadbeater, several of their marks for
retailers include the words (see WILLOW ART CHINA). Until more
models are recorded this can only be a theory.

Macintyre

Trademark used by James
Macintyre and Co. Ltd,
Washington China Works,
Burslem.

See ARGONAUTA PORCELAIN for further details.

The Macintyre mark *Argonauta Porcelain* is exactly the same as the one
above with the addition of Argonauta Porcelain printed above. It is very
probable that this mark found on a 62 mm Vase is just a badly printed
version of that.

Mayfair

Trademark used for a retailer
by Hewitt and Leadbeater,
Willow Potteries, Longton.

For details of this china and manufacturer see WILLOW ART CHINA.

The only model recorded with this mark carries a Northampton crest
and it is quite possible that the mark was used for a retailer in that county.
The Bulldog is from the same mould as one marked 'Tudor Arms', this
mark was used by Hewitt and Leadbeater.

Mayfair Model

Animal
Bulldog, standing. 125 mm long.

Right Milton. Chick No. 325
65 mm

Left Leadbeater. Large
walking lion 120 mm long.

Milton. Lucky black cat transfers
on a bottle, hair pin box and
small vase

Right Milton. Cartoon character
impressed 'Mr. Beetle'

Left Mosanic. Christchurch Priory
133 mm long

Left Mosanic. The College,
Aberystwyth. 110 mm long

Maxim China

Trademark used by Max
Emanuel and Co., Mitterteich. (Bavaria)

This German firm was established around 1900 and as early as 1901 were advertising their hard paste china miniatures in the Pottery Gazette. (The wares were shown in Shoe Lane, Holborn and do not appear to be crested.) Max Emanuel and Co. were well known producers of pink souvenir wares and obviously turned to making the crested souvenirs as soon as they would sell. The models illustrated in 1901 include comic or grotesque cats and dogs, which English manufacturers were not making at this early date. Many of the unmarked animals and buildings of German origin were probably made by this firm.

The two items found with this mark are a 43 mm vase and a trinket box.

1912–1930

Meir Arms China

Trademark used by Barker
Bros Ltd, Meir Works, Barker
Street, Longton.

Barker Bros, manufacturers of china and earthenwares, were established in 1876 and are still working today. Like most established firms they made a range of arms china during the Great War when skilled labour was unavailable. They did not advertise this time and it probably accounted for very little of their production. By 1919 they were advertising 'Teddy Tail' Nursery China and had obviously turned their attention to the new child market.

Most models found are 'smalls' or domestic ware. The arms ware is more pot than china.

Meir Models

Historical/Folklore
Mary Queen of Scots Chair, no details of size.
Mons Meg. Edinburgh Castle, Model of.
57 mm.

Seaside Souvenirs
Eddystone Lighthouse, not named.
109 mm.

Animals
Pig, standing. 88 mm long.

Great War
Tank. No details of size.

Miscellaneous
Sabot. No details of size.

Mermaid

Trademark used by William
Ritchie and Sons Ltd, 24, 26
and 28 Elder Street, Edinburgh.

For further details of this china and manufacturer see PORCELLE.

This mark is only found on domestic items including plates, egg cups, sugar bowls and jugs.

The Milton China

Trademark used by Hewitt
Bros, Willow Potteries,
Longton.

For details of this china and manufacturer see WILLOW ART CHINA.

This trademark appears to have been used after the Great War, until at least 1926. No view ware has been found with this mark which indicates its later date, *Willow* view ware was made before the war. One military 'crest' has been recorded, this is the Royal Flying Corps Badge. Many 'Lucky Black Cat' transfer devices are found, usually with red or blue edging and rims.

*Numbering System.*Stock numbers where recorded are not necessarily the same as those found on *Willow Art* pieces. Milton China was probably offered as a separate range. Stock numbers where known are listed below. Single painted numbers found on models are paintresses' marks.

Milton Models

Ancient Artefacts
Ancient tyg, not named. 2 handled. No details of size.

Monuments
Drake statue, Plymouth. 160 mm.

Animals
Donkey with saddle. No. 904. 120 mm long.
Elephant, with trunk in the air. 80 mm long.
Elephant Jug. 70 mm (Trunk is handle).
Frog, with open mouth. 60 mm.
Lion. 83 mm long.
Ram, with curly horns. 90 mm long (quite rare).

Birds
Chicken, very fluffy. No. 325. 65 mm.

Great War
Nurse, inscribed: *A friend in need.* 130 mm.
Aeroplane Propellor. 150 mm long.
Submarine, impressed: *E4*. 116 mm long.
Bandsman's Drum with cording. 60 mm.

Kit Bag with verse: 'Pack up your troubles' 74 mm.

Home/Nostalgic
Wheelbarrow. 105 mm long.

Comic/Novelty
Girl in dress and bonnet. 78 mm.
A truck of coal from . . . Wagon of black coal. 90 mm long.

Sport
Racehorse. 102 mm.

Musical Instruments
Guitar. 163 mm long.

Miscellaneous
Dagger, in decorative scabbard. 135 mm long (rare).
Ladies' 18th century shoe. 90 mm long.

Miniature Domestic
Mug, one handled. 38 mm.

Mosanic

Trademark used by a Bavarian Manufacturer, possibly Carl Schumann, Arzberg or Max Emanuel and Co. Mitterteich.

MOSANIC
MADE
IN
BAVARIA

Impressed mark

Both of the above firms were known to produce souvenir china for the British Market. The buildings marked *Mosanic* are unusual in that they are usually a drab brown colour and are unglazed. The models although very attractive and detailed are rather heavy. They were made before the war and several models have been found with the mark defaced, one can only speculate whether this was done by unhappy owners or disgruntled retailers who still held German stock at the beginning of the war. These models are usually found without crests, but some crested examples exist.

Numbering System. Stock numbers are impressed above the mark, registration numbers at the side. Where these have been recorded they are listed below.

Mosanic Models

Buildings—Unglazed
Birmingham Town Hall. 72 mm long.
Canterbury Cathedral. 112 mm long.
Chester Cathedral Rd. No. 566854. 100 mm long.
Edinburgh Castle. Rd. No. 359939. 113 mm long.
Exeter Cathedral. 150 mm long.
St. Patricks Cathedral. 103 mm.

St. Tudno's Church, Llandudno. Rd. No. 854747. 84 mm.
Ye olde town house of ye Abbots of Buckfast, ye close Exeter. No. 0372. Rd. No. 876827.92 mm long.

Seaside Souvenirs
Corbierre Lighthouse, Jersey, Model of. No. 0719. Rd. No. 558636. 84 mm.

MOSCHENDORF
BAVARIA

Moschendorf

Trademark used by unknown
German Manufacturer.

This mark has only been found on a crested 6 inch tea plate.

Mother Shipton China

Trademark used for the
retailer J. W. Simpson,
Dropping Well, Knaresboro',
by Wiltshaw and Robinson
Ltd, Carlton Works,
Stoke-on-Trent.

For details of this china and manufacturer see CARLTON CHINA.

All models found with this mark have either a crest of Knaresboro' or Mother Shipton, accompanied by the inscription: 'Near to the Knaresboro Dropping Well. I first drew breath as records tell'. Some 'smalls' and models are found with a hand coloured transfer print of Mother Shipton surrounded by a ship, aeroplane, train, telephone or radio wires, inscribed: *Prophecies of Mother Shipton*.

Such items usually have the following verse on the reverse: 'Around the world thoughts shall fly. In the twinkling of an eye. In the air shall men be seen, carriages without horses shall go, iron in the water shall float, as easy as a wooden boat'. No wonder Mother Shipton was so popular a folklore figure in 1920.

Stock Numbers where found seem to be those found on Carlton models.

Mother Shipton Models

Historical/Folklore
Mother Shipton, with some colouring. 2
  sizes: 92 mm & 190 mm. (Large size can
  be found in lustre.)
Mother Shipton with some colouring
  standing on lustre oval base. Inscribed:
  Good luck. 90 mm. (This model has an
  alternative inscription to the common
  one recorded above. 'Near this petrifying
  well, I first drew breath as records tell'.)

Animals
Deer, with antlers, sold as a pair one facing
  right and one left. 217 mm to top of
  antler.

Great War
Munitions worker, inscribed: *Doing her bit.
  Shells and more shells.* Some colouring.
  140 mm.

Edith Cavell, statue, inscribed: *Brussels dawn
  October 12th 1915. Sacrifice, Humanity.*
  163 mm.

Home/Nostalgic
Frying Pan. Rd. No. 537474. 110 mm long.
Warming Pan. Rd. No. 497685. No. 392.
  127 mm long.

Comic/Novelty
I'm forever blowing bubbles, Pears advert blue
  boy blowing bubbles. Clothes blue,
  bubble and bowl lustre. Rd. No. 681378.
  110 mm.

Alcohol
Toby Jug, with inscription: 'This is an exact
  copy in miniature of the old Toby Jug'.
  70 mm.

Musical Instrument
Upright Piano. 64 mm.

Nautilus Porcelain

Tradename used by The
Nautilus Porcelain Co., Possil
Pottery, Glasgow.

1903–1913

This firm, established in 1896, and for sometime restyled the Possil Pottery Co., was disbanded in 1913. Based in Glasgow, the Nautilus Porcelain Co. made many Scottish crested pieces, but English Crest can be found, the firm having showrooms in 47, Holborn Viaduct, London. The Company specialized in producing ornamental porcelain, tea sets, dessert services,

Leadbeater 'Nurse Cavell'
Memorial and 'Harrogate War
Memorial'

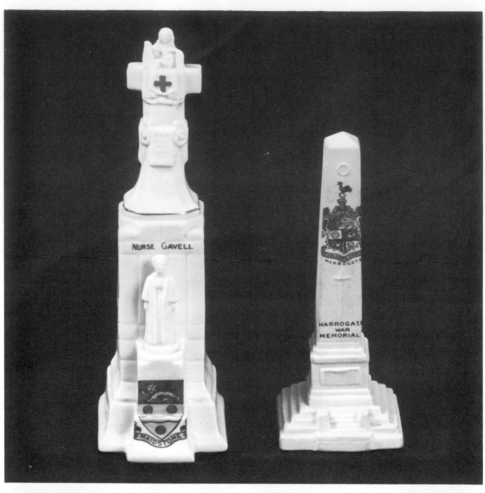

Right Mother Shipton. Vase with
Mother Shipton crest

Left Mother Shipton. Mother
Shipton on the usual Carlton
oval base. Some colouring

Right Nautilus. 56 mm Vase with
colour transfer of 'House of John
Knox'. Coloured thistle on
reverse. Reverse of crested spill
vase showing tudor rose 110 mm

Left Nautilus. Old Boot 63 mm
long

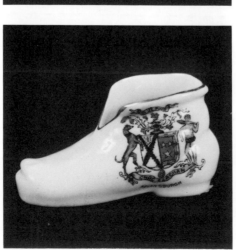

NAUTILUS

PORCELAIN
GLASGOW

c1907–1913

trinket sets and figures, so naturally they quickly turned to arms and view ware. The Nautilus Porcelain Co. were making a special feature of these as early as 1903, and by 1907 were producing large quantities. Crests were applied to a range of domestic porcelain ware as well as a 'large assortment of small fancy china pieces'.

Nautilus is fine china and some pieces of 'egg shell' lightness can be found. The crests and the very small quantity of view ware that has survived are very well produced. 'Smalls' with the early mark often have a black transfer print of a tudor rose, thistle or tartan shield on the reverse, and these can be found hand painted.

Obviously the range of models is small as the firm went out of business before the Great War, but there are many 'smalls' and much domestic ware to be found, and these are well worth looking for as they are of such good quality.

Numbering System. No stock numbers are printed on the china. The painted numbers on the base are paintresses' works numbers, 10 and 14 being most often found.

Nautilus Models

Ancient Artefacts
Loving Cup, three handled. 2 sizes: 39 mm and 50 mm.
Puzzle Jug. 70 mm.

Traditional/National
Irish Wooden Noggin. 57 mm.
Highland Whisky Bowl. 60 mm dia.
Thistle Jug. 64 mm.

Animals
Pig, fat and standing. 70 mm long.

Home/Nostalgic
Coal scuttle, cylindrical on bow feet. 70 mm long.
Garden Urn. 63 mm.
Milk Churn. 76 mm.
Miner's Lamp. 63 mm.

Miscellaneous
Dutch Sabot. 90 mm long.
Old Boot. 63 mm long.
Top Hat. No details of size.

Miniature Domestic
Beaker. 39 mm.
Cheese Dish, 2 pieces. 70 mm long.
Cup. 39 mm.
(It is quite probable that a complete range of miniature domestic items was offered for sale.)

Norfolk Crest China

Trademark used for W. H. Smith and Sons by Hewitt and Leadbeater, Willow Potteries, Longton
—subsequently Hewitt Bros.

For details of this china and manufacturer see WILLOW ART CHINA.

This is the second mark used by Hewitt and Leadbeater for W. H. Smith and Sons, the other being *Kingsway Art China*. This appears to be a later mark, used from the end of the Great War to the mid-twenties. A half pint mug has been recorded with the *Norfolk* mark, it has a colour transfer print of H.M.S. Iron Duke, an Aeroplane, the Flags of the Allies and a peace inscription. Black Cat transfers are also found indicating the later date and some models could have come from *Arcadian* moulds once the firms had combined.

Stock numbers where found would be the same as WILLOW ART models.

Norfolk Models

Monuments
Sir Robert Peel statue. With inscription and history. 168 mm.

Traditional/National Souvenirs
Lancashire clog. 88 mm long.
Welsh Hat, with blue band. No. 75. 57 mm.

Animals
Dog, Bull terrier, standing. 60 mm.
Elephant, walking. 52 mm.
Pig, standing. 85 mm long.

Birds
Hen egg cup. 76 mm long.

Great War
Battleship, impressed: H.M.S Lion. 140 mm long.
British Tank. Rd. No. 658588. 102 m long. (Usual Willow Art version is around 92 mm long. This could be from the same mould but it is rather larger than one would expect. It is possible that another mould was used, possibly *Arcadian*.)
Kitbag with verse: 'Pack up your troubles'. 74 mm.
Matlock Bath War Memorial, inscribed: *He blew with his winds and they were scattered.* 182 mm.

Home/Nostalgic
Grandfather Clock, inscribed: *Make use of time let not advantage slip. Shakespeare.* 128 mm.

Comic/Novelty
Jester, double faced bust. Some colouring. 2 sizes: 65 mm & 90 mm. (Could be *Arcadian* mould.)
Monk, jovial and plump. No glass. 90 mm.

Alcohol
Monk, jovial and holding glass. 70 mm.

Nornesford China

Trademark thought to have been used by Edwin Leadbeater, Brewery Place, Commerce Street, Longton.

This mark was registered in 1920, by a firm given as Nornesford Ltd, Commerce Street, Longton. No Company of this name ever seems to have been registered. In 1920 Edwin Leadbeater had left Hewitt and Leadbeater and had opened his own business in Commerce Street, Longton. (See LEADBEATER ART CHINA.) It is very possible that Edwin Leadbeater decided to use this title and registered the work early in 1920 and then decided that the Leadbeater name was worth trading under. The mark was used very little and only one model has been found so far. No Top Hat with a Leadbeater Art Mark has been recorded but the stock number on the Nornesford hat is very much in the style of Leadbeater stock numbers.

Nornesford Model

Miscellaneous
Top Hat. No. 173. 45 mm.

One and All

Trademark used by an unknown British Manufacturer.

Most china found with this mark are 'smalls' with 'Lucky Black Cat' transfers, and could have been made by any of the firms active in the mid-twenties. The models recorded below are very similar to *Willow Art* models but it is more likely that the mark was used by the huge CAULDON empire which combined the *Willow Art* and *Arcadian* moulds and marks. (See ARCADIAN CHINA.) This mark is very like a mark used by Cauldon for Pearsons of Blackpool. (See PALATINE CHINA.)

One and All Models

Ancient Artefacts
Salisbury sack, not named. 50 mm.

Buildings—White
Anne Hathaway's Cottage. 105 mm long.

Animals
Teddy Bear. No. 27. 65 mm.
Goose. No. 114. 95 mm. (Not found marked *Willow Art* but found marked *Kingsway Art*, another mark used by Hewitt and Leadbeater/Hewitt Bros.)

Oxford Art China

Trademark used for a retailer
by Hewitt and Leadbeater.

For details of this china and manufacturer see WILLOW ART CHINA.

The only model found with this mark has a Barrow-in-Furness crest which seems to indicate that the W. & Co. in the mark had a chain of gifts shops. One would expect the original shop to have been in Oxford.

Oxford Art Model

Historical/Folklore
Sir Walter Scott's Chair, Abbotsford, Model of.
   80 mm.

P

Trademark used by an
unknown German
Manufacturer

This mark is found on 'smalls', ancient artefacts and domestic ware with crests from all over Great Britain. The ware is the continental hard china, and the models recorded indicate that the mark was used before the Great War.

P Models

Ancient Artefacts
Ancient Tyg, 2 handled. No details of size.
Loving Cup, 3 handled. No details of size.

Home/Nostalgic
Cauldron. No details of size.

Miniature Domestic
Cheese dish and cover, 2 pieces. 55 mm.
Teapot. 65 mm.

Palatine China

Trademark used by Pearsons
of Blackpool, manufactured
by J. A. Robinson Ltd,
subsequently Cauldon Ltd.

For details of this china and manufacturer see ARCADIAN CHINA.

This mark has been found on only two models, one of which is from an ARCADIAN mould. This mark was probably used for a 'Palatine Bazaar' in Blackpool, as only Blackpool crests have been recorded. This mark is very similar to one used in the mid-Twenties, on *Willow Art* moulds indicating that both marks were used by the Cauldon group. (See ONE AND ALL). The models below seem to be earlier than the 'One and All' models, indicating that the mark was re-used later.

Palatine Models

Animals
Dog, sitting with a tear on cheek. 80 mm.

Great War
Tank, Model of. Rd. No. 658588. 115 mm
   long (*Arcadian mould*).

P.A.L.T.

Trademark used by an
unknown German
Manufacturer after the Great
War.

This mark has been found on domestic ware with crests from all over Great Britain. The use of 'Czecho-Slovakia' as the country of origin proves that the mark was used after 1920.

Right Panorama. 'Model of Sir Walter Scott's Chair at Abbotsford'

Left Panorama. 76 mm flask with coloured transfer of 'War Memorial Stoke-under-Ham'. Colour transfer of 'Old Bridge Billinghay' on a welsh hat

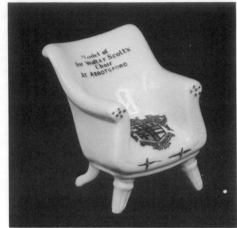

Right Porcelle. Glengarry showing coloured thistle, crest on reverse

Left Pearl. Lighthouse 'Pepper' pot 100 mm

Porcelle. Duck, begging puppy and pig. Three from a range of small and rather unexciting animals and birds

Right Norfolk. 75 mm vase with lucky black cat transfer inscribed 'Jazz Waltz'

Left Norfolk. Plump monk. 90 mm

Panorama

Trademark used by Wagstaff
and Brunt on china
manufactured by Edwin
Leadbeater, Commerce
Street, Longton.

For details of this china and manufacturer see LEADBEATER ART
CHINA.

Wagstaff and Brunt were registered as pottery manufacturers from 1880
to 1927 but most of the wares stamped with their name appears to have
been made by other manufacturers. They specialised in commemorative
china, and it could well be that they were dealers rather than
manufacturers. The miniatures marked 'Panorama' were definitely made
by Edwin Leadbeater, who could possibly have taken this contract with
him from Hewitt and Leadbeater. I suspect the trademark *Panorama* was
chosen because the range was intended to be only view ware. Many pieces
marked Panorama carry coloured transfer views rather than a crest, but
crests do occur. Apart from the usual views of castles and sea fronts there
are some transfers of War Memorials to be found, including The
Cenotaph, Stoke under Ham and Hemyock War Memorials. Stock
numbers where they are used coincide with *Leadbeater Art* stock
numbers.

Panorama Models

Unglazed/Parian
Burns and Highland Mary. 125 mm.

Monuments
Sir Robert Peel statue on large plinth with
  inscription 'the eighth Honorable Sir
  Robert Peel Bart born Feb. 18th 1788.
  Erected in the year 1830 member of
  Parliament—Tamworth—which town he
  continued to represent until his death
  July 2nd 1850'. 165 mm.

Historical
Bunyans Chair, Model of. 95 mm.
Sir Walter Scott's Chair at Abbotsford. No. 85.
  80 mm.

Traditional/National
Welsh Hat. No. 57. 60 mm.

Birds
Chick. 33 mm.

Great War
Red Cross Van. No. 103. 88 mm long.

Home/Nostalgic
Anvil   No. 78. 58 mm.

Miscellaneous
School Boy's Cap. 67 mm long (Some
  collectors are sure this is a cricket cap and
  not as listed).

Patriotic China

Trademark used during the
Great War by Birks, Rawlins
and Co (Ltd), Vine Pottery,
Stoke.

For details of this china and manufacturer see SAVOY CHINA.

The items with this mark so far recorded carry military crests and were
obviously made to commemorate the Great War. The teapot listed below
has a colour transfer with the verse 'A soldier of the King' and a crest of the
'11th Welsh'. Some domestic ware has also been found with this transfer
and crest. Another pot has the crest of Seaford Camp. These pieces are
obviously of great interest to the Great War collector and one would
assume that there must be further crests to record.

Patriotic Model

Miniature Domestic
Teapot. 65 mm.

Pearl Arms China

Trademark used on china
manufactured by Hewitt
Bros, Willow Potteries Ltd. Longton.

The middle initial could possibly
be a 'C' and not a 'G'

For details of this china and manufacturer see WILLOW ART CHINA.

The initials A. G. R. & Co Ltd were used by the firm of A. G. Richardson and Co, Gordon Pottery, Tunstall, Staffs, established in 1915. This firm manufactured *Crown Ducal* ware and did not advertise crested miniatures. The models with the *Pearl Arms* mark are undoubtedly from the same moulds as those marked *Willow Art*. Whether this range was made for another manufacturer or retailer or was an alternative trademark used by Hewitt Bros must remain a mystery. The use of the initials A. G. R. or A. C. R. and the diversity of crests seems to indicate that the range was made for another manufacturer.

No military crests, transfer devices or views have been recorded on china with this mark. Domestic ware and 'smalls' are often found. Stock numbers where they occur coincide with those found on *Willow Art* models.

Pearl Arms Models

Historical/Folklore
James V Chair, Stirling Castle. 100 mm.

Traditional/National Souvenirs
Blackpool Big Wheel. 100 mm.
Lancashire Clog. No. 152. 88 mm long.

Seaside Souvenirs
Lighthouse, not named. 110 mm.

Animals
Cat, sitting. 70 mm.
Bulldog, black, emerging from kennel, inscribed: *The Black Watch*. No. 288, 70 mm long.
Dog, Collie, standing. 85 mm.
Elephant, walking. No. 113. 52 mm.
Mouse. 62 mm.
Pig, standing. 85 mm long.

Birds
Canary on rock. No. 27. 98 mm.
Swan, with head on breast. 58 mm.

Great War
Monoplane, with fixed prop. 146 mm long.
Battleship, 4 funnels. No. 213. 127 mm long.
British tank, Model of, with trailing wheels. Rd. No. 358588. 130 mm long.
Kit Bag with verse: 'Pack up your troubles in your old kit bag'. 74 mm.
Officer's Peaked Cap. 70 mm dia.

Pickelhaube. (German spiked Helmet). 50 mm.
Fireplace, inscribed: *Keep the home fires burning.* Some colouring. 100 mm long.

Home/Nostalgic
Basket, oblong with handle. No. 224. 76 mm long.
Grandfather Clock, inscribed: *Make use of time let not advantage slip. Shakespeare.* No. 149. 128 mm.
Sundial, circular on square base, with inscription: 'I mark not the hours'. No. 205. 98 mm.

Comic/Novelty
Billiken, the God of Luck, often found unnamed. 73 mm.
Billiken, the God of Luck, sitting on high-backed chair. 100 mm.

Alcohol
Whisky Bottle with cork, inscribed: *One special scotch.* 88 mm.

Miscellaneous
Hand holding a tulip. No. 74. 80 mm.
Policeman's Helmet. No details of size. (Not found marked Willow Art.)

Miniature Domestic
Cheese dish and cover. 45 mm.

Pheonix China

Trademark used by an
unknown English
Manufacturer.

This obscure mark has only been recorded on a plate, 60 mm diameter, with an Eastbourne crest. Until more items are found it is impossible to determine who used the mark.

Podmore China

Trademark used by Podmore
China Co., Elm Street,
Hanley.

1921–c1927 on crested china

A Mr A. J. Podmore of the Tunstall Art Pottery Co. in 1920 announced that in consequence of the expiration of his lease the blocks, moulds and cases and other implements connected with his range of useful and ornamental pottery were for disposal. In 1921 The Podmore China Co. was established in Hanley and one can only assume that Mr A. J. Podmore had found new premises. (This indication of the sale of moulds in Staffordshire helps to explain why so many firms produced similar if not identical models during this period.) The Podmore China Co. continued until 1941 when it became Sylvan Pottery Ltd.

Podmore China Co. produced crested china miniatures from 1921 to at least the middle if not late twenties. No early historical shapes have been recorded and the whole range of models seems to be from the twenties and not the Nineteen hundreds. The range includes some coloured models including two delightful children at the seaside which would have sold well in the mid-twenties. The models are rather on the large and heavy side but well finished and painted. Some 'Lucky White Heather' transfers have been found on models and 'smalls' but no other transfer devices, views or commemoratives have been recorded.

(No stock numbers are found on Podmore China, the small dots and dashes in colour found on the base are paintresses' marks.)

Podmore Models

Unglazed/Parian
Bust of Burns, on square unglazed base with crest. Impressed *Burns* and *Podmore China Co* on reverse. 150 mm.

Buildings—Coloured
Bell Hotel, Abel Fletcher's house in John Halifax gentleman. Not crested. 67 mm (can also be found uncoloured).

Buildings—White
Bell Hotel, Abel Fletcher's house in John Halifax Gentleman. 67 mm (can also be found coloured).
Big Ben. 101 mm.
God's Providence House AD 1652. 2 sizes: 70 mm & 90 mm.
King Charles Tower Chester. 88 mm.
Leicester, Clock Tower. 191 mm.
Lincoln Cathedral, west front. 106 mm.
Margate, Clock Tower. 143 mm.
St. Pauls Cathedral. 105 mm.
Westminster Abbey. 127 mm.

Monuments (including Crosses)
Banbury, The Cross. 158 mm.
Bunyans Statue, Model of. 2 sizes: 173 mm & 206 mm.

Historical/Folklore
Burns Chair, Model of. 93 mm.
Mary Queen of Scots Chair in Edinburgh Castle, Model of. No details of size.
Mother Shipton, standing figure. 75 mm.
Tewkesbury Cross Stocks and Whipping Post. 105 mm (rare).

Traditional/National Souvenirs
Chester Imp, recumbent. 100 mm long. (This is a rare model, the Imp is in the Nave of Chester Cathedral.)
Lancashire Clog. 73 mm long.
Lincoln Imp sitting on round base. 105 mm.

Seaside Souvenirs
Lifeboatman on plinth. 142 mm.
Beachy Head Lighthouse, with black band. 120 mm (size varies).
North Foreland Lighthouse, Broadstairs. 128 mm.
Oyster shell on log base. 80 mm.
Whelk shell, inscribed: *Listen to the sea.* 100 mm long.
Child, sitting with knees under chin, wearing bathing suit. Impressed: *Splash me.* Some colouring. 140 mm (rare).
Child, standing on rock draped in towel. Some colouring. 115 mm.

Animals
Cat, grotesque with almost human face and wearing a black cap. Inscribed: *Puss Puss.* 105 mm.
Cat with long neck. 120 mm.
Dog, Scottie, looking out of kennel. Inscribed: *Black Watch.*
Dogs, black with green bow. 70 mm.
Dog, Scottie, wearing a Tam O'Shanter. 75 mm.
Elephant. 64 mm long.
Pig, standing. 100 mm long.
Shetland Pony. 110 mm long.

Birds
Hen, with red comb. 66 mm.
Penguin. 88 mm.

Right Podmore. Penguin 88 mm
and hen with red comb 66 mm

Left Podmore. A very clumsy
model of a pig showing how
crude models from this pottery
can be

Right Podmore. Fireplace with
clock on mantlepiece. Some
colouring

Left Podmore. 'Beachy Head'
Lighthouse with black band and
'North Foreland Lighthouse
Broadstairs'

Right Podmore. 'War Memorial,
Matlock Bath' 190 mm

Left Podmore. 'Clock Tower
Hastings' with matching crest

Great War
Bust of *HRH, Prince of Wales*, in uniform, on square base. 155 mm.
Cenotaph, inscribed: *The Glorious Dead. MCMXIV–MCMXIX*. Green wreaths. 3 sizes: 84 mm, 130 mm & 165 mm
Edith Cavell Memorial, London. Inscribed: *Edith Cavell Brussels dawn October 12th 1915. Humanity Sacrifice.* 2 sizes: 142 mm & 170 mm.
Edith Cavell Statue, Norwich. 3 sizes: 102 mm, 138 mm & 165 mm.
Matlock Bath War Memorial. Often found un-named. 190 mm.
Blackpool War Memorial, inscribed: *1914 in memory of our glorious dead 1918.* 145 mm.

Home/Nostalgic
Grandfather Clock, with inscription: 'Make use of Time'. 123 mm.
Fireplace with clock on mantelpiece, inscribed: *Home sweet home. East or west home is best.* Some colouring. 98 mm.

Comic/Novelty
Billiken, sitting on high backed chair, inscribed: *The God of things as they ought to be.* 102 mm.
Sack of Coal, some colouring. 2 sizes: 60 mm & 95 mm. Large size inscribed: *If you can't afford a truck—buy a sack.*

Cartoon/Comedy Characters
Mr Pussy Foot. All water we don't think. Standing figure, some colouring. 96 mm. (Mr. Pussy Foot was an American Prohibitionist.)

Transport
Charabanc. 127 mm long.

Miniature Domestic
Cheese Dish, 1 piece. 50 mm.

Porcelle
Trademark used by William Ritchie and Son Ltd, 24, 26 and 28 Elder Street, Edinburgh.

From c1910–1924

This mark was registered in 1910 and published in the Pottery Gazette in October of that year. William Ritchie and Son Ltd were described as Porcelain and Earthenware manufacturers. No information or record of this firm can be found in standard works on the pottery industry or in the Pottery Gazette and therefore for the moment we have little other information. The firm seems to have begun producing a large range of crested china before the Great War and could appear to have stopped doing so before the mid-twenties, as no coloured models or 'lucky' transfers have been found. Most crests recorded are from Scotland, Ireland and the North of England and obviously the firm concentrated its sales efforts in these areas.

No commemorative transfer items, view ware or any other form of decoration on miniatures or domestic ware has been recorded. A great deal of crested domestic ware has been recorded including teapot stands, plates, butter dishes and trays of various kinds. These sometimes are found with a buff instead of a white body. *Porcelle* china is more cream or ivory than white, and is fairly fine. The crests are rather well produced.

Numbering System. Stock numbers are sometimes found painted on the base of models and these are listed where known.

Porcelle Models

Unglazed/Parian
Bust of Robbie Burns on glazed plinth. 135 mm.

Ancient Artefacts
Newbury Leather Bottle. (not named.) 65 mm.
Whisky Quaich. (not named.) No. 2. 30 mm.

Buildings—White
Burns Cottage, Model of, with inscription: 'Robert Burns the Ayrshire Poet was born in this cottage on 25th Jan AD 1759. Died 21st July 1796. Age 37½ years. 70 mm long.
Cottage. 75 mm long.
Windmill, with revolving sails. No. 470. 108 mm (including sails).

Historical/Folklore
Hindu God or Pixie (variously described) on circular base. No. 35. 88 mm.

Traditional/National Souvenirs
Irish Harp with moulded shamrocks. 105 mm.
Thistle Vase. No. 329? 48 mm.

Seaside Souvenirs
Bathing Machine, inscribed: *Morning dip*.
 No. 428. 87 mm.
Fisherman, with Tub, inscribed: *Waiting for
 the smacks*. 67 mm.
Scallop Shell. 70 mm long.
Whelk Shell. 100 mm.

Animals
Cat, sitting. No. 992. 51 mm.
Dog, puppy begging. 68 mm.
Duck, 70 mm long.
Pig, lying down. 80 mm long.
Pig, standing. 70 mm long.
Rabbit, crouching with flat ears. 30 mm.
Rabbit, sitting. 80 mm.
Seal. 50 mm.
Grotesque animal/bird. 105 mm.

Great War
Sailor, standing with hands on hips.
 130 mm.
British Airship on stand. 130 mm long.
HMS Queen Elizabeth. 165 mm long.
Torpedo Boat Destroyer, Model of. 140 mm
 long.
Submarine, inscribed: *E1*. 150 mm long.
Armoured Car with 2 guns. 127 mm long.
British motor searchlight, Model of. 90 mm
 long.
Red Cross Van. 110 mm long.
Tank with 2 steering wheels, inscribed:
 HMS Donner Blitzen and *Model of British
 tank first used by British troops at the Battle of
 Ancre Sep 1916*. 160 mm long.
Field Gun. 170 mm long.
Howitzer. 2 sizes: 140 mm & 168 mm long.

Machine gun, Model of, on tripod (2 pieces).
 80 mm.
Trench Mortar, no details of size.
Shell inscribed: *Iron rations for Fritz*. 78 mm.
Glengarry. 2 sizes: 70 mm & 100 mm long.
 Larger model has coloured heather in
 band.
Colonial soldiers Hat. 90 mm long.
Tommy's Steel Helmet. 82 mm long.
Fireplace, inscribed: *Keep the home fires
 burning*. No. 629. 70 mm.

Home/Nostalgic
Baby's Cradle. 55 mm.
Iron and stand. 70 mm long.
Milk Churn with fixed top. 60 mm.
Wooden tub. 39 mm.

Sport
Golf Club Head. No. 442. 65 mm.

Musical
Banjo. 137 mm long.

Transport
Open Motor Car. No details of size.

Miscellaneous
Boot. No. 14. 58 mm long.
Sabot with turned up toe. No. 312. 88 mm
 long.
Top Hat. 45 mm.

Miniature Domestic
Cup and Saucer. 40 mm.
Mug. 47 mm.

Premier

Trademark used by a
wholesaler on china
manufactured by Taylor &
Kent (Ltd), Florence Works,
Longton.

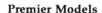

For details of this china and manufacturer see FLORENTINE CHINA.
   This china was made by the great mass producers of crested ware, Taylor & Kent. H. H. & Co. were probably a London firm of wholesalers, as crests are found from all over Britain but mostly from the South of England. No view ware or transfer devices have been found on china with this mark but one military crest has been recorded. 'Royal Military College, Camberley' (This must be the most common military crest—presumably everyone bought a souvenir of their stay there!) Domestic ware, including Bagware and 'smalls' are often found.

Premier Models

Traditional/National Souvenirs
Welsh Hat. 57 mm.

Seaside Souvenirs
Suitcase. 77 mm long.

Animals
Manx cat. 61 mm.
Frog. 72 mm long.
Pig, standing, inscribed: *The pig that won't
 go*. 95 mm long.

Home/Nostalgic
Coal scuttle, helmet shaped. 65 mm.
Oriental lamp. (Aladdin's Lamp). 100 mm
 long.

Musical
Tambourine, 70 mm dia.

Miscellaneous
Shoe, Ladies', 18th Century. 95 mm long.

Miniature Domestic
Coffee Pot. 55 mm.

Princess China

Trademark used for a
Blackpool retailer by an
unknown manufacturer.

The models recorded with this mark are unusually detailed and finished.
All models found, several of each of the two below have been recorded,
have a Blackpool crest. The mark one can only assume was used for a
Blackpool retailer with the initials J.B. & Co. The manufacturer is much
more difficult to identify, and could even be German. Until further models
are found it is not possible to make a suggestion.

Princess Models

Buildings—White
Blackpool Tower, with buildings. Very
    detailed all domes and pinnacles are fully
    gilded. 155 mm.

Birds
Bird standing on rock, tail and wings have
    black markings. 80 mm.

Queens China or Ware

Trademark used by Birks,
Rawlins and Co. (Ltd), Vine
Pottery, Stoke.

For further details of this china and manufacturer see SAVOY CHINA.

Birks, Rawlins & Co. manufactured china and earthenware and
advertised Queens China as a line of tableware. This mark is found on
much heavier models generally than those marked *Savoy* so one can only
assume that this was a cheaper range. (The lack of the usual initials B.R. &
Co. seems also to indicate that the firms were not very proud of this
range.) The mark appears to have been used during the same period as
Savoy, but no models of buildings have been recorded. Some of the models
below have not been recorded in the Savoy range.

'Smalls' have been found with the same Great War commemorative
inscriptions and crests as recorded on *Savoy* models. No other transfer
devices or views have been found.

Stock numbers were used and do not coincide with Savoy stock
numbers. (Birks & Rawlins use of stock numbers is often unreliable—see
SAVOY CHINA for details.) Stock numbers are given where known in the
following lists.

Queens Models

Ancient Artefacts
Shakespeare's Jug, not named. 63 mm.

Historical/Folklore
Burns Chair, not named. 76 mm.

Traditional/National Souvenirs
Welsh Hat, 50 mm.

Seaside Souvenirs
Bathing machine, No. 425, 60 mm.
Rowing Boat, 127 mm long.

Countryside
Beehive, 70 mm.

Animals
Bear, dancing, with muzzle. No. 307.
    102 mm (rare model).
Dog, angry and barking. 100 mm long.
Fish, No. 640. 102 mm long.
Hare, No. 235. 74 mm.

Lion, sitting on base. No. 239. 104 mm.
Pig, lying down. 80 mm long.
Seal. 55 mm long.

Birds
Birds on tree trunk, no details of size.
Duck, swimming, 40 mm long.
Penguin, 76 mm.

Great War
Ambulance, Red Cross Van. 108 mm long.
Ambulance, with Rolls Royce front.
    115 mm long.
Field Gun. 140 mm long.
British Trench Mortar Gun. 110 mm long.
    (The 'Savoy' version is only 98 mm long
    but the difference in size could be
    accounted for by the use of a different
    earthenware body.)
Shell. 70 mm.
Airman's Hat. 72 mm long.
Colonial Hat. 92 mm long.

Right Podmore. Child wearing bathing suit impressed 'Splash me'. Some colouring, pink cheeks, blue eyes and red mouth

Left Podmore. Parian bust of Burns, impressed on reverse 'Podmore China Co'

Queens. Hare and angry dog, two rather detailed models

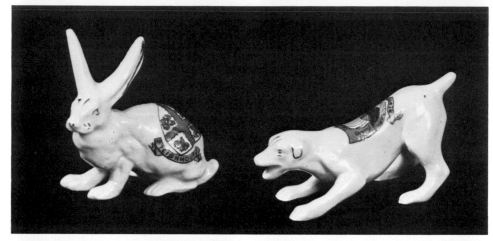

Right Queens. An unusual model, a lion sitting on a small square base

Left Queens. Policeman with hands behind back holding truncheon 105 mm

Left Queens. Humpty Dumpty salt and pepper pots

French Trench Helmet. 72 mm long.
Glengarry. 70 mm long.
Officer's Peaked Cap. 72 mm long.
(These hats are unnamed and vary in size
from 'Savoy' models.)
Bandman's Drum. 55 mm dia.

Comic/Novelty
Humpty Dumpty Salt and Pepper Pots.
80 mm.
Policeman holding truncheon. No. 327.
105 mm.

Musical Instruments
Banjo. 136 mm long.

Queens Crest China

Trademark used for S. P. & Co.
Ltd of 57 King St, Manchester,
by Arkinstall & Son Ltd,
Arcadian Works, Stoke-on-Trent.

For details of this china and manufacturer see ARCADIAN CHINA.

As models with this mark have been found with crests from all over Great Britain, and also of Paris, one must assume that S. P. & Co. Ltd of Manchester was a wholesaler. (Obviously some wares printed with this mark would also have been used by Arkinstall to supply other retailers if they had production problems.)

Arkinstall produced a range for this firm that was much finer and more carefully finished than their own *Arcadian* range. Most items found with this mark are 'smalls', some of which may well be un-named ancient artefacts. The models recorded indicate that the mark was used before the Great War, several pieces have been found with the crest 'La Ville-de-Paris' and the addition to the mark of 'Importe D'Angleterre'.

Numbering System. Stock numbers found on Queens Crest models do not coincide with *Arcadian* numbers. Queens Crest was obviously offered as a completely separate range. Stock numbers where known are given in the following lists.

Queens Crest Models

Ancient Artefacts
Colchester Vase, inscribed *Model of Famous Colchester Vase now in Museum.* No. 504. 50 mm. (This stock number is likely to be an 'Arcadian' number.)
Fountains Abbey Cup, inscribed *The Abbots cup from the original at Fountains Abbey.* No. 23821, 50 mm.
Irish Bronze Pot, Model of Ancient. No. 1834. 45 mm.
Jersey Milk Can. Model of Ancient No. 2424, 60 mm.
Lincoln Jack from original in museum, model of. No. 1564, 65 mm.

Animals
Tortoise. Rd. No. 456065, 72 mm long.

Numbered Ornamental Wares
Some of these could be un-named ancient artefacts.
No. 1724. Small pot on three feet, 43 mm.
No. 1774. Fluted Vase, 43 mm.
No. 1824. Ewer, 60 mm.
No. 3164. Pot, 50 mm.
No. 3594. Vase, 50 mm.
No. 3884. Vase, 54 mm.
No. 7061. Vase, 65 mm.
No. 14715. Vase, with Narrow neck, 100 mm.

R & L

Trademark used by Robinson
& Leadbeater, Wolfe Street,
Stoke-on-Trent, and
subsequently a branch of
J. A. Robinsons Ltd.

Impressed mark

Robinson & Leadbeater was established in 1850 and specialised in the production of Parian statuary imitation antique ivory and Ecclesiastical statuary. R & L busts are becoming exceedingly popular with Parian collectors, the firm having made a large and well produced range, including busts of heroes (of the South African War), Royalty, Celebrities and literary figures. These busts were obviously made before the craze for crested china and cannot be considered to be 'crested china'.

The firm became insolvent in 1904, no explanation was given, but possibly one of the partners died. Robinson & Leadbeater was taken over by Harold Taylor Robinson (see ARCADIAN CHINA) in 1906, and was formed into a Limited Company, Robinson & Leadbeater Ltd in 1908. In 1910 the firm became a branch of J. A. Robinson Ltd.

It is probable that the small amount of crested china found marked R & L was produced after 1904. Some R & L moulds including busts are found overstamped 'Arcadian'. The mark was not used after 1924.

Most recorded crested pieces with this mark are 'smalls' or domestic items such as trinket boxes and parian match strikers. One transfer print has been found, this being a colour transfer of a battleship on a shallow bagware bowl. (No numbering system appears to have been used.)

R & L Models

Ancient Artefacts
Chester Roman Vase, not named. 2 sizes, 63 mm & 76 mm.
Loving Cup, 3 handled, not named. 39 mm.

Bird/Eggs
Egg Flower Holder, 80 mm long.

Miscellaneous
Thimble Salt Pot. 37 mm.

R & M

Trademark used by Roper & Meredith, Garfield Pottery, Longton.

Roper & Meredith was established in 1913 and manufactured earthenwares until 1924, when the firm went out of business. This firm, like most other manufacturers, would have turned to crested models during the Great War, when skilled labour needed to make tableware was in short supply. The firm did not advertise as makers of crested china and it would be correct to assume that this was a small side line. The models recorded are however very interesting and not just copies of other manufacturers wares. R & M also made a range of unglazed busts of poets, composers and other historic personalities.

R & M Models

Unglazed/Parian
March War Memorial. 174 mm.

Bird
Bird, with open wings. 75 mm long.

Great War
St. Ives War Memorial Cross, inscribed: *Men of St. Ives who have fallen in the Great War MDCGCCXIV–MDCCCCXVIII.* 135 mm.

Comic/Novelty
Truck of coal, inscribed: *Black Diamonds.* Black coal. 79 mm long.

Sport
Rugby player, holding rugby ball, on oval ashtray. Inscribed: *Play up.* Fully coloured. 126 mm.

Raleigh China

Trademark used by a retailer, manufacturer unknown.

The models found with this mark give no clues as to their manufacturer. No stock numbers or registration numbers have been recorded, and the models could have been made by any well known firm. Only two crests have been recorded, Southsea and Portsmouth, and it is possible that a retailer had shops there.

Raleigh Models

Historical/Folklore
Ark. 92 mm long.

Great War
Submarine, inscribed *E4.* No details of size.
Field Gun. 125 mm long.

Miniature Domestic
Cheese Dish. 45 mm.

Raphael

Trademark used by an
unknown manufacturer.

Mark unknown

This mark has been reported found on two un-named Kendal Jugs, 76 mm, one has the crest of Austria, the other Switzerland. Having been unable to see an example of the mark or a model, one cannot even begin to guess who manufactured this china. (It is interesting that the countries were reported spelt in the usual English way. This would not have been the case on German souvenirs unless they were made specially for English tourists.)

Regency Ware

Trademark used for a
wholesaler on china thought
to have been manufactured by
Sampson Hancock (& Sons),
Bridge Works, Stoke.

Mark can sometimes be found
without the 'S' after the initials
'J.B.'

For details of this china and manufacturer see THE CORONA CHINA.

No known manufacturer used the initials J. B. S. B. and so one can assume that this was a retailer's or wholesaler's mark. Crests are found from all over the South of England and so a wholesaler seems more likely. The *Regency* mark is identical to the *Grosvenor* mark used by Sampson Hancock with the addition of the initials. Some of the models listed below were made by Hancocks for other wholesalers including CEB.L. (see ALEXANDRA CHINA) so it seems probable that Hancocks used this mark for another wholesaler during the Great War.

Regency Models

Animals
Cat, sitting with ruff of fur round neck.
 100 mm (identical model found in
 'Alexandra' range).
Cat, standing. 60 mm.

Great War
Zeppelin. 153 mm long. (This is larger than
 the usual 'Corona' model.)
Flash Lamp. 85 mm.

Miscellaneous
Pawn, Chess Piece. No details of size.
 (Other chess pieces are found marked
 Corona.)

Regis

Trademark used by Hewitt
Bros, Willow Potteries,
Longton.

For details of this china and manufacturer see WILLOW ART CHINA.

Models found with this mark have crests from all over Great Britain, but many pieces have crests from Jersey, Ireland and Scotland. It seems very probable that the mark was offered to retailers in these areas as an alternative to *Willow Art*. Many 'Weymouth' crests have also been recorded and why this seaside resort and port should have been sold 'Regis' is a mystery. (Did the Willow traveller stay in Weymouth on his way to Jersey and manage to get an order from a local retailer?) The mark seems to have been used for some time; from before the Great War until the early Twenties. No view ware, commemoratives or transfer devices have been recorded with this mark.

Numbering system. Where stock numbers are found they are the same as *Willow Art* models. Stock numbers where known are listed below.

Right Regis. Standing dog, described by collectors as a collie 85 mm long

Left Regis. 'British Tank' with trailing wheels 127 mm

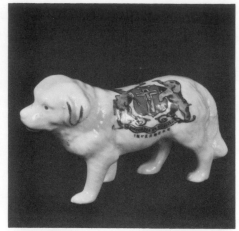

Right Regis. 'Jubilee Clock Tower, Weymouth'

Left Regis. Highland Mary Statue on plinth 150 mm

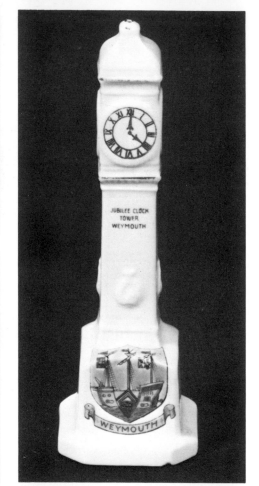

Left Regis. 'Mary Queen of Scots Chair'

Right Rita. 'Glastonbury Tor' 85 mm

Left Rialto. Battleship with Great War inscription

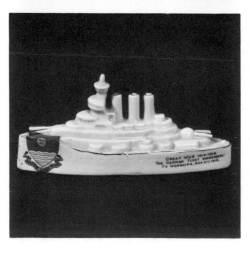

Regis Models

Parian/Unglazed
Bust of Lord Beatty. 165 mm.

Buildings—White
Weymouth Jubilee Clock Tower. 126 mm.

Monuments
The Blackwatch Memorial, Edinburgh.
127 mm.
Highland Mary statue. 155 mm.

Historical/Folklore
Mary Queen of Scots Chair, Edinburgh
Castle, Model of. 75 mm.

Seaside Souvenirs
Lifeboat, coloured ropes. 118 mm long.
Lighthouse, not named. 100 mm.
Corbiere Lighthouse, with coloured rock
base. 96 mm.

Animals
Dog, Collie, standing. 85 mm.
Dog, Scottie, wearing a Glengarry, some
colouring on hat. 85 mm.

Great War
Airship (Observation Balloon), inscribed:
Beta. 80 mm long.
British Tank, model of. 92 mm.
British Tank, model of, with trailing
wheels. 2 sizes: 95 mm & 127 mm long.
Large size No. 201. (Smaller size has not
been found marked 'Willow Art'.)
Kit Bag with verse: 'Pack up your troubles in
your old kit bag'. 74 mm.
Forage Cap. 83 mm long.
Cenotaph, inscribed: *The glorious dead,*
MCMXIV–MCMXIX. 145 mm.
Florence Nightingale Statue, inscribed:
Florence Nightingale 1820–1910. 160 mm.
Weymouth War Memorial, inscribed: *To our*
glorious dead. 152 mm.

Home/Nostalgic
Anvil, 76 mm.
Shaving Mug, 55 mm.

Comic/Novelty
Billiken, not named. No. 24. 73 mm.
Billiken, the God of Luck, sitting on high
backed chair. 100 mm.

Alcohol
Toby Jug. 83 mm.

Miscellaneous
Hand holding tulip. No. 74. 80 mm.

Rex China
Trademark used by an
unknown manufacturer.

Only two items have been found with this model, only one crest has been
recorded and that was of Ayr. The models are not identifiable as having
been made by any well known manufacturer, but the china is translucent
and quite fine. From the evidence available the mark was used in Scotland
and could have been used on Scottish or even German china. Until further
models are recorded it is impossible to be more precise.

Rex Models

Traditional/National Souvenirs
Tam O'Shanter. 72 mm dia.

Miniature Domestic
Cheese Dish, with gilded rope handle.
70 mm.

REX
CHINA

Rialto China
Trademark used by British Art
Pottery Co. (Fenton) Ltd,
Rialto Works, High Street, Fenton.

This small firm was established in 1920 and manufactured china.
Although the 'Rialto' mark was registered and the firm appeared in the
lists of manufacturers, they did not advertise and one can only guess from
the name of the firm that they produced novelty wares. The firm went into
voluntary liquidation in May 1926, so could have only produced crested
china between 1920 and 1926.

Some domestic ware has been found with the mark and one coloured
transfer view of 'Plas Newydd' has been recorded.

1920–6

Rialto Models

Ancient Artefacts
Salisbury Kettle, not named. 88 mm.

Great War
Battleship with inscription: *Great War*
1914–1918. The German Fleet surrendered 74
warships Nov. 21st 1918. 153 mm long.

Home/Nostalgic
Watchman's Lamp. No details of size.

Rita China Series

Trademark used by an
unknown manufacturer.

The initials L. & L. were used by Lovatt & Lovatt, the makers of Langley Ware which was stoneware and earthenware, and they were therefore not likely to have made crested china. The 'W. S. Mare' in the mark indicates a retailer or wholesaler based in Weston-Super-Mare but crests are found from all over England, and many of the models are Scottish souvenirs. However, the most commonly found crest is Cheddar, which again indicates a retailer in Weston-Super-Mare as the two places are both in Somerset.

The models recorded are not recognisably made by any well known manufacturer. Taylor & Kent (see FLORENTINE CHINA) and Wileman & Co. (see SHELLEY CHINA) made some similar models. Wileman & Co. do not appear to have used retailers' marks on their wares, Taylor & Kent often did, so they are the most likely manufacturer. (It is possible that several manufacturers used the same retailer's mark.)

Rita Models

Unglazed/Parian
Llangynwyd Church. 107 mm long (not found with a crest).

Buildings—White
Ann Hathaway's Cottage. 55 mm long.

Monuments
Glastonbury Tor. 83 mm.
Great Rock of Ages, Burrington Coombe, Near Cheddar, Som. Model of, with verses of hymn. 125 mm.
King Alfred's Statue. 160 mm.

Historical/Folklore
Burns Chair, model of. 88 mm.
James V Chair, Stirling Castle. No details of size.

Animals
Fish, 115 mm long.

Comic/Novelty
Clown. No other details available.
Jester, double faced, inscribed *Awake. Asleep*. No details of size.

'Modern' Equipment
Horn Gramophone. 90 mm.

Miscellaneous
Dutch Sabot, model of. 85 mm long.
Schoolboy's Cap. 65 mm long.

Rosina Queens China

Trademark used by George
Warrilow (& Sons) (Ltd),
Queens Pottery, Longton.

George Warrilow was established in 1887. They specialised in the production of Teasets, Badged Ware and Queens White Ware. Most firms making badged ware were capable of producing crested china, but this firm does not seem to have produced any quantity. One plate with four egg cups with an Exmouth crest has been recorded, it is very probable that the company made a range of crested domestic ware.

Rowena China

Trademark used by an
unknown manufacturer but
thought to be a branch of
J. A. Robinson, Ltd.

For details of J. A. Robinson, Ltd see ARCADIAN CHINA.

This mark is thought to have been designed to be used on the series of cartoon characters listed below. (Only one other model has been recorded marked *Rowena*). The mark was not registered but its similarity to the *Arcadian* mark is very noticeable. *Arcadian* was only one trademark used by

J. A. Robinson Ltd. Others include *Swan, Clifton* and *R & L*. These characters are much more likely to have been made by R. & L., as they specialised in parian ware. (See R. & L.). These models are exceptionally well produced.

Rowena Models

Ancient Artefacts
Gastrica Cyprian Bottle, not named. 71 mm.

Cartoon Characters
These four models form a series. All are inscribed: 'Copyright by permission of the Proprietors of the Daily Sketch'. They are unglazed, the characters are very subtly tinted and are mounted on square parian pedestals. Although all are extremely rare and very desirable the boy 'Don' is the most commonly found.

Don, little boy in short trousers and blue cardigan. 130 mm.

Dr Dromedary, camel, in black top hat and suit. 130 mm.

Oo Jah, Flip Flap, Elephant, in pink striped pyjamas. 130 mm.

Pa Piggins, Pig, in Edwardian Sporting clothes. 130 mm.

Mark used 1905–7

Royal Albert Crown China

Trademark used by Thomas
C. Wild, Crown China Works,
High St, Longton.

This mark used by Thomas C. Wild, the well established china manufacturers is found on domestic ware and 'smalls' made between 1905 and 1907. This firm obviously did not need to turn to model making during the Great War but survived by selling the table wares and fine china they specialised in.

Royal China

Trademark used by
E. Hughes and Co., Opal
Works, Fenton.

For details of this china and manufacturer see FENTON CHINA and E. HUGHES & CO. CHINA.

This mark has only been found in one model with a crest, which is listed below. The mark is usually found on badged hotel ware and domestic china.

Mark used 1912–41

Royal Model

Miniature Domestic
Cheese dish and cover, 50 mm.

Royal China Works, Worcester

Trademark used by Grainger,
Worcester when taken over
by the Worcester Royal
Porcelain Co. Ltd.

The very famous firm of George Grainger at Worcester was taken over by the Worcester Royal Porcelain Co. Ltd in 1889. This mark was only used after the takeover and not after 1902, so china with this mark can be accurately dated. A small number of 'smalls' have been found and the one model listed below. The china, as one would expect, is very fine and the crest well produced.

1889–1902

Royal China Works Model

Miniature Domestic
Mug, with one handle, 40 mm. (This is often listed as a loving cup with one handle, which cannot be correct as by definition a loving cup must have more than one handle.)

Royal Coburg

Trademark used by an
unknown manufacturer.

This mark was not registered and there are no initials or country of origin given to help with identification. Most pieces found are 'smalls' and carry crests of the South of England. It is possible that the china was manufactured in Germany, but unlikely. The Royal Family's connection with Coburg would have made this a respectable name before the Great War and this mark was probably used before 1914.

Royal Coburg Model

Miniature Domestic
Cheese dish and cover. 50 mm.

Mark used from 1902

Royal Doulton

Trademark used by Doulton
& Co. (Ltd), Nile St, Burslem.

This well-known firm produced a very small range of crested ware. Most of its seems to have been for export, crests recorded including New Zealand, Seal of Wellington and Jamaica. Most pieces of Doulton with crests are small vases, jugs or domestic ware. As one would expect the china is well produced.

Royal Doulton Model

Ancient Artefacts
Loving Cup, 3 handled. 49 mm.

Royal Ivory Porcelain

Trademark used by Robinson
& Leadbeater Ltd and for the
London Wholesalers E. B. &
Co.

For details of this china and manufacturer see R. & L.

Royal Ivory Porcelain was the printed mark used on small crested wares by Robinson & Leadbeater Ltd, Wolfe Street, Stoke-on-Trent, which subsequently became a branch of J. A. Robinson Ltd. The same mark occurs with the initials E. B. & Co., these same initials appearing with another mark used by a London wholesaler (see THE DAINTY WARE).

E. B. & Co. china with the Royal Ivory mark is much finer than the *Dainty Ware* range, and probably was more expensive. Most items which are recorded are found with both sets of initials, indicating that E. B. & Co. sold the whole R. & L. range.

Most pieces with this mark are 'smalls' or domestic ware, including pill boxes. No view ware, commemoratives or transfer devices have been recorded. *Royal Ivory* was exported and some foreign crests have been found. Crests of the Allies are found on 'smalls' with the E. B. & Co. initials.

Royal Ivory Models

Ancient Artefacts
Chester Roman Vase, not named. 63 mm.
Loving Cup, 2 and 3 handled. 45 mm.

Miscellaneous
Bishop's Mitre, no details of size.

It is more than probable that many of the smalls are in fact un-named ancient artefacts.

ENGLAND

Mark used from 1912

Mark used from 1929–40

Royal Stafford China

Trademark used by Thomas
Poole, Cobden Works,
Longton.

This firm obviously turned to crested china production for a short time during the Great War as many firms did. Why they produced crested domestic ware with the later mark is rather a mystery, unless the wares were for export. (One item has been found with a Bulawayo Municipal Council crest but the exact mark was not recorded). Most items recorded are domestic, including the inevitable ashtrays.

Royal Stafford Models

Animals
Elephant, walking. 52 mm.

Great War
Submarine, inscribed *E4*. 115 mm long.

Miscellaneous
Spade, playing card suit. 68 mm. (Found with stock number 286 indicating a much larger range of models than the items recorded would suggest!)

ENGLAND

Mark used from 1908

Royal "Vale" China

Trademark used by H. J.
Colclough, Vale Works,
Goddard Street, Longton.

This mark is very rare on crested china, only one model having been recorded, and this found twice, once with a Margate crest, and once with a St. Alban's crest. View ware can be found on the domestic and table ware which this firm made. (In 1907 the firm advertised 'Best English China at Foreign prices. Seaside and present ware or Bazaar Goods in Views, plain or coloured or gilt'.)

Royal Vale Model

Great War
Water Bottle. 70 mm.

Royal Worcester

Trademark used by Worcester
Royal Porcelain Company Ltd
(Royal Worcester).

The majority of small items carrying the famous *Worcester* mark were made at the turn of the century. Items of domestic ware and pierced vases and dishes can all be found with well produced crests. It seems that well established firms only made crested ware when it was considered tasteful and new, in other words a 'middle class' souvenir. Some pieces have been found with a cream instead of a white body. One 39 mm mug has been recorded with a transfer print of the Manx legs and a black bird (thought to be the Manx Shearwater).

Royal Worcester Models

Ancient Artefacts
Chester Roman Vase, not named. 60 mm.
Loving Cup. 2 and 3 handled. 40 mm.

Miniature Domestic
Mug, one handled. 45 mm.

Rowena. The 'Rowena Two Seater,' ashtray with inscription 'No tax on this car' on reverse.

Right Royal Worcester. Two handled loving cup with a commemorative transfer

Left Royal Vale. Ladies slipper, a rather charming model

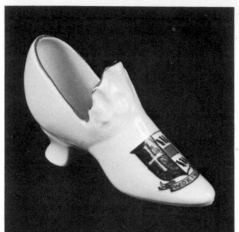 

Savoy. Machine gun on tripod, the model is in two separate pieces so the gun swivels

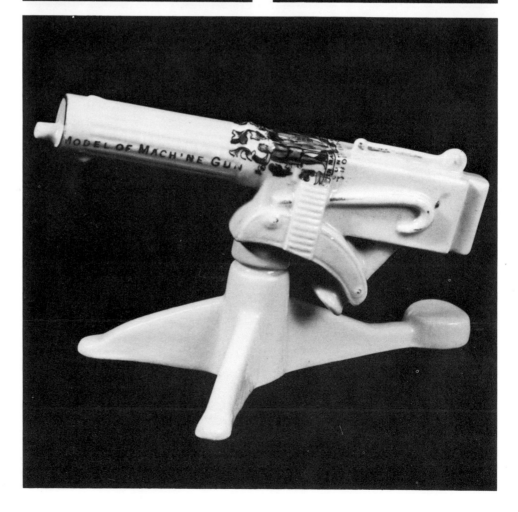

Ryecroft China Series

Trademark used by an unknown manufacturer.

This mark was not registered and no known manufacturer used the initials C.P.W. It has been suggested that the crested models listed below were not made in the same period as other crested china but much later, i.e. after the Second World War. I have not been able to see these models for myself but an owner hotly denies this suggestion, saying that they are very much pre-war. I can offer no suggestions as to the manufacturer.

Ryecroft Models

Buildings—White
Roche Abbey, ruins, unglazed. 85 mm.
Town Hall, Stockton-on-Tees, glazed.
    94 mm.

S

Trademark used by P. Donath, Tiefenfurt (Silesia).

P. Donath was a manufacturer of the imported pink view ware that preceded crested china as the popular souvenir. The company was nationalised after the last war, now being in the State of Poland. Very little crested china of this manufacture has been found and all known pieces are small domestic items.

SR

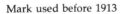

ENGLAND

Mark used before 1913

Trademark used by Samuel Radford (Ltd), High St, Fenton.

This China Manufacturer established in 1879 did not produce a large range of crested china. Only one piece of miniature domestic ware has been recorded and this was made at the turn of the century.

SR Model

Miniature Domestic
Cheese dish and cover. 64 mm long.

St. George China

AUSTRIA

Trademark used by an Austrian Manufacturer.

This mark is found on some typically German comic animal models. The Elephants on the slide are often found unmarked, and it is possible that this manufacturer usually left his models unmarked. One small jug has been recorded with a black transfer view of 'The Old Curiosity Shop' on one side and 'Charles Dickens' on the other. (German Manufacturers specialised in transfer view production and exported a great deal to Great Britain before the Great War.)

St. George Models

Seaside Souvenirs
Lighthouse. 121 mm.

Animals
Cat, with drumstick, sitting on a drum.
    90 mm.
Elephants, two on a sledge or slope. Comic and very attractive model. 70 mm.

San Juan

Mark used by an unknown
manufacturer.

One model has been found with this mark; it carried a MADRID Crest. It would have been made by any English firm that exported to tourist areas. The initials S. M. & Co were not used by any manufacturer working during the 'crested china' period and so are probably the initials of the retailer.

San Juan Model

Ancient Artefact
Portland Vase, not named. 51 mm.

1910–1933

Savoy China

Trademark used by Birks,
Rawlins and Co. (Ltd), Vine
Pottery, Stoke.

The firm Birks, Rawlins and Co., China Manufacturers, was founded in 1900. It had previously been known as L. A. Birks and Co. (founded 1896). Who Mr Rawlins was will probably remain a secret but Mr L. A. Birks managed the Pottery and was responsible for the designs. The firm's early products were 'breakfast and teas' in the usual number of printed patterns and other decorative domestic ware including pierced white pieces.

Birks, Rawlins and Co. began producing what were described as china miniatures for the seasonal souvenir trade around 1910 using the trade-name *Savoy China*. The production of this work was stepped up in 1919 to take advantage of the gap left in the market by the banning of German goods. It was reported in the Pottery Gazette in 1919 and 20 that the firm were producing miniature architectural models and could execute models of any well known building to order. Aberystwyth University, St. Paul's, Westminster Abbey, Truro Cathedral, King Charles Tower, Hastings Clock Tower and Portsmouth Town Hall were all said to be in production. (Only the last two have been found so far.) Even more perplexing to the collector is a list printed in 1920 of 'Small figures which aim at filling a need that was created when German supplies to this country ceased. 'Birks Grotesques' included 'Old Bill' in camouflage or in khaki, 'Sunny Jim', 'Weary Willy', 'Artful Eliza', 'Saucy Sue', 'Peter Pan', 'Conchy', 'Blighty' and 'C3'—all well known cartoon and comic strip characters of the time. None of these have been reported with or without crests or marked *Savoy* and one wonders if they were ever produced in any numbers.

Many coloured novelties were made in the 1920s including figures, birds, floating bowl decorations (butterflies and other insects) and plump pixies sitting on toadstools. These were not crested so have not been listed here.

In 1925, Birks, Rawlins and Co. exhibited at the British Empire Exhibition, showing Parian China and novelties. Presumably the return of cheap continental souvenir ware and the effect on trade of the Depression were too much for the firm, for by 1931 the company was put into the hands of the Receiver. F. W. Carder ceased to act as Receiver on 7th March 1932 and it was announced that Birks, Rawlins and Co had merged with Wiltshaw and Robinson Ltd (Makers of Carlton China). Wiltshaw and Robinson continued to use the *Savoy* trade mark for a short time and some *Carlton* moulds can be found with the *Savoy* mark.

The *Savoy* range, although described as 'china' and even 'porcelain miniatures', cannot really be considered delicate or even fine, and the crests are not at all well produced. It is obvious that Birks, Rawlins and Co. lowered their standards to produce cheap items for the lower end of the souvenir market. Very few Savoy models are found with transfer prints of any kind and these are mostly domestic pieces.' 'Lucky Black Cat' transfers are occasionally encountered but no 'Lucky White Heather' devices have as yet been recorded.

Birks, Rawlins and Co. seemed to have produced very few Military Crests either, the Royal Military College, Camberley being the only one known. They did however print the most interesting range of Great War Commemorative inscriptions sometimes found in Military models but more often on 'smalls'. These celebrate, if that word can possibly be used to described such carnage, battles and events in the war and carry matching crests. The following are known:

Antwerp Crest 'Antwerp invaded Oct. 1st 1914. Bombarded 1914, evacuated Oct. 7th 1914. Captured Oct. 13th 1914.'

Armentiers Crest 'Desperate Battles between British and Germans, Nov. 1914, June 1915.'

Arras Crest 'Great Battle between French and Germans. French gain trenches June 1915.'

Belgium Crest No details of inscription available.

B. E. Africa Crest 'South Togoland seized by Great Britain August 7th 1914.'

Bucharest Crest 'Rumania declares war on Austria–Hungary August 27th 1916.'

Calais Crest 'German life and death advance.'

Dunkerque Crest 'Dunkerque bombarded by long range German guns.'

French Republic Crest 'French Territory invaded by German troops August 2nd 1914. Battle of the Marne Sept. 8th to Sept. 12th.'

Lille 'Lille captured by the Germans Sept. 1914.'

Louvain Crest 'Louvain burned and destroyed by the Germans, August 25th 1914.'

Mons Crest 'Battle of Mons, Historic Retreat begun August 23rd 1914.'

Namur Crest 'Namur Forts destroyed by the huge German guns August 23rd 1914.'

Neuve Chapelle Crest 'Brilliant British Victory over Germans at Neuve Chapelle March 10th 1915.'

Paris Crest No details of inscription available.

Russia Crest 'War declared upon Russia by Germany Aug. 1st 1914.'

Verdun Crest 'German defeat before Fort Douardmont February 26th 1916.'

Ypres Crest 'German push stemmed by the Valour of the British troops October 27th 1914. 2nd battle of Ypres the Canadians gallantry saved the situation April 24th 1915.'

Commemoratives can also be found of the Scottish Exhibition, Glasgow 1911 and the Wembley British Empire Exhibition 1924/5.

Numbering System. Savoy models tend to be over endowed with printed and painted numbers on their bases. Many models have a very clear printed number which was obviously a stock number. Unfortunately for the collector the same low numbers often appear on different models. There are possibly one or two reasons for this, one theory being that as models were deleted from the range new models were given their numbers. Another theory for which there is some evidence is that the numbers were badly printed and often only the first or last one or two are in evidence. Sometimes where this has happened a larger stock number is painted in black beside the printed number. Other coloured painted numbers found near the mark seem to be paintresses' marks, these often

Right Savoy. Grotesque animal, No. 398. This model was obviously popular in its day as it appears in several ranges

Left Savoy. Pixie on rock or Hindu god? blue beads

Right Savoy. Tiny Welsh Hat with full wording around brim

Left Savoy. Dutch sabot No. 424

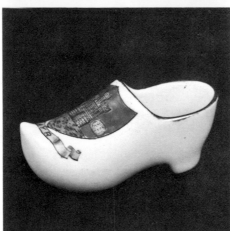

Savoy. Portsmouth Town Hall 80 mm

appearing directly under the painted stock number also in black.

Where stock numbers have been found consistently (printed or painted on models) they have been recorded in the following lists.

Savoy Models

Parian/Unglazed
All known unglazed Savoy models are commemoratives of the Great War. They are the only firm that appear to have made a range of unglazed personnel. All unglazed models, with the exception of the nurse and John Cornwell are found on glazed circular bases, and do not normally carry crests.

Busts
Bust of Albert King of the Belgians. 150 mm.

Bust of Admiral Sir David Beattie, found with inscription 'British Naval Victory, German Cruiser Blucher sunk January 24th 1915. England declared War on Germany August 4th 1914.' 150 mm.

Bust of Lord Kitchener, found with inscription 'Lord Kitchener of Khartoum Field Marshal KG KP Secretary for War. Born 1851. June 15th, drowned at sea off the Orkneys 1916.' 120 mm.

Bust of Sailor, can be inscribed: *HMS Iron Duke, HMS Tiger,* or *HMS Warspite.* 108 mm.

Bust of John Travers Cornwell, inscription 'John Travers Cornwell, age 16. Faithful unto death. Hero Battle of Jutland. (He was the first Boy V.C.) Rd. No. 662782. 108 mm.

Figures
Highland Infantryman, with pack, rifle and bayonet. 165 mm.

Nurse with red cross on chest. No. 531. 165 mm.

(Both of these figures can be found glazed. See Great War.)

Exeter Cathedral, tinted brown, no crest. No details of size.

Ancient Artefacts
Many of these models have been taken from Dealers' stock and sales lists; the size, stock numbers and other information are not always available. Some of the inscriptions are extremely brief and uninformative. These models are often found unnamed.

Ancient Jug, Model of. No. 87. 74 mm.

Bottle (not named) No. 408. 90 mm.

Carlisle Elizabethan Measure, no details.

Carlisle Vase, no details.

Celtic Vase in British Museum, Model of. No. 25. 45 mm.

Chester Roman Vase, no details.

Chinese Vase, Model of, no details.

De Nevers model of vase, no details.

Globe Vase, Model of. No. 62. 42 mm.

Greek Vase, inscribed: *Model of very ancient Greek vase in British Museum.* No. 77. 69 mm.

Hastings Kettle, inscribed: *Model of Hastings kettle in Hastings Museum.* No. 140. 60 mm.

Itford Urn, inscribed: *Model of British urn dug up at Itford now in Lewes Castle.* 44 mm.

Launceston Bottle, inscribed: *Model of bottle dug up in ploughed field about 200 years old now in Launceston.* No. 173. No details of size.

Loving Cup. 3 handled. (Not named.) 38 mm.

Maltese fire grate, Model of. No. 721. 45 mm.

Newbury Leather Bottle, inscribed: *Model of leather bottle found at Newbury 1044 on battlefield. Now in museum.* No. 14. No details of size.

Pear bottle, Model of. No. 17. No details of size.

Penrith Salt Pot, inscribed: *Model of 14th Century salt pot found at Penrith now in Carlisle Museum (By permission of Com. Tullie House).* No. 182. 60 mm. Rare example has distinctive floral decoration.

Persian bottle, Model of. No. 68. 85 mm.

Portland vase, Model of. No details.

Salt maller, Model of. No details.

Scarborough Jug inscribed: *Model of jug found in moat at Scarborough.* No. 454. No details of size.

Silchester Roman Urn, inscribed: *Model of Roman urn from Silchester in Reading Museum.* No. 74. 51 mm.

Buildings—Coloured
Savoy do not appear to have made a range of coloured buildings, only one unnamed cottage has been recorded.

Tumbledown cottage, not named, highly coloured and glazed. Impressed 1800. 105 mm long.

Building—White
As Savoy specialised in buildings it is quite clear that the list of recorded models is very incomplete.

Burns cottage, Model of. No details.

Clifton Suspension Bridge. 132 mm long.

Hastings Clock Tower. No. 274. 156 mm.

Margate Clock Tower. 160 mm.

Monnow Gate, Monmouth. Found numbered 86 and 305. 112 mm.

Portsmouth Town Hall. No. 7. 80 mm.

Historical/Folklore
Burns Chair, Dumfries. 81 mm.

Mary Queen of Scots Chair, Edinburgh Castle, Model of. 77 mm.

Traditional/National Souvenirs
Ripon Horn Blower. No. 497. 110 mm.

Bagpipes. 110 mm long.

Thistle Vase. 47 mm.

Welsh Hat with longest place name round brim. No. 6. 35 mm. (Very tiny and not often found.)

Right Savoy. Model of a mouse 65 mm long

Left Savoy. Amusing hippopotamus with protruding teeth

Savoy. Scottie wearing glengarry with red and black checked band and fully coloured yellow scottie wearing green tam o'shanter

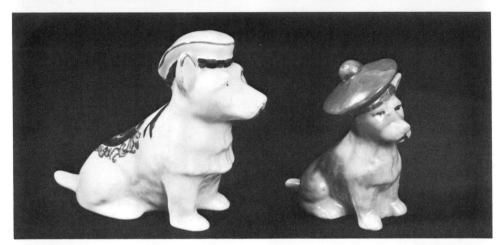

Right Savoy. Top row: Dachshund or Basset dog
Middle row: Bulldog with inscription on reverse 'Another Dreadnought'
Bottom row: Lion walking with inscription on reverse 'Another Dreadnought'

Left Savoy. Comic Elephant No. 218

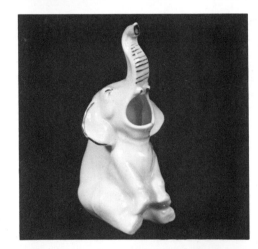 

Left Savoy. Toad, rather a detailed model

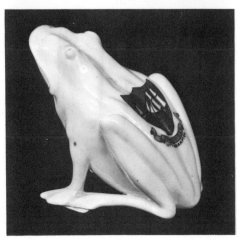

Right Savoy. No. 719 an ugly
little duckling model.

Left Savoy. Penguin 76 mm
marked No. 549

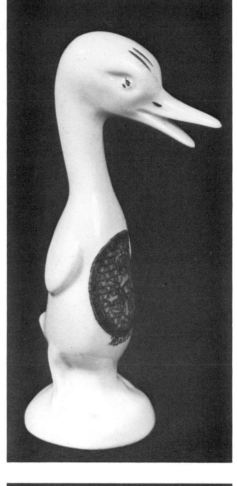

Left Savoy. Winkie the Gladeye
Bird not named 68 mm

Right Savoy. Model of a fat pig.
70 mm long

Left Savoy. Fireplace with Great
War inscription

Savoy. Twenty-four seater
charabanc

Seaside Souvenirs
Bathing Machine, inscribed: *Morning dip*. No. 126 or No. 5. 62 mm.
Yacht. 115 mm long.
Beachy Head Lighthouse. No. 371. 130 mm.
Eddystone Lighthouse, Model of. 92 mm.
Crab Ashtray or dish. 52 mm long.
Lobster pintray with lid. 97 mm long.

Countryside
Acorn, Model of. No. 110. 56 mm.

Animals
Cat, Cheshire (not named). No. 17. 80 mm.
Cat, angry with arched back, inscribed: *Me backs up*. No. 195. 100 mm long.
Cat with long neck. No. 217. 105 mm.
Dog, (no particular breed) sitting. 55 mm.
Dog, (curly tail) standing. 65 mm.
Dog, Basset/Dachshund (variously described). No. 296. 132 mm long.
Bulldog, standing, with verse: 'Be Briton still to Britain true. Among ourselves united. For never but by British hands, May British wrongs be righted.' *Burns* or sometimes inscribed: *Another Dreadnought*. No. 364. 130 mm long. (This model is often found in Great War Collections.)
Dog, crouched and barking. No. 253. 100 mm long.
Dog, Scottie, wearing Glengarry. Can be found numbered 447 or 777. 86 mm.
Dog, Scottie, wearing Tam o'Shanter. 2 sizes: 63 mm & 80 mm. Smaller size can be found fully coloured.
Dog, Spaniel begging. 65 mm.
Elephant, sitting with trunk in the air. No. 218. 63 mm.
Elephant, walking with trunk curled overhead. No. 253. 108 mm long.
Fish. 104 mm long.
Grotesque animal (a horrid looking creature which could be a pig or a dog). No. 398. 102 mm.
Hare, crouching. No. 177. 63 mm long.
Lion, sitting on square base. 108 mm.
Lion, walking sometimes inscribed: *Another Dreadnought*. No. 788. 135 mm long. (See also British Lion in Great War section.)
House. 65 mm long.
Pig, lying down. 80 mm long.
Pig, standing and fat. 70 mm long.
Piglet with long ears, found marked 'Series 3' and numbered 99 or 198. 65 mm long.
Rabbit. 88 mm long.
Seal. 2 sizes: 63 mm & 80 mm long.
Toad. No. 331. 75 mm.

Birds
Duck, swimming. No. 562. 2 sizes: 40 mm & 65 mm long.
Duck, in dress, singing. 82 mm.
Duckling, grotesque. 2 sizes: 130 mm & 170 mm.
Goose in full length cloak. 72 mm.
Penguin. No. 549. 76 mm.

Great War
Savoy made many more serviceman's hats than other firms, but very few personnel. Many models carry the Victory inscription. 'Victory, Peace, Honour, 1919.'
British Lion, wearing puttees, inscribed: *Another Dreadnought*. 130 mm long.
Nurse, with red cross on chest. (Also found unglazed.) Can be found inscribed: *Nurse Cavell*. No. 531. 165 mm.
Sailor, bust, inscribed on cap badge: *HMS Warspite* or *HMS Lion*. No. 532. 135 mm.
Scottish soldier on circular base. 160 mm. (Also found unglazed.)
Biplane, with fixed prop. inscribed: *RAF*. 153 mm long.
Monoplane, with fixed prop. 128 mm long.
Monoplane, pointed wings and revolving prop. No. 521, or No. 28. 130 mm long.
Zeppelin with revolving 2-bladed propellor, can be found with inscription 'Zeppelin destroyed by Lt. Robinson V.C. at Cuffley Essex Sept. 3rd 1916. No. 567. 175 mm long.
Battleship, found inscribed with the name of one of the following: *HMS Lion: HMS Iron Duke: HMS Warspite* or *HMS Queen Elizabeth*. Rd. No. 652617. No. 524. 168 mm long.
British Minesweeper, Model of. No. 644. 146 mm long.
Torpedo Boat Destroyer, Model of. Rd. No. 651546. 140 mm long.
Submarine, inscribed: *E1*. Usually found with inscription 'Commander Noel Laurence, large German transport sunk July 30th 1915. German Cruiser Moltke torpedoed August 19th 1915.' No. 575. 150 mm long.
Ambulance, with 3 red crosses—one on cab top. Found numbered 17 or 28 or 520. 108 mm long.
Ambulance (with 'Rolls Royce' front). No. 520. 115 mm long.
Armoured Car (reputedly a 'Talbot' but not named). 125 mm long.
British motor searchlight, Model of. No. 123. 103 mm long.
Tank with trailing steering wheels, inscribed: *HMS Donner Blitzen* and 515 on side, with further inscription on base: 'Model of British Tank first used by British Troops at the Battle of Ancre Sept. 1916.' Numbered 132, 152 & 586. Sizes vary but there seem to be mainly 3 sizes: 125 mm, 140 mm & 155 mm long.
Tank with inset steering wheels, inscribed as above. 2 sizes: 125 mm & 115 mm long.
Tank with no trailing wheels, inscribed exactly as above. No. 597. 135 mm long.
Field Gun. Found numbered 416 & 616, 140 mm long.
Howitzer. Rd. No. 651545. No. 536 & 518. 170 mm long.
Machine Gun, 2 pieces, swivels on tripod. No. 402. 153 mm long.
British Trench Mortar Gun. Rd. No. 658483. No. 613. 98 mm long.
Shell, inscribed: *Iron rations for Fritz*. No. 5. 66 mm.

Right Savoy. Red Cross nurse on round base

Left Savoy. Parian bust of John Cornwell the boy hero of Jutland. Rare

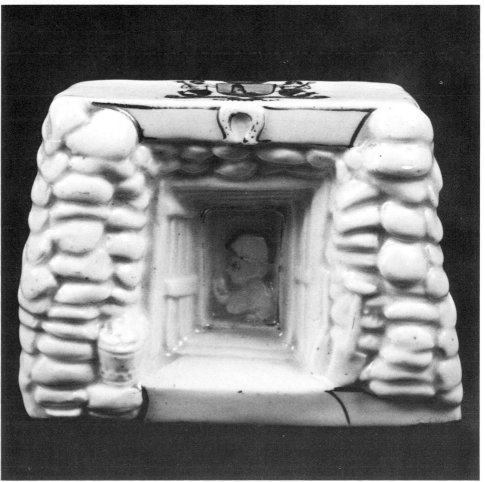

Left Savoy. Shell usually found inscribed 'Iron rations for Fritz' and hand grenade not named No. 556

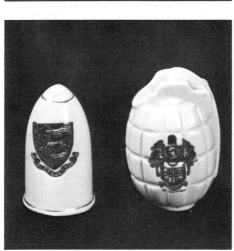

Savoy. Tommy in his dug out, this model is not named

Right Savoy. Howitzer with solid wheels. Numbered 518. 170 mm long

Left Savoy. British Trench Mortar Gun 98 mm long

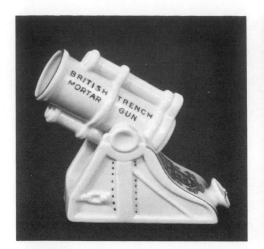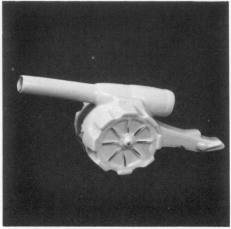

Savoy. Field Gun numbered 616. Note the excellent detailing

Savoy. 'Model of Torpedo Boat Destroyer' 140 mm long. (see Great War)

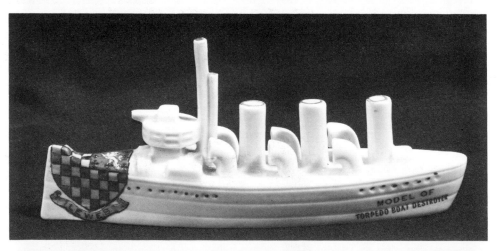

Savoy. Battleship inscribed 'H.M.S. Lion'

Savoy. Glengarry, sailors hat inscribed 'H.M.S. Queen Elizabeth' and RFC cap'

Savoy. 'French Trench Helmet' and 'New Zealand Hat'

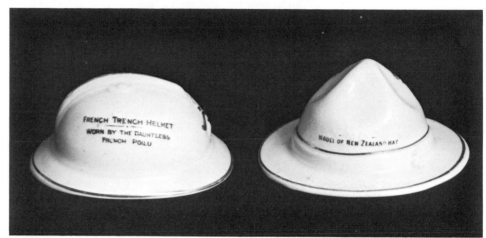

Savoy. Zeppelin with revolving 2 bladed propeller

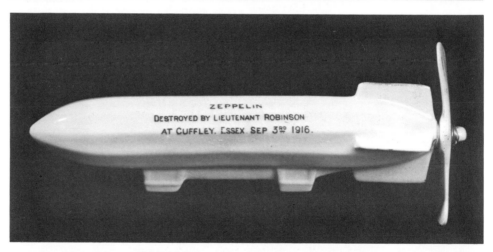

Savoy. 'H.M.S. Donner Blitzen' with and without trailing wheels

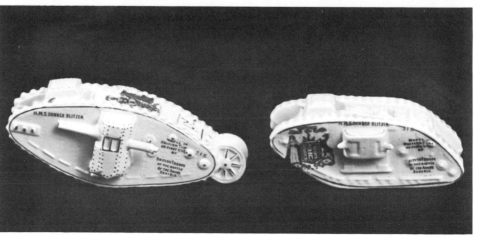

(Shell 'Salt' and 'Pepper' pots also found. 80 mm.)

Trench Mortar Bomb. Often found not named. 2 sizes: No. 574, 65 mm. No. 575. 86 mm.

Hand Grenade, not named. No. 556. 75 mm.

Anzac Hat, Model of. No. 111. 90 mm long.

Balmoral Bonnet, Model of. Rd. No. 661741. 74 mm long.

Colonial Hat. No. 48. 82 mm long.

French Trench Helmet, worn by the Dauntless French Poilu. No. 69. 82 mm long.

Glengarry. No. 508. 78 mm long.

New Zealand Hat, Model of. No. 612. 80 mm long.

Officer's Peaked Cap. 72 mm long.

Rumanian soldier's steel helmet, Model of, found with Bucharest Crest and Rumanian War declaration inscription. 82 mm long.

R.F.C. Cap, Model of, cap badge clearly moulded. No. 577. 80 mm long.

Sailor's Hat, inscribed on band: *HMS Lion* or *HMS Queen Elizabeth.* Blue bow. No. 533. 71 mm dia.

Tommy's Steel Helmet, not named. 82 mm long.

Bandsman's Drum. 55 mm dia.

Bell Tent, can be found in full camouflage colours. No. 118. 65 mm.

Water Bottle. No. 219. 57 mm.

Tommy in Dug Out, not named. (Could be from Carlton Mould.) No. 669. 85 mm. (rare)

Cenotaph, inscribed: *The Glorious Dead.* 130 mm.

Edith Cavell Memorial, Norwich, inscribed: *Nurse Cavell.* Red Cross on apron. No. 110. 168 mm.

Home/Nostalgic

Grandfather Clock, inscribed: *Nae man can tether time nor tide.* No. 622. 146 mm.

Watering Can. No. 455. 76 mm.

Comic/Novelty

Billiken, not named. (Flat, grotesque faced type.) 75 mm.

Caterpillar with human face. No. 543. 74 mm.

Choirboy. No. 542. 85 mm.

Hindu god sitting on rock, blue beads. No. 28 or No. 554. 90 mm. (This model is often described as a pixie.)

Policeman, short and fat. 103 mm.

Cartoon/Comedy Characters

Bonzo, dog. (1920's cartoon character.) No. 927. 80 mm.

Winkie the Gladeye Bird, not named. 68 mm.

Sport

Golf ball, Model of, No. 111. 40 mm.

Musical Instruments

Upright Piano. No. 887. 83 mm long.

Violin. 136 mm long.

Transport

Charabanc, (24 seater). No. 811. 134 mm long.

Modern Equipment

Gramophone, square with large horn. 102 mm.

Miscellaneous/Miniature Domestic

Cheese Dish, one piece. 40 mm.

Cheese stand, Model of, with lid. No. 200. 55 mm long.

Extinguisher, Model of (Candle Snuffer). No. 42. 51 mm.

Top Hat. 44 mm.

Scotch Porcelain

Trademark used by an unknown manufacturer.

A 62 mm tankard has been found with this mark. It has a coloured transfer print of 'John Knox's House, Edinburgh' on its side. The china is fine and the print well produced. Unfortunately the mark offers no clue to the manufacturer.

Shamrock China

Trademark used by Belleek Pottery, (David McBirney and Co), Belleek, Co. Fermanagh, Ireland.

For further details, see BELLEEK.

This mark could have been used for a cheap range of crested souvenir ware but as only one model has so far been recorded this can only be an assumption.

Shamrock Model

Bird

Cockerel, with orange face and yellow beak. 100 mm.

Shamrock Crest China

Trademark used for a Belfast
wholesaler by an unknown
manufacturer.

The initials N.P.O. were not used by any known manufacturer and are
likely to be those of a Belfast wholesaler. Only two 'smalls' with this mark
have been recorded, a jug with the crest of Newtownards and a vase with a
transfer print of 'The Irish Jaunting Car' and an Irish harp in a wreath of
shamrocks. Neither of these pieces gives us any clue as to their
manufacturer.

J. Shaw

Trademark used by J. Shaw
and Sons, Longton,
subsequently John Shaw and
Sons (Longton) Ltd, Willow
Pottery, Longton.

One most unusual model has been found with this mark from a firm
usually concerned with producing tableware and fine bone china. I can
offer no explanation for this oddity, most firms producing small quantities
of crested ware usually stuck to 'smalls'. It is possible that this model was
used in advertising.

J. Shaw Model

Novelty
Biscuit impressed: *Huntley and Palmer*.   68 mm long. (Has been recorded with a
   Biscuit coloured on white shaped base.   Dolgelly crest.)

Shell China

Trademark used by an
unknown Staffordshire
Pottery.

This mark has only been recorded on one miniature domestic model listed
below. It could have been manufactured by any of the Staffordshire
Potteries.

Shell Model

Miniature Domestic
Cheese dish and cover. 45 mm.

Shelley China

Trademark used by Wileman
and Co, Foley Potteries and
Foley China Works, Fenton,
Longton and subsequently
renamed Shelleys Ltd.

The firm of Wileman and Co was founded in or around the year 1860 by Mr
J. F. Wileman and Mr J. E. Shelley. From 1883 the business was run
entirely by the Shelley family; the founder and his son Percy Shelley, and
later his grandsons. Wileman and Co were well known and respected
manufacturers of fine china, specialising in tea and breakfast sets for the
comfortable middle class market both at home and abroad. Several other
firms used the tradename 'Foley' (notably E. Brain and Co) and this can be
confusing for the collector looking for early pieces. Obviously the
tradenames were causing confusion in the 1900's for in 1910 the company
decided to change its tradename to 'Shelley', using the name of the
owners rather than the pottery. In its advertising to the trade the company

1890–1910 On small,
decorative and domestic
items

Trade Mark
Late Foley

SHELLEY

ENGLAND

1910–1923/4 On small, decorative
and domestic items

CHINA

SHELLEY

ENGLAND

1923/4–1925+

THE FOLEY CHINA

1890–1910. On numbered models

SHELLEY CHINA
LATE FOLEY

1910–1920+ On numbered
models

SHELLEY CHINA

c1920–1925+

announced, perhaps rather unfairly, 'The World Wide reputation of *Foley* china has caused many cheap imitations, and in future to protect the public the real genuine *Foley* china will always be indelibly marked Shelley'.

For sometime the tradename *Shelley* was accompanied by the title *late Foley* and one suspects that this was dropped from the markings on 'Crest China' before other domestic wares. It is not clear exactly when the new trademarks, without *late Foley*, first appeared. The firm changed its name legally to Shelleys Ltd in 1925, but the new mark seems to have been used before this date.

The Shelley family produced commemorative and view ware before 1900, and seem to have begun producing *Crest China* as they called it in 1903 as a sideline. One suspects that this was in direct competition with W. H. Goss. Foley, and later Shelley fine crest china was sold in the best China shops, rooms and halls and not in bazaars, post offices, cafes and other dubious tourist outlets. At first crests were applied to domestic wares (the same shapes can be found decorated in the usual styles of the day) and small trays and vases. Early models include simple small shapes such as books, hats, animals and some souvenir items of the South African War. All of these being rather more in line with the cheaper crested china firms than Goss, but by 1906 the Shelleys were producing small models of ancient artefacts, very like the Goss products. Over the next few years the firm produced the most interesting range of these, always in the delicate white china for which they were well known and with carefully painted crests.

With the coming of the war years, and the loss of skilled men to the battlefields of France, the production of moulded models obviously became financially more important to the firm. (Models made during and after the Great War tend to be heavier and cruder than other products of the firm—obviously the work of unskilled labour.) In 1920 at the British Industries Fair the Shelley family showed 'Crest China' and advertised it in that year for the first time. Great War souvenirs and some novelty items were added to the range, but they never quite reached the vulgarity displayed by other manufacturers. Shelley stopped producing crested china much earlier than other firms, in fact they appear to have added very few items to their range after 1923 and do not mention its production in advertising after that date. Obviously they continued to produce the domestic ware which was always the speciality of the firm and made a feature of children's ware in the later 1920's as did many other manufacturers' Shelley Potteries Ltd is now part of the Doulton Group.

The Shelley models are not very exciting for those who like the colourful and bizarre. A few half-hearted 'novelties' can be found, but basically Shelley crest china was produced to sit politely in the china cabinets of the 'respectable' and not to amuse on the mantleshelves of the 'working classes'. However, collectors of fine china are very drawn to Shelley/Foley pieces, especially to the named historic shapes which are so like Goss. (New collectors should be warned that the less common of these already change hands among seasoned collectors for more money than the common Goss models.)

Early Foley/Shelley view ware is very beautiful, both monochrome (red, black and brown) and polychrome transfers can be found. Later Shelley transfers are rather disappointing being very highly coloured and not so attractive. The firm also produced models with transfer prints of a regional nature instead of crests. (A few early models marked FOLEY or SHELLEY/LATE FOLEY can be found with deep tinted pictorials printed all over. These are numbered but not named.)

Foley/Shelley also produced commemorative ware and souvenirs of most Royal events from 1860 onwards can be found. Commemoratives, view ware and crested pieces were also made for the American, Australian, New Zealand and South African markets but examples of these are difficult to find in Britain.

Shelley do not appear to have produced Military Crests but a 1914 War Inscription can be found on some models. Commemoratives of the Boer War, although not crests, are of great interest to the Military Collector as they name Generals and Colonial Supporters. (These are naturally marked *Foley*.)

Some late Shelley models do carry 'Lucky Black Cat' transfers but these are rare so it seems likely that they were only made in a limited way. No 'Lucky White Heather' pieces have been found and the firm made very few coloured crested models. 'How Ink is Made' being a noticeable exception. Other coloured models were made in the 1920's, including a striking range of birds. These however were not crested and are not listed here.

Very keen Shelley collectors are probably already aware of the wonderful range of crested domestic ware made by the firm. Collectors of 1920's and 30's china can find vases and bowls in lustred finishes and very evocative nursery ware designed by Hilda Cowham and Mabel Lucie Atwell.

Numbering System This was the only firm to *print* (paint in the case of low numbers) a stock number on every model and to do so throughout that model's production. They appear to have begun to do so from around 1906 onwards, and so some early pieces marked *Foley* are not numbered.

From registration numbers and trade names found on numbered models one can deduce the approximate date of original production. The following is offered as a rough guide to dating:

Models 1–120 designed 1903–1910

Models 130–413 designed 1910–1923/24

Models 500–507+ designed after 1923/24

Stock numbers 91–99, 121–129, 216–299 (with the exception of a Bulldog which is found numbered 238), 390–399 and 414–499 do not appear to have been used. It seems that in four of the above five cases when a new series of models was added to the range the numbering recommenced at the nearest hundred above the last number used. The exception, the gap between stock numbers 121 and 129, seems to have been caused by the introduction of the new *Shelley/late Foley* mark.

Real Shelley addicts may like to make their own list of models in numerical order—if they do they will find that 60 individual numbers have not yet been found. These unrecorded numbers must have been used and hopefully these models will eventually be recorded. Almost certainly a numbered model not listed here is rare.

Shelley Models
NB. These lists include models marked FOLEY and SHELLEY/LATE FOLEY.

Unglazed/Parian
All busts are on square glazed bases and do not normally carry crests. Most of these are marked Shelley/late Foley and are not numbered.

Bust of HM King George V. 130 mm.

Bust of French, with inscription: 'Field Marshall Sir John French, Commander in Chief of the Expeditionary Force'. 118 mm.

Bust of Jellicoe, with inscription: 'Admiral Sir John Jellicoe. In Supreme Command of the North Sea Fleet'. 118 mm.

Bust of Joffre, with inscription: 'General Joffre, Commander in Chief of the French Army 1915'. 130 mm.

Bust of Kitchener, with inscription: Field Marshall Earl Kitchener, Secretary of State for War'. 118 mm.

Bust of *The Rt Hon David Lloyd George*. 2 sizes: 118 mm & 130 mm.

(It is probable that all the above busts were offered for sale in these two sizes.)

Shelley. No. 88 Hanley Eygptian Vase, No. 107 Silchester Urn and No. 207 Phoenician Water Jar

Right Shelley. 'Mode of Persian Wine Server 13th Century' No. 308

Left Shelley. No. 301 'Model of Italian Vase 16th Century

Right Shelley. Burns and Highland Mary 118 mm. Not as yet found numbered

Left Shelley. No. 302 Persian Cafeterre, No. 303 Indian wine vessel and No. 309 Italian 15th Century Vase

Shelley. Penmeanmawr Urn with Welsh spinning wheel (Foley), Top hat with map of the Isle of Wight (Foley) and a Penmeanmawr Urn with a lucky black cat holding poppies (Shelley/late Foley). Two examples of early coloured transfers and one late device

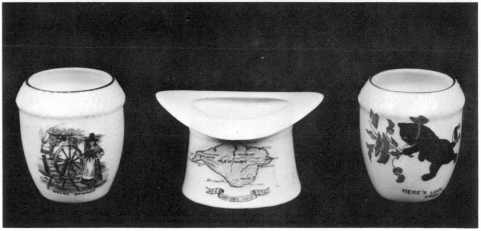

230

One exceptional 'parian' model has been reported, it is marked Shelley/late Foley and has not been found glazed:

Sailor standing with hands on hips, square base. Inscribed: *Ready! Aye! Ready!* and impressed: *HMS Lion.* Coloured. 170 mm.

Ancient Artefacts

Early models (marked Foley) are sometimes found with no printed number or inscription. Models can be found with coloured transfer views, etc, instead of crests. *All* inscriptions begin: *Model of* so this will not be repeated throughout the list.

Ancient Cyprian water bottle. No. 140. 45 mm.

Antique tea caddy—Queen Anne. No. 153. 70 mm.

Aqua Mivel for pouring water over the hands of the priest. No. 137. Rd. No. 595630. 74 mm wide.

Arabian wine vessel. No. 203. 75 mm.

Caerswys roman vessel. No. 204. No details of size.

Cauldron with two handles. Unnamed Foley model. No. 31. Rd. No. 400929. 35 mm.

Celtic jar (an ancient). No. 200. 65 mm.

Celtic water bottle. No. 205. 63 mm.

Chester Roman Urn, inscribed: *A very rare Roman urn found near Chester now in possession of J. W. Salt Esq.* No. 118. 54 mm.

Chinese jar 12th Century. No. 304. 121 mm.

Chinese vase of great antiquity and beauty, date about 5000 BC. Belongs to the nation. No. 115. 62 mm.

Chinese vase, about 500 AD. No. 213. 60 mm.

Cinerary urn of rare form. No. 134. No details of size.

Cleopatra's Vase, inscribed: *An Egyptian vase taken from the tomb of Cleopatra.* No. 144. 50 mm.

Colchester Famous Vase, inscribed: *Famous Colchester vase in the museum.* No. 110. 48 mm.

Cyprian vase about 5000 BC. No. 206. No details of size.

Cyprian water bottle. No. 192. 76 mm.

Derby Roman Vase, inscribed: *Roman vase found at Little Chester, Derby.* No. 83. No details of size.

Dorset Cinerary Urn, inscribed: *Cinerary urn with handles found at Dorset.* No. 132. 56 mm.

Dover Cinerary Urn, inscribed: *Cinerary urn found in Dover.* No. 141. 63 mm.

Eastern Olive jar. No. 208. 53 mm.

Egyptian Vase, inscribed: *Ancient Egyptian vase about 250 BC.* No. 84. 43 mm.

Ely Saxon Vase, inscribed: *Ancient Saxon vase, found in Ely.* No. 310. 88 mm.

Exeter Vase, Unnamed Foley model. No. 117. No details of size.

Flemish jug 14th Century. No. 312. 70 mm.

Gastrica Vase, inscribed: *Vase or bottle found at Gastrica. Ancient Cyprian pottery 900 BC.* No. 138. Rd. No. 595629. 51 mm.

Glastonbury Bowl, inscribed: *Bowl from the ancient British lake village near Glastonbury.* No. 101. 34 mm.

Glastonbury Vase, inscribed: *Vase from the ancient British lake village near Glastonbury.* No. 104. 50 mm.

Hanley Chinese Vase, inscribed: *Chinese vase, original in Hanley Museum.* No. 80. 63 mm.

Hanley Egyptian Vase, inscribed: *Ancient Egyptian vase now in Hanley Museum.* No. 88. 63 mm.

Herpes Jug, inscribed: *Jug from cemetery at Herpes, Charente.* No. 183. 45 mm.

Horsham Jug, unnamed Foley model. No. 20. 65 mm.

Indian wine vessel from Temple, Delhi. No. 303. 152 mm.

Irish bronze pot. No. 109. 35 mm.

Italian vase. 15th Century. No. 309. 100 mm.

Italian vase. 16th Century. No. 301. 100 mm.

(The) Kai.—Ping vase, date about 2500 BC. No. 119. 63 mm.

Kang Hi tea caddy. No. 144. 63 mm.

Kang Hi vase, presented to George V. No. 305. 120 mm.

Kent Roman Urn, inscribed: *Roman urn from warriors grave, Kent.* No. 211. 51 mm.

Lesser Pyramid Vase, inscribed: *Vase taken from a tomb under the Lesser Pyramid about 3500 BC.* No. 117. 57 mm.

Letchworth Celtic Urn, inscribed: *Celtic urn found in Letchworth.* No. 199. 80 mm.

Lord Byron's Vase, inscribed: *Fine model of a Greek vase presented to the nation by Lord Byron. Now in South Kensington Museum.* No. 116. 57 mm.

Loving Cup. 3 handled. Not found numbered. 40 mm.

Malta Chatty. No. 89. 44 mm.

Maltese firegrate. No. 39. No details of size.

Newbury Leather Bottle, inscribed: *Leather bottle found on battlefield of Newbury. 1644. Now in museum.* No. 103. 60 mm.

Notre Dame Candlestick, inscribed: *Altar candlestick in church of Notre Dame.* No. 306. 115 mm.

Penmaenmawr Urn, inscribed: *Ancient urn found on Penmaenmawr.* No. 108. 48 mm.

Persian cafeterre (fine), 15th Century. No. 302. 118 mm.

Persian scent bottle 700 AD. No. 212. 55 mm.

Persian Wallace vase. No. 82. No details of size.

Persian wine server. 13th Century. No. 308. 105 mm.

Phoenician vase, original in Stoke-on-Trent Museum. No. 86. 57 mm.

Phoenician water jar. 1000 BC. No. 207. 65 mm.

Pompeian vessel in Burslem Museum. No. 87. 60 mm.

Potters vessel, found in Temple to Buda. No. 150. 54 mm.

Roman money box, found at Lincoln AD307. No. 131. 53 mm.

Roman tear vase, 200 BC. No. 201. 63 mm.

Roman wine vessel 500 BC. no. 142. 51 mm.

Sacred vessel found in Bethlehem. No. 146. 68 mm.

Salami's Lampshade, inscribed: *Lampshade found at Salami's ancient Cyprian pottery.* No. 130. 60 mm.

Salonika Vase, inscribed: *Ancient Greek vase found at Salonika by the British troops when entrenching Jan 1916.* No. 170. 70 mm.

Right Shelley. The 'Ripon Horn Blower'

Left Shelley. No. 409 Mother Shipton and No. 158 Model of the Ripon Hornblower

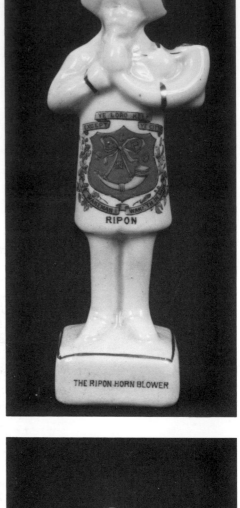

Left Shelley. No. 351 'Model of Legs of Man'

Right Shelley. Cenotaph No. 368 with inscription 'The Glorious Dead'

Left Shelley. No. 318 'Southport Lifeboat Memorial'

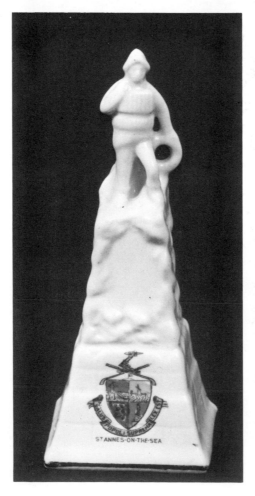

Scandinavian water bottle. No. 143. 83 mm.
Sevres vase, 18th Century. No. 300. 88 mm.
Silchester Urn, inscribed: *Roman urn, from Silchester in Reading Museum.* No. 107. 50 mm.
Silchester Vase, inscribed: *Vase from Silchester in Reading Museum.* No. 102. 51 mm.
Silver rose bowl. No. 147. 63 mm.
Sofia Cup, inscribed: *Very quaint cup found with silver belt, Sofia, Bulgaria.* No. 139. 42 mm.
Staffordshire cow cream jug. No. 317. No details of size.
Swindon Vase, inscribed: *Vase dug up near Swindon.* No. 105. 58 mm.
Tara vase, now in the Vatican, Rome. No. 113. 50 mm.
Tibet Sacred Vase, inscribed *Sacred vase from Temple in Tibet.* No. 209. 60 mm.
Turkish scent jar S.K. No. 202. 66 mm.
Vatican Urn, inscribed: *Golden urn in the Vatican.* No. 145. 78 mm.
Vestel Lamp, inscribed: *Roman vestal lamp. 500 BC.* Has been found with a black boy's head popping out of lamp. No. 149. 90 mm.
Water Bottle, inscribed: *Ancient water bottle of rare form.* No. 136. No details of size.
Weymouth Vase, inscribed: *Roman vase found at Jordan Hill, Weymouth now in Dorset Museum.* No. 85. No details of size.
York Roman Ewer, inscribed: *Roman ewer from original in Hospitium, found in York.* No. 81, 63 mm.

Buildings—White

The Tower, Blackpool, Model of. No. 322. 140 mm.
Blackpool Tower with buildings. No. 412. 160 mm.
Burns cottage, Model of. No. 189. 68 mm. long.
Douglas, Queen Victoria Jubilee Clock 1887. No. 388. 145 mm.
Ross, Town Hall, with Clock Tower (not found numbered). 123 mm. *Shelley.*
Skegness, clock tower, can also be found inscribed: *Monmouth clock tower.* No. 371. 155 mm.
Windsor round tower. No. 372. 88 mm.

Monuments

King Alfred, Statue (not found numbered). 165 mm. *Shelley.*
Southport Lifeboat Memorial. No. 318. 140 mm.
Rock of Ages, with verse (not found numbered). 125 mm. *Shelley.*
Rufus Stone, with lengthy inscriptions (not found numbered). 95 mm. *Shelley.*

Historical/Folklore

Bunyan's Chair (also found inscribed *The old armchair*). No. 347. 90 mm.
Burn's Chair. No. 336. 86 mm.
Mayor jug 1870, Model of. No. 326. No details of size.
Mother Shipton with black hat and cat. With verse: 'Near to the Knaresboro Dropping Well. I first drew breath as records tell'. No. 409. 110 mm.

Sir Walter Scott's chair at Abbotsford, Model of. No. 325. 68 mm.

Traditional/National Souvenirs

Lancashire Clog. No. 162. 57 mm.
Legs of Man, model of. No. 351. Rd. No. 673247. 90 mm.
Lincoln Imp, model of the. No. 160. 122 mm.
Ripon Horn Blower, model of the, with inscription: *The old time custom of sounding the horn at 9 pm each day is still observed.* No. 158. 110 mm.
Kathleen Mavourneen, standing figure of Irish Lady. No. 405. 98 mm.
Pat's Hat and Dudeen, model of. (Irish Topper with pipe moulded on top.) No. 159. 53 mm. (Both of these 'Irish' models are elusive.)
Burns and Highland Mary, an oval base (not found numbered). 118 mm. Shelley.
Thistle Vase, can be found inscribed: *Just a wee deoch-an-Doris.* No. 181. 2 sizes: 50 mm & 65 mm.
Welsh Lady, seated, inscribed: *Cymru-Am-Byth.* No. 404, 95 mm (rare).
Welsh Hat, model of the. Can be found with longest Welsh place name around brim. (Very occasionally the hat can be found painted black with a red hat band.) No. 154, 35 mm.
Swiss Cattle Bell. No. 314. 95 mm.

Seaside Souvenirs

Bathing Machine. No. 320. 70 mm long.
Lifebelt. No. 47, Rd. No. 412402. 100 mm dia.
Lifeboatman, standing by Capstan, inscribed: *Lifesaver.* No. 410. 112 mm (scarce).
Lifeboat, with gold anchor, inscribed: *Maud pickup.* No. 323. 115 mm long.
Motor Boat, model of. No. 343. Rd. No. 671552. 112 mm long.
Paddle Steamer, model of. No. 362. 160 mm long.
Yacht in Sail. No. 401. Rd. No. 659668. 112 mm.
Fisherman's Basket, inscribed: *A good catch.* No. 186. 88 mm long.
Beachy Head Lighthouse. No. 178. 100 mm.
Pharos Lighthouse (not named). No. 73. 98 mm.
Scallop Shell. No. 166. 78 mm wide.
Whelk Shell, inscribed: *What are the wild waves saying.* No. 168. 70 mm long.
Whelk Shell. No. 169. 70 mm long.
Cabin Trunk. No. 167. 75 mm long.
Valise, half open. No. 58. Rd. No. 412403. 73 mm long.

Animals

Bear, walking. No. 67. Rd. No. 447231. 80 mm long.
Camel, kneeling (1 hump). No. 64. Rd. No. 447227. 102 mm long.
Cat, angry, inscribed: *He backs up.* Rd. No. 673247. 2 sizes. No. 195, 90 mm and No. 198, 76 mm.
Cat, comical, and sitting with red bow. No. 333. 132 mm.
Cat, sitting. No. 68, Rd. No. 447139. 64 mm long.

Right Shelley. A very large and appealing comic puppy inscribed on reverse 'some pup'. No. 382

Left Shelley. No. 386 Inscribed 'Scots Guards' on reverse. Mauve tam and black glengarry

Left Shelley. Scottie dog with pink ears and black collar No. 505

Left Shelley. Top row: No. 70 Elephant and No. 64 Camel Bottom row: No. 505 Scottie with pink ears and black nose, No. 62 Fox, and No. 61 Monkey with no inscription

Right Shelley. 'Putney on a Pig', this inscription is not always found on this pig. No. 60

Left Shelley. No. 384 Penguin with book, black markings and orange beak

Right Shelley. No. 63 Model of a plump goose 93 mm

Left Shelley. Comical cats with red bows, two versions of No. 333 which can be found with right or left ear up

Shelley. No. 148 'Model of the Real Cheshire Cat' impressed 'Tim' with pink features and one green eye, standing cat No. 381 with pink ears, green eyes and red mouth, and another 'Tim' exactly the same model as the one on the left but with features picked out in gilding

Shelley. Welsh group. No. 154 'Model of the Welsh Hat' in black with a red band. No. 404 'Cymru-am-byth' a seated Welsh lady and No. 154 an ordinary Welsh Hat

Shelley. 'Blighty is the place for me-e-e'

Shelley. Britannia and Marianne, two rare patriotic models

Cat, standing with long neck. No. 381. No details of size.

Cheshire Cat, model of the Real, impressed: *Tim*. No. 148. 82 mm.

Bulldog, seated, inscribed: *Another Dreadnought*. No. 233. 63 mm.

Bulldog, black, in kennel, inscribed: *Blackwatch* (Also found with Bulldog not painted and no inscription.) No. 316. 95 mm.

Pup standing on hand mirror, inscribed: *Some pup!* No. 382, no details of size. (This number 382 is also found on a large comical Pup, inscribed: *Some pup!* It has black ears and spots. 116 mm.)

Dog, alert terrier. No. 377. 80 mm.

Dog, Scottie, sitting. No. 505. 76 mm.

Dog, Scottie, wearing tam o'shanter. No. 507, no details of size.

Dogs, 2 Scotties, sitting, one wearing tam o'shanter and other wearing a glengarry. Both hats beautifully coloured. Can be found inscribed: *Scots Guards*. No. 386. 88 mm.

Donkey. No. 367. 115 mm long.

Elephant, lying down. No. 70, Rd. No. 447138. 80 mm long.

Elephant, standing. No. 363. 105 mm long.

Fish Jug (tail forms handle). No. 350. 105 mm.

Fox, sitting. No. 62. Rd. No. 447229. 78 mm.

Monkey, sitting, can be found inscribed: *Who hung the monkey?* No. 61. Rd. No. 447230. 64 mm.

Mouse, sitting with paws raised. No. 65. Rd. No. 447226. 70 mm.

Pig, standing with inscription: *You can push, you can shuv but I'm hanged if I'll be druv*. No. 74. 2 sizes: large and small (no other details).

Pig, sitting, with folded arms, found inscribed: *Very umble* or *Sussex pig, won't be druv* or *Putney on a pig*. No. 60. Rd. No. 447312. 80 mm.

Piglet, standing. No. 90. No details of size.

Toad. No. 71. Rd. No. 447141. 47 mm.

Terrapin. No. 69. Rd. No. 447142. 85 mm long.

Birds

Goose, plump. No. 63. Rd. No. 447228. 93 mm.

Penguin, with black beak, and holding newspaper. No. 384. 100 mm (rare).

Swan, with coloured beak. No. 321. 85 mm long.

Swan Posy Holder. No other details available.

Great War

Shelley made quite a small range of Great War souvenirs compared with other manufacturers, however, they did make them for some time and included one of everything. None of these models could really be described as rare except the model of the head of the German Torpedo and the rather patriotic figures marked below. (These were probably quite expensive—3 or 4 shillings—at the time and so did not sell in great numbers.)

Scottish soldier, standing figure, inscribed: *Scotland for ever*. No. 402. 114 mm. (It is difficult to decide if this model is a Great War souvenir or a souvenir of Scotland, but most collectors would include it here. This is not a great problem to many as the model is quite rare.)

Soldier, playing concertina outside a tent, inscribed: *Blighty is the place for Me-e-e*. No. 341. Rd. No. 664306. 108 mm long. (Very evocative of the Great War).

Biplane, usually found with a fixed prop, but can be found with a movable one. No. 344. 150 mm long.

Bleriot Warplane, model of. Monoplane with fixed prop. No. 311. 150 mm long.

Zeppelin, model of. No. 332. 154 mm long.

Battleship, not found named. No. 319. 125 mm long.

Submarine, inscribed *E9*. No. 328. 150 mm long.

Armoured car, model of. No. 329. 120 mm long.

British Tank, model of, with trailing steering wheels. No. 400 (but can be found wrongly numbered 400A). Rd. No. 658588. 140 mm.

Red Cross Van, model of. No. 330. 95 mm long.

Fieldgun. No. 340. 148 mm long.

Howitzer. No. 331. 132 mm long.

Trench Mortar, model of. inscribed: *For freedom*. No. 179. 63 mm.

Trench Mortar, not named, inscribed: *For freedom*. No. 327. 45 mm.

9.2 mm Shell, model of. No. 175. 90 mm.

German Zeppelin Bomb, model of. No. 177. 85 mm.

Mills Hand Grenade, model of. No. 334. 78 mm.

German Mine washed up on the East Coast, model of. Can be found wrongly inscribed: *Head of German torpedo, Model of. German Mine*. No. 188. *German Torpedo*. No. 187. 68 mm. (Torpedo inscription being rare.)

Bandsman's Drum. (Probably originally made as a souvenir of the Boer War, as there are many un-numbered Foley drums around. This model was obviously made for many years.) No. 57. Rd. No. 412407. 32 mm.

Bugle. No. 354. 112 mm.

Fieldglasses. No. 343. 83 mm.

Peaked Cap. (Collectors describe this as an Army Service Cap; it was also probably made as a souvenir of the Boer War.) No. 54. 53 mm dia.

Glengarry. No. 176. 86 mm long.

Anti Zeppelin Candlestick as used during the Great War—souvenir. No. 348. 83 mm (Smaller Arcadian model has light shield on wrong side!).

Fireplace, inscribed: *Keep the home fires burning*. No. 338. 70 mm.

Britannia, standing figure, inscribed: *Rule Britannia*. Some colouring. No. 403. 108 mm (rare).

Marianne. (Stylised female figure representing France—as found on the cover of French comic paper La Baionnette during the Great War),

Right Shelley. Parian bust on
square glazed base

Left Shelley. No. 354 Bugle 2 mm

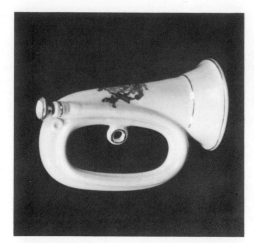

Right Shelley. 'Anti-Zepplin
candlestick as used during the
Great War'

Left Shelley. No. 316
'Blackwatch', a joke item
produced by many firms

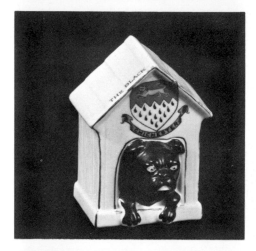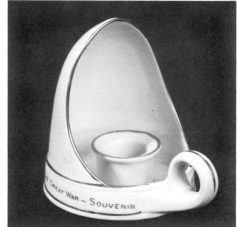

Right Shelley. No. 187 'Head of a
German Torpedo and No. 188
'German mine washed up on the
east coast'. 188 can be found
wrongly inscribed 'Head of a
German Torpedo'

Left Shelley. Howitzer, not
named

Shelley. No. 311 'Bleriot War
Plane' a monoplane with fixed
prop. and Biplane with fixed
prop

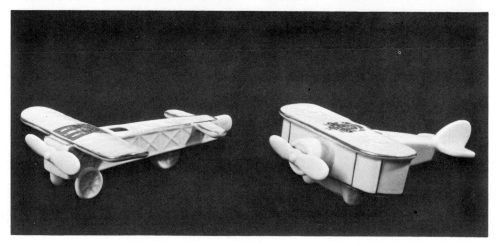

Right Shelley. No. 400 Model of 'British Tank'

Left Shelley. No. 400A 'Model of British Tank'

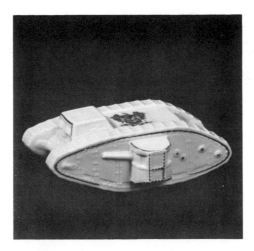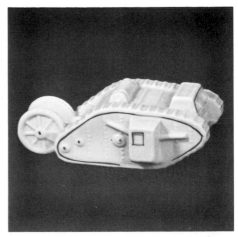

Shelley. No. 329 'Model of Armoured Car'

Shelley. No. 332 Model of Zeppelin

Shelley. No. 328 Submarine usually found inscribed 'E9'

239

Right Shelley. No. 178 'Beachy Head Lighthouse'

Left Shelley. No. 412 Blackpool Tower

Right Shelley. No. 410 a Lifeboatman, black hat and boots

Left Shelley. 'Model of Kang Hi Tea Caddy' with colour transfer print of 'Peterborough Cathedral, West Front' No. 144.

Right Shelley. No. 500 Trilby with black band

Left Shelley. No. 168 Whelk shell with inscription and No. 166 scallop shell

Right Shelley. No. 160 Model of the Lincoln Imp 122 mm

Left Shelley. No. 353 'Model of Motor Boat'

Right Shelley. Fireplace inscribed 'Keep the home fires burning'

Left Shelley. No. 345 Upright piano 76 mm

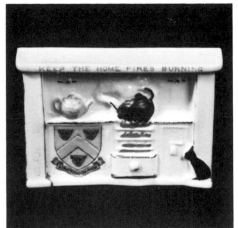

Right Shelley. No. 346 'Model of ye olde lanterne'

Left Shelley. No. 342 a bicycle lamp, only very occasionally found named

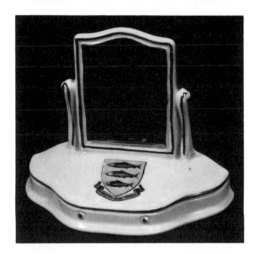

Right Shelley. No. 337 Horn Gramophone 95 mm

Left Shelley. No. 376 Swing mirror on stand with silvered mirror

Right Shelley. No. 347 Bunyan's chair

Shelley. No. 196 a miniature cheese dish

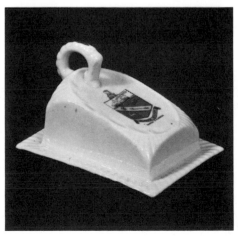

Right Shelley. No. 194 Tennis racquet and three tennis balls

Left Shelley. 'England's Hope' No. 375 A very untypical Shelley model

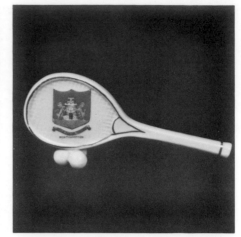

Right Shelley. No. 361 Open motor car

Left Shelley. Model No. 358 a garden roller

Shelley. No. 362 Paddle Steamer

Shelley. No. 365 Locomotive 150 mm long

242

inscribed: *Vive la France*. Some colouring. No. 406. 108 mm (rare).

Cenotaph, flags in relief. No. 368. 2 sizes: 130 mm & 152 mm.

Florence Nightingale, sitting figure. No. 408. 102 mm (rare).

Matlock Bath War Memorial, not found numbered. Rd. No. 417592. 180 mm. *Shelley*.

Home/Nostalgic

Anvil. No. 189. 78 mm long.

Anvil, inscribed: *Every morning sees some task to be done*. No. 183. 183 mm long.

Armchair, inscribed: *The old armchair*. (Also found inscribed 'Bunyan's Chair'.) No. 347. 90 mm.

Baby's Cradle. (Often found not numbered when marked *Foley*.) Found No. 50 and No. 503 (Shelley). 80 mm long.

Bellows. No. 35. Rd. No. 412409. 95 mm long.

Book. No. 56. Rd. No. 412405. 63 mm.

Clock, long case, inscribed: *Model of 14th Century clock in Wallace collection*. Can also be found further inscribed: *Wake up and get to business* (The first inscription is rather odd as there were no longcase clocks in the 14th century.) No. 307. 130 mm.

Desk, roll-topped. No. 380. 80 mm long.

Garden Roller. No. 358. 104 mm long.

Kennel. No. 49. Rd. No. 412408. 55 mm.

Lantern, inscribed: *Model of ye olde lanterne* and *Ancient lights*. No. 346. 105 mm.

Milk Churn. No. 46. Rd. No. 412410. 71 mm.

Shaving Mug. No. 164. 54 mm.

Sundial, octagonal. No. 359. 120 mm.

Swing Mirror on stand. No. 376. 88 mm.

Victorian Pillar Box, model of. No. 137. 90 mm.

Watering Can. No. 163. 63 mm.

Water Pump. No. 51. Rd. No. 412406. 83 mm.

Wheelbarrow. No. 355. 110 mm long.

Comic/Novelty

Black Boy in bath, inscribed: *How ink is made*. Fully coloured. No. 374. Rd. No. 685378. 108 mm long.

Box of Matches, open to reveal contents. Some colouring. No. 190. 74 mm long.

Cigarette Case holding 6 gold-tipped cigarettes. No. 349, no details of size (rather rare).

Coal Hod, inscribed: *Coal rations, Yours to a cinder* or *Your rations to a cinder*. No. 185, no details of size.

Tobacco Pouch, 2 crossed pipes in relief on front. No. 501. 98 mm long (rather rare).

Truck of black coal, inscribed: *Black diamonds from* . . . No. 389. 62 mm long.

Alcohol

Beer barrel. No. 48. Rd. No. 412404. 63 mm.

Beer Barrel on stand. No. 161. 65 mm.

Bottle with cork, inscribed: *All scotch*. No. 214. 90 mm.

Toby Jug, with verse 'No tongue can tell' etc. No. 335. 95 mm.

Sport

Boxer, inscribed: *England's hope*. Brown boxing gloves. No. 375. 100 mm (Thought to be Wally Thom.)

Golf Bag and Clubs. No. 197. 108 mm.

Golf Ball on Tee. No. 215. 52 mm.

Tennis Racquet with 3 Balls. No. 194. 116 mm long.

Musical Instruments

Banjo. No. 72. 127 mm long.

Piano, upright. No. 345. 76 mm.

Transport

Charabanc, inscribed: *The Monarch*. No. 352. 125 mm long.

Cycle Lamp, very rarely found inscribed: *Model of cycle oil head lamp*. No. 342. Rd. No. 664308, 83 mm.

Locomotive. No. 365. 150 mm long.

Open Motor Car. No. 361. 135 mm long. (Scarce.)

Single decker closed Motorbus 'K' type. 125 mm long. No. 370. (Very rare.)

'Modern' Equipment

Flash Lamp, model of. No. 191. 70 mm.

Horn Gramophone. No. 337. Rd. No. 662040. 95 mm.

Miscellaneous

Bishop's Mitre. No. 58, 70 mm.

Top Hat, found numbered 11 and 35. 60 mm wide.

Trilby Hat, with black band. No. 500, no details of size.

Bell, not found numbered. 63 mm. *Foley*.

Dutch Sabot. No. 36. Rd. No. 409599. 84 mm long.

Elephant's Foot, not found numbered, no details of size. *Foley*.

Handbag. No. 184. 85 mm.

Horse's Hoof. No. 52 (often found not numbered marked *Foley*). 45 mm.

Leather Highboot, not found numbered, no details of size. *Shelley*.

Shield on stand, not found numbered. 52 mm. *Foley*.

Miniature Domestic

Cheese Dish. No. 196. 50 mm.

Tea Pot, inscribed: *Take a cup of tea*. (not numbered). 50 mm. *Shelley*.

Numbered Ornamental Wares

This list is included for Shelley Collectors who may be interested: obviously all of these objects were made to carry crests or views, as other domestic ware produced by the firm was not numbered. Some of the vases and jugs below may well be unnamed ancient artefacts, and hopefully named models will be discovered.

No. 1. Pin Tray.

No. 3. Dish with ribbed sides. 120 mm dia.

No. 7. Vase, 2 handled with crinkle top. 56 mm.

No. 21. Vase. 70 mm.

No. 22. Vase, shaped. 38 mm.

No. 24. Pot, with lid. 50 mm dia.

No. 25. Vase, 2 handles, with bulbous base. 60 mm.

No. 26. Vase, 2 handles. 40 mm.
No. 27. Vase, 2 handles, with crinkle top. Rd. No. 380408. 85 mm.
No. 28. Jug, square. 35 mm.
No. 30. Jug. Rd. No. 409600. 72 mm.
No. 32. Jug, small, no details of size.
No. 33. Vase, 2 handles. 54 mm.
No. 40. Cream Jug. 55 mm.
No. 41. Jug. 63 mm.
No. 42. Jug. 65 mm.
No. 43. Vase, 2 handles. 54 mm.

No. 44. Jug, 2 handles. 50 mm.
No. 45. Vase, crinkle top. 52 mm.
No. 106. Vase. 65 mm. (Must be unnamed ancient artefact.)
No. 112. Taper Vase. 60 mm.
No. 120. Box, heart-shaped, no details of size.
No. 165. Pen and Ink Stand. 60 mm long.
No. 173. Salt Pot, circular. 100 mm.
No. 174. Pepper Pot, circular. 100 mm.
No. 339. Candleholder. 102 mm.

Signal Series

Trademark used by an unknown manufacturer.

There is so much information on this mark that at first glance it seems that it will be easy to identify. Unfortunately the mark does not seem to have been registered or advertised. The initials E. & S. Ltd and G. & S. were not used by known manufacturers. The small 45 mm bulbous vase found with this mark has a Cork crest, so it is possible that the china was made in Ireland. (The style of the mark is late, perhaps 1920 onwards.)

Snowdon China

Trademark used for the Snowdon Mountain Tramroad and Hotels Co Ltd on china manufactured by Arkinstall & Sons Ltd, Arcadian Works, Stoke-on-Trent.

For further details of this china and manufacturer see ARCADIAN CHINA.

All crests found on china with this mark are either of Snowdon or Snowdon Mountain Tramroad & Hotels Co Ltd. (This is a most striking red, white and black crest with the initials S.M.T.) The china, which appears to have been made before the Great War, is very fine and well produced.

Snowdon Models

Traditional/National Souvenirs
Welsh Hat, model of, with longest Welsh place name round brim. (That is Llanfairpwllgwyngyllgogerychwyrndrob willantysiliogogogoch). 52 mm.

Home/Nostalgic
Umbrella, open. 50 mm dia.

'Modern' Equipment
Camera folding. 60 mm.

Souvenir Series

Trademark used by an unknown manufacturer for a London wholesaler or retailer.

H. & S. London must have commissioned a series of commemoratives of the Great War. Two 'smalls' have been found with transfer prints of four flags of the Allies with the inscription: *We are fighting for a just cause.*

Spencer Art China

Trademark used for a retailer
by a Fenton manufacturer.

SPENCER
ART
CHINA
FENTON
STAFFS

The models below both have Isle of Wight crests and one would assume that 'Spencer' was a retailer or wholesaler on that Island. (No potter or pottery named Spencer was working in Fenton from 1900–1920.) The three Fenton manufacturers known to have produced a quantity of crested china were E. Hughes Ltd, A. G. Harley Jones and James Reeves. E. Hughes mostly made domestic ware so they were hardly likely to have produced two odd buildings. The other two manufacturers could have used this mark but A. G. Harley Jones is possibly the most likely candidate as he used the term *Art China* in his marks (see WILTON CHINA).

One 'small' has been found with a Leeds crest, which could have been used to fill another order.

Spencer Art Models

Buildings—White
Osborne House. 150 mm long.

Monuments
Arch Rock, Freshwater Bay. 82 mm.

Stanley China

Trademark used by Charles
Amison (& Co Ltd), Stanley
China Works, Wedgwood St.
Longton.

STANLEY CHINA
C·A
L

This firm was established in 1889 and manufactured porcelain. (The factory closed in 1941 and was reopened in 1946, and continues to make *Stanley fine bone china* today.) Like most fairly successful firms. Amison made a small range of crested china wares when these were very fashionable. The models made seem to have sold well in the North of England.

Charles Amison did not make commemoratives or miniature souvenirs of the Great War. No view ware or transfer devices have been recorded.

Stanley Models

Traditional/National Souvenirs
Lancashire Clog. 135 mm long.

Home/Nostalgic
Pillar Box. 76 mm.

Miniature Domestic
Cheese dish and cover. 50 mm.

Star Bazaar Art China

Trademark used for the Star
Bazaar, Douglas, Isle of Man,
on china thought to have
been manufactured by
Hewitt & Leadbeater, Willow
Potteries, Longton.

STAR BAZAAR
ART CHINA
DOUGLAS
I OF M

For details of Hewitt & Leadbeater see WILLOW ART CHINA.

This mark is only found on china with Douglas or Isle of Man crests. Hewitt & Leadbeater often used *Art China* in marks designed for retailers, and the models below could have been produced by them.

Star Bazaar Models

Animals
Manx cat with collar, not named.
63 mm.

Home/Nostalgic
Anvil 50 mm.

Right Shelley. No. 190 Box of matches, slightly opened to reveal contents

Left Savoy. 'Model of extinguisher' (candle snuffer) with Battle of the Marne, Great War inscription

Right Ryecroft. 'Town Hall, Stockton-on-Tees'

Left Snowdon China. 'Model of Welsh Hat'. The usual 'Arcadian' model but with the superb Snowdon crest

Right Star Bazaar. Manx cat with 'Star Bazaar' mark and Isle of Man crest

Left Syren. This rather comic duck marked 'Syren' is an unpainted version of the Carlton model usually found with green coloured base and yellow beak.

Right St. George. 60 mm jug with black transfer print of 'The Old Curiosity Shop' and a print of Charles Dickens on the reverse

Left St. George. Cat on drum 90 mm and two elephants on sledge 70 mm

Strand China

Trademark used for a London
retailer by Podmore China
Co, Elm Street, Hanley.

For details of this china and manufacturer see PODMORE CHINA.

All models with this mark carry a City of London crest, presumably the retailer having premises in the Strand. The two Memorials are found in the *Podmore China* range but the Woodpecker is not.

Strand Models

Birds
Woodpecker. No details of size.

Great War
Cenotaph, inscribed: *The glorious dead
  MCMXIX* Green wreaths. 130 mm.
Edith Cavell Memorial, London. inscribed:
  *Edith Cavell Brussels dawn October 12th
  1915. Humanity Sacrifice.* 142 mm.

Success (Art) China

Trademark used by an
unknown manufacturer, or
manufacturers.

The fact that two quite different marks are found can either indicate that the tradename was used for a long time or that the name was used by more than one manufacturer. There are so few models found with these marks (and unfortunately the two were not recorded separately) that one must accept that they could be from two manufacturers.

The Art China mark could have been used by Hewitt & Leadbeater (see WILLOW ART CHINA). The Garter mark is much more difficult, for several firms used this device, including Hewitt & Leadbeater in retailers' marks. No models have stock numbers or inscriptions which give clues to the manufacturer so until such a piece is found the marks must remain unidentified.

The Salisbury Kettle listed below has a coloured transfer print of Beachy Head.

Success (Art) Models

Ancient Artefacts
Salisbury Leather Kettle, not named.
  61 mm.

Home/Nostalgic
Anvil. 58 mm.
Grandfather Clock. 121 mm.

Sussex China

Trademark used for an
Eastbourne retailer by
Sampson Hancock (& Sons),
Bridge Works, Stoke.

For further details of this china and manufacturer see THE CORONA CHINA.

All models with this mark carry an Eastbourne Crest. For the most part the models are identical to those found in the Corona range, except that there were two versions of Beachy Head Lighthouse made specially for this retailer. The models were probably made during the Great War.

Sussex China Models

Historical/Folklore
Ark. 90 mm long.

Traditional/National Souvenirs
Harp. 90 mm.

Seaside Souvenirs
Lighthouse. 104 mm.
Beachy Head Lighthouse, black band. 2
  sizes: 102 mm & 118 mm.

Animals
Teddy Bear, sitting. 85 mm.

Great War
British Airship on base, 128 mm long.
Lusitania. 163 mm long.
Submarine, inscribed *E4*. 102 mm long.

Sussex China S.P. Co.

Trademark used for a Sussex
wholesaler by Arkinstall &
Son Ltd, Arcadian Works,
Stoke-on-Trent.

SUSSEX CHINA

MADE IN ENGLAND
S. P. C⁰

For further details of this china and manufacturer see ARCADIAN
CHINA.

S.P.Co. must have been a wholesaler in fancy goods or had a chain of
shops because china models with this mark have crests from all over
Sussex. Coloured transfer prints of Sussex views have been recorded but
no other transfer devices, indicating that the mark was probably only
used between 1914 and 1920.

Sussex S.P. Co. Models

Ancient Artefacts
Newbury Leather Bottle, inscribed: *Model
of leather bottle found on battlefield of
Newbury 1644 now in museum.* 65 mm.

Buildings—White
Cottage. 55 mm.

Seaside Souvenirs
Whelk Shell. 100 mm long.

Animals
Dog, Staffordshire bull terrier, sitting.
72 mm.
Pig, sitting. 63 mm long. (It is very odd
that none of the named 'Arcadian'
Sussex pigs have been recorded with
this mark.)
Rabbit, lying, ears along back. 70 mm long.

Great War
Battleship, 3 funnels and tiny gun fore and
aft. 120 mm long.

Red Cross Van. 85 mm long.
Howitzer. 140 mm long.
Mills Hand Grenade, model of. 62 mm.
Bell Tent. 64 mm dia.
Sandbag, model of. Rd. No. 638678.
73 mm long.
Trench Dagger, model of. Rd. No. 637649.
102 mm long.

Home/Nostalgic
Old Armchair, not named. 90 mm.

Comic/Novelty
Pea pod, curved and split to reveal four
peas. 133 mm long. (This model has not
been recorded with an 'Arcadian' mark
and is rare.)
Policeman, no inscription. 140 mm.

Musical Instruments
Piano, upright. 70 mm long.

Miscellaneous
Knight, chess piece. 63 mm.

Sussex Ware

Trademark used for
Cheesman & Co., Brighton
by Hewitt & Leadbeater,
Willow Potteries, Longton.

No details of mark available

For further details of this china and manufacturer see WILLOW ART
CHINA.

The sixth edition of the Goss Record published in 1906–7 carries an
advert for the Goss Agent in Brighton, Cheesman & Co, 169 North
Street, Brighton. In the advert the firm announces the sale of their
'Sussex Ware' including 'Ye Olde Sussex Pig', green with ivory
decoration or brown with hop decoration. In 1905 when the new firm of
Hewitt & Leadbeater was given a write-up in the Pottery Gazette, 'Hop
Ware' was one of their newly invented lines. Hewitt & Leadbeater
obviously went on to make heraldic china for Cheesman & Co until well
after the Great War.

No 'Ye Olde Sussex Pigs' have been recorded but would be a delightful
novelty to look out for. They would probably not carry the Sussex China
Garter mark.

Swan China

Trademark used by Charles
Ford, Cannon St, Hanley,
subsequently a branch of
J. A. Robinson & Sons Ltd.
(see ARCADIAN CHINA).

The original firm, known as T. & C. Ford at this address, was formed in
1854. By 1871 it was known as Thomas Ford, and in 1874 it became
Charles Ford. (Presumably all these Fords were members of the same
family.) Production of view ware and crested china seems to have begun
at the turn of the century. Very shortly after this, in 1904, Mr Harold
Taylor Robinson gained control of the firm and merged it with Robinson
& Beresford in 1907. In 1910, Charles Ford was made a branch of J. A.
Robinson & Sons Ltd, and production of Swan China was moved to the
Arcadian Works. It is very difficult to distinguish original Charles Ford
moulds from Arkinstall moulds, as both were used at the Arcadian
Works and models were marked *Swan* or *Arcadian*. (Pieces are often
found with both marks.) Early *Swan* models seem to be heavier than
Arcadian China, these include miniature domestic items, small vases and
animals. Later *Swan* and *Arcadian* models are identical. The *Swan* mark
does not seem to have been used after 1925.

Early Charles Ford models can be found with views, monochrome
only, and crests, often accompanied by suitable long and learned historic
details concerned with the place or person. These do not appear on
Arcadian China. An interesting range of all the crests of English
Monarchs (about forty) can be found, each crest on a different small
piece, with this kind of historical information printed on the reverse.

Polychrome view ware is the same as *Arcadian*, as are other transfer
decorations including tropical birds, cockerels and Raphael Tuck
Cartoons. (These are always found with 'By special permission of
Raphael Tuck & Sons Ltd' printed on the base when marked *Swan*.)

Great War commemoratives and inscriptions are the same as Arcadian
including crests of the Allies, but as yet the only military crest recorded is
that of the Lincolnshire Regiment. A Lucky Black Cat transfer has been
found, but these are not common. No Lucky White Heather devices have
been recorded.

Numbering System. Original Charles Ford models carry painted stock
numbers, but few of these have been recorded. Models made at the
Arcadian Works have printed stock numbers which do not correspond to
the numbers found on similar *Arcadian* pieces. Stock numbers are given
where known in the following lists.

Swan Models

NB. *Arc* indicates that models are also
found marked *Arcadian*.

Unglazed/Parian

These busts can be found with crests on
their glazed bases.
Bust of King Edward VII on circular glazed
base. 140 mm. *Arc*.
Bust of Queen Alexandra, on circular
glazed base. 140 mm. *Arc*.
Bust of King George V, on circular glazed
base. 135 mm. *Arc*.
Bust of Queen Mary, can be found
inscribed: *Queen Mary, born May 26th
1867*. 135 mm. *Arc*.
Bust of Sir John Jellicoe, on square glazed
base. 155 mm. *Arc*.

Bust of General Joffre, on square glazed
base. 155 mm. *Arc*.
Bust of Lloyd George, on circular glazed
base. 135 mm. *Arc*.

Ancient Artefacts

These models are all found in the Arcadian
range but Swan models sometimes carry
slightly different inscriptions (probably
indicating that they were original
Charles Ford models). It should be noted
that even on identical models the stock
numbers are not usually the same as
Arcadian. (These are given where
known.) All inscriptions begin: *Model of*,
so this will not be repeated throughout
the list.

Right Swan. Dog lying with crossed paws 108 mm long

Left Swan. 'Swan' Polar Bear 130 mm long, is not at all like the usual 'Arcadian' model and has not as yet been found with that mark

Right Swan. 'Novel collecting box for the Royal National Lifeboat Institution, Robin Hoods Bay'

Left Swan. Cock with some colouring inscribed 'Cock o'the North'

Left Swan. Ripon Hornblower with Ripon crest

Right Swan. 'Model of Egyptian Water Bottle'

Left Swan. Yellow tinted vase with Raphael Tuck cartoon 'None but the brave deserve the fair'

 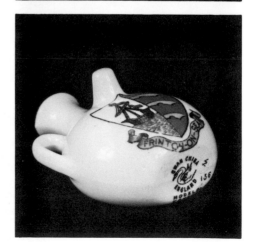

250

Butter Pot, old, of 17th Century (not found numbered). 45 mm. *Arc.*
Canterbury Roman Vase, inscribed: *Roman vase found near Canterbury original in Canterbury Museum.* No. 282. 65 mm. *Arc.* No. 24.
Chinese Vase, Original in Hanley Museum (not found numbered). 58 mm. *Arc.* No. 127.
Devon Oak Pitcher, inscribed: *Oak pitcher peculiar to Devon.* No. 192. 60 mm. *Arc.* No. 165.
Fountains Abbey Cup, inscribed: *The Abbots cup from the original at the Fountains Abbey.* No. 709. 50 mm. *Arc.*
Glastonbury Vase, inscribed: *Vase from the ancient British lake village near Glastonbury.* (Number not known.) 50 mm. *Arc.* No. 642.
Highland Whisky Bowl (not found numbered). 134 mm wide. *Arc.*
Kendal Jug, inscribed: *Jug in Kendal Museum* (number not known). 75 mm. *Arc.* No. 9.
Lincoln Jack from Original in Museum. No. 50. 62 mm. *Arc.* No. 50.
Loving Cup originated by Henry of Navarre King of France. 3-handled (not found numbered). 2 sizes: 40 mm & 52 mm. *Arc.* 40 mm. No. 579.
Phoenician Vase, Original in Stoke on Trent Museum. No. 217. 60 mm. *Arc.* No. 25.
Puzzle Jug, Original in South Kensington Museum, with verse: 'Try how to drink and not to spill'. No. 147. 70 mm. *Arc.* No. 147.
Shakespeare's Jug, not found named or numbered. 54 mm. *Arc.*
Toby Jug, not found named or numbered. 61 mm. *Arc.* No. 253.
Winchelsea Vase, inscribed: *Vase found in Winchelsea.* (Number not known.) 82 mm. *Arc.* 75 mm. No. 87.
Winchester Vase, inscribed: *Vase found near Winchester.* No other details available. *Arc.*
York Roman Ewer, inscribed: *Roman ewer from original in Hospitium found at York.* (Number not known.) 55 mm. *Arc.* No. 57.
York Roman Urn, no other details available. (Not as yet found in Arcadian but it is very probable that they made this model.)

Buildings—Coloured
Only one such building has been found, the same model being made by Arcadian but in different sizes.
Shakespeare's House. 84 mm long.

Buildings—White
All models are also found marked Arcadian but inscriptions and size can differ.
Anne Hathaway's Cottage, Shottery, Near Stratford-on-Avon, Model of. 83 mm long. *Arc.*
First and Last Refreshment House in England. 73 mm long. *Arc.*
Highland Cottage, model of. 80 mm. *Arc.* 50 mm–63 mm.

Irish Round Tower. 106 mm. *Arc.*
Marble Arch. 65 mm. *Arc.*
Southampton Bargate, not found named. 66 mm. *Arc.*

Crosses
Celtic Cross, not named. 125 mm.
Iona Cross, not named. 120 mm. *Arc.* 142 mm.

Historical/Folklore
Ancient Coaching Hat, model of. 65 mm long. *Arc.* No. 687.
Davey Safety Lamp 1836. 85 mm. *Arc.* but no inscription.
Judge, bust, with inscription: *Defend the children of the poor and punish the wrong doer.* Copy of inscription of New Bailey Court, London. 2 sizes: 55 mm & 70 mm. *Arc.*
Mother Shipton, with verse: 'Near to Knaresboro dropping well'. 115 mm. *Arc.*
Man in Stocks. 88 mm. *Arc.*

Traditional/National Souvenirs
Luton Boater, not named. 78 mm dia. *Arc.*
Melton Mowbray Pie, The. Pie with moulded pastry adornments, with verse Though you travel by train or by liner, in search of a pie that is finer. North, South, East or West, Melton Mowbray's the best' and inscribed: *Here's a genuine one 'Made in China'.* Rd. No. 610084. 50 mm. (A late model has been found marked *Clifton,* but not as yet found marked *Arcadian*—Rare.)
Ripon Hornblower with inscription: *The ancient custom etc.* Rd. No. 535941. 130 mm.
Welsh Lady, bust. 65 mm. *Arc.*
Welsh Leek, can be found with inscription: *King Henry V. The Welshmen did goot servace (at Crecy) in a garden where leeks did grow. Shakespeare.* 98 mm. *Arc.*

Seaside Souvenirs
Bathing Machine with '32' above the door. 85 mm. *Arc.*
Lifeboat with blue band and yellow rigging. Can be found inscribed: *John Birch.* 118 mm long. *Arc.* but not with this inscription.
Novel Collecting Box for the Royal National Lifeboat Institution Robin Hoods Bay, model of. Fish standing on square base inscribed: *My diet is £.s.d.* Rd. No. 284246. 128 mm. (A very early model made for W. A. Smith, Robin Hoods Bay—very rare.)
Rowing Boat, with coloured rope. 115 mm long.
Fishing Basket, found inscribed: *A good catch.* Rd. No. 629116. 50 mm.
Beachy Head Lighthouse, not found named. 102 mm. *Arc.*
Eddystone Lighthouse. 105 mm. *Arc.,* but not named.
Pharos Lighthouse, Fleetwood, model of. 88 mm. *Arc.* not this size. (Lighthouse also found not named 127 mm, could possibly be Cove Sea Lighthouse, *Arc.*)
Scallop Shell. 70 mm dia. *Arc.*

Right Swan. 'Model of colonial Hat'

Left Swan. 'Model of clip of bullets with a colour transfer print of 'Ollerton church', rather an odd model to carry such a transfer

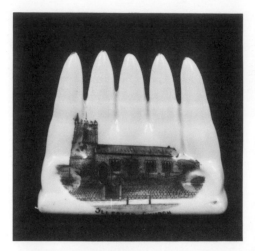

Swan. Two sailor busts, unnamed Great War bust with no inscription and the older 'Sailor Beware', in this case also inscribed 'Dreadnought'

Swan. Rare whippet tank, with large hexagonal turret

Scallop Shell Menu Holder. 62 mm.

Shell Ink Well, one open shell inverted on another, inscribed: *We are always glad to hear from you.* 105 mm. *Arc.*

Countryside

Beehive on Table. Rd. No. 629167. 78 mm. *Arc.* but not named.

Haystack, rectangular. 50 mm. *Arc.*

Animals

Cat, angry, standing with arched back and green eyes, no inscription. 63 mm long. *Arc.*

Cat, long necked and sitting. Inscribed: *My word if your not off.* 108 mm. *Arc.*

Cat, sitting, and smiling (grotesque, rather similar to Cheshire Cat). 75 mm. *Arc.*

Cat, sitting, with bow round neck. 56 mm. *Arc.*

Black Cat, sitting in octagonal dish. 100 mm wide. (Must be *Arc.* mould but no example found marked *Arcadian*.)

Dog, Collie, lying down, inscribed: *Shetland Collie.* 78 mm long. *Arc.*, no inscription.

Dog, lying, with crossed paws. 108 mm long.

Dog, King Charles Spaniel, begging on cushion. 68 mm. *Arc.*

Dog, Pup, with one ear raised. 68 mm. *Arc.*

Dog, Scottish Terrier. 66 mm long. *Arc.*

Elephant, African (big ears). 58 mm.

Elephant, trunk modelled free from body, inscribed: *Baby Jumbo.* 50 mm. *Arc.*

Fish, open-mouthed. 108 mm long. *Arc.*

Frog, open-mouthed and green eyes. No. 10. Rd. No. 535943. 80 mm long. *Arc.*

Hare. 73 mm long. *Arc.*

Lion, walking. 110 mm. *Arc.*

Monkey, sitting, hand to mouth. 65 mm. *Arc.*

Pig, lying down, alert ears. 78 mm long.

Pig, sitting and fat. No. 587. 90 mm long.

Pig, standing, with drooping ears. No. 300. 90 mm long.

Sussex Pig, model of, standing thin pig, inscribed: *You can push or you can shuv but I'm hanged if I'll be druv.* 78 mm long. *Arc.* No. 148.

Piglet, standing, with erect ears. No. 277. 73 mm long.

(It would seem that Charles Ford were great Pig makers.)

Polar Bear. 2 sizes: 100 mm & 136 mm long. *Arc.* 100 mm size.

Teddy Bear. 68 mm. *Arc.*

Tortoise. 72 mm long. *Arc.*

Welsh Goat, model of, inscribed: *Yr Afr Cymreig.* 100 mm long. *Arc.*

Birds (including Eggs)

Chick breaking out of egg, can be found inscribed: *Just out* or *Latest out.* 63 mm long. *Arc.*, but not with 2nd inscription.

Egg, with flattened base. 44 mm.

Cock, standing, legs modelled separately, inscribed: *Cock o'th North.* Some colouring to head. 100 mm. *Arc.*

Hen, roosting. 54 mm. *Arc.*

Owl, baby. 40 mm. *Arc.*

Swan. 70 mm long. *Arc.*

Great War

All models were made in the Arcadian Works so items not also found marked Arcadian are inevitably rare. Many of these models are found with the inscription: *War Edition AD 1914*, as are Arcadian models.

'Arry, bust of airman. 83 mm (very rare).

British Soldier, model of, on oval domed base. Often unnamed. 135 mm. *Arc.*

Despatch Rider, model of, on motorbike. Rd. No. 657737. 120 mm long. *Arc.*

Nurse and Wounded Tommy, model of. Rd. No. 658674. 108 mm long. *Arc.*

Nurse, inscribed: *Soldier's friend.* Red Cross on chest. 132 mm. *Arc.*

Russian Cossack, model of, on horseback. 122 mm. *Arc.*

Sailor, bust, found with hatband impressed: *HMS Dreadnought* or *HMS Queen Elizabeth.* Inscribed: *The handyman.* Rd. No. 652244. 92 mm. *Arc.*

Sailor, bust, inscribed: *Sailor beware* and with verse 'Hearts of Oak'. Rd. No. 539930/8. 95 mm. (This was registered well before the Great War in 1910, and should not really be included here. It has also been found marked *Clifton*.)

Sailor, standing with hands on hips. 132 mm. *Arc.*

Sailor, winding Capstan, model of. Rd. No. 658875. 105 mm. *Arc.*

Scotch Soldier, model of, on domed oval base. 135 mm. *Arc.*

Soldier, bust, inscribed: *Tommy Atkins* with verse: 'Soldiers of the King'. Some colouring. 90 mm. *Arc.*

Soldier with respirator, bust, inscribed: *Model of new gas mask.* 95 mm. *Arc.* (see Arcadian listings for comment).

Tommy Driving a Steam Roller over the Kaiser, inscribed: *To Berlin.* 120 mm long. *Arc.* (see Arcadian listings for comment).

Tommy in Bayonet Attack, model of. Rd. No. 658676. 130 mm. *Arc.*

Tommy on Sentry Duty, model of. 110 mm. *Arc.*

Tommy Throwing his Grenade, model of. 130 mm. *Arc.*

New Aeroplane, model of. Biplane with fixed prop, and roundels in relief. 120 mm long. *Arc.*

New Aeroplane, model of, with revolving prop. 153 mm long. *Arc.*

British Airship, model of. 120 mm long. *Arc.*

British Airship on stand. 128 mm long. *Arc.*

Observer or Sausage Balloon, model of. 84 mm. *Arc.* (Rare.)

Super Zeppelin, model of. 127 mm long. *Arc.*

Battleship, inscribed: *HMS Queen Elizabeth.* 115 mm long. *Arc.*

Battleship, 3 funnels. 120 mm long. *Arc.*

Torpedo Boat Destroyer, model of. Rd. No. 658687. 126 mm long. *Arc.*

Submarine, inscribed: *E4.* 95 mm long. *Arc.*

Submarine, inscribed *E5.* 126 mm long. *Arc.*

Armoured car, model of. 95 mm long. *Arc.*

Red Cross Van, red cross on each side and rear. 'EH 139' printed on radiator. 85 mm long. *Arc.*

Tank, model of, with inset steering wheels. Rd. No. 658588. 115 mm long. *Arc.*

Tank, model of, with trailing steering wheels. Found inscribed: *Original made in Lincoln* with Lincoln crest. Rd. No. 658585. 144 mm long. *Arc*, but no inscription.

Field Gun. 140 mm long. *Arc.*

German Howitzer, not named. 140 mm long. *Arc.*

Trench Mortar, model of. 70 mm long. *Arc.*

Anti Aircraft Shell, model of. 98 mm. *Arc.*

Cannon Shell. 2 sizes: 70 mm & 90 mm. The 90 mm size is often inscribed: *Jack Johnson. Arc.*

Clip of Bullets, model of. Rd. No. 657648. 57 mm. *Arc.*

Bomb dropped from Zeppelin, model of. 75 mm. *Arc.*

Cannister Bomb, model of. Rd. No. 657700. 60 mm. *Arc.*

German Aerial Torpedo, model of. 88 mm long. *Arc.*

Bandsman's Drum. 53 mm. *Arc.*

Capstan. 56 mm. *Arc.*

Ghurka Knife, model of. 110 mm long. *Arc.*

Pair of Field Glasses, model of, often found not named. 78 mm long. *Arc.*

Sandbag. 70 mm long.

Tommy's Hut, model of. 105 mm long. *Arc.*

Waterbottle, model of. Rd. No. 657995. *Arc.*

Colonial Hat, model of. Rd. No. 657738. 88 mm wide. *Arc.*

Glengarry. 90 mm long. *Arc.*

Officer's Peaked Cap, with coloured badge and hatband. 65 mm dia. *Arc.*

Home/Nostalgic

Anvil. 66 mm. *Arc.*

Bellows. 95 mm long. *Arc.*

Chair, highbacked. 90 mm. *Arc.*

Firebucket. 55 mm. *Arc.*

Fruit Basket. 63 mm. *Arc.*

Grandfather Clock, model of a, usually found inscribed: *Make use of time let not advantage slip. Shakespeare.* Can be found inscribed: *The time of day.* 110 mm. *Arc.* No. 209, but not with 2nd inscription.

Milkchurn. 63 mm. *Arc.*

Pillar Box, inscribed: *GRV* and *If you haven't time to post a line here's the pillar box.* 63 mm. *Arc.*

Stool, 3 legged. 40 mm. *Arc.*

Comic/Novelty

Clown, bust, inscribed: *Put me amongst the girls,* some colouring. Rd. No. 522477. 80 mm. *Arc.*

Jester, double faced, happy and sad, and eyes open and closed. Can be found inscribed: *Ye jester awake, ye jester asleep.* Rd. No. 473172. 65 mm. *Arc.*

Policeman on duty, with verse: 'A Policeman's lot is not a happy one'. Can occasionally be found inscribed: *Controlling the traffic.* 148 mm. *Arc.*

Suffragette handbell, double-faced. Front, sour old lady, inscribed: *Votes for women.* Back, pretty young girl, inscribed: *This one shall have the vote.* Some colouring. No details of size. *Arc.*

Cartoon/Comedy Characters

Harry Lauder, bust, not named. Inscribed: *Stop ye're tickling Jock.* 83 mm. *Arc.* (rare).

Mrs Gummidge, standing figure, with inscription: *A lone lorn creetur and everything goes contrary with her.* 112 mm. *Arc.* (rare).

Alcohol

Beer Barrel, on stand. Rd. No. 607828. 40 mm.

Monk, jovial and holding glass, with verse: 'A Jovial Monk am I'. 2 sizes: 70 mm & 112 mm. *Arc.*

Soda Syphon. 100 mm. *Arc.*

Sport

Cricket Bag. 80 mm long. *Arc.*

Golf Ball, inscribed: *The game of golf was first played in the year 1448.* 42 mm. *Arc.*

Tennis Racquet. 90 mm long. *Arc.*

Musical Instruments

Guitar. 153 mm long. *Arc.*

Piano, Upright. 70 mm long. *Arc.*

Tambourine. 70 mm dia. *Arc.*, but not this size.

Transport

Car, Saloon, inscribed: *EH 139.* 76 mm long. *Arc.*

Can of Petrol, impressed: *Motor spirit.* 55 mm. *Arc.*

Miscellaneous

Fireman's Helmet. 82 mm long (rare).

Mortar Board. 66 mm long (rare).

Handbell, no clapper. 53 mm. *Arc.*

Rook, chess piece. 55 mm. *Arc.*

Sabot, pointed toe. No. 352. 103 mm long.

Miniature Domestic

Cheese dish, one piece. 50 mm. *Arc.*

Cheese dish and cover. 50 mm. *Arc.*

Teapot and Lid. No. 145. 40 mm (early).

1919–1921

Sylvan China

Trademark used by Dura Porcelain Co. Ltd, Empress Pottery, Hanley.

This very short lived firm, established in 1919 and closed in 1921, seems to have been created to make crested souvenirs and dolls' heads to fill the market for cheap German wares that could no longer be imported. An advert for the firm in the Pottery Gazette of September 1920 illustrates some of their products including dolls' heads, and crested china boot, monoplane, red cross van, Florence Nightingale statue, hen and Shetland Pony. (None of the models illustrated have been recorded.) Presumably when German goods returned to Britain after the war they were still cheaper than the Dura Company could manage—a constant problem for British manufacturers except during the war.

The china is actually quite reasonable and the crests are very well produced.

Sylvan Models

Historic/Folklore
Burns Chair, Model of. No details of size.
Mary Queen of Scots Chair, Edinburgh Castle, Model of. 76 mm.

Traditional/National Souvenirs
Welsh Hat. 55 mm.

Animals
Scottie Dog, black, looking out of Kennel. Inscribed: *Black Watch.* Green bow. 68 mm.

Birds
Cockerel. No details of size.

Home/Nostalgic
Fireplace, inscribed: *East or West home is best, Home Sweet Home.* Some colouring. 95 mm long.

Comic/Novelty
Billiken sitting on throne, inscribed: *The God of things as they ought to be.* 100 mm.

Alcohol
Toby Jug, with verse. 88 mm.

Sport
Golf Ball, inscribed: *The ancient game of golf was first played in 1448.* No details of size.

Miniature Domestic
Cheese dish and cover. 45 mm.

Syren China

Trademark used by Wiltshaw & Robinson Ltd, Carlton Works, Stoke on Trent.

For details of this china and manufacture see CARLTON CHINA.

This mark has only been found on one small vase and the model listed below. As the duck is normally painted and rather more delicate when marked *Carlton*, one suspects that this mark was used for a cheap range for a small retailer or a mark used by the company on wares which were not good enough to be marked *Carlton*.

Syren Model

Birds
Duck on base. 102 mm. (This duck is from the same mould as the one in the series of birds with green bases and coloured beaks. This one has no colouring.)

Talbot China

Trademark used for a retailer by Sampson Hancock (and Sons), Bridge Works, Stoke.

For further details of this china and manufacturer see THE CORONA CHINA.

The models listed below are obviously from the *Corona* range. H. B. and Co. must have been a retailer, the only crest recorded being Castle Coombe, so it is probable that he had a shop in that area.

Talbot Models

Animals
Fish Vase. 60 mm.

Miscellaneous
King. Chess Piece. 115 mm.

TAYLOR & KENT
LONGTON
ENGLAND

1912+

Taylor and Kent

Trademark used by Taylor
and Kent (Ltd), Florence
Works, Longton.

For details of this china and manufacturer see FLORENTINE CHINA.

Taylor and Kent only used this mark on coloured buildings without crests. I suspect these were finished to a higher standard than the *Florentine* range and so the company were happy to have their name on them. The mark was registered in 1912 so it is probable that these models were made before the Great War. Taylor and Kent made some models of buildings after 1930 but these have a slightly different mark, with the addition of a new trade name for the china.

Taylor and Kent Models

Buildings—Coloured
Ann Hathaway's Cottage. 3 sizes: 50 mm, 70 mm & 115 mm long.

Shakespeare's House: 2 sizes 70 mm & 115 mm long. (It is possible that a 50 mm long size was made but it has so far not been recorded.)

Temple Porcelain

Trademark used by an
unknown manufacturer.

Crests from all over the South of England and Wales are found on crested china with this mark. Most items found are 'smalls' and the models listed below do not appear to be from the range of any well known manufacturer. One can only assume that this mark was used by a British manufacturer who did not bother to register it.

The china is for the most part quite fine and the crests are reasonably well produced. No view ware or any other transfer devices have been recorded.

Temple Models

Ancient Artefacts
Loving Cup. Three handled. 39 mm.

Home/Nostalgic
Bellows. No details of size.
Coal scuttle, shell shaped, on two ball feet. No details of size.

Sport
Curling Stone. No details of size.

Miniature Domestic
Cheese dish and cover. 50 mm.

L. M. MACK
AYR.

Thistle China

Trademark used for L. M.
Mack, Ayr, by Hewitt and
Leadbeater, Willow Potteries,
Longton.

For details of this china and manufacturer see WILLOW ART CHINA.

China with this mark has always been recorded with the crest of Ayr, with the exception of one vase which had an Edinburgh crest. The models listed below and 'smalls' are from the *Willow Art* range.

Thistle Models

Parian/Unglazed
Bust of *Burns*. 150 mm (with Ayr crest).

Great War
Monoplane with fixed prop. 146 mm long.

T.M.W. and Co. Ltd and S. Ltd

Trademark used for a
wholesaler by an unknown
manufacturer.

This mark can also be found with
the initials TMW & S Ltd.

The three models listed below have been found with the following crests:
Leatherhead, Lee-on-Solent and Chichester, indicating that this was a
wholesaler's mark. (The mark seems to be a print of the Bargate
Southampton which may provide a clue.) No known potters used the
initials T.M.W. and the models below could have been made by any
British manufacturer.

T.M.W. Models

Historical/Folklore
Mother Shipton. 105 mm.

Birds
Chick. 65 mm.

Alcohol
Barrel. 33 mm.

Tourist Art China

Trademark used for Frank
Duncan Ltd, Auckland, by
Hewitt and Leadbeater Ltd,
Willow Potteries, Longton.

For details of this china and manufacturer see WILLOW ART CHINA.

Models with this mark are invariably Kiwi miniatures. The crests
found include New Zealand and Wellington. The New Zealand crest is
often accompanied by the inscription: 'A Souvenir from Auckland'
or 'Wellington'. A vase and the lighthouse below have been found with
transfer prints of a view of the 'New Bath Building, Rotorua, N.Z.'
Fortunately this view is recognisably a product of Willow Potteries.
Hewitt and Leadbeater were the only firm to outline their views with a
black scroll border, so the mark can be identified. Frank Duncan Ltd was
no doubt a New Zealand fancy goods wholesaler.

Tourist Art Models

Seaside Souvenirs
Lighthouse. 110 mm.

Birds
Kiwi. 66 mm.

Towy China

Trademark used for a Welsh
retailer by Hewitt and
Leadbeater Ltd, Willow
Potteries, Longton.

This mark has only been found on a Welsh Hat with an unrecognisable
crest which has not been named on the model but is obviously Welsh.
The hat fortunately is not only identical to the *Willow Art* model but
carries the same stock numbers, so one can confidently assume that this
mark was used for a Welsh retailer by Hewitt and Leadbeater.

Towy Models

Traditional/National Souvenirs
Welsh Hat. No. 75. 57 mm.

Right Sylvan. Jokey model of the American Prohibitionist 'Mr Pussy Foot'

Left Swan. Reverse of kettle with black pictorial transfer of 'Maentwrog Church', showing long inscription

Right Tourist Art. Lighthouse with coloured transfer 'New Bath Building Rotorua N.Z.'. Note the scroll edging as found on some Willow Art transfers

Left Tourist Art. The Kiwi made by Hewitt & Leadbeater is marked 'Tourist Art' for sale in New Zealand

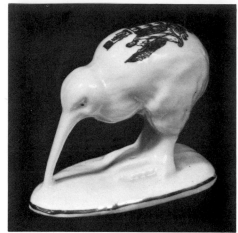

Right Tuscan. Tomato with green leaves, this model does not appear in other ranges

Left Tuscan. Fish with open mouth and glass eyes.

Right Tuscan. Grandfather Clock 128 mm

Left Tuscan. 75 mm triple mouthed vase with delightful pierrot and pierette colour transfers

From 1919

Triood

Trademark used by Hoods
Ltd, International Works, Fenton.

Hoods Ltd was established in 1919 and manufactured earthenwares.
Obviously the firm made crested china souvenirs of the Great War very
early in their history and probably only made a range of such wares until
the early twenties, when German competition returned. The models
produced are very ordinary and do not carry inscriptions. The range
includes domestic items and 'smalls', which, like the models, tend to be
rather heavy.

Crests recorded are from all over the Midlands and south of England.
One military crest, The Worcestershire Regiment, has been found.

Triood Models

Traditional/National Souvenirs
Lancashire Clog. No details of size.

Seaside Souvenirs
Lighthouse. 108 mm.

Animals
Collie Dog, sitting. No details of size.

Great War
Airship on base. 130 mm long.
Battleship. 120 mm long.
Submarine, impressed: *E4*. 104 mm long.
Tank, with inset steering wheels. 102 mm
 long.
Field Gun. 130 mm long.
Bell Tent, with open flaps. No details of
 size.

Home/Nostalgic
Grandfather Clock. 125 mm.

Tudor Arms China

Trademark used for a
wholesaler by Hewitt and
Leadbeater Ltd, Willow
Potteries, Longton.

For details of this china and manufacturer see WILLOW ART CHINA.

Most models with this mark have Welsh Crests and it is possible that
C. J. and Co. were Cardiff wholesalers. All models listed below are from
the *Willow Art* range and stock numbers where they occur are the same.

Tudor Arms Models

Buildings—White
Lloyd George's Home, inscribed: *The old
 home of the Right Hon D. Lloyd George Esq.
 M.P. Llanystymdwy near Criccieth.*
 102 mm long.

Traditional/National Souvenirs
Welsh Hat, with blue ribbon and longest
 place name around brim. No. 75.
 57 mm.

Seaside Souvenirs
Bathing Machine. 80 mm.

Animals
Bulldog, standing. 125 mm long.
Elephant, walking. 52 mm.

Great War
Kit Bag with verse: 'Pack up your troubles
 in your old kit bag'. 74 mm.
Church Bell, inscribed: *Curfew must not ring
 tonight.* 70 mm.

Home/Nostalgic
Coal Scuttle, helmet shaped. 53 mm.

Miscellaneous
Boot. 112 mm long.

Tuscan China

Trademark used by R. H. and
S. L. Plant (Ltd), Tuscan
Works, Longton.

Mr Richard Hammersley Plant was born in Longton in 1847 and began
work at the Daisy Bank Pottery at the age of seven. He was employed
there for twenty five years, eventually becoming the Manager. In 1880 he
started his own business with his brother which was known as R. H. and
S. L. Plant. Mr R. H. Plant died in 1904, and his two sons and his brother
carried on the business which is still in existence today.

Messrs Plant were known for their tea and breakfast wares produced for the home, colonial and foreign markets. They were represented in London by Messrs Mogridge and Underhay. 10, Barletts Buildings, Holborn Circus, EC. In 1906 R. H. and S. L. Plant added Arms Ware in 'superb ivory porcelain, with the arms of all Nations, the Colonies and the United Kingdom', to their range using the Tuscan trademark. In 1908 they were advertising 'Heraldic Ware' in Tuscan China, adding that arms of towns could be applied to small fancy pieces and teaware.

During the Great War the company obviously made china miniatures a speciality and by 1916 were also producing 'Present from . . . Ware' and 'Nursery Rhyme Ware'. In 1919 the firm could offer 'Heraldic Ivory China, Heraldic Bone China, View Ware, Nursery Rhyme Ware and Present from . . . Ware'. Like so many high and medium class china manufacturers they had to turn to cheaper wares during the war years. By the 1920 British Industries Fair the company was showing 'High Class Services' as well as 'Seaside Ware'. The firm continued to produce Heraldic Wares until at least 1925 but no mention is made of them however in adverts after that date.

Tuscan China is quite fine and well produced, the range of models is however rather unimaginative and the majority of crested china made by the firm appears to have been domestic ware, little of which survives as it would have been in constant use. A large number of small pots and vases have survived and unless numbered, these have not been listed as they are of interest only to collectors specialising in crests of specific areas or towns. Miniatures and 'smalls' can be found with views and other 'twenties' transfer decorations, but no 'Lucky Black Cats' or 'Lucky White Heather' transfers have been recorded.

Foreign and colonial crests were obviously made but the only recorded one is 'British Honduras'. Great War Commemoratives can be found on 'smalls' and models, these being 'Flags of the Allies' transfers with the inscription: *Freedom and Honour*. ('Tuscan' advertised ashtrays decorated with planes and flags in 1938 but it is not known if these were ever made.)

In the thirties the firm made a range of coloured animals and 'Crinoline Ladies' and these appeal to collectors of the Goss and Arcadian Ladies, but obviously they have nothing whatsoever to do with crested china.

Numbering System. Stock numbers do appear on the base of some models and can be painted in any colour. These are recorded in the following lists where known. Paintresses' marks are painted initials or dots and dashes.

Tuscan Models

Ancient Artefacts
Loving Cup, 3 handled. No. 82. 39 mm.

Historical/Folklore
Coronation Chair, not named. 80 mm.
The Chertsey Abbey or Curfew Bell, cast circa 1370. With clapper. Rd. No. 466813. 88 mm.

Seaside Souvenirs
Lighthouse, not named. 90 mm.

Animals
Camel with two humps, kneeling. No. 18. 125 mm long.
Cat, winking. No details of size.
Dog, Bulldog. 702mm long.
Dog, Hound, running. 200 mm long.

Fish, open mouthed with green glass eyes. No. 95. 120 mm long. (A surprise to find glass beads being used by this firm who do not appear to have made many novelties.)
Rabbit, no details of size.

Birds/Eggs
Egg, cracked open and lying on side. No. 53. 65 mm. long.

Great War
Kit bag, with no inscription. 63 mm.

Home/Nostalgic
Grandfather Clock, inscribed *Time for tea 5 o'clock* 128 mm.
Milk Churn, no details of size.

Comic/Novelty
Boy Scout, saluting. 140 mm (not a
    common model).
Man in nightshirt and nightcap. 90 mm.
Sun with face. 100 mm.
Tomato with green leaves. 60 mm dia.

Miscellaneous
Top Hat Matchstriker. 45 mm.

Miniature Domestic
Cheese dish and cover. 2 pieces. 50 mm.
Shaving Mug. 57 mm.

'Smalls' with known Stock Numbers
The following list of numbered 'smalls' is
    given for 'Tuscan' collectors. Some of
    these shapes are probably unnamed
    ancient artefacts.
No. 5. Vase. 65 mm.
No. 6. Vase. 60 mm.
No. 10. Ewer. 70 mm.
No. 22. Vase. 50 mm.
No. 24. Jug. 45 mm.
No. 57. Ewer. 58 mm.
No. 59. Vase. 43 mm.
No. 71. Vase. 63 mm.
No. 72. Jug. 63 mm.
No. 89. Vase. 55 mm.
No. 110. Jug. 51 mm.

Union K

Trademark used by an
unknown German
manufacturer.

The use of the term *Czechoslovakia* indicates that this mark, used on
domestic ware, was produced after the Great War. One interesting item
recorded is a card box with the four suits on the sides.

Unity China

Trademark thought to have
been used by Max Emanuel
and Co., Mitterteich.
(Bavaria.)

See MAXIM CHINA for further details of this manufacturer.

This mark is identical to one used by Max Emanuel and Co. on pink
view ware china, with the addition of the words *Unity China*. If, as I
suspect, this mark was used after the Great War the use of the word
Unity is very apt, if not, a little tactless, as no mention of the country of
origin is made.

Even more surprisingly, the only recorded model carries a
commemorative to Field Marshall Sir John French.

Unity Model

Miniatures Domestic
Cheese Dish. 50 mm.

Universal Series

Trademark used by an
unknown manufacturer.

The one small urn and the drum below could have been made by any
manufacturer. The mark offers no clue whatsoever but the crests are both
Scottish, which may indicate a Scottish manufacturer.

Universal Model

Great War
Bandsman's Drum. 57 mm dia.

Right Vectis. 'Arch Rock, Freshwater Bay' a souvenir of the Isle of Wight

Left Vectis. 'Needle Rocks and Lighthouse, Isle of Wight' 125 mm long

Right Venetia China. 46 mm jug with colour transfer of 'Imperial International Exhibition'

Left Vectis. A very rare model, 'Sleep of Innocence, Osborne House, Cowes', Isle of Wight

Victoria. Two Welsh Hats and an Aberdeen Bronze Pot with colour transfers inscribed 'Welsh Costume'. Identical transfers can be found on items marked 'Florentine'

Victoria. Monoplane with roundels and moveable prop.

Venetia China

Trademark used by Charles
Waine (and Co) (Ltd), Derby
Works, Longton.

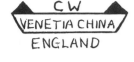

Charles Waine and Co worked in Longton, manufacturing china from 1891 to 1920, but only used the initials C. W. until 1913. The firm made a range of 'smalls' and small models probably at the turn of the century when many other established firms added crests to their shapes. One commemorative has been found on a small jug, this being a coloured transfer view of the 'Imperial International Exhibition'. *Venetia* is rather heavy and more like earthenware than china, the view and crests are adequate but by no means exceptional.

Venetiá Models

Ancient Artefacts
Loving Cup. 3 handles. 40 mm. (It is quite
  possible that many of the 'smalls' are
  unnamed ancient artefacts.)

Birds
Swan Posy Bowl. 80 mm.

Miniature Domestic
Cheese Dish and cover. 55 mm.

Vectis/Victis Models

Trademark used for an Isle of
Wight retailer by J. A.
Robinson and Sons,
subsequently Cauldon Ltd.

VECTIS
MODELS
NIGH
VENTNOR
I.O.W.

VICTIS
MODELS
NIGH
VENTNOR
I.O.W.

For details of this china and manufacturer, see ARCADIAN CHINA.

There seems to have been some indecision in the Arcadian Works as to how to spell Vectis, which is of course the Roman name for the Isle of Wight. The models with this mark could have been made by any of the branches of J. A. Robinson, which included Arkinstall ('Arcadian'), Robinson and Leadbeater (R. and L.) and Wardle's Art Pottery Ltd. The parian models listed below would almost certainly have been made by R. and L.

All the models are souvenirs of the Isle of Wight, and carry Isle of Wight crests. A number of 'smalls' have been recorded with the coloured transfers of tropical birds on *Arcadian* and *Cauldon* wares.

Vectic Models

Parian/Unglazed
Osborne House, Isle of Wight. 140 mm long.
*Sleep of innocence. Osborne House. Cowes.
  I.O.W.* Two babies lying on a couch
  96 mm long. (Both of these models carry
  crests.)

Buildings—White
Osborne House. Cowes. Isle of Wight. 48 mm.

Monuments
Arch Rock, Freshwater Bay, I.O.W. 80 mm.

Traditional/National Souvenirs
Donkey in well, Carisbrooke Castle. 90 mm
  Donkey treads wheel to draw water.
Map of Isle of Wight. A coloured map
  standing upright on an oval ashtray.
  106 mm long.

Seaside Souvenirs
Needles Rocks and Lighthouse. 125 mm long.

Victoria China

Trademark thought to have
been used on crested wares
by James Reeves, Victoria
Works, Fenton.

J.R.C'
Mark used approx 1910–1924

James Reeves was established in 1870 and produced tableware and ornamental earthenware. It seems likely that the firm began making some miniatures just before the Great War and continued to do so as the craze for war souvenirs grew and the supply of skilled operatives diminished. The firm continued in business until 1948, but seems not to have made crested ware and other miniatures after the mid-Twenties.

Marks used approx 1910–1924

They obviously saw such production as a sideline, as they never advertised it or bothered to register the mark used on their range.

Victoria china is rather heavy as one would expect from an earthenware manufacturer but it is quite well finished. Some models showed a marked similarity to *Botolph China* (probably manufctured by J. Wilson and Sons, Fenton). It is possible that there was some connection between the two firms apart from the obvious one of them both being based in Fenton. Other models show a great similarity to *Florentine China* (Taylor and Kent) but there is no known connection between the two firms. No view ware, 'Lucky White Heather' or 'Lucky Black Cats' have been recorded with this mark but two different coloured transfers entitled 'Welsh Costume' have been found on Welsh Hats. (J. Reeves seemed to have found a good market in Wales, many Welsh crests have been recorded and were the 'Welsh' models in the following lists.) Two military crests have also been recorded. 1st Herefordshire Regiment and 5th Battalion, The Queen's Surrey Regiment. No other commemoratives have been found with this mark.

Numbering System. No stock numbers are found on crested models. The painted numerals, dots and dashes found on the base are paintresses' marks. A few items of crested domestic ware have been recorded and some of these carry stock numbers, e.g. Salt Pot 148 and Candlestick 144. It is possible that the firm offered a range of these items, but very few have survived.

Victoria Models

Ancient Artefacts
Carlisle Salt Pot, not named. 70 mm.
Fountains Abbey Cup, not named. 50 mm.

Buildings—White
Blackpool Tower, with buildings. 142 mm.

Monuments (including Crosses)
Cross on base (Possibly Irish). 108 mm.
Wallace Monument, Stirling. 120 mm.

Historical/Folklore
Man in pillory. 101 mm.
Mother Shipton. 70 mm.

Traditional/National Souvenirs
Ripon Hornblower. 90 mm.
Welsh Bardic Chair. 86 mm (identical to Old Arm Chair.)
Welsh Harp. 90 mm.
Welsh Hat with thin blue ribbon band. 48 mm.
Welsh Hat, two different moulds, one with twisted cord band, and the other with blue band with gold tassels. Can be found with Llanfair . . . etc, around brim. 62 mm.

Seaside Souvenirs
Canoe. 102 mm long.
Houseboat, rectangular. 90 mm long.
Fisherman bust. 87 mm.
Fisherwoman bust. 87 mm. (These two probably sold as a pair.)
Whelk Shell, inscribed: *Listen to the sea.* 95 mm long.
Gladstone Bag. 45 mm.
Portmanteau. 55 mm.

Animals
Cat, with long neck. 115 mm.
Cat, The Cheshire. Inscribed: *Always smiling.* 80 mm.
Cat, Manx. 80 mm long.
Dog, King Charles Spaniel, begging on cushion. No details of size.
Fish, inscribed: *Caught at . . .* 102 mm long.
Frog. 39 mm.
Monkey, crouching, hands to mouth. 88 mm.
Pig, sitting. Copyright. Rd. No. 417593. 39 mm.
Pig, standing. 88 mm long.
Teddy bear, sitting. 98 mm.

Birds
Hen, roosting. 92 mm long.
Parrot. 76 mm.
Pelican Jug. 63 mm.
Swan. 2 sizes: 70 mm & 90 mm long.
Swan Posy Bowl. 80 mm long.

Great War
Bust of Sailor. 90 mm.
Airship on base. 128 mm long.
Zeppelin. 132 mm long.
Monoplane with roundels and movable prop. 165 mm long.
Battleship. 120 mm long.
Torpedo Boat Destroyer. 110 mm long.
Submarine, inscribed *E4*. No details of size.
Submarine, inscribed *E9*. 147 mm long.
Red Cross Van 102 mm long.
Renault Tank. 82 mm long.
Tank, with inset steering wheels. 100 mm long.
Tank, with large side turrets. 120 mm long.
Field Gun. 127 mm long.
Trench Mortar. 65 mm.

Torpedo ,fixed prop. 155 mm long.
Colonial Soldier's Hat. 73 mm long.
Grandfather Clock, usual model but with
  clock transfer at 3.25. With inscription:
  'World War 1914–1919. Peace signed 3.25
  pm. June 28 1919'. 110 mm. (Difficult to
  find, as sought by Clock and Great War
  Collectors.)
Cenotaph. 135 mm.
Matlock Bath War Memorial. 178 mm.
Ripon War Memorial. 118 mm.

Home/Nostalgic
Baby in bath. 100 mm long.
Garden Roller. 85 mm long.
Lady in Bonnet, salt pot. 93 mm.
Lamp. 70 mm.
Lantern. 86 mm.
Milk Churn, no details of size.
The old armchair, with inscription: 'I live it, I
  love it and who shall dare to chide me for
  loving the old Armchair'. 83 mm.
Pillar Box, inscribed *I cant get a letter from
  you, so send you the box.* 70 mm.
Watering Can. 70 mm.

Comic/Novelty
Boy on Scooter. No details of size.
Jack in the Box. 95 mm.
Screw, inscribed: *You could do with a big fat
  screw.* 76 mm.
Suffragette Handbell, two sided. One side
  ugly old lady, inscribed: *Votes for women.*
  Reverse, a pretty young girl, inscribed:

This one shall have a vote. 108 mm (much
  sought after).

Cartoon/Comedy Characters
Harry Lauder, bust not found named.
  63 mm.

Alcohol
Champagne Bottle in ice bucket, inscribed:
  Something good—a bottle of the boy. 83 mm.
Whisky Bottle. No details of size.

Musical Instruments
Grand piano, with closed lid. 80 mm long.

Transport
Charabanc, with driver. 115 mm long.
Motor Horn, inscribed: *Pip Pip.* 90 mm
  long.

'Modern' Equipment
Gramophone, square without horn.
  58 mm.
Radio Horn. 95 mm.

Miscellaneous
Carboy. 72 mm.
Chess Pawn. 60 mm.
Sabot, with pointed turned-up toe. 95 mm
  long.

Miniature Domestic
Cheese Dish, 2 pieces. 50 mm.
Shaving Mug. 50 mm.

Victoria (China)

Trademark used by Schmidt
and Co, Carlsbad, (Bohemia).
For further details of manufacturer see GEMMA.

This mark is usually found on domestic wares but the models listed
below have been recorded. The ware is very fine and one would assume
that Schmidt and Co made this china in another works or offered it as an
alternative range to *Gemma*.

Victoria Models

Miscellaneous
Sabot. 84 mm long.

Miniature Domestic
Cheese Dish and cover. 30 mm.

Victorian Porcelain

Trademark used by Robinson
and Leadbeater, Wolfe
Street, Stoke-on-Trent.
For further details of this china and manufacturer see R. and L.

This mark was definitely used before Robinson and Leadbeater were
taken over by Harold Taylor Robinson in 1906 and subsequently a branch
of J. A. Robinson. The china found with this mark is very fine and
translucent, and was obviously made at the turn of the century.
Robinson and Leadbeater would have offered a small range of crested
wares while they were still a refined souvenir.

Waterfall. Hull 'Fishermans Memorial', Hull South African War Memorial and 'Statue of Sir William de la Pole' All with Hull crests

Right Wembley. Welsh Teaparty with B.E.E. 1924 crest. No colouring

Left Waterfall. Cheshire cat with inscription, has a red mouth and nose and one open green eye.

Right W. Swan Posy Bowl 80 mm long.

Left W. 70 mm Vase with two handles. This piece illustrates well the high quality of china with this mark

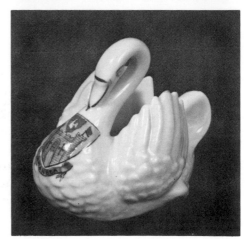

Most of the items recorded with this mark are 'smalls' or small domestic pieces such as beakers. One loving cup has been found with a colour transfer print of a ship in full sail.

Victorian Porcelain Models

Ancient Artefacts
Loving Cup. 2 and 3 handled. 39 mm.
Oxford Jug, not named. 83 mm.

Home/Nostalgic
Bellows. 110 mm long.

W

Trademark used by H. M.
Williams and Sons, Bridge
Pottery, Longton.

BRITISH MADE

BRITISH MADE

This firm established in 1858, according to an advert in the Pottery Gazette, were well known for their china tea and dinner sets. They used the mark above on cheaper wares from 1900 and probably for only a short time. (The mark is shown in an advert in the Pottery Gazette in 1903.) Their range of crested china is quite well produced, but by no means exceptionally so, and most of the items found could be described as 'smalls'. Many models are recorded with the commemorative transfer 'The Triple Entente' which consists of shields of the flags of France, Great Britain and Russia.

W Models

Ancient Artefacts
Salisbury Kettle, not named. 102 mm.

Seaside Souvenirs
Portmanteau. 80 mm long.

Animals
Pig, standing. 100 mm long.
Seal, no details of size.

Birds
Bird Jug, no details of size.
Swan Posy Bowl. 80 mm long.

Home/Nostalgic
Old Lantern. 71 mm.

Wade

Trademark used by Wade
and Co, Union Pottery,
Burslem, subsequently
Wade, Heath and Co (Ltd).

No details of mark available except that marks incorporate the name WADES

This company which went on to make coloured cartoon models in the thirties and later Wade miniature animals and Disney characters, (Hat Box series), did not surprisingly make a large range of crested china. The odd items found with their name are domestic pieces, the crest almost appearing to have been added as an after thought. The firm before 1927, when it became Wade, Heath and Co., manufactured earthenwares so the crested wares tend to be heavy and useful rather than ornamental.

Warwick China

Trademark used for W. H.
Smith and Sons by Arkinstall
and Son Ltd, Arcadian
Works, Stoke-on-Trent.

For further details of the china and manufacturer see ARCADIAN CHINA.

This range of china made for W. H. Smith is of a higher quality than one normally associates with *Arcadian China* and the crests are boldly and beautifully produced. The models are, however, made from *Arcadian* moulds and if one can judge from the models recorded, seem to have been made before and during the Great War, but not afterwards.

Numbering System. Numbers can either be printed or written and are usually in the style of a fraction. The lower numbers occur on many different models and could possibly be an order number. The following lower numbers have been recorded: 010, 01½, 06½, 09, 012, 014, 015 and 030. The upper numbers appear to be stock numbers and where recorded they coincide with *Arcadian* stock numbers. Stock numbers where known are given in the lists below.

Warwick Models

Ancient Artefacts
Ancient tyg, Model of. No. 58. 70 mm.
Chester Roman Vase, inscribed: *Model of roman vase now in Chester Museum.* No. 136. 60 mm.
Newbury Leather Bottle, inscribed: *Model of leather bottle found on battlefield of Newbury 1644 now in museum.* No. 83. 65 mm.

Buildings—White
Rowton Tower, with inscription: 'King Charles I stood on this tower Sept 24th 1645 and saw his army defeated on Rowton Moor'. 105 mm.

Historical/Folklore
Yorick's Skull, inscribed: *Alas poor Yorick.* No. 22. 57 mm.

Seaside Souvenirs
Fishing Basket, inscribed: *A good catch.* 70 mm long.

Animals
Otter, holding fish in mouth. 120 mm long.
Pony, Shetland. 105 mm long.
Teddy Bear, sitting. Rd. No. 548705. 90 mm.

Birds
Chick breaking out of egg. 63 mm long.
Hen, roosting. 54 mm.

Great War
British Airship on stand. 128 mm long.
Red Cross Van, red cross on each side and rear. 'EH 139' inscribed on radiator. 85 mm long.

Miniature Domestic
Cheese dish and cover. 50 mm.

Waterfall Heraldic China

Trademark used for a
Northern Wholesaler by
Hewitt and Leadbeater,
Willow Potteries, Longton.

For further details of this china and manufacturer see WILLOW ART CHINA.

All crests and model souvenirs of monuments and buildings found with this mark are northern. The most commonly found crests are Withernsea, Grimsby, Hull and Filey, indicating that the models were sold in Northern towns, resorts and ports. Most models are identical to those found in the *Willow Art* range but some models were obviously made especially to be sold in Hull, Grimsby and Hedon.

Stock numbers where they occur, coincide with *Willow Art* numbers.

Waterfall Models

Buildings—White
Grimsby Hydraulic Tower. 165 mm.

Monuments (including Crosses)
Hull fishermans memorial, with inscription. 2 sizes: 135 mm & 160 mm.
Hull South African War Memorial, with inscription. 165 mm.
Kilnsea Cross Hedon with inscription: 'Erected at Ravenspurne 1338 by King Henry IV. Re-erected at Hedon'. 134 mm (quite rare).
Sir William de la Pole, Statue of, with long inscription. 160 mm.

Historical/Folklore
Skull. 60 mm long.

Traditional/National Souvenirs
Bagpipes, with turquoise ribbon. No. 138. 118 mm long.

Seaside Souvenirs
Grimsby fisherman, bust. 83 mm (rare).
Spurn lighthouse, with inscription: 'Radius of Light 20 miles, candle power 519,000. Erected 1895. Height 128 feet'. 130 mm.
Withernsea Lighthouse, with inscription: 'Radius of Light 17 miles, Candle power 90,000. Erected 1894. Height 127 feet'. 2 sizes: 105 mm & 130 mm.

Animals
Cat, Cheshire inscribed: *Still smiling.* 95 mm.
Dog, Bull Terrier, standing. 60 mm.
Elephant, walking. 52 mm.

Fish with open mouth. No. 36. 103 mm
long.
Teddy Bear, sitting. 76 mm.

Great War
Monoplane, with revolving prop. 150 mm
long.
Battleship, impressed: *HMS Lion*. 140 mm
long.
Submarine impressed: *E4*. 116 mm long.
Red Cross Van. Red Cross on side. 84 mm
long.
British Tank, Model of. 92 mm long.
British Tank, Model of with trailing wheels.
Rd. No. 658588. 130 mm long.

Field Gun. 120 mm long.
Field Gun, with screen. 115 mm long.
Howitzer. 115 mm long.
Glengarry, some colouring. 83 mm long.

Home/Nostalgic
Milk can with lid. 60 mm.
Watering Can. 75 mm.

Comic/Novelty
Billiken, not named. 73 mm.
Dutch Boy. 80 mm.

Alcohol
Beer Barrel on stand. 58 mm.

Waverley China

Trademark used for Wyman
and Sons Ltd, by Arkinstall
and Son, Ltd, Arcadian
Works, Stoke-on-Trent.

For further details of china and manufacture see ARCADIAN CHINA.

This mark has only been found on 'smalls' and ancient artefacts, and was probably only used before the Great War.

Waverley Models

Ancient Artefacts
Glastonbury Bronze Bowl, inscribed: *Model of bronze bowl from the ancient British lake village near Glastonbury*. No. 74. 40 mm.

Hastings Kettle, inscribed: *Model of ancient kettle dredged up off Hastings. 1873 in Hastings Museum*. No. 237. 62 mm.

WEDGWOOD
ENGLAND
Used after 1900

WEDGWOOD
ETRURIA ENGLAND
c1900

Wedgwood

Trademark used by Josiah
Wedgwood (and Sons Ltd),
Etruria.

The very famous firm of Wedgwood made a few very small vases with crests at the turn of the century. The china is very fine and the crests are beautifully enamelled. These heraldic wares were obviously also exported, as crests of La Havre and Monaco have been recorded.

WEMBLEY CHINA

Wembley China

Trademark used on china for
sale at the British Empire
Exhibition of 1924 and 1925
by the Cauldon Group of
Companies.

For further details of this china and manufacturer see ARCADIAN CHINA.

This mark is found on china from *Arcadian* moulds with BEE crests. Cauldon had stands at the exhibition and have used the 'Wembley Lion' symbol in their mark.

Wembley Models

Parian/Unglazed
George V statue on glazed plinth inscribed:
A souvenir from Wembley, with
inscription: 'King George V—Born June
3rd 1865—Ascended the throne May 6th
1910'. 2 sizes: 125 mm & 140 mm.

Prince of Wales, (Edward VIII) bust on
glazed plinth, with inscription: 'HRH
The Prince of Wales, Born June 23rd
1894'. 135 mm.

Historical/Folklore
Miner's Lamp. 70 mm.
Mother Shipton. 115 mm.
Man in Stocks. 88 mm.

Traditional/National Souvenirs
Thistle Vase. 70 mm.
Welsh Hat. 52 mm.
Welsh Teaparty group. 98 mm.

Seaside Souvenirs
Bathing Machine. 65 mm.
Yacht. 125 mm long.
Lighthouse, not named. 2 sizes: 110 mm &
    140 mm.

Countryside
Beehive on table. 78 mm.

Animals
Black Cat, sitting on Armchair. 55 mm.
Fawn. 50 mm.
Pig, sitting and smiling. 63 mm long.

Great War
Nurse and Wounded Tommy. 108 mm
    long.
Soldier Bust, unnamed Tommy Atkins.
    Some colouring. 90 mm.

Tank, Model of 115 mm long.
Capstan. 56 mm.
Pair of field glasses, Model of. 78 mm long.
Officer's Peaked Cap. 65 mm dia.

Home/Nostalgic
Fireplace, no inscription but much
    colouring. 90 mm.
Grandfather Clock, without inscription.
    108 mm.
Kennel. 50 mm.
Lantern, horn. 85 mm.

Comic/Novelty
Hand holding pig's trotter. 110 mm long.

Sport
Curling Stone. 49 mm.

Transport
Car, open tourer, (2 seater). 110 mm long.

Miscellaneous
Boy Scout's Hat. 73 mm dia.

The White House
Trademark used for a
Manchester retailer by an
unknown manufacturer.

Only one 'small' has been found with this mark and it is frankly impossible to suggest a manufacturer. A. H. and S. M. Manchester was not a manufacturer so one can assume that the White House, Manchester was a retail outlet.

W. H. H. and S
Trademark used by an
unknown manufacturer.

The initials *W. H. H. and S. P.* were not used by any known manufacturer, so one must assume that these are retailer's initials. The inclusion of the Sir Francis Drake Statue indicates that the P under the mark may stand for Plymouth. The mark could have been used by a German manufacturer.

W. H. H. and S. Models

Buildings—White
Clock Tower, not named. 125 mm.

Monuments
Sir Francis Drake, statue. Plymouth.
    163 mm.

Animals
Elephants, two on a sledge or slope.
    76 mm long.

Sport
Cricket Cap. 70 mm long.

Wilco Series
Trademark used by an
unknown manufacturer.

Only one item has been recorded with this mark and unfortunately the crest was not noted. The cheese dish could have been made by any known manufacturer.

Wilco Model

Miniature Domestic
Cheese dish and cover. 50 mm.

Willow Art and Willow China

Trademark used by Hewitt
and Leadbeater, Willow
Potteries, Longton,
subsequently Hewitt Bros,
and eventually Willow
Potteries Ltd, a branch of
Cauldon Ltd.

WILLOW
ART CHINA
LONGTON

Early mark 1905–c1910

Can have STAFFORDSHIRE
added

Marks used between 1907 and
1925. (Models with these marks
can also be found impressed H &
L 1907–1920 and Hewitt Bros.
1920–1925)

Hewitt and Leadbeater joined in partnership in 1905 as manufacturers of 'artistic and useful specialities in great variety'. Mr Edwin Leadbeater was the son of the senior partner of Robinson and Leadbeater (R. and L. makers of Parian busts), and brought his experience to the new business. Arthur Hewitt was his brother-in-law. Edwin Leadbeater , as already mentioned (see: Leadbeater Art China), always received a good press from the Pottery Gazette and so we have more information about the products of the Willow Pottery than any other 'arms ware' firm.

As well as flower holders and vases in many shapes and colours, the new firm produced ecclesiastical and art statuary in plain white, antique ivory and art colours. (These were marked H. and L.) The firms early ornamental wares are very beautiful, vases were made in the form of open flowers, the most striking being an arum lily with green leaves. 'Hop Ware' and 'Vine Ware' were also made, these vases and jugs having moulded bunches of green hops on dark green grounds or purple grapes and green vine leaves on cream grounds. They are delightful and delicate. (These early items are very rare and carry the earliest *Willow Art* mark.)

But 'Heraldic Ware' was one of the firms leading lines from the beginning and its production helped Hewitt and Leadbeater to establish themselves. The company supplied miniatures with crests, views and other decorations including poppies. The range at this time was called 'Daisy Arms China' but this title does not appear on the models. By 1914, the firm was heavily involved in the production of heraldic novelties, and were said to specialise in models of churches, crosses and buildings of historic interest, also introducing models of a car, battleship, aeroplane, soldier, sailor and nurse to their range. A quote from the Pottery Gazette of December 1914, will give some idea of the firms production:

'For a town such as Stratford, for instance, they have a model of Shakespeare's house in five sizes, Ann Hathaway's Cottage in five sizes, three distinct bust models of Shakespeare embracing in all ten different sizes, Shakespeare's font and desk, and a bust of Ann Hathaway in three sizes'.

(The Parian models would have been marked H. and L. Not all the Ann Hathaway's cottages have been found.)

The war years were very kind to this firm as they could easily manufacture the cheap souvenirs usually supplied by the German China Industry. Hewitt and Leadbeater produced a range of topical interest, but cannot be said to have made many original Great War souvenirs. They did begin to produce dolls' heads but this seems to have been short-lived. They had become well known in the trade as specialists in the production of miniatures and parian, but their real speciality in terms of originality was coloured buildings. These sold cheaply at the time but are becoming particularly sought by collectors today. It is perhaps blasphemy to say so, when Goss Cottages change hands for hundreds of pounds, but the *Willow Art* coloured buildings are much more interesting and typical of the period, showing the same good eye for design and colour that was used on the early decorative vases. By 1920 the firm offered a range of 200 different miniatures from stock and offered to

Right Willow Art. Sugar Caster with E.P.N.S. top and lucky black cat transfer

Left Willow Art. A lighthouse with an unusual and rather unsuitable Christmas transfer

Right Willow Art. A very early biscuit tinted unglazed model of Bill Sykes and a small cream vine ware vase. Both carry the earliest Willow Art mark

Left Willow Art. Small dish with colour transfer in the usual Willow Art scroll border

Right Willow Art. Club vase with coloured butterfly transfer. Very similar prints are found on china marked 'Arcadian'

Left Willow Art. Two small vases, white china with transfer print of red poppies and mother of pearl lustre with green shamrock and harp transfer

Right Willow Art. 60 mm yellow lustre vase with brown monochrome transfer 'Norman Tower Bury St. Edmunds'

Left Willow Art. Very unusual and beautiful art deco vase with hand coloured transfer print of tango dancers

272

Can be found with "ware" rather than "china"

Can be found with "china" omitted. Marks used between 1925–1930

WILLOW CHINA

Mark found on late coloured models from 1925

Mark found on domestic ware, 1925–1930

H & L

Impressed mark 1905–1919

H. BROS WILLOW ENGLAND

Impressed mark 1919–25

make copies of any building of which a photograph or postcard was supplied.

In November 1919 Edwin Leadbeater left the firm to start a pottery business on his own account. (See: Leadbeater Art China for details). The remaining Mr Hewitt took his brother into partnership and the firm at Willow Pottery became known as Hewitt Bros. Hewitt Bros continued to use the same tradename on heraldic china and described themselves as 'Novelty Potters'. They produced the usual post-war memorials, figures and comic items. In 1922 they introduced their 'Teddy Tail' and 'Black Cat China'. Teddy Tail transfers, from the original drawings by M. Charles Folkard, creator of the cartoon for the Daily Mail, were applied to nursery ware. (Very few if any of these mugs and plates have survived.) Black Cat transfers, from the original drawings by Mr H. H. Hosband were applied to domestic ware such as plates, hair tidies, trinket boxes and small vases.

Hewitt Bros did not survive the Depression but it is difficult to understand why the firm came to grief so early, except that they produced only novelties which were the last things people could afford. By 1925 Mr Harold Taylor Robinson had bought the firm and had formed a new company. Willow Potteries Ltd, using the tradename 'Willow Crest'. Willow Potteries Ltd became part of the Cauldon group almost immediately. By 1927 *Willow China* was produced along with *Arcadian* at the Arcadian Works. It is difficult to tell if late models were originally Hewitt Bros or Arkinstall moulds. The *Willow* mark was not used after 1930 but many recognisably Willow buildings are found marked *Goss England*, so the Willow moulds obviously were being used after that date.

The Pottery Gazette of December 1914 tells us that 'Willow Art Arms Ware, is of a warm, ivory caste, of an excellent body and well treated both as regards the potting and the painting'. Praise indeed! Very few exceptionally fine pieces of *Willow Art* arms ware are found, for the most part the ware is heavy and the painting of the crests is just about adequate. This heraldic china sold well because it was cheaply produced and novel. The early wares, especially the parian and coloured buildings made by the firm however, would have sold on their technical merit, and early view ware is found on very fine china.

Very little view ware has been recorded. Early coloured views are found on small dishes and vases, they are pleasant but unremarkable. More exciting are monochrome (brown) pictorials found on small Willow Art pieces, occasionally finished in yellow lustre, and coloured transfers of a regional nature which include Peeping Tom (Willow Art) and Kiaora from Maoriland, Tiki, New Zealand, (Willow).

Willow Art was exported too, so foreign crests are found: Australia, New Zealand and Gibraltar have been recorded. A Jerusalem Crest is often found but this is an indication that the model was purchased from the 'Jerusalem and Oriental Bazaar, Great Yarmouth' and not from the Middle East.

Military crests were also produced by Hewitt and Leadbeater, these include The Army Service Corps; Royal Engineers, Longmoor Camp; Royal Army Medical Corps and The Somerset Light Infantry. 'Flags of the Allies' Great War Commemoratives are found inscribed, 'United We Stand'. Other Willow Art commemoratives found are 'Franco British Exhibition 1908' and 'BEE'.

Willow Art and Willow China can be found decorated with red poppies and 'Lucky Black Cat' transfers. Willow Art 'smalls' can be found with a coloured transfer of a Kingfisher and edged in blue, these have the inscription 'Happy Days at . . .'.

Willow Art. 'Round Tower, Windsor Castle' and 'Windsor Castle' a choice of souvenir of a day spent in the town

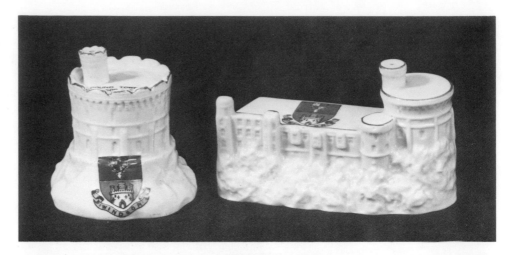

Willow Art. 'Old London Bridge' and 'Hampton Court Palace' on ashtray bases

Willow Art. 'St. Botolph's Church, Boston' and 'Chesterfield Parish Church' with crooked spire

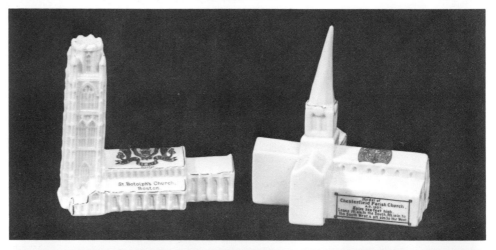

Willow Art. 'Westgate' Canterbury with two crests and Canterbury Cathedral West Front' with the more usual single crest

274

Numbering System. Willow Art models in general production, not made for a specific retailer, do sometimes have painted stock numbers, and these have been listed where they are known. Paintresses' marks are usually initials found under these numbers.

Some late models usually marked *Willow* have impressed stock numbers, for example the Willow black cat on a pouffe is impressed 539. These numbers are very difficult to spot and equally difficult to read clearly as they are usually covered in thick glaze and more often than not have the trademark printed over them. They have not yet been recorded, it is hoped that as clear examples are found they will be noted.

Willow Art and Willow Models
NB. All models are Willow Art unless indicated. *Willow* after the size indicates that the model has only been found with the Willow or Willow China mark. *Also Willow* indicates that the model can be found with both marks.

Parian/Unglazed
All the busts can be found impressed H. and L. (Hewitt and Leadbeater). The known busts form an odd group and one suspects that there are more Great War personalities to be recorded.

Busts
Bust of Albert King of the Belgians, not named on square glazed base. 170 mm.
Bust of French, not named, on square glazed base. 170 mm.
Bust of Burns impressed *Burns* and impressed on reverse *H. Bros* on square unglazed base with a crest. 150 mm.
Bust of Burns, not named, on circular glazed base. 170 mm.
Bust of Sir Walter Scott, not named, on circular glazed base. 130 mm.
Bust of Gladstone, not named, on circular glazed base. Can be found with crest of W. E. Gladstone on glazed base. 160 mm.
Peeping Tom Coventry. 2 sizes: 130 mm & 160 mm.

Buildings
St. Nicholas Church, Great Yarmouth. 140 mm long.
Shakespeare's House, with red roof. 125 mm long.
Wilberforce Museum with inscription. Coloured grey. 115 mm long. *Willow.*

Monuments
Burmah Cross, Taunton, inscribed: *Burmah 1885-6-7* and *Somerset Light Infantry.* 118 mm. (Scarce).
Statue of Viking, not named. 128 mm.

Ancient Artefacts
Chester Roman Jug, not named. 55 mm. Loving Cup. 2 and 3 handled. 40 mm. Also *Willow.*
Phoenician Water Jar, not named. 66 mm.
Puzzle Jug with verse: 'Try how to drink'. 70 mm *Willow* (probably an Arcadian Mould).

Buildings—Coloured
Coloured Buildings can be found glazed or unglazed. Some of these models can also be found white.
Ann Hathaway's Cottage. 2 sizes: 60 mm & 105 mm long. *Also Willow.*
Bell Hotel, Abel Fletchers House in John Halifax Gentleman. 2 sizes: 55 mm & 84 mm long. *also Willow.* 124 mm long. *Willow.*
John Bunyans cottage. 75 mm long. *also Willow.*
Burns Cottage, Model of. 105 mm long.
Feathers Hotel, Ludlow. No details of size. *Willow.*
Godalming Old Town Hall. 100 mm.
Knox's House, inscribed: *Model of the house in Edinburgh where John Knox the Scottish reformer died 24th Nov 1572.* 102 mm. *also Willow* (not common).
Old Blacksmiths shop and marriage room, Gretna Green. 85 mm long. *also Willow.*
Old Curiosity Shop. No. 14, Portsmouth Street. 80 mm long.
Old Maids Cottage, Lee near Ilfracombe. 59 mm long.
Old Ostrich Inn, Colnbrook 80 mm (scarce).
Historical, Old Mint House, Pevensey 1342 AD. 120 mm long. *also Willow.*
St. Bernards Monastery, Coalville. 102 mm long.
Shakespeare's House. 4 sizes: 65 mm, 110 mm, 125 mm & 135 mm long. *also Willow.* 50 mm long size (Probably *Arcadian* mould).
Tan House, Little Stretton. 120 mm long.
Whittington Inn, with inscription: 'Whittington near Stourbridge. This Manor House of the D. R. Whittingtons (ancestors of the famous Dick Whittington) was built by that family early in the 14th Century and additions made in Tudor Times, with secret chapels and Jesuit hiding places'. 100 mm long. *also William.* (Scarce).

Buildings—White
Bath Abbey. 106 mm.
Bath Abbey, West Front. 110 mm.
Battle Abbey Gateway. 95 mm. *also Willow.*
Bell Hotel, Abel Fletchers House in John Halifax Gentleman. 84 mm long. *also Willow.*
Bell Hotel, Abel Fletchers House in John Halifax Gentleman, on ashtray's base. Some colouring. 75 mm long.
Big Ben. 146 mm.
Blackpool Tower. 125 mm. *also Willow.*
Blackpool Tower, with buildings. 150 mm.

Right Willow Art. 'Hay Castle', Brecon 94 mm

Left Willow Art. 'Town Hall Wallingford' 84 mm

Right Willow Art. 'Monnow Bridge, Monmouth' 92 mm

Left Willow Art 'Model of Town Hall, Chatham'

Right Willow Art. Parian St. Alban on glazed base, inscribed 'Statue of St. Alban'

Left Willow Art. 'Hope Pole Inn' Tewkesbury on ashtray base

Left Willow Art. Parian bust of 'Burns' marked 'H. Bros' on reverse

Right Willow Art. 'Saxon Church Bradford on Avon'

Left Willow Art. 'Solomon's Temple' erected on the site of a prehistoric barrow 88 mm

Right Willow Art. 'Maiwand Memorial, Forbury Gardens' this memorial for obvious reasons often appears in animal collections

Left Willow Art. 'Bunyan' statue and Issac Newton Statue

Willow Art. C.S. Rolls Memorial, Carnegie Statue and the Hughes Monument three impressive monuments

Right Willow Art. 'Peter Pan' Statue 140 mm

Left Willow Art. 'Lincoln Imp'. This model is so ugly one wonders why so many people bought them yet most ranges include a version

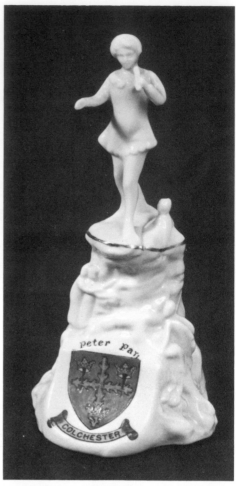

Left Willow Art. A 27th Century Puzzle 'A rubbing stone for asses'

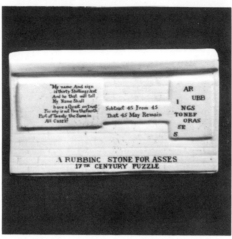

Right Willow Art. Model of Flamborough Lighthouse

Left Willow Art. 'Flodden Cross 1513' inscribed 'To the brave of both nations'

Left Willow Art. Gibbet Cross, Hindhead and sailor's stone, Hindhead both with Hindhead crests

Blackpool Tower, with buildings, impressed: *Variety, Dancing, Concert.* 165 mm. *Willow* (rare).

Bourne Abbey, West Front. 108 mm.

John Bunyan's Cottage, Model of. 75 mm long.

Burns Cottage, Model of, with inscription: 'The Robert Burns the Ayrshire Bard was born at Alloway near Ayr on 25th Jan'y 1759. He died on 21st July 1796 at Dumfries, where he was buried. 105 mm long. *also Willow.*

Bury St. Edmunds, Abbey Gate. 80 mm.

Canterbury Cathedral, West Front. 125 mm. *also Willow.*

Canterbury, West Gate. 90 mm. *also Willow.*

Chantry Front, Model of, otherwise not named. 95 mm.

Carillon Tower. 159 mm.

Carnegie's Birthplace, inscribed: *The birthplace of Andrew Carnegie.* 115 mm long.

Castle Hill Tower, Huddersfield. 115 mm.

Chatham, Town Hall, Model of. 146 mm. *also Willow.*

Chesterfield Parish Church, Model of, found with inscription: 'AD 103 Spire 228 feet. Leans 6 ft. south and 4 ft 4 ins s. west' or 'Leans 7 ft 6 ins to the south. 7 ft 10 ins to the south west and 3 ft 2 ins to the west'. 125 mm. *also Willow.* (Amazingly the spire is still standing.)

Clifton Suspension Bridge, Model of, with long inscription. 120 mm long. *also Willow.*

Conisborough Castle, The Keep. 95 mm (rare).

Cottage, inscribed: *Built in a day 4th June 1819.* 43 mm long. *Willow.*

Crofter's Cottage. 55 mm long.

First and last house in England. 83 mm long.

First and last house in England, with annex. 95 mm long.

Grimsby Hydraulic Tower, with details of size etc. 165 mm.

Hamsfell Hospice. Grange over Sands. (Often found not named). 72 mm (odd square building with outside stairs and flat roof, and with impressed Greek inscription over door) (rare).

Hampton Court Palace. 85 mm.

Hampton Court Palace, flat frontage on ashtray base. 108 mm long. *also Willow.*—No. 525.

Hastings Clock Tower. 165 mm. *Willow.*

Haycastle, Brecon. 94 mm.

Hop Pole Inn, flat frontage on ashtray base, with long quotation referring to the Inn from Chapter 50 'The Pickwick Papers' by Charles Dickens, on ashtray. 60 mm long.

Lancaster, Castle Gateway. 90 mm.

Leicester, Clock Tower. 175 mm. (This model was obviously made for some time and the transfer used for the clock face varies. It can be 12.45 or 3.55.)

Lincoln Cathedral, West Front. 118 mm.

Lincoln, Stonebow. 104 mm long.

Lloyd George's Home, inscribed: *The old home of the Right Hon D. Lloyd George Esq M.P. Llanystymdwy near Criccieth.* 102 mm long.

Old London Bridge on ashtray base, small. 105 mm long.

Mickle Gate Bar, York. 116 mm.

Monnow Bridge, Monmouth. 92 mm. *also Willow.*

Morpeth Castle, Model of. 78 mm (scarce).

Nottingham Castle, Model of. 92 mm long.

Old Bridge House, Ambleside. 88 mm.

Old London Bridge, Model of, on ashtray base. 100 mm long. *also Willow.*

Old Nottingham Inn. Ye Olde Trip to Jerusalem, 1199 AD, Model of. 95 mm (specially commissioned by a former landlady Mrs Ward) (scarce).

Old Ostrich Inn, Colnbook. 80 mm.

Peterborough Cathedral, West Front. 80 mm long.

Peveril Castle. 115 mm long.

Pier Entrance, Skegness. 88 mm long.

Priory Gate House, Worksop. 88 mm long.

Pump Room, Harrogate. 75 mm. *also Willow.*

St. Albans Clock Tower. No details of size known.

St. Ann's Well, Great Malvern. 2 sizes: 85 mm & 102 mm long. *Willow.*

St. Botolph's Church, Boston. 112 mm. *also Willow.*

Saville Fountain. No. 730. 140 mm (scarce).

Saxon Church, Bradford on Avon. 74 mm.

Shakespeare's House. 2 sizes: 120 mm & 160 mm long.

Shakespeare's House, on brown base. 208 mm long.

Skegness, Clock Tower. 2 sizes: 125 mm & 165 mm. *also Willow.*

Soloman's Temple, Grinlow Tower, inscribed: 'erected on site of a prehistoric barrow. Buxton. 88 mm. *also Willow.*

Tudor Gabled House, Taunton AD 1878. 100 mm.

Upleatham Church. 88 mm. *also Willow.*

Wainhouse Tower, Halifax. 130 mm.

Wallingford, Town Hall. 84 mm.

West Malling, Abbey Tower. 94 mm.

Whittington Inn with inscription (see coloured buildings). 100 mm long. *Willow.*

Wilberforce House, Hull. 86 mm.

Windsor Castle. 125 mm long. *also Willow.*

Windsor Castle. Round Tower. 76 mm.

Worcester Cathedral. 144 mm long.

Monuments (including Crosses)

Banbury Cross. 140 mm.

The Blackwatch Memorial. Edinburgh. 127 mm. (This monument is in the form of a Scottish soldier on a square base and is often not named—it is frequently found in Great War collections.)

Burns statue, on square base. 170 mm. *Willow* version 150 mm.

Bunyan statue. 165 mm. *also Willow.*

Burton statue, inscribed: *Michael Arthur, first Baron Burton.* 128 mm. *also Willow.*

Caister-on-Sea Lifeboat Memorial: moulded in relief: 1903 and *Caister Lifeboat* on lifebelt. 162 mm. *also Willow.*

Carnegie, statue. 150 mm.

Cleethorpes Fishermans' Memorial, with inscription: 'Erected by Public Subscription to the memory of George Henry Smith (skipper) and William Richard Leggatt (Third Hand) etc. unveiled August 30th 1908'. 155 mm.

Sir William de la Pole, Statue of, with long inscription of its presentation and the history of Sir William. 160 mm.

Drake, Statue, Plymouth. 160 mm.

Flodden Cross, inscribed: Flodden 1513, to the brave of both nations. 136 mm.

Gibbet Cross, Hindhead, inscribed: Post Tenebras Lux In Luce Spes In Obrtu Pax Post Obitum Salus. 136 mm.

Hector Macdonald Memorial, Dingwall. 112 mm.

Highland Mary Statue, Dunoon, on plinth. 150 mm.

Huddersfield, Market Cross. 150 mm. also Willow.

Hughes Monument Rugby School. 140 mm.

Hull Fisherman's Memorial. 2 sizes: 135 mm & 160 mm.

Hull South African War Memorial, with inscription: 'Erected to the memory of the men of Hull who fell in the late South African War'. 165 mm.

Keppels Columm 1778. 140 mm (rare).

King George Statue, Kingstown. 135 mm (rare).

Laceby, The Monument. 2 sizes: 120 mm & 150 mm. also Willow.

Lowestoft Fisherman' Memorial. 130 mm.

Maiwand Memorial Forbury Gardens Reading. Lion sometimes coloured brown or black. 98 mm.

Margate Surf Boat Monument, with usual lengthy inscription. 115 mm.

Nelson's Column. 160 mm. Willow.

Issac Newton, statue. 165 mm. also Willow.

Peter Pan, statue. 140 mm. Willow (rare).

Queen Victoria's Statue. 163 mm (rare).

C. S. Rolls Memorial, inscribed: Memorial to the late Honourable C. S. Rolls. 128 mm. also Willow. (This Motor Car Manufacturer was the first English victim of aviation: he was killed in 1910.)

Rufus Stone, with lengthy inscription on all 3 sides. 110 mm. also Willow.

Runic Cross, Ancient. Bakewell. 115 mm. Willow (rare).

Ruskin Memorial, Friars Crag, with inscriptions. 180 mm.

Sailor's Stone, Hindhead, with very lengthy and bloodthirsty inscriptions. 95 mm. also Willow.

St. Alban, Statue of. 146 mm (also found unglazed on glazed base).

Toad Rock, Tunbridge Wells. 83 mm. also Willow.

Historical/Folklore

Archbishops Chair, Canterbury Cathedral. 100 mm.

Bill Sykes and his dog, standing figure on base. Coloured beige, no crest. 128 mm. (An early model.)

Bishops Jester, Wells Cathedral. Fully coloured. No crest. 115 mm (rare).

Bunyan's Chair, Model of. 90 mm. also Willow.

Bunyan's Cushion, Model of. 105 mm long.

Burn's Chair, Dumfries. 85 mm.

Cauldron, 2 handles. 36 mm.

Cauldron, on 3 feet. 60 mm.

Daniel Lambert, sitting in chair. With long inscription. 118 mm. also Willow (quite rare—Daniel Lambert was the heaviest man who ever lived in England).

The Ducking Stool, with inscription as Arcadian. 120 mm long. Willow. (Very rare, possibly Arcadian mould.)

Font, not named. No. 228. 87 mm.

James V Chair, Stirling Castle. 100 mm. also Willow.

Man in the Moon. 55 mm. also Willow. Can be found with yellow lustre face marked Willow.

Mary Queen of Scots Chair. Edinburgh Castle, Model of. No. 163. 75 mm. also Willow.

Mermaid, seated on rock, combing hair. 105 mm (quite rare).

Mons Meg, Edinburgh Castle. 130 mm long.

Mother Shipton. 2 sizes: 80 mm & 105 mm. also Willow.

Peeping Tom, bust. 130 mm.

A rubbing stone for asses, a 17th century puzzle printed on a brick wall. 100 mm long.

Sir Walter Scots Chair, Abbots Ford, Model of. 80 mm.

Skull, can be inscribed: Alas poor Yorick. 60 mm long. also Willow.

Trusty Servant, with verse on both sides, fully coloured. 132 mm.

Traditional/National Souvenirs

Banbury cake. 105 mm wide.

Bolton Trotter. No details of size. Willow.

Blackpool Big Wheel. 100 mm. also Willow.

Cornish Pasty. 93 mm long. also Willow.

Lancashire Clog. 88 mm long.

Leaking boot. Grimsby. No details of size.

Lincoln Imp. 63 mm.

Lincoln Imp, on pedestal. 102 mm.

Melton Mowbray Pie with verse. 55 mm. also Willow.

Reading Biscuit, with verse: 'Than Reading biscuits there are no finer, Here's a good one reproduced in china'. Coloured fawn. 85 mm long (rare).

River Thames pleasure punt, with or without coloured cushions. 175 mm long. also Willow (rare).

Yarmouth bloater. 121 mm.

Irish Harp. 105 mm.

Bagpipes. 118 mm long. (Can be found with ribbon painted turquoise blue.)

Blacksmiths Anvil, Gretna Green, often found not named, with inscription: 'The famous old Blacksmiths Anvil over which marriages were and still are performed'. 76 mm. also Willow.

Scotsman, bust, Some colouring. 80 mm.

Scotsman matches holder. Comic fully coloured figure. Inscribed: Matches. 90 mm.

Souter Johnny, sitting figure, with verse: 'Here's to all of us! For there's as much good in the worst of us, and so much bad in the best of us that it hardly behoves any of us to talk about the rest of us'. Can be found with some colouring. 130 mm.

Tam O'Shanter, sitting figure, with verse as Souter Johnny. Can be found with some colouring. 135 mm.

Thistle Vase. 50 mm.

Welsh Hat, can have blue hat band. Found
    with longest Welsh place name printed
    round brim. No. 75. 57 mm.
Welsh Lady, bust, with black hat. 110 mm.
Welsh Leek. 55 mm. *Willow.*
Welsh tea party, a figure group, some
    colouring. 50 mm. *Willow.*

Seaside Souvenirs
Bathing Machine, inscribed: *A morning dip.*
    2 sizes: 65 mm & 80 mm.
Lifeboat, coloured ropes. 118 mm long.
    also Willow.
Motorboat, with driver, at sea. 115 mm
    long.
Paddlesteamer. 154 mm long (rare).
Rowing boat on rocks. 114 mm long. *also
    Willow.*
Yacht in full sail. 122 mm.
Lifeboatman, standing on plinth (hand
    raised to hat). No details of size.
Fisherman's Basket with handle. 77 mm
    long.
Lighthouse, not named. 100 mm. *Willow.*
Lighthouse, not named. No. 135. 110 mm.
Lighthouse on rocks with brown rowing
    boat. 133 mm.
Beachy Head Lighthouse, with black band.
    136 mm. *also Willow.*
Flamborough Lighthouse. 110 mm.
North Foreland Lighthouse. 135 mm.
Scarborough Lighthouse, with inscription:
    'This lighthouse was damaged in the
    bombardment by German Warships on
    Wednesday December 16th 1916'. This
    model has two shell holes in its side.
    132 mm. *also Willow.* Is of interest to
    World War I collectors (rare).
Scarborough Lighthouse, with rectangular
    buildings. Inscription as above. 110 mm.
    also Willow. (rare).
Spurn Lighthouse, with details of size and
    power. 125 mm. *also Willow.*
Withernsea Lighthouse, with details of size
    and power. 127 mm.
Crab. 83 mm long.
Scallop Shell flower holder, on rocky base.
    92 mm.
Open bag with four feet. No details of size.
    Willow.
Great Yarmouth Rock, pink stick with
    wording: *Great Yarmouth.* 75 mm (very
    rare).
Sand for the kiddies from Brighton: same
    model as truck of coal but with coal
    painted yellow. No. 292. 40 mm long.
    (Sand from Brighton? this model is very
    rare and has only been recorded 'from
    Brighton' but it must have been made for
    other seaside resorts.)

Countryside
Pinecone. 90 mm.
Treetrunk vase, four necks. No. 259.
    80 mm.

Animals
Many of the Willow animals are found
    marked Arcadian.
Boar, standing on rocky base. 102 mm long
    (rare).
Cat, angry, with tail in the air. Blue Bow.
    80 mm long. *also Willow.*

Cat, in Boot. 88 mm long.
Cat, Cheshire, with coloured face.
    Inscribed: *Always smiling.* 95 mm. *Willow*
    (not often found).
Cat, sitting, bow round neck. No. 17 or 27.
    80 mm.
Cat, sitting, blue bow. No. 62. 60 mm.
Cat, sitting, large red bow, and red and
    green eyes. No. 70. 70 mm.
Cat, sitting, detailed thick coat, and tail
    round paws. 57 mm.
Cat, standing, chubby. No. 61. 70 mm.
Cat, standing (long back), green eyes and
    red tongue. 117 mm long.

Black Cats
Two types of black cat are found with the
    Willow or Willow Art mark. The true
    Willow Art Black Cat is large and very
    realistic, and can be found sitting on a
    number of 'bases'. The other Black Cat is
    an imp-like creature which very much
    resembles the *Arcadian* Registered
    Series. (These models usually marked
    Willow are not found with the *Arcadian*
    mark however.) One must assume that
    these Willow models were moulded by
    the same hand that modelled the
    Arcadian range when Cauldon were
    using the Willow mark. Whether
    originally employed by Willow or
    Arcadian is hard to say. All have red
    bows. *Willow Art* sitting Black Cats are
    found on the following:
Curling Stone. Rd. No. 709314. 60 mm.
    also Willow.
Cushion. 100 mm. *also Willow.*
Diamond Ashtray, inscribed: *Ashtray* and
    Good luck. 120 mm long.
Pouffe, inscribed: *Good luck.* Can be found
    with blue bow. 85 mm. *Willow* version,
    impressed, No. 539. 95 mm.
(All of these are completely coloured black,
    with blue, green eyes on white cushions
    etc.)
Arcadian type Black Cats. All are of a
    regional nature.
Black Cat, playing Bagpipes. 60 mm.
    Willow.
Black Cat, wearing kilt and sitting on a
    curling stone.
Black Cat, playing Bagpipes, and wearing
    kilt, standing on thistle ashtray. Rd. No.
    71546? 88 mm long. *Willow.*
Black Cat, standing beside thistle vase. Rd.
    No. 708645. 57 mm. *Willow.*
Black Cat, playing Harp. Rd. No. 709314.
    60 mm. *Willow.*
Black Cat, wearing a Welsh Hat, standing
    beside a leek. Rd. No. 708647. 67 mm.
    Willow.
(All of these cats have one green eye and
    one yellow. The Rd. No's are probably as
    unreliable as most Arcadian numbers.
    All of these models must be considered
    rare.)
Black Cat, climbing into cup, inscribed:
    May your cup of Good Luck brim over.
    90 mm. *Willow.* (The only other cat
    found on a domestic item (a dish) is
    marked *Swan.*)

Right Willow Art. Three legged dog with the Isle of Man Crest inscribed 'Prince Toby Mary'

Left Willow Art. Sitting bulldog and dachshund sitting 95 mm long

Willow Art. Scottie dog wearing a blue glengarry 60 mm, Scottish terrier standing 90 mm long and bulldog sitting, black collar 55 mm

Right Willow Art. Large Deer 115 mm long

Right Willow Art. Shetland Pony inscribed on reverse 'A native of Shetland'. The ponies can be found facing right or left

Right Willow Art. A model of a ram with wonderfully curly horns which can easily be damaged.

Left Willow Art. Long cat with red tongue and green eyes

Willow Art. Highland bull with inscription 'King of the Herd' and Cow. Both models are rare

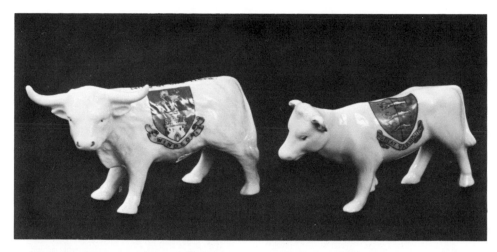

Right Willow Art. Crouching lion with red mouth

Left Willow Art. Unglazed jockey on racehorse, yellow and blue silks. Newmarket crest

Right Willow Art. Polar Bear 96 mm, a very realistic model

Left Willow Art. Wild Boar on base, a particularly handsome model

Right Willow Art. This really grotesque bird posy bowl is very unlike the other bird models in the Willow Art range and could possibly have been copied from some other manufacturer's model.

Left Willow Art. Pelican with inscription on his side

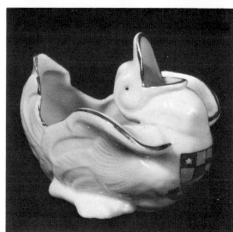

Cow. 105 mm long (rare).

Deer, sitting. 2 sizes: 64 mm & 115 mm long. *also Willow*.

Bulldog, sitting, feet moulded separately. Black Collar and red mouth. 55 mm.

Bulldog, sitting, feet internally moulded. 50 mm.

Bulldog, black, emerging from kennel, inscribed: *The Black Watch*. 70 mm long. *also Willow*.

Dog, Bull terrier, standing. 60 mm. *also Willow*.

Dog, Collie, standing. 85 mm.

Dog, Dachshund, sitting, long ears and rather comic. 75 mm.

Dog, The Manx three legged dog, often found not named. Inscribed: *Prince Toby Orry*. 70 mm. (Toby was a fighting dog belonging to a Douglas publican, he lost a leg in an accident but continued quite happily. Because he had three legs the title of Prince Orry was added to his name. Prince or King Orry founded TynWald.)

Dog, Scottie, wearing a glengarry. 2 sizes: 60 mm & 100 mm. *also Willow*.

Dog, Scottie, wearing a tam o'shanter. 60 mm. *also Willow*.

Dog, Scottish Terrier, standing. 90 mm long.

Donkey in harness. No. 294. 100 mm long (not often found).

Elephant, with trunk in the air. 80 mm long.

Elephant, walking. No 113. 52 mm. *also Willow*.

Elephant Jug. 70 mm.

Fish Ashtray, in shape of plaice. 78 mm long. *Willow*

Fish, curved. 75 mm long. *Willow*.

Fish, straight. 130 mm long. *also Willow*.

Fish, straight, with open mouth. 115 mm long.

Hare. 77 mm long.

Highland Bull, inscribed: *King of the Herd*. No. 342. 115 mm long. *Willow* (rare).

Lion, crouching. Red open mouth. 82 mm long.

Lion, walking. No. 47. 105 mm long.

Monkey, holding coconut. 85 mm. *also Willow*.

3 Monkeys on diamond shaped ashtray. Monkeys inscribed: *See not evil, speak not evil, hear not evil*. 130 mm long.

Mouse (very fat and often described as a hamster or guinea pig—it could be either!) 62 mm.

Pig, sitting on haunches. 60 mm.

Pig, standing. 85 mm long. *also Willow*.

Pig, standing. Very fat, with double chin. 96 mm long.

Polar Bear. 96 mm.

Polar Bear, sitting. 83 mm.

Pony, inscribed: *A Native of Shetland*. No. 127. 108 mm long.

Rabbit, lying down. 54 mm long.

Rabbit, sitting, alert ears. 60 mm long. *also Willow*.

Ram, with curly horns. 90 mm long (not often found).

Teddy Bear, sitting. 65 mm. *Willow* version 76 mm.

Tortoise. 88 mm long.

Isnt this rabbit a duck: On its base a rabbit, turned on its side, a duck. 75 mm (also found marked *Arcadian*. Really a novelty item).

Birds (including eggs)

Bird (reputedly a tit). 77 mm long.

Bird, on plinth. 103 mm.

Bird Posy Holder. 104 mm long.

Canary on rock, can be found coloured yellow on green base. No. 27. 98 mm.

Chicken, very fluffy, 65 mm.

Chicken—Pepper Pot. 70 mm.

Chicken, emerging from egg, inscribed: *Every little helps mother will be pleased*. Rd. No. 740912. 50 mm. *Willow*.

Cock. 100 mm. *Willow*.

Goose, some colouring. 143 mm.

Pelican; with inscription: 'A wonderful bird is the pelican, his beak will hold more than his belican.' 75 mm (usually found marked Arcadian).

Swan, with yellow beak. 60 mm. *also Willow*.

Swan, with head on breast. 58 mm.

Swan Posy Holder. 65 mm long. *Willow* version 93 mm long.

Wise Owl with verse: 'An aged owl sat in an oak etc.' 98 mm. *also Willow*.

Great War

It is quite likely that the *Willow* models listed here are from *Arcadian* moulds and not *Willow Art. (Arc Mould)* indicates that the model is recorded as being the Arcadian version.

Airman, standing to attention. 140 mm.

Air Force Officer, a hero holding medal. Coloured. 140 mm (rare).

Nurse, inscribed: *A friend in need*. 130 mm. *also Willow*.

Sailor, at attention, inscribed: *Our brave defender*. 2 sizes: 130 mm & 170 mm. *also Willow*.

Soldier, with rifle, inscribed: *Our brave defender*, 132 mm. *also Willow*.

Monoplane, with fixed prop. No. 67. 146 mm long.

Monoplane with revolving prop., coloured roundels on wings, and stripes on tail. 150 mm long.

Aeroplane Propeller. 150 mm long. *Willow (Arc Mould)*.

Airship (Observation Balloon), inscribed: *Beta*. No. 70. 80 mm long.

Battleship. 4 funnels. 2 sizes: 127 mm & 140 mm long. *also Willow*

Battleship, impressed: *HMS Lion*. 140 mm long.

Troop Carrier, Liner converted. 140 mm long. *also Willow*. (scarce)

Submarine, impressed: *E4*. 116 mm long.

Submarine, inscribed: *E4*. 95 mm long. *Willow (Arc Mould)*.

Red Cross Van, red cross on side. No. 218. 84 mm long. *also Willow*.

British Tank, Model of. 2 sizes: 92 mm & 120 mm Long. *also Willow*.

British Tank, Model of, with trailing wheels. Rd. No. 658588. No. 201. 130 mm long.

Field Gun. 120 mm long. *also Willow*.

Field Gun, with screen. 115 mm long. *also Willow*.

Right Willow Art. Model of an airman, obviously a hero as he is holding a medal. Rare

Left Willow Art. Airman standing to attention. 140 mm

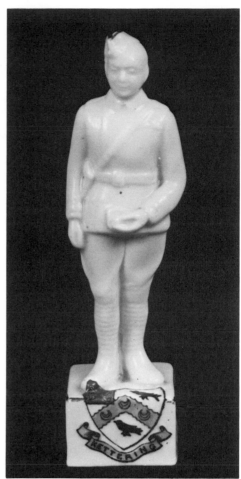

Willow Art. Sailor at attention, red cross nurse and soldier with rifle

Right Willow Art. 'Scarborough Lighthouse' showing two shell holes caused by German bombardment

Left Willow Art. Great Yarmouth War Memorial with inscription 'They gave their all, these nobly played their part, they heard their country's call for God and King and right'

Left Willow Art. 'Caister-on-sea lifeboat memorial' a beautifully modelled memorial, with a great deal of detail

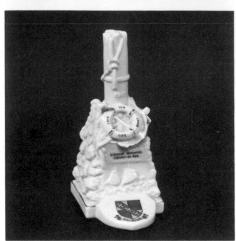

Willow Art. Portsmouth 'Royal Naval War Memorial', 'War Memorial, Matlock Bath' and 'Edith Cavell' Memorial, London

Right Willow Art. Fireplace with coloured kettle and cat

Left Willow Art. Baby inscribed 'Cheerio' Probably a model of 'Pooksie' a Great War Cartoon character

Right Willow Art. Observation Balloon 'Beta' 80 mm long

Left Willow Art. Small Bugle and Kit Bag with verse

Willow Art. Liner converted to a troop ship, not found named

Willow Art. Aeroplane propellor with a Kingsbury crest and the RFC badge

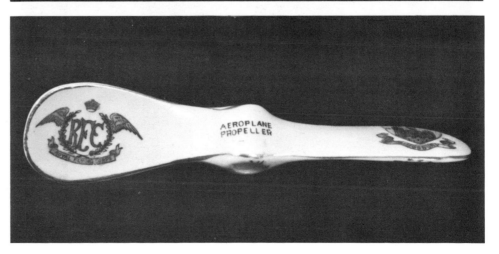

Right Willow Art. Dutch boy with hands in pockets

Left Willow Art. 'Souter Johnny' with blue tam and brown tankard and verse

Right Willow Art. 'Box of chocolates' with no colouring

Left Willow Art. 'Box of chocolates' with pink faces and brown hair

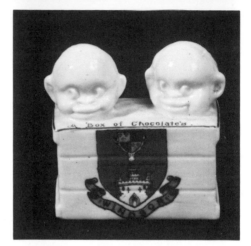

Right Willow Art. The massive figure of Daniel Lambert, a very rare model

Left Willow Art. 'Billiken The God of Luck'. This Willow Art version is modelled sitting on a high backed chair

Right Willow Art. Grotesque Billiken 73 mm

Left Willow Art. Man in the Moon, this model is not found in other manufacturers ranges

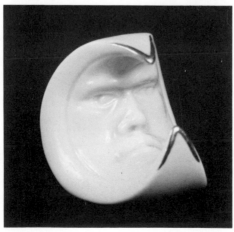

Howitzer. 115 mm long. *Willow.*
Bandsman's Drum, with cording. 60 mm.
Bugle. No. 379. 2 sizes: 70 mm & 115 mm long.
Field glasses. 83 mm. *also Willow.*
Kit Bag with verse: 'Pack up your troubles in your old kit bag'. 74 mm. *also Willow.*
Tent, cone shaped with open flaps on base. 70 mm.
Tommy's Steel Helmet. 76 mm long. *also Willow.*
Church Bell, inscribed: *Curfew must not ring tonight.* 70 mm.
Fireplace, inscribed: *Keep the home fires burning.* Some colouring. 100 mm long.
Kitchen range, with pot on fire, inscribed: *Keep the home fires burning.* Some colouring. 78 mm long.
Trench Lamp. 70 mm. *also Willow.*
Forage Cap. 83 mm long.
Glengarry. Some colouring. 83 mm long. *Willow.*
Officer's Peaked Cap. 70 mm dia. *also Willow.*
Pickelhaube (German Spiked Helmet). 50 mm. *also Willow.*
Edith Cavell. Memorial, London, inscribed: *Brussels dawn Oct 12th 1915. Sacrifice, Humanity.* 3 sizes: 110 mm & 150 mm. *also Willow.* 175 mm *Willow*
Edith Cavell, Nurse. Patriot and martyr, memorial statue, Norwich. 3 sizes: 115 mm, 155 mm & 175 mm. *also Willow.*
Cenotaph, inscribed: *The Glorious Dead MCMXIV–MCMXIX* with green wreaths. 3 sizes: 70 mm, 145 mm & 184 mm.
Chatham *Naval War Memorial.* 160 mm.
Florence Nightingale Statue, Model of. Can be found inscribed: *Florence Nightingale 1825–1910.* 2 sizes: 120 mm & 160 mm.
Great Yarmouth War Memorial. With inscription: 'They gave their all, They nobly played their part, They heard their country's call. For God and King and right.' 166 mm. *also Willow.*
Ilkeston War Memorial, with inscription: 'To the Glory and to the memory of the men of Ilkeston who gave their lives in the Great War 1914–1918'. 135 mm.
Loughborough War Memorial. 155 mm. (Carillon tower).
Matlock Bath *War Memorial,* inscribed: *Duty nobly done.* 182 mm. *Willow.*
Portsmouth. *Royal Naval War Memorial.* 160 mm. (Chatham, Plymouth and Portsmouth War Memorials were all built from the same prize-winning design.)

Home/Nostalgic
Ali Baba Storage Basket, very detailed. 75 mm. *Willow.*
Basket, oval with handle. 70 mm long.
Book, Model of. 57 mm.
Child smiling, bust. 60 mm (rare).
Coal Scuttle, helmet shaped. No. 101. 53 mm.
Fireplace, inscribed: *There's no place like home.* 70 mm. *also Willow.*
Flat Iron. 64 mm.
Flat Iron, on stand. (2 pieces) 66 mm.
Garden Roller. 51 mm.

Grandfather Clock, found inscribed: *Make use of time let not advantage slip. Shakespeare,* or much more rarely: *Nae man can tetha time or tide. Burns.* No. 149. 2 sizes: 112 mm (rare) and 128 mm.
Milk Can with lid. 60 mm. *Willow.*
Pail, with moulded rope handle. 63 mm.
Pillar Box, impressed GR. No. 207. 90 mm.
Shaving Mug. No. 125. 2 sizes: 55 mm & 70 mm.
Sundial, circular on circular base, with inscription: 'I Mark not the hours'. 118 mm. *also Willow.*
Sundial, circular on square base, with inscription: 'I Mark not the hours'. No. 205. 98 mm.
Watering Can. 75 mm. *also Willow.*
Wheelbarrow. No. 300. 105 mm long.

Comic/Novelty
Many of the highly coloured models were made very late in the firm's history and will be found grouped together at the end of this listing:
Billiken, The God of luck, often found unnamed. 73 mm.
Billiken, The God of luck, sitting on high backed chair. 100 mm.
Broadbean pod splitting open, inscribed: *Good old bean.* 130 mm long (scarce).
Dutch Boy. Can be found fully coloured. 80 mm.
Dutch Girl. Can be found fully coloured. 80 mm. (A pair to the Dutch Boy.)
Fat Lady on weighing scales, scale registers 20 stone, inscribed: *Adding weight.* Blue Bonnet. Rd. No. 740919. 90 mm. *Willow* (from Arcadian mould).
Policeman, very jolly. 80 mm. *Willow* version found fully coloured. Rd. No. 752238.
Sack of Meal with Mouse, inscribed: *May the mouse ne'er leave yer mealpoke wi' a tear-drop'n its e'e.* 63 mm. *Also Willow.*
A truck of coal from . . . Wagon of black coal, also found with coal painted grey and inscribed: *A truck of iron ore from . . .* 90 mm long.

Black Boys
All of these boys are fully coloured but sit on white boxes etc. Some of these were obviously original Willow Art Moulds, later used by Cauldon and are found with Arcadian marks. Boys marked *Willow* are from Arcadian moulds. (The highly glazed and coloured models are late.) All rare.
Black Boy, playing drum. Rd. No. 72881? 70 mm. (Only found marked Willow Art.)
Black Boy, in bath of ink, inscribed: *How ink is made.* 110 mm. *also Arcadian.*
Black Boy, in bed with spider, inscribed: *A little study in black and fright.* Boy can have red or blue pyjamas. 70 mm long. *Willow.*
Black Boy, eating slice of melon, sitting on soap box. 80 mm. *Willow* (late).
Black Boy, at table eating a boiled egg which has chicken popping out. 70 mm. *Willow.*

Right Willow Art. Open topped double decker tram 108 mm long

Left Willow Art. Hand holding tulip, a rather tasteful model in the 'Willow Art' range

Right Willow Art. 'River Thames Pleasure Punt' Windsor crest. Can also be found with striped seats

Left Willow Art. Open four seater tourer 114 mm long

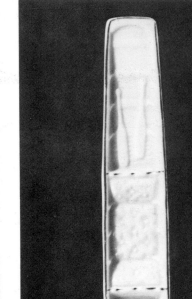

Left Carlton. Truck of Coal, coal was heavily rationed during the Great War and so became very precious

Willow Art. Open tourer 115 mm long

Two Black Boys, heads popping out of box, inscribed: *Box of chocolates*. Can be found with boys painted as white children, yellow hair and blue eyes and is often found not coloured at all. 60 mm. *also Arcadian.*
Black Boy, holding container for matches. 100 mm. *Willow* (late).

Little Birds
From Arcadian moulds. Head fully coloured, eggs white.
Flapper's head hatching from egg, inscribed: *A little bird from* . . . 50 mm long. *Willow.*
Black boy's head hatching from egg, inscribed: *A blackbird from* . . . 50 mm long. *Willow.*

Comic Ashtray
From Arcadian mould
Scotsman, really grotesque, fully coloured sitting on white bench on white ashtray. 95 mm. *Willow.*

Cartoon/Comedy Characters
Baby, with arms outstretched, inscribed: *Cheerio*. Some colouring on face. 125 mm. *also Willow.* (Great War cartoon character, could be 'Pooksie'.)
Baby, saluting, inscribed: *One of the b'hoys*. Can be found with A.W.W.H. on chest. Some colouring on face. 125 mm. *also Willow.* (Great War cartoon character as above.)
Harry Lauder, bust. Brown Hat with thistle. No. 116. 80 mm.
Mr Beetle (impressed). 142 mm. (Daily Mail comic strip. Strip began 1915.)
Teddytail (impressed). 142 mm. (Daily Mail comic strip character as above.)
Two Cartoon characters sitting in Armchair. 90 mm. (Thought to be Mr Beetle and Sunny Jim.)

Alcohol
Barrel. 50 mm.
Barrel on stand. No. 35. 58 mm.
Barrel with opening on one side. 54 mm long.
Beer Bottle and Tankard on horseshoe ashtray, with inscription: 'The more we are together the merrier we'll be'. Silver Tankard. 85 mm. *Willow* from Arcadian mould.
Hand, holding beaker, inscribed: *Good health*. 50 mm.
Tankard, foaming. 58 mm.
Thimble, inscribed: *Just a thimbleful.* 50 mm. *also Willow.*
Thistle Vase, with verse: 'A wee Deoch on Doris'. 56 mm. *also Willow.*
Whisky Bottle, inscribed: *One special scotch.* 63 mm.
Whisky Bottle, with cork, inscribed: *One special scotch.* 88 mm. *also Willow.*
Whisky Bottle and Soda Syphon on Tray, inscribed: *Scotch and soda.* 88 mm dia. *Willow* from Arcadian mould.
Whisky Bottle, Soda Syphon and Tumbler on horseshoe ashtray. With inscription: 'The more we are together, the merrier we will be.' Some colouring. 87 mm long. *Willow.*

Sport
Golf clubs in bag. 108 mm.
Football. 50 mm dia.
Jockey on Racehorse, found in different coloured silks. Can be found coloured but unglazed. 112 mm. *also Willow.*
Racehorse, impressed. No. 6001. 102 mm.

Musical Instruments
Banjo. 160 mm long.
Guitar. 163 mm long. *also Willow.*

Transport
Car, open 4 seater. 114 mm long.
Tram, single deck, enclosed top. Inscribed: *Life on the ocean wave.* No. 333. 104 mm long.
Tram, double decker, open top. Inscribed: *Life on the ocean wave.* No. 334. 108 mm long.
Can of Petrol, impressed: *Motor spirit.* 55 mm. *Willow* from Arcadian mould.

'Modern' Equipment
Camera, folding. 60 mm.
Horn Gramophone. square. 95 mm. *also Willow.*
Radio Horn, inscribed: *Hello* . . . (name of town) *calling.* 70 mm. *Willow.*

Miscellaneous
Shoes
Boot. 112 mm long.
Ladies' Riding Shoe, square toe and blue tie. 115 mm long.
Slipper Wall Pocket, blue bow. 178 mm long.
Bell. 60 mm.
Hammer Head, Matchholder, inscribed: *My speciality is striking* or *Matches.* No. 301. 80 mm long.
Hand holding a tulip. No. 74. 80 mm. *also Willow.*
Pipe. 76 mm long (rare).

Miniature Domestic
Cheese dish, one piece. 45 mm. *also Willow.*
Cheese dish and cover. 45 mm. *also Willow.*
Coffee Pot with lid. 70 mm. *also Willow.*
Teapot with lid. 60 mm. *Willow.*

Interesting Domestic Items with Crests
Bridge Trump indicator. Coloured suit symbols on circular base, spinning cover allowing only one suit to be seen. Very ornate. Rd. No. 693774. 104 mm dia.
Hair Pins, box. 105 mm.
Hat Pins, curved fluted holder. No. 154. 125 mm.
Pin Box, horseshoe shaped. 62 mm.
Pin Box, oval, with safety pin in relief on lid. 90 mm long.
Playing cards, box. 154 mm long.
Trinket Box, oval on eight collar stud feet with moulded cufflinks placed between each stud. Border of moulded cufflinks and tie pin in relief on lid. 90 mm long (quite rare—very silly and most desirable).

Right Wilton. Vase 62 mm with very vivid colour transfer of 'Plunge Bath, Holywell'

Left Wilton. Reverse of 72 mm yellow lustre pot showing Pathe trademark. Manufacturers had to pay the film agents fees for using Felix on their wares

Wilton. Welsh Hats, two extra large showing coloured transfers and a tiny crested model

Right Wilton. Long necked cat with red mouth and green eyes inscribed 'Luck' Photographed to show the 'Felix the film cat' transfer. These souvenirs of Felix can be found on many Wilton models

Left Wilton. 72 mm yellow lustre pot with black transfer print of 'Felix the film cat'. This is often found on Wilton pieces

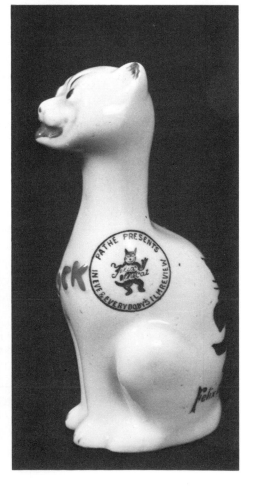

Left Wilton. 57 mm Vase with lucky black cat transfer print

1903+

Williamsons

Trademark used by H. M.
Williamson and Sons, Bridge
Pottery, Longton.

For more details see W.

This mark was used by Williamson and Sons on domestic china with the usual patterns, and has also been found on domestic ware with crests. It also appears on the one model listed below.

Williamson Model

Ancient Artefacts
Guernsey Milk Can, with lid. 105 mm
(found with a Guernsey crest).

Willper Heraldic China

Trademark used by an
unknown Hanley
manufacturer.

No Hanley manufacturer registered *Willper* as a tradename. Ford and Pointon (THE CORONET WARE), Charles Ford (SWAN CHINA) and The Podmore China Co. (PODMORE CHINA) all were working in Hanley during the period crested china was made. Of these three, the mark is more likely to have been used by the Podmore China Co. The other two became branches of J. A. Robinson and so moved out of Hanley eventually.

Two 'smalls' have been recorded with this mark, one has a Derby crest and the other Bristol. Until recognisable models are discovered with the mark one cannot determine the manufacturer.

c1923–1934

WILTON
ART
CHINA

in gilt 1232–1934

Wilton China

Trademark used by A. G.
Harley Jones at Wilton
Pottery, Fenton.

Mr A. G. Harley Jones started his business in Fenton in 1905, and until 1920 seems to have concentrated on producing ornamental wares. After 1920 he diversified production, adding general earthenwares and crested china to his range. In 1923 he advertised 'Wilton heraldic china' and registered the mark in 1927. Mr Harley Jones was quite successful before 1920, expanding his business and extending his premises. After this date he seems to have had great difficulty in surviving, snatching at any craze or passing whim in the china trade to make money. This makes his wares very appealing to collectors as he produced a small but very original and innovative range of crested china models, tending towards the vulgar but reeking with nostalgia. Unfortunately he turned to crested china at the end of its popularity and even this new venture could not stem the tide of his insolvency. His turnover dropped from £22,062 in 1927 to £8,915 in 1932. By 1933 he had turned his hand to making glazed tile fireplaces but to no avail: he was declared bankrupt in June 1934. The account of his bankruptcy proceedings is a sad record of business losses from 1927 onwards, enlivened only by the Official Receiver's questions regarding a marriage deed made on the eve of his bankruptcy settling his household effects on a lady he married three days later. The Official Receiver doubted whether the settlement held good in law.

Right Wilton. Comic Bookmaker, a very original model only found in the 'Wilton range

Left Wilson. 'Black Diamonds' from in this case Tonypandy 87 mm long

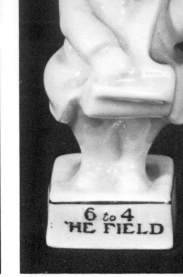

Left Wilton. Dick Whittington and his cat on ashtray base. This particular model has a very odd inscription

Right Unmarked. Delicate parian Luton boater with blue band, Luton crest inside crown. These boaters are invariably found unmarked

Left Unmarked. The Castle, Guildford

Wilton. Small lustre Bonzo Dog, found as an individual model and also set on a lustre ashtray with a coloured transfer print. Both sold by same agent in Hastings, N. Magnus

Found on models with Felix
transfer or inscription

Wilton China is for the most part rather heavy and is better described as
'pot'. This does not however mean that models are not attractive: they
are particularly 'modern', amusing and often unique to this pottery.
There are obviously very few ancient artefacts or Great War souvenirs in
the range as there was little call for these after 1923, but the novelty and
comic items produced are particularly exciting. Mr Harley Jones shows
the same awareness of public taste as the manufacturers of *Carlton China*
and he also made many models in lustre ware. Unlike Carlton he does
not seem to have made models of Felix the Cat but he used a transfer
print of him with the inscription: 'Felix the film cat' on many different
models and small vases. He did make models of that other popular
twenties animal 'Bonzo Dog'.

'Lucky Black Cat' transfers, transfer prints of a regional nature such as
Welsh Tea Party groups and the Devil at Devil's Bridge and view ware
(both monochrome, red, black or blue and polychrome) can all be found.
No lucky white heather devices or commemorative pieces have yet been
recorded.

Numbering System. No stock numbers were printed or painted on
Wilton models. Painted numbers, such as 018 or 012 are found on a large
number of different models and must be the paintresses' marks.

Wilton Models

Ancient Artefacts
Ancient Tyg, 1 handle. 70 mm.
Loving Cup, 3 handles. 39 mm.

Buildings—Coloured
These can be found with crests
Feathers Hotel. 1600. Ludlow. 80 mm long.
Shakespeare's House. 53 mm long.

Buildings—White
Christchurch Priory. 108 mm.
Cottage, Thatched. (Probably unnamed
   Anne Hathaway's Cottage.) 56 mm
   long.
Druids well. Sutton Park, Sutton Coldfield.
   50 mm.
Shakespeare's House. 53 mm long.

Monuments
Liberty Statue. 175 mm.

Historical/Folklore
Dick Whittington and cat on ashtray base,
   inscribed: *IV miles to London* on milestone
   and *Turn again Whittington* on ashtray.
   110 mm (rare).

Traditional/National Souvenirs
Blackpool Big Wheel. 105 mm. Found with
   the Felix transfer and Pathe trademark,
   inscribed: *Felix the cat comes to Blackpool.*
Irish Harp, with green shamrocks.
   105 mm.
Welsh Hat. 35 mm. (Much smaller than the
   usual Welsh Hat—rare.)
Welsh Hat. 70 mm (A Giant among Welsh
   Hats!)

Seaside
Bathing Machine with girl in doorway.
   Lustre and some colouring. Large, but
   no other details of size.
Lighthouse, inscribed: *Sailor beware.* Found
   in lustre. 155 mm.

Sailing Yacht, inscribed: *Saucy Sue.*
   125 mm.

Animals and Birds
Cat, sitting, inscribed: *Luck.* Red tongue.
   102 mm.
Terrier Dog, sitting, lustre. 85 mm.
Duck, sitting. Found lustre. 50 mm.
Pig, inscribed: *You may push.* No details of
   size.

Great War
Sailor, kneeling, and holding submarine.
   Blue cap band. 75 mm.
Battleship, tall top mast and no forward
   guns. 115 mm long.
Fieldglasses. 83 mm.
Folkestone War Memorial, inscribed: *Road
   of Remembrance.* 78 mm.
St. Anne's *War Memorial.* 152 mm.
Thetford *War Memorial.* 150 mm.
Walsall *War Memorial.* No details of size.

Home/Nostalgic
Grandfather Clock, inscribed: *Make use of
   time let not advantage slip.* Can be found
   completely red, but this is rare. 128 mm.
Sundial, inscribed: *What o' clock* and *Serene
   I stand among the flowers and only count
   life's sunny hours.* 146 mm.

Comic/Novelty
Bookmaker, standing figure, inscribed: *6 to
   4 the field.* 80 mm (rare).
Broke to the wide, man standing with head
   and shoulders bowed. 82 mm (rare).
Open Razor Ashtray, inscribed: *Got me
   through many a scrape.* 95 mm long (rare).
Truck of Coal, inscribed: *Black Diamonds.*
   Black coal, sometimes found unpainted.
   Found lustre. 98 mm long.

Right Wil Wat. Leaking Boot, Cleethorpes. This model is also marked 'Grafton'

Left W.H.H. & S. This model of two elephants on a slide is more often found unmarked. It is very charming and one suspects that the model was originally copied from a comic drawing for children

Left Wy Knot. 'Model of Burns Chair'

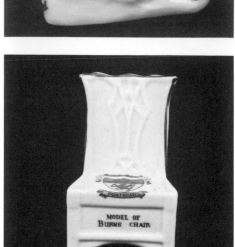

Willow Art. 'Bunyan's Chair', 'Walter Scott's' armchair and the 'Archbishop's Chair, Canterbury Cathedral'

Right Wilton. Lustre dog inscribed 'Terrier Dog'.

Left Wilton. Thetford 'War Memorial' and Folkestone 'Road of Rememberance' War Memorial

Cartoon/Comedy Characters
Bonzo Dog (G. E. Studdy's popular 1920's cartoon dog). Lustre. 48 mm. Can also be found sitting on a lustre ashtray base. 110 mm long. (Both quite rare.)
Comedian, standing figure wearing brown Oxford bags, black jacket, blue tie, brown trilby hat and black shoes. 96 mm. (Obviously an easily recognisable figure in the 1920's as it was not necessary to name him. Now unfortunately he cannot be identified.)
Mutt and Jeff, on rectangular base. 105 mm long. (Rare model of these comic strip characters. They first appeared in America in 1908 and in Britain in 1923. The strip is still drawn today.)

Alcohol
Barrel of Beer. 53 mm
Barrel of Beer, on stand. 55 mm.
Whisky Bottle. 98 mm.

'Modern' Equipment
Radio operator, inscribed: *Listening in.* Some colouring, Found lustre. 80 mm.
Telephone, upright. 105 mm.

Miscellaneous
Pastry Cutter, clover shaped. 90 mm long.
Thimble. 43 mm.

Miniature Domestic
Cheese dish, 1 piece. 50 mm.
Cheese dish and cover, horseshoe shaped. 45 mm.

Wil-Wat China

Trademark used for a retailer by Alfred B. Jones and Sons Ltd, Grafton China Works, Longton.

WIL-WAT
W.W
G
CHINA

For further details of this china and manufacturer see GRAFTON CHINA.

Fortunately for the researcher, models with this mark are found with the *Grafton* mark printed alongside. WWG must have been a retailer, but it is difficult to draw any conclusion about when the models were made.

The two models made specially for this retailer do not carry stock numbers but the fish does, presumably being taken from the *Grafton* range.

Wil-Wat Models

Monuments
The Monument, Laceby. 150 mm.

Traditional/National Souvenirs
Leaking boot, Cleethorpes. (Statue of boy, boot joined to hand by string.) 156 mm.

Animals
Fish, straight, with open mouth. No. 97. 100 mm long.

W and R

Trademark used for a London wholesaler by Hewitt and Leadbeater, Willow Potteries, Longton.

For details of this china and manufacturer see WILLOW ART CHINA.

Models and 'smalls' with this mark usually carry crests of the South of England. All models are found in the *Willow Art* range and seem to have been made during the Great War.

W and R Models

Seaside Souvenirs
Lighthouse, not named. 110 mm.

Animals
Pig, standing. 85 mm long.

Great War
Soldier, with rifle, inscribed: *Our brave defender.* 132 mm.
Battleship, impressed: *HMS Lion.* 140 mm long.

Comic/Novelty
Billiken, not named. 73 mm.

Transport
Car, open 4 seater. 114 mm long.

Miscellaneous
Hand holding a tulip. 80 mm.

W R and S

Trademark used by William
Ritchie and Son Ltd, 24, 26
and 28, Elder Street,
Edinburgh.

For details of this china and manufacturer see PORCELLE.

This mark is identical to the *Porcelle* mark but the word Porcelle and the visor have been omitted.

W R and S Models

Seaside Souvenirs
Whelk shell. 100 mm.

Great War
Bell Tent. 74 mm (not found marked
    Porcelle).

Miscellaneous
Top Hat. 45 mm.

Wy Not? Crest China

Trademark used for a
wholesaler by Hewitt and
Leadbeater, Willow Potteries,
Longton.

For details of china and manufacturer see WILLOW ART CHINA.

This mark is often badly printed and can be read as IVY NOT. Crests on models with the mark are from all over England and Wales, and all the models are from *Willow Art* moulds, so it is impossible to suggest what the last D in the initials underneath the mark stands for.

Stock numbers where found coincide with *Willow Art* numbers.

Wy Not Models

Ancient Artefacts
Loving Cup, 3 handles. 39 mm.

Historical/Folklore
Burn's Chair, Dumfries. 85 mm.
*Mary Queen of Scots Chair, Edinburgh Castle,
    Model of.* 75 mm.

Traditional/National Souvenirs
Lancashire Clog. 88 mm long.
Welsh Hat. No. 75. 57 mm.

Animals
Cat, sitting, blue bow. No. 62. 2 sizes:
    60 mm & 75 mm. (The 75 mm size has
    not been found marked 'Willow Art'.)
Dog, Collie, standing. 85 mm.

Elephant, walking. 52 mm.
Mouse (very fat, often described as a
    guinea pig). 62 mm.

Great War
Nurse, inscribed: *A friend in need.* 130 mm.
Sailor, inscribed: *Our brave defender*, and
    carrying a flag on his chest instead of a
    crest. The flag transfer is inscribed: *Good
    Luck. The boys in blue.* 130 mm.
Battleship, 4 funnels. 127 mm long.
Red Cross Van, red cross on side. No. 218,
    84 mm long.
Field Gun. 120 mm long.
Tommy's Steel Helmet. 76 mm long.

Miniature Domestic
Cheese dish and cover. 50 mm.

Unmarked Wares

Many models are found without marks but can often be recognised as the products of the major firms which for some reason escaped from the pottery without the trademark. (Some, but by no means all, of these pieces can be substandard and collectors would rather have a marked model.) There are however vast quantities of unmarked crested china around which cannot be attributed to any one manufacturer. This china, mostly very simple models, could have been made by several firms known to have made crested china but do not appear to have used a mark. These firms include:

George Proctor and Co., High Street, Longton.
Advertised arms ware in 1907 but their initials G. P. and Co. L. have not been found on recorded marks.

Barkers and Kent Ltd, The Foley Pottery, Fenton.
Were said in 1921 to be doing much to fill the gap left by the German manufacturers. An illustrated article in the Pottery Gazette shows a range of Great War souvenirs and animals. The initials B. and K. L. used by the firm are not found in known marks.

Biltons (1912) Ltd, London Road Works, Stoke-on-Trent.
Biltons had at one time made little else except teapots but when they lost male operatives during the Great War they changed to making 'small fancies' (why women could not be taught to make teapots has perhaps more to do with male vanity than their own capability). 'Small fancies' included models of soldiers, sailors, nurses, pierrots, pierrettes and animals. They were offered coloured, but look very suitable for the applying of crests. Biltons did register marks but none have been found on crested china.

C. J. Bisson and Co., 82 Liverpool Road, Stoke-on-Trent.
During the Great War the firm specialised in heraldic china and the company also owned The British Doll Manufacturing Co. Both of these lines were tackled to take advantage of the lack of German competition. C. J. Bisson do not seem to have registered a mark but a photograph of their range of heraldic novelties shows Great War souvenirs, a piano, and animals.

Unmarked Models

Some models are more often found unmarked or with a simple 'British Manufacture' stamp than marked. These include arks, anvils, cottages, elephants on a slope, footballs, grandfather clocks, lighthouses, petrol cans, parian straw boaters, pillar boxes, propellers, puzzle jugs and top hats. These often have coloured transfer views instead of crests.

The models listed below are not to my knowledge found marked although it is quite possible that marked models will eventually be recorded. They are well worth listing because most of them are quite unusual, many of them possibly being of German manufacture.

All of these models are quite rare as they are not found in the usual marked ranges.

BRITISH MANUFACTURE

Buildings—Coloured
Mason Croft, The House of Miss Marie Corelli. 90 mm long.
Old Falcon Tavern, Bidford on-Avon. 115 mm.
The Feathers Hotel Ludlow. 112 mm.
Plas Newyd House, impressed: *The House of the Ladies of Llangollen.* Rd. No. 521568. 115 mm long.
Pump room and baths, Trefriw Wells, plus long inscription. 95 mm long.

Buildings—White
British Government Pavilion B.E.E. Wembley 1924–5. 60 mm.

Monuments
Captain Scott, figure on square base. 150 mm (rare).

Historical/Folklore
Bust of General Booth, can be found inscribed: *Salvation Army.* 75 mm.

Right Unmarked. The wonderfully ferocious sabre toothed tiger, very rare and as yet not found marked.

Left Unmarked. Pigs with pink muzzles dressed as a barrister and possibly a witness. Although they have not been recorded during my researches collectors are sure that there are a court room set of these pigs

Right Unmarked. A delightful, slightly comic elephant found unmarked.

Left Unmarked. Two Pharo Hounds beautifully modelled but unmarked

Right Unmarked. Dog with bandaged face and leg and cat with bandage round jaw

Left Unmarked. An unmarked elephant complete with white hunter and two Indian bearers

Right Unmarked. Unmarked cat putting crown on, lucky black cat transfer on base making this a late and probably English model

Left Unmarked. Washer woman with basket of washing, unmarked

Jacobean Font at Newport I.W., Model of.
70 mm.
Knight's Helmet and Visor, with reclining
animal on top. 80 mm.
Mary Bell, witch, holding black cat.
108 mm.
Sanctuary Chair, Beverley Minster. 68 mm.
Scold's Bridle, bust of old woman wearing
bridle, with story of gossiping women.
64 mm (very rare).
*Ulphus Horn, Original in York Minster, Model
of.* 110 mm long.

Traditional/National Souvenirs
Cheddar Cheese, Model of, with inscription:
'This famous cheese has been made in
and around Cheddar for centuries, and
to this day no country in the world has
been able to equal it.' 60 mm dia.
Jersey Milkmaid. 80 mm.
Melton Mowbray Pie, A, with pastry rose
and leaves. With verse: 'If a Melton
Mowbray Pie should ever meet your eye.
My advice is hurry up! Make haste. And
at once The dainty buy. Learn why
epicures sigh. Longing for another
scrumptuous (sic) non such taste'.
55 mm.
Plate o'Bolton Trotters, A. Three pigs' trotters
on a plate. No details of size.

Seaside Souvenirs
Deep Sea Diver. 115 mm.
Jack Ashore, boy sailor on round base.
Coloured face. 153 mm.
Whelk Shell, with a green frog sitting on it.
105 mm long.

Animals
Bear, playing a mandolin. No details of
size.
Cat, in holdall. 55 mm long.
Cat, with toothache, bandage round jaw.
95 mm.
Cat, wearing coat and bandages. 90 mm.
(Looks like a Great War casualty.)
Cat, Egyptian, with long ears. 90 mm long.
Cat, Posy Bowl, no details of size.
Cat, sitting on square base putting on
crown. 130 mm.
Cat and Rabbit, in high boot, inscribed: *A
jolly place for a jolly couple.* 83 mm.
Dog with bandaged face and leg. 75 mm.
Dogs, two Bulldogs, one seated and the
other standing. 57 mm.
Dogs, two Pharo Hounds, on oblong base.
76 mm long.
Elephant, with hunter and two Indian
Bearers on his back. 90 mm.
Elephant, circus, with front feet on drum.
102 mm.
Elephant sitting, rather comical.
Lion wearing coat and trousers, holding
telescope. 132 mm.
Pig, wearing barrister's wig and glasses,
muzzle pink. (This is probably an
unmarked *Gemma* model.) 85 mm.

Pig, sitting, wearing monocle and bowler
hat, muzzle pink. 82 mm. (This is also
probably an unmarked *Gemma* model.)
Rabbits, 2 on sledge or slope. No details of
size.
Tiger, sabre-toothed. 128 mm long (a very
impressive model).

Birds
Ducks, 2 with coloured beaks and feet on
an oval stand. 185 mm (an enormous
model).
Kingfisher. 60 mm.
Parakeet, fully coloured on plinth.
215 mm.

Comic/Novelty
Artist's easel on stand. 65 mm.
Cook, holding wooden spoon. 115 mm.
Girl, sitting on horse by tree trunk.
110 mm.
Monk, carrying lantern and basket.
135 mm.
Washer Woman, holding a basket of
washing. 118 mm.

Cartoon/Comedy Characters
Crested faced man, fully coloured. 80 mm.
Felix, standing cat on oval base, no
colouring. 87 mm. (This is a really nice
Felix.)
The Sprinter. Comic figure with corkscrew
legs—wound up for action. 100 mm.
Sunny Jim, bust. 85 mm.

Alcohol
Two drunks on an ashtray, inscribed:
Another little drink wouldn't do any harm.
Rd. No. 700992. No details of size.

Sport
Footballer, with ball, no colouring.
130 mm. (*Savoy* range advertised a
coloured version of this model.)
Rugby Ball. 74 mm long.

Musical Instruments
Drum set with cymbals. 65 mm.

Transport
Aeroplane with pilot, size varies usually
100 mm long. (Almost certainly
German.)
Open racing car.. 138 mm long.

'Modern' Equipment
Cash Register. 44 mm.
Typewriter inscribed: *My little typewriter.*
No details of size.

Miscellaneous
Top Hat, with umbrella across. No details
of size.
Loving Cups, 3 handled, with lithophanes
of King Edward, Queen Alexandra, King
George or Queen Mary in base. 39 mm.

Right Unmarked. Large
uncoloured Felix, unmarked

Left Unmarked (Biltons). Clown
or Pierrot playing banjo, pink
face. 125 mm. This model is very
like the wares appearing in
Biltons adverts during the period
they were making crested china.
This model is unmarked

Right Unmarked. 'Jack Ashore' a
delightful unmarked model

Left Unmarked. Deep sea diver, a
very rare model and not as yet
found marked

JACK ASHORE

Unmarked. Two monoplanes
with pilots, both white German
china but unmarked

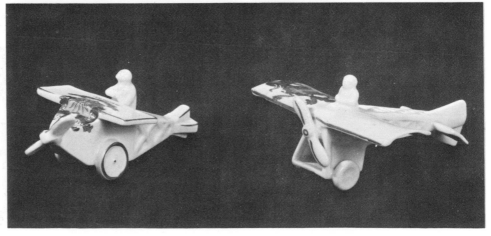

Right German. Bathing belle in basket chair with crossed flags on the top. Yellow/brown shaded lustre

Left Unmarked. Bust of General Booth only found unmarked

Right German. Bathing beauty on slide in yellow/brown lustre

Left German. Bell hop girl on suitcase in yellow/brown shaded lustre

Right German. Open tourer in shaded yellow/brown lustre

Left German. Yellow/brown shaded lustre girl on a donkey with the lucky white heather device

Right Saxony. Locomotive with the initials of the Romney Hythe and District Railway

Left Saxony. Cat singing and cat in Gladstone Bag 'Good Night'

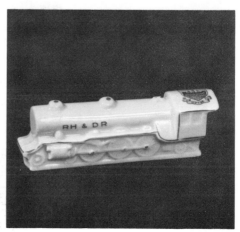

Country of Origin Marks

Germany

Foreign

Impressed marks

This mark is found on many small models, the china is usually heavy. The most common models are arks and top hats, but sabots, boots, animals and a huge quantity of 'smalls' are all recorded with this mark.

Both of these impressed marks are normally accompanied by an impressed stock number. They were both used by the same firm. All the models listed below can be found with a lustre finish, usually yellow shaded through to rust, but sometimes mother-of-pearl. These normally have the 'Lucky White Heather' device rather than a crest. Impressed stock numbers are listed where known. Unfortunately, I have to list most of these models without size.

Germany/Foreign Models

Ancient Artefacts
Southwold Jug. No. 4687 (lustre).

Buildings
Bandstand. No. 3972 (lustre).
Clock Tower. No. 7727 (lustre).

Traditional/National Souvenirs
Cleethorpes Leaking boot, with arm moulded holding boot to chest.

Seaside Souvenirs
Yacht. No. 3482 (lustre).
Yacht, with waves. No. 4422 (lustre).
Girl, riding donkey. No. 4840. 115 mm (lustre).
Mermaid, on a shell (lustre).

Animals
Jaguar, open mouthed, crouching on oval base. No. 934. 125 mm long.
Seal, on rectangular base. 127 mm long.

Great War
Monoplane, with pilot. No. 7207 (lustre).
War Memorial Clacton on Sea. No. 6999.

Home/Nostalgic
Chair. No. 3567 (lustre).
Milk Pail. No. 5185 (lustre).
Shepherd and lamb in hollow tree trunk. No. 846. 76 mm.

Comic/Novelty
Bride and groom, in a large shell. No. 5795 (lustre).
Boy with flag. No. 5795—pair with girl below (lustre).
Girl with flag. No. 5795—pair with boy above (lustre).
Girl, dressed as bell hop, sitting on suitcase. No. 5804. 75 mm long (lustre).
Children, Two, ski-ing down slope. No. 5805 (lustre).
Stile, with heart and initials.
Sultan, sitting on bowl. No. 4834 (lustre).

Twenties Flappers
Found decorated in two styles: white ware with clothes edged in rust/brown and the face and hair are coloured, or yellow/rust shaded lustre.
Bathing girl, sitting on ashtray. Whiteware. 75 mm.
Bathing girl, on slide. Lustre.
Bathing girl, lying on turtle. Lustre.
Girl, in basket beach chair. White ware and lustre. 115 mm.
Girl with parasol in a basket beach chair. White ware. Two sizes: No. 4165. 120 mm. No. 4074. 104 mm.

Transport
Motorcar (lustre).

'Modern' Equipment
Gramophone. No. 3563 (lustre).

Another German mark which could have been used by any of the firms working in Saxony. The most likely manufacturer is Unger and Schilde, Roschützer Porzellanfabrix (Saxony), who was known to have made a great quantity of pink souvenir wares for the British Market.

Saxony Models

Buildings—White
Weymouth Clock Tower. 124 mm.

Animals
Three puppies, in a basket. 65 mm.
Cat, singing, holding book. 74 mm.

Great War
Monoplane, figure in the plane. 100 mm long.

Transport
Steam Locomotive, inscribed: R.H. and D.R. 118 mm long. (Romney Hythe and District Railway.)

Equipment
Gramophone. 60 mm.